THE NEW EUROPEAN ECONOMY REVISITED

Loukas Tsoukalis

Oxford University Press
1997

Oxford University Press, Great Clarendon Street, Oxford OX2 6DP

Oxford New York

Athens Auckland Bangkok Bogota Bombay
Buenos Aires Calcutta Cape Town Dar es Salaam
Delhi Florence Hong Kong Istanbul Karachi
Kuala Lumpur Madras Madrid Melbourne
Mexico City Nairobi Paris Singapore
Taipei Tokyo Toronto

and associated companies in
Berlin Ibadan

Oxford is a trade mark of Oxford University Press

Published in the United States
by Oxford University Press Inc., New York

British Library Cataloguing in Publication Data
Data available

Library of Congress Cataloging-in-Publication Data
Tsoukalis, Loukas.
The new European economy revisited / Loukas Tsoukalis. — 3rd ed.
p. cm.
Rev. ed. of: The new European economy. 2nd ed. 1993.
Includes bibliographical references
1. European Union.   2. European Union countries—Economic policy.
I. Tsoukalis, Loukas. New European economy.   II. Title.
HC241.2.T74   1997   337.1´42—dc 21   96–51593

ISBN 0–19–877562–8
ISBN 0–19–877477–X (pbk)

10 9 8 7 6 5 4 3 2 1

Typeset by BookMan Services, Ilfracombe
Printed in Great Britain
on acid-free paper by
Biddles Ltd, Guildford & King's Lynn

PREFACE

The first edition of *The New European Economy* came out in 1991. It attempted to capture the new phase of European integration marked by the internal market programme, an ambitious budgetary deal with a significant redistributive dimension, and an ever-expanding agenda in which social policies and monetary union began to feature. Markets responded favourably (almost enthusiastically) to European political initiatives. High investment ratios and rapid economic restructuring were the main characteristics of the second half of the 1980s. Those economic developments were taking place against the background of dramatic political changes on the European continent, following the collapse of communist regimes and the disintegration of the old Soviet empire. The European Community (the term generally used to refer to the three existing Communities until then) appeared as the only solid piece of the European architecture.

The book had a strong policy orientation; economic issues were therefore examined in their political context. It was also an attempt to present a synthetic view of the many different aspects of regional integration, which required a dangerous kind of navigation between the Scylla of overgeneralization and grand theorizing on the one hand, and the Charybdis of narrow empiricism on the other. The book argued that the continuous expansion and deepening of regional integration already justified the use of the term 'European economy' which was qualitatively different from the set of highly interdependent national economies we had known until then; hence the title of the book.

It was, perhaps, inevitable that the book would, to some extent, reflect the mood of its time. The 'Euro-scepticism' of the early 1980s had been quickly swept away by strong waves of optimism and euphoria which were characteristic of both political and business circles, apparently working together in harmony and thus providing the necessary ingredients for a new virtuous circle of economic growth and further integration. The book did not, however, adopt a starry-eyed approach to the future of European construction. It pointed to the overselling of the internal market programme, the elements of instability in monetary integration, and, even more importantly, the widening gap between economic and political integration.

The events of the early 1990s had a sobering effect: Maastricht had a difficult birth, European populations showed hardly any enthusiasm for the newborn, while international markets openly challenged the official plan for an economic and monetary union. And the economic environment deteriorated rapidly. The second, revised edition of *The New European Economy* appeared in 1993 in times of crisis and growing 'Euro-scepticism'. Popular moods change very rapidly, and so do the 'animal spirits' in the financial markets.

Under gentle but continuous pressure from Oxford University Press, I have been long torn between writing a third edition and a completely new book. So much has happened in recent years that made it virtually impossible to add small bits here and there. A third edition would therefore require a radical revision. I have opted for the middle road. *The New European Economy Revisited* is precisely what it says: a new book on an old theme, namely about the nature and shape of the regional economic system in Europe. Except for the historical parts, the book has been completely rewritten and virtually all the tables and figures are new. The structure of the book has not, however, changed much, even though the contents of each chapter are different. And many of the basic arguments remain similar, although hopefully richer and better documented.

The book has been rewritten in the light of more recent developments in a large number of policy areas, while also drawing on the burgeoning literature in different academic disciplines. From the very early stages, political scientists and lawyers had turned their attention to European integration issues, also developing new analytical tools in the process. It had been very different with economists: European integration had remained for many years a subject for a small number of eccentrics in the profession. Things have changed radically in recent years and economists have been rapidly catching up. There is now, undoubtedly, an embarrassing wealth of information and analysis which becomes increasingly difficult to assimilate; but still, interdisciplinary boundaries are very infrequently crossed.

The European agenda has changed with time. When I was writing the first edition of *The New European Economy*, the main emphasis was unavoidably on the 1992 programme and the establishment of the internal market. This is history now, even though many people begin to discover (with surprise?) that the elimination of all remaining barriers in the European single market may be a very long process. In the second half of the 1990s, the game is different: it is mostly about economic and monetary union, redistribution, enlargement, and flexibility. None of them is a completely new item on the European agenda, yet each has acquired another dimension in a rapidly changing political and economic context. *Changement dans la continuité*; or *continuité dans le changement*.

I am grateful to my students and to numerous colleagues and active participants in the European construction who have over many years helped me to develop and refine the ideas contained in this book. I am also grateful to readers of the earlier work for their comments and constructive criticism. In recent years, I have been actively involved as an outside consultant in the work of different directorates-general of the European Commission: in the academic panel of experts for the assessment of the effects of the internal market programme; in the advisory board for the evaluation of structural policies; as joint coordinator of the study on the cohesion aspects of Community policies which forms part of the preparatory work for the first cohesion report; as adviser for the preparation of the paper on industrial cooperation with the countries of Central and Eastern Europe; and in the provision of technical assistance to the same group of countries as well as to the newly independent states of the former Soviet Union. I have benefited a great deal from this experience through the exchange of ideas and the privileged access to information, which I hope I have not abused. It has also helped me to keep my feet on the ground. There is no limit to the amount of nonsense that one can produce when working in isolation. I trust that my friends in the Commission and other European institutions have a high threshold of tolerance for criticism directed at the policies for which they are responsible.

I am also grateful to the University of Athens and the College of Europe in Bruges for the spiritual home with which they have provided me for years (the two institutions being thousands of kilometres apart may in turn explain my frequent absence from both); to the Robert Schuman Centre in the European University Institute in Fiesole which offered me generous hospitality and a stimulating environment as Visiting Jean Monnet Professor, when I started working for this book; and to many other academic and policy institutions for opportunities to try out half-baked ideas.

Special thanks are due to Beatriz Knaster, Antonia Carzaniga, Carmen Suárez, Andrea Rossi, Volker Stehmann, Martin Foeth, and Nikos Koutsiaras for valuable research assistance; to David Young for compiling the index; and to Vivian Politou who has helped me to keep the loose threads of many different activities together. I should also like to thank Nikiforos Diamantouros and Helen Wallace for their very useful comments on earlier drafts of the introductory and concluding chapters. Tracy Mawson and Andrew Schuller from Oxford University Press have offered continuous support and encouragement which I gratefully acknowledge. As for the more personal debts of gratitude, they will remain nameless.

L.T.

September 1996

CONTENTS

List of Figures and Maps   ix

List of Tables   x

List of Abbreviations   xi

1. Searching for Things New and European   1

2. The Early Ups and Downs of European Integration   9

   The Foundations of European Regionalism   9
   Economic Growth, Trade Liberalization, and the Mixed
      Economy   15
   No Longer Small and Carefree   24

3. Treaty Revisions and the New Economic Orthodoxy   33

   The Rediscovery of Europe and the Market   34
   Virtuous Circles are not Forever   40
   The Post-Maastricht Blues   50

4. From Customs Union to the Internal Market   61

   Non-Tariff Barriers and the Mixed Economy   61
   Supply-Side Economics and the Labours of Implementation   68

5. The Political Economy of Liberalization and Regulation   79

   Breeding Euro-Champions: Competition or Industrial Policy?   81
   Deregulation in Financial Services: Efficiency and Stability   92
   Tax Harmonization: This Side of Eternity?   102
   The Race Between National and European Standards   108

6. Social Policies and Labour Markets   114

   Free Movement and Little Mobility   117
   Charters, Protocols, and White Papers: Battles on the Ideological
      High Ground   121
   Subsidiarity and the European Model   132

7.   Building a Regional Currency System   138

     Much Ado About Nothing: The Early Years   138
     Monetary Stability and the EMS   143
     Free Markets, Policy Coordination, and Asymmetry   152

8.   Towards Monetary Union   163

     Negotiating EMU: The Primacy of High Politics   164
     A Long and Bumpy Road Leading to Narrow Gates   172
     Living in an EMU   179

9.   Cohesion and Redistribution   187

     The Regional Problem   188
     A New Package Deal   196
     Structural Funds: Development Policies in Europe's Periphery   202
     The Budget: Small and Beautiful?   209

10. European or Global Power?   223

     The EU and International Economic Interdependence   225
     Trade Policies and the World Trade Organization   233
     The Changing World of Preferences   241
     Preparing for a New Enlargement   248

11. Ten Theses on Integration   259

References   277
Index   293

LIST OF FIGURES

2.1. Intra-EU Trade in Goods, 1960–1994   19

3.1. Unemployment Rates in EU-15, the USA, and Japan, 1972–1994   35

3.2. General Government Expenditure, Receipts, and Net Lending (Borrowing) in the EU, 1960–1994   39

3.3. Economic Growth and Popular Support for European Unification, 1982–1994   57

5.1. Mergers and Acquisitions of Majority Holdings in Industry, 1983/4 to 1991/2   82

5.2. Mergers and Acquisitions of Majority Holdings in Services, 1984/5 to 1991/2   83

7.1. Bilateral Exchange Rates of the US Dollar and the Yen against the ECU, 1980–1995   148

7.2. Price Deflator Private Consumption, 1979–1995   149

7.3. Nominal Long-Term Interest Rates, 1979–1995   151

7.4. Real Effective Exchange Rates, 1979–1995   154

7.5. Bilateral DM Rates of ERM Currencies, Mar. 1979–Aug. 1993   157

7.6. Depreciation of Currencies against the DM, Sept. 1992–Jan. 1996   161

8.1. Convergence Criteria: Inflation and Long-Term Interest Rates, 1995   177

8.2. Convergence Criteria: Government Net Borrowing and Gross General Government Debt, 1995   178

9.1. GDP per Inhabitant by Member Country, 1983–1993   193

9.2. Regional Disparities in GDP per Inhabitant by Member Country, 1993   196

9.3. Structure of EU Budget Expenditure, 1958–1996   212

9.4. Structure of EU Budget Revenue, 1971–1996   215

10.1. Exports and Imports of Goods of EU-12, USA, and Japan, 1960–1994   226

LIST OF MAPS

9.1. Regional GDP per Inhabitant, 1993   190

9.2. Unemployment Rates by Region, 1995   194

LIST OF TABLES

2.1. Growth Rates, 1960–1994   16
2.2. Unemployment Rates, 1960–1995   17
2.3. Consumer Price Indices, 1960–1995   18
2.4. Government Expenditure, 1960–1994   21
4.1. Macroeconomic Consequences of the
     Completion of the Internal Market   70
7.1. Composition of the ECU   144
7.2. EMS Realignments: Changes in Central Rates   147
8.1. Openness of EU Economies, 1960–1994   182
9.1. Net Transfers through the EU Budget, 1980–1994   218
10.1. Breakdown of EU Trade by Trading Partners   226
10.2. Sectoral Breakdown of EU External Trade, 1970–1994   228

LIST OF ABBREVIATIONS

ACP	African, Caribbean, and Pacific countries
AFNOR	Association Française de Normalisation
ASEAN	Association of South-East Asian Nations
BRITE	Basic Research in Industrial Technologies for Europe
BSI	British Standards Institution
CAP	Common Agricultural Policy
CCP	Common Commercial Policy
CEEC	Central and Eastern European country
CEN	Centre Européen de Normalisation
CENELEC	Centre Européen de Normalisation Électrotechnique
CEPR	Centre for Economic Policy Research
CET	Common External Tariff
CFSP	Common Foreign and Security Policy
CIS	Commonwealth of Independent States
CMEA	Council of Mutual Economic Assistance
COMETT	Community Programme for Education and Training for Technologies
COREPER	Committee of Permanent Representatives
CSF	Community Support Framework
DIN	Deutsches Institut für Normung
DM	Deutschmark (Deutsche Mark)
EA	Europe Agreement
EAEC	European Atomic Energy Community
EAGGF	European Agricultural Guidance and Guarantee Fund
EBRD	European Bank for Reconstruction and Development
EC	European Community
ECB	European Central Bank
ECJ	European Court of Justice
ECOFIN	Council of Economic and Finance Ministers
ECSC	European Coal and Steel Community
ECU	European Currency Unit
EDC	European Defence Community
EDF	European Development Fund
EEA	European Economic Area
EEC	European Economic Community
EFTA	European Free Trade Association
EIB	European Investment Bank
EMCF	European Monetary Cooperation Fund
EMI	European Monetary Institute
EMS	European Monetary System

EMU	Economic and Monetary Union
EOTC	European Organization of Testing and Certification
EPC	European Political Cooperation
EPU	European Payments Union
ERASMUS	European Community Action Scheme for the Mobility of University Students
ERDF	European Regional Development Fund
ERM	exchange rate mechanism
ESC	Economic and Social Committee
ESCB	European System of Central Banks
ESF	European Social Fund
ESPRIT	European Strategic Programme for Research and Development in Information Technology
ETSI	European Telecommunications Standards Institute
ETUC	European Trade Union Confederation
EU	European Union
EUREKA	European Research Co-ordinating Agency
FDI	foreign direct investment
GATS	General Agreement on Trade in Services
GATT	General Agreement on Tariffs and Trade
GDP	Gross Domestic Product
GFCF	gross fixed capital formation
GNP	Gross National Product
GSP	Generalized System of Preferences
HDTV	high definition television
IGC	Intergovernmental Conference
ILO	International Labour Organization
IMF	International Monetary Fund
IMP	Integrated Mediterranean Programme
MCA	monetary compensatory amount
MEP	Member of the European Parliament
METS	minimum efficient technical scale
MFA	Multifibre Arrangement
MFN	Most Favoured Nation
NAFTA	North American Free Trade Agreement
NAIRU	non-accelerating inflation rate of unemployment
NATO	North Atlantic Treaty Organization
NIC	newly industrializing country
NIEO	New International Economic Order
NIS	New Independent States
NTB	non-tariff barrier
NUTS	nomenclature of territorial units for statistics
OECD	Organization for Economic Cooperation and Development
OEEC	Organization for European Economic Cooperation
OPEC	Organization of Petroleum Exporting Countries
OSCE	Organization for Security and Cooperation in Europe
PETRA	Action Programme for the Vocational Training of Young People and their Preparation for Adult and Working Life
PHARE	Pologne, Hongrie assistance pour la restructuration économique

PPS	purchasing power standard
QR	quantitative restriction
R&D	research and development
RACE	Research in Advanced Communications for Europe
RTD	research and technological development
SDI	Strategic Defence Initiative
SEA	Single European Act
TACIS	Technical Assistance to the Commonwealth of Independence States
TEU	Treaty on European Union
TRIM	Trade-Related Investment Measure
TRIP	Trade-Related Intellectual Property Right
UN	United Nations
UNCTAD	United Nations Conference on Trade and Development
UNICE	Union des Confédérations de l'Industrie et des Employeurs d'Europe
VAT	value added tax
VER	voluntary export restraint
WEU	Western European Union
WTO	World Trade Organization

1

SEARCHING FOR THINGS
NEW AND EUROPEAN

This book is about the process of European economic integration. It concentrates mainly, although not exclusively, on the more recent phase which started around the mid-1980s and which has been characterized by a continuous expansion of the European agenda, the strengthening of intra-European economic ties, the transfer of new powers to common institutions, as well as the geographical extension of what we may call the European economic system. The highly ambitious programme for the establishment of the internal market, aiming at the elimination of all remaining barriers in the economic transactions between member countries of the European Community (EC),[1] helped to transform radically the political and economic climate back in the 1980s. Thus, 'Euro-optimism' came to replace the pessimism of earlier years. The internal market programme was backed by a budgetary deal with a strong redistributive dimension, something completely unprecedented. More and more issues entered the European agenda as political decisions and the sustained improvement of the economic environment fed into each other. And this led to the revival of the most ambitious plan of all, namely the creation of an economic and monetary union (EMU).

The process of integration has always been characterized by fits and starts, by

---

[1] Before the Treaty on European Union (TEU), the term EC was generally used to refer to the three existing Communities, namely the European Coal and Steel Community (ECSC), the European Economic Community (EEC), and the European Atomic Energy Community (EAEC). With the TEU, signed at Maastricht in February 1992, the old EEC dropped one of the 'E's and became the European Community. Together with the other two, which have kept their old names, it now constitutes the so-called Community pillar of the European Union (EU) construction; and by far the most important one. To simplify matters, the term EC will be used to refer to all three Communities, except when specific reference needs to be made to one of them. In practice, there is very little difference, since the old EEC (and now EC) has always dominated the scene, while the other two Communities became marginalized early on. Since the book concentrates on economic integration, there is very little to say, and only indirectly, about the other two pillars created at Maastricht, one on common foreign and security policy and the other on cooperation in the fields of justice and home affairs (see also Chapter 3). The term European Union (EU) will be generally used for the post-Maastricht period. The reader should, however, be warned that a neat separation between the EC and the EU is practically impossible, especially when policies are discussed in a historical context.

bursts of activity which have often been followed by crisis and relative inaction. In the early 1990s, the economic and political climate changed once again, the deterioration of the macroeconomic environment being accompanied by successive crises in the exchange markets and growing scepticism about the future of European integration. Unemployment rates reached dangerous heights, while economic growth receded. And the armies of unemployed began to seriously threaten Europe's welfare systems. Yet the process of integration did not stop; far from it. And the plan for EMU has remained on the table with a treaty seal on it. The remaining years until 1999 are therefore most likely to be dominated by preparations for the historic rendezvous with the single currency, a rendezvous which, if it does take place as scheduled, some countries at least are bound to miss.

During the same period, the EU has gone through two more rounds of enlargement, with the accession of five new members (without counting the accession of the Eastern *Länder* following Germany's unification). And it now prepares for an even bigger enlargement which may, however, take place in different stages extended over a relatively long period. It has also gone through two major treaty revisions, linked to the internal market programme and EMU respectively, while a third one is under negotiation while this book goes to press.

The early stages of European integration were mainly about the elimination of trade barriers, and this eventually brought about a, still incomplete, customs union in goods and the rapid growth of trade interdependence. Developments since the mid-1980s constitute a major qualitative change: European integration is now largely about economic regulation, redistribution, and increasingly through the locking of exchange rates, macroeconomic policies. This has an immediate and highly recognizable impact on an ever-growing number of economic agents and citizens alike. The European economic system can be seen as a superstructure built on top of already densely knit national economies.

We argue that those developments, which will be examined in depth in subsequent chapters, justify the use of the term 'new European economy', even though the nation-state and, by implication, national economies, show hardly any signs of withering away. On the other hand, there is the allegedly unstoppable trend of economic globalization which, according to so many experts and laymen, leaves little room for public regulation and effective intervention (see for example, Ohmae, 1990; and for a more sceptical view, Hirst and Thompson, 1996; and Boyer and Drache, 1996). Will the European economy soon lose any practical meaning because of increasingly global market forces?

European integration has indeed evolved within the context of growing international economic interdependence, a term still often used instead of globalization by the less exuberant representatives of the economics profession. Intra-European developments have always been strongly influenced by changes in the international economy. Yet, a basic argument in this book is that European integration should not be seen as simply another manifestation of the phenomenon of international interdependence. The difference between the European and the world level is both quantitative and qualitative. It lies in the different degree and nature of economic interaction between national units as well as in the advanced form of joint rule-setting, side-payments, and management at the European level of governance in the words of Helen and William Wallace (H. Wallace, 1996; W. Wallace, 1996). Autonomous economic processes and policy cooperation have been mutually reinforcing. Thus, there has been and still remains a clear discontinuity, in terms of the intensity of the economic interaction and joint policy-making, between the European economic system and the rest of the world.

Any talk about discontinuity implies the existence of boundaries. And in this case boundaries have never been clearly marked. Economic transactions have a life of their own and are not entirely determined, although still strongly influenced, by institutional arrangements. Thus, for example, countries which formed part of the European Free Trade Association (EFTA) used to be more closely integrated in the European economic system, in terms of monetary policy and exchange rates and also in terms of trade and production interpenetration, than some of the members of the EU. With successive enlargements, and notably the most recent one in 1995, the boundaries of the European economic system have become almost identical with the boundaries of the Union. Yet, there are still countries such as Switzerland and Norway which form an integral part of the European economic system, although they are still not strictly bound by many of the rules and regulations produced in Brussels.

Until 1989, the *annus mirabilis* for the countries of Central and Eastern Europe, regional integration was meant to refer to the EC and sometimes to Western Europe more generally (Western Europe being defined in political and not strictly geographical terms). Countries to the east of the notorious Iron Curtain were left outside this process, being involved in their own, and not particularly successful, form of integration. The collapse of communist regimes has put an end to this division. Participation in the process of European integration presupposes pluralist political systems and market economies. The countries of Central and Eastern Europe have been going through a difficult transition in both political and economic terms and each one with different degrees of success. The extension of the European economic system to the whole of the continent, the boundaries to the east having shifted while still remaining uncertain, is now a concrete possibility; but the process is bound to be rather long.

European integration has been and continues to be largely about economics; but economics which has wider political ramifications. The distinction made by traditional theories of international relations between high politics, referring to matters of national security and prestige, and low politics, reserved for more mundane issues such as trade and even money (thus relegating economic issues to the second division of international affairs) has always looked suspect. Although, perhaps, understandable when seen through the eyes of superpowers at the peak of the cold war, such a distinction can be positively misleading when applied to the contemporary European reality, where politics and foreign policy are largely about economics.

In this book, the study of economic issues will be placed in its proper political context. It will also be set against a historical background in order to facilitate a better understanding of the evolution of the attitudes and policies of the parties concerned. In other words, a political economy approach will be adopted in an attempt to obtain a deeper insight into the ongoing process of economic integration in Europe, the linkages between different issues, and the trade-offs, even though not always explicit. Policies imply choices, and there is strong emphasis in the book on the wider implications of economic integration and some of the choices which need to be made. We shall discuss the effects of integration on economic order, thus shedding light on the changing interaction between the state and the market. The efficient allocation of resources and the maximization of global welfare have been the almost exclusive concern of neoclassical economics. However, politics in the real world is not only about efficiency. Economic policies will be discussed in this book with a close eye on their distributional aspects among countries, regions, and social classes, in full awareness of the strong limitations in this respect of the available data and our tools of analysis. Attention will also be devoted to a very different, albeit highly sensitive, dimension of distribution, namely the distribution of economic power between different levels of decision-making. Repeated references will also be made to questions of legitimacy and public accountability of European institutions.

With the years, European integration has extended to a very large number of areas. In view of the complexity of the issues involved and also the fact that patterns of decision-making often vary considerably from one area of activity to the other, depending on historical circumstances, the nature of the activity, and the internal as well as external balance of forces, most observers of the European scene have long since abandoned any attempt to analyse the phenomenon of integration as a whole, opting instead for narrow specialization. The relative failure of earlier attempts at general theorizing to contribute much to our understanding of the whole process, not to mention their predictive capacity, has acted as a further disincentive against the search for the overall view.

Puchala (1972) issued an early warning: he likened the process of integration to an elephant and researchers to blind men who by touching different parts of the body try to draw conclusions about the shape of the whole animal. This book is an attempt to provide a general picture of economic integration and the European economic system, by concentrating especially on the links between different areas of policy and the real economy. The aim of this book is not towards grand theorizing nor is it to engage in an exercise in futurology. On the contrary, there is a strong policy orientation and as much reliance as possible on 'hard facts'. It is hoped that the search for the overall shape of the elephant will not lead to too much of a fuzzy picture.

The book starts with a historical section which is intended to provide a *tour d'horizon* of European economic integration and its different phases. Chapter 2 covers the period between the end of the Second World War and the 'dark years' of the prolonged post-1973 economic recession, when the whole European edifice looked in danger of collapsing. It traces the evolution of the integration model from the period of the economic boom to the years of the recession, its links with national and international developments, and the effects of regional integration in terms of trade and welfare. It also examines the apparent contradiction between the trade liberalization of early years and the development of the mixed economy and the welfare state in individual Western European countries; a contradiction which proved manageable only in the years of rapid economic growth. Changing economic circumstances and successive enlargements of the EC have had a noticeable effect on the overall package deal which has sustained the process of integration, thus also having a direct impact on common policies and institutions.

The next chapter concentrates on the events of the 1980s and the first half of the 1990s in an attempt to understand the dramatic transformation of the political and economic climate associated mostly with the implementation of the internal market programme. The 1992 programme, as it came to be known, offers a fascinating case-study of political leadership, excellent marketing skills, and, perhaps, also luck, that necessary ingredient of success. Luck could not, however, last for ever. We have witnessed a transition from the 'Euro-pessimism' of earlier years to the virtuous circle of higher growth and closer integration in the second half of the decade, and then back to a new kind of 'Euro-pessimism' provoked by a deteriorating economic environment and the serious problems encountered in the process of ratification of the Maastricht treaty. The last section of this chapter is devoted to the treaty revision which came into force in November 1993 and the main developments which have taken place since then.

The nature of the remaining barriers and the large gap still separating the EC in the mid-1980s from a true internal market are discussed in Chapter 4. In the context of mixed economies, integration is a long process and the old distinction between the different stages loses much of its meaning. The emphasis gradually shifts from border controls, mainly in the form of tariffs, to domestic government intervention and the multitude of manifestations of the mixed economy. It also shifts from goods to services and factors of production. The internal market programme was about stronger competition and the freer interplay of market forces, in turn consistent with the general shift to liberal economic ideas during this period. Its effects will be felt over several years. We shall discuss the difficulties of implementation of the internal market programme and we shall also attempt to draw a provisional balance sheet of its effects, drawing on the results of some recent studies.

The next chapter goes into the heart of the internal market programme by examining specific attempts to eliminate remaining barriers in the intra-EU movement of goods, services, and factors of production. Since integration does not take place in a *laissez-faire* environment, the elimination of those barriers raises delicate questions about the appropriate mixture of liberalization and regulation in the context of mixed economies; in other words, about the interaction between the state and the market. What is also at stake in this respect is the distribution of power between national and European levels of authority.

This chapter contains four case-studies. The first one examines the growth of cross-border mergers and acquisitions and their influence on the development of a new EU regulatory framework as part of the common competition policy. There has undoubtedly been a major restructuring of the European manufacturing sector and also services. Yet, are we really witnessing the emergence of European champions and what are the policy instruments which European institutions can use to this effect? On the other hand, hostile takeovers and pressures for the creation of 'level playing fields' in different countries raise more general questions about different kinds of capitalism. The second case-study deals with the liberalization of financial services and the new supervision rules adopted at the Union level. With respect to financial services, there seems to be a trade-off between efficiency and stability which has not yet been seriously addressed at the policy level. The third one examines the difficulties encountered in terms of tax harmonization and the implications for public finances in a world of growing mobility of goods and factors of production. The fourth case-study tries to make sense of the highly technical world of standards and regulations as potent instruments of industrial policy and external protection. Has mutual recognition and/or the application of the so-called 'new approach' led to a 'race to the bottom'? The conclusions drawn from each case-study in terms of the mixture of liberalization and regulation are not identical; and why should they be? There is no single pattern of integration followed in each and every sector of economic activity. Those case-studies offer some insight into the complexity of the integration process and the changing economic order in Europe.

Given the special characteristics of labour markets, the attempts to agree on a common regulatory framework at the European level are discussed separately in Chapter 6. As with social policy more generally, regulation is essentially market-correcting. This is an area where national differences have largely survived the impact of economic integration, and intra-EU labour mobility remains limited. Attempts to add a social dimension to the internal market came almost as an afterthought. In the debate which has ensued, ideology and political symbols seem to have taken precedence over concrete measures. Is deregulation inevitable/desirable in a world of high unemployment and what are the implications of the latter for European welfare systems? Should there be any specific role reserved for European institutions? The answers to those questions largely depend on the answer to be given to a more general and politically loaded question: is there an economic and social model specific to Europe, and how should we go about defending it in the context of rapidly growing international economic interdependence? The answer to this question can only be given in the political market-place.

The discussion about new forms of regulation in product and labour markets is followed by an examination of monetary integration and macroeconomic policies at the European level. The Community started from virtually zero and gradually developed over the years mechanisms for policy coordination centred on a system of fixed but adjustable exchange rates. The snake was the precursor to a much more successful and durable European Monetary System (EMS) which did, however, come close to a complete breakdown in the early 1990s as EU governments were starting preparations for a complete EMU. Stable intra-EU exchange rates have generally been considered as a necessary ingredient of the European internal market. On the other hand, a link has been established between asymmetrical relations and monetary stability. Does it matter? Chapter 7 will examine the development of a regional currency system in Europe and the lessons to be drawn from it.

Chapter 8 examines the project of EMU, the most ambitious project in the context of European integration. It traces what appears to be a long and bumpy road leading to the adoption of a single European currency scheduled for 1999. Is monetary union an end in itself or is it rather an economic means to a political end? After all, a complete EMU will radically transform the European economic system and may also bring political union through the back door. Will European societies and international markets conform to political exigencies? What will be the economic cost of abandoning the exchange rate instrument and are there any effective substitutes at the national or European level? The strict criteria adopted at Maastricht for the admission of countries to the final stage of EMU raise the question of different tiers or speeds inside the Union; what will happen to those left out? The chapter also discusses the institutional mechanism provided for in the Maastricht treaty for the final stage of EMU: a centralized system for the conduct of monetary policy together with a still highly decentralized system for the coordination of national fiscal policies.

The discussion of EMU is followed by an examination of redistributive policies at the Union level. Redistribution is one of the central elements of the European mixed economy; it can also be considered as an indicator of the degree of internal cohesion of a political system. Chapter 9 discusses the nature and size of inter-country and inter-regional disparities inside the EU, and the development of redistributive policies at the European level. Particular emphasis is laid on the role of Structural Funds and their impact on peripheral countries and regions. Intra-EU transfers are already significant; but how effective are they in terms of economic development and how much can they justify a close involvement of EU institutions in the formulation and implementation of development policies in the recipient countries and regions? The last section of this chapter is devoted to an examination of issues pertaining to European public finance, with particular emphasis on its redistributive dimension. It also examines the various forces pushing the EU budget in the direction of change; and those forces do not always push in the same direction.

The next chapter is devoted to the EU's role as an international actor. It concentrates mostly on external economic policies, although reference is also made to the links between economic diplomacy and the more traditional aspects of political power. Chapter 10 starts by examining the range of policy instruments at the EU level which enable the latter to play an active part in the context of international economic interdependence, with particular emphasis on trade policies which remain the principal instrument in relations with the rest of the world. Is globalization a reality and is there any economic sense in European regionalism? The launching of the internal market programme initially provoked fears about the creation of a 'Fortress Europe'; were those fears really justified? Protectionism is one issue; trade preferences another. The use of such preferences by the EU as an instrument of both low and high policy is also discussed in this chapter. The last section is devoted to the Union's rapidly changing relations with countries in Central and Eastern Europe, the many difficulties experienced in developing a coherent European policy (a need which has emerged as a result of the breakdown of the old political order), and the preparations for further enlargement which may eventually lead to almost doubling of the present membership and a very different political and economic entity.

The final chapter attempts to pull together the loose threads of the argument. The conclusions are presented in the form of ten theses on integration, with the emphasis on the interaction between economic and political factors. So far, we seem to have asked our economic feet to run much faster than our political heart could take. And this presents serious risks. More generally, there is a growing mismatch between the goals set by European politicians and the public at large on the one hand, and the ability of the European political system to deliver on the other. This chapter examines the broad economic changes brought about by the process of integration, the relationship between public power and market forces, and the ability of European institutions to provide an effective level of governance between a weakened, but still very much alive, nation-state and an increasingly (but not yet) global economy. It ends by raising some general questions about further integration and the challenges which lie ahead for Europe.

2

THE UPS AND DOWNS OF
EUROPEAN INTEGRATION

The Foundations of European Regionalism

European economies emerged from the Second World War faced with enormous physical destruction. For many countries, 1936 production levels were only recovered in 1949, the year which is considered by most historians as marking the end of the reconstruction phase. The latter was relatively short and successful. It was characterized by high economic growth and rapid expansion of intra-European trade, with both trends continuing, without any major interruption, for almost thirty years.

The foundations of regional economic cooperation were laid during the reconstruction period. The initiative and the money came from the Americans, in the form of the Marshall Plan. American aid to the dollar-hungry economies of Western Europe provided the finance for the large payments deficits, which were in turn the inevitable outcome of the ambitious growth strategies pursued by European governments. At the same time, US aid was conditional on effective cooperation among European governments and the progressive liberalization of intra-European trade and payments. Both the Organization for European Economic Cooperation (OEEC), which was later transformed into the Organization for Economic Cooperation and Development (OECD) with the entry of non-European, Western industrialized countries, and the European Payments Union (EPU) were the result of American pressure on the European recipients of Marshall aid. The aim was to achieve a more effective use of the money given and also promote the economic and political integration of the old continent.

Through the Marshall Plan, the United States offered Europe what it had adamantly refused to do at Bretton Woods only three years earlier. The refusal to become 'the milch cow of the world in general' (MacBean and Snowden, 1981: 38), by agreeing to the large amounts of unconditional liquidity envisaged by the Keynes plan, was replaced by a US initiative for large bilateral aid for Europe. True, it was now bilateral aid and not drawing rights with an international clearing bank. Furthermore, the granting of Marshall aid and the creation of the

OEEC and the EPU meant that the American Administration appeared ready to accept, albeit reluctantly, that the principle of multilateralism would have to be put in cold storage. Multilateralism had been one of the main planks of US policy with respect to the new postwar economic order.

European governments continued with their extensive system of trade controls, and the slow process of liberalization, mainly through the OEEC and the EPU, was carried out at the regional level, thus implying a discrimination against American exporters. Economic necessity and long-term political objectives were behind the pragmatism and the generosity of the new US policy towards Europe. The European Recovery Programme and the creation of the first regional organizations also marked the institutionalization of the political division of Europe, established by the armies of the allied powers, as they converged on Germany from the east and the west.

The refusal, or more precisely the inability, of the European countries which had come under Soviet control to accept US aid and participate in the new regional organizations led to the first institutionalized form of a Western European system. The early divisions among members of the OEEC and its political counterpart, the Council of Europe, which had been mainly along supranational–intergovernmental lines as well as the nature and extent of economic cooperation–integration, quickly created the basis for a further division. And this time, the line cut across the Western European region.

The OEEC and the EPU contributed significantly towards the rapid expansion of intra-European trade and economic recovery in general. They also provided the initiation stage for economic cooperation at the regional level, which was later taken further through other organizations. The war had followed the protectionism of the 1930s, thus further severing the economic links across national frontiers. Gunnar Myrdal (1956) aptly described the 1930s as the period of national economic integration and international disintegration, thus referring not only to autarchic national policies but also to the expanding economic role of governments during that period. The first efforts at regional cooperation in the early years of reconstruction marked a conscious attempt to reverse an earlier trend which had, obviously, acquired a much larger dimension during the war. The disastrous experience of the past and the considerable disillusionment with the nation-state provided a fertile ground for new ideas on European cooperation, and even federalism, to grow.

However, external liberalization, conducted with much caution and conditioned by the fragile state of European economies, did not signify the adoption of more general *laissez-faire* attitudes by the governments concerned. On the contrary, the early postwar years were characterized by a much wider acceptance of Keynesian ideas regarding the role of governments in manipulating aggregate demand and managing the national economy more generally. It was exactly those ideas, backed by popular expectations, and the weak state of their economies which explained the strong reluctance of European governments to go along with the liberal vision of the postwar economic order held by the Americans. Interestingly enough, American power and money were largely unsuccessful in shaping the European economic order according to Washington's preferences (Milward, 1984).

The next step was taken with the Schuman Plan of May 1950, which led to the signing of the Treaty of Paris one year later and the establishment of the European Coal and Steel Community (ECSC). This also marked the further division of Europe, with the Federal Republic of Germany, the Benelux countries, and Italy following the French initiative, while Britain, still the most powerful country on the western side of Europe's dividing line, decided to stay out of this new organization. Different interests and priorities were coupled with a complete misjudgement by the government in London of the intentions of the Six (Camps, 1964; Monnet, 1976). This was to be repeated several times subsequently; a reassuring sign that people rarely learn any lessons from history.

The Schuman Plan was a French initiative intended to deal essentially with the 'German problem' which belonged to the sphere of high politics. It was also directly related to the emergence of the cold war, and it was for long perceived as such by the Soviet Union. The Schuman Plan laid the foundations of Franco-German reconciliation which later developed into close cooperation, thus providing the cornerstone and the main driving force of regional integration. Wider political considerations were behind the decision of the other four countries to join. The compatibility of economic interests was not always obvious. Hence, for example, the special provisions made in the treaty for Belgian coal and Italian steel. This also explains the complicated nature of many of the legal provisions intended to safeguard different national interests in a very complex package deal.

The ECSC was about the integration of two sectors with central importance for both economic and defence reasons. Two decades later, they would have been among the least likely candidates to be chosen in the first step towards the integration of industrialized economies. However, their strategic importance was hardly in doubt at the time. Although the main objective of the Treaty of Paris was the elimination of barriers and the encouragement of competition in the sectors of coal and steel, many specific provisions were hardly compatible with economic liberalism. This was virtually inevitable in view of the long history of direct government intervention and restrictive business practices in both sectors.

The High Authority, the supranational executive organ of the ECSC, was given extensive powers including the right to levy taxes, influence investment decisions, and also impose minimum prices and production quotas in times of 'imminent' and 'manifest crisis' respectively. Walter Hallstein referred to the economic system set up by the Paris Treaty as one of 'regulated competition' (Haas, 1958: 247), and this was clearly very different from the liberal order dreamt of by postwar US administrations. On the other hand, the development of an international organization, and for that matter any political system, cannot be determined solely by the specific provisions contained in a treaty or a constitution. In fact, Alan Milward (1984: 420) has referred to the ECSC as a protoplasmic organization which could take virtually any shape the High Authority and the member countries would eventually wish to give it. Flexibility and suppleness are after all the main weapons of legal documents in the battle against time. Milward's observation is supported by the actual development of the ECSC.

There was a clear discrepancy in the treaty between the institutional framework envisaged and the specific economic tasks which those institutions were expected to perform. The discrepancy was intentional, since the integration of the two sectors was only partially an end in itself; it was also a means towards the achievement of wider and more long-term political objectives. Subsequent attempts to explain and analyse the Schuman Plan relied heavily on functionalist ideas about the central role of economic issues in Western pluralist systems and their potential use in promoting international cooperation and world peace (Haas, 1958; Lindberg, 1963). And this often led to exaggerated expectations about the influence and the scope of functionalist strategies which were allegedly behind the whole process of integration. Many academics appeared to be only too ready to write off the old nation-states of Europe as the undisputed protagonists of the political scene. The failure of an even more ambitious French plan, also put forward in 1950 by the Defence Minister, Mr Pleven, for the creation of a European Defence Community (EDC), should have served as an early warning sign for those who hoped to find European political union around the corner. The failure of the EDC had another consequence, namely to place defence cooperation firmly within an Atlantic framework (Fursdon, 1980).

The establishment of the ECSC came in the aftermath of the economic reconstruction period. Output continued to grow fast, and external trade, especially between European countries, grew even faster. The OEEC and the EPU helped to liberalize European trade and also multilateralize the system of payments. Meanwhile, following the 1949 devaluation of several European currencies and the economic boom associated with the Korean War, domestic prices began to stabilize. Soon, new plans were put forward for the integration of other sectors, and especially agriculture. European governments were slowly regaining their confidence and were looking for new ways of extending their cooperation in the economic field.

With the signing of the Treaty of Rome in 1957, two new Communities were created: the European Economic Community (EEC) and the European Atomic Energy Community (EAEC—better known as Euratom). The latter was the favourite child of the French who continued their search for strategically placed sectors in the economy, following the earlier example of coal and steel. Interestingly enough, France was later instrumental in placing Euratom in a permanent state of hibernation.

The EEC is by far the most important and far reaching in terms of scope and instruments among the three Communities which constitute what used for years to be generally referred to as the European Community (EC). Through its contents and, perhaps even more sharply through its omissions, the EEC treaty reveals the combination of economic preferences and political objectives as well as the balance of power which prevailed during the negotiations leading to its signing in 1957.

The central element of the 1957 treaty was the creation of a common market, meaning an economic area within which there would be free movement of goods, services, persons, and capital. The main emphasis was on the progressive elimination of tariffs and quantitative restrictions and the suppression of any form of discrimination based on nationality. The stress on the abolition of trade barriers, the provisions made for an EEC competition policy, along the lines of the US anti-trust model, and the negative attitude expressed on the subject of state aids, despite the qualifications included in Article 92, all pointed towards a more liberal economic approach than the one found in the Treaty of Paris. This could be explained in terms of the much wider scope of the new treaty. It was also a reflection of the greater confidence of European governments in the efficacy of market mechanisms; a confidence which had been gradually gained through the successful economic performance of previous years.

There were, however, important exceptions, and the most notable one was agriculture which at the time represented more than one-fifth of the total labour force in the six member countries. Given the special characteristics of this sector and the long history of extensive government intervention, the inclusion of agriculture in the common market could not be achieved through the simple elimination of existing barriers, but only through the adoption of a common policy at the EEC level. On the other hand, the incorporation of agriculture was an essential part of the overall package deal on which the Treaty of Rome was based. Hence the provisions made for a common policy, which were, however, kept at a very general level; thus, basically, registering a joint commitment and providing a framework for the negotiations which were to follow. A similar comment could be made about transport policy, also mentioned in the treaty. As regards the common commercial policy, it was essentially the inevitable outcome of the establishment of a customs union and the adoption of a common external tariff.

Industrial policy and regional policy were most notable by the absence of any specific provisions in the treaty. This absence was striking, especially in view of the importance attached to those policies by European governments during the 1960s. But this reflected the inability of the six signatories to agree on anything specific, because of political and ideological differences. Although Article 2 of the treaty referred to the 'harmonious development of economic activities' and to 'a continuous and balanced expansion', there were hardly any instruments created to ensure the achievement of those general objectives.

The European Investment Bank (EIB) and the European Social Fund (ESF), together with provisions made for the free movement of labour, were designed to work mainly in favour of the Mezzogiorno, the least developed area of the EEC of Six. But there was virtually nothing else to ensure a 'harmonious development' and a 'balanced expansion'. There was a lack of correspondence between objectives and instruments. It could be argued that the signatories may have hoped or believed that those objectives could be achieved through the working of the market mechanism; but this must, surely, have required strong faith and little regard to historical experience. A more plausible explanation would be that the complicated package deal, expressed through the various provisions made in the treaty, was expected to bring about a fairly equal distribution of gains and losses among participants, and that this was the main thing that counted; or perhaps that this was the maximum that could be agreed by the founding members at the time. The fundamental point is that the treaty made virtually no provision for redistributive instruments of policy.

On the other hand, despite various pious wishes about the coordination of economic policies and the consideration of the exchange rate as a problem of common interest, there were virtually no specific provisions regarding cooperation in the macroeconomic field. Furthermore, the objective of the common market was accompanied by a very clear caution regarding the liberalization of capital movements which was to take place only 'to the extent necessary to ensure the proper functioning of the common market' (Article 67).

National differences were one explanation behind the legal void in the macroeconomic area. Considerations of economic and political feasibility were another. The creation of a common market was in itself an extremely ambitious objective. Trying to go beyond that might stretch dangerously the limits of the politically possible, and thus jeopardize the success of the whole enterprise. On the other hand, the predominance of the US currency in the international monetary system and the remaining perception of the 'dollar gap' among European policy-makers made the creation of a regional monetary system in Western Europe virtually unthinkable at the time of the signing of the treaty (Tsoukalis, 1977*a*).

There was still another important reason. The influence of Keynes's ideas meant that governments were keen on retaining direct control over fiscal and monetary policies to be used for the attainment of the objective of full employment at home. Therefore, there should be no readiness for the transfer of real powers to the European or international level. Greater mobility of capital across national frontiers would undermine the effectiveness of national monetary instruments. Hence the caution regarding the liberalization of capital movements in the Treaty of Rome, which could also be found in the Articles of Agreement of the International Monetary Fund (IMF).

The emphasis in the treaty was clearly on the creation of a common market, and more precisely on the establishment of a customs union for goods, with the addition of a limited number of sectoral policies. In view of its much wider scope, the Treaty of Rome was generally less specific in its provisions, when compared with the Treaty of Paris. This explains the distinction sometimes made between *traité-cadre* and *traité-règle* (Lagrange, 1971). The heavy institutional framework provided for in both treaties, when seen in relation to the concrete economic tasks undertaken, can be largely explained in terms of the more long-term political ambitions of the authors. It was evident that some federalist ideas had infiltrated the higher echelons of government in at least a number of Western European countries.

The division created by the ECSC inside Western Europe, resulting from the refusal by a group of countries, led by the UK, to accept the supranational aspects of the Treaty of Paris, and which was further strengthened by the establishment of two new Communities in 1958, was taken to its logical conclusion with the creation of the European Free Trade Association (EFTA) in 1960. As the name implies, this was a much less ambitious initiative than the EEC. The seven members of EFTA (Austria, Denmark, Norway, Portugal, Sweden, Switzerland, and the UK) retained their independence in the conduct of external trade policies, hence the problem of trade deflection and the need to introduce rules of origin in intra-EFTA trade. Agricultural goods were virtually excluded from the free trade area, and again, as the name implies, there was no attempt to extend cooperation beyond trade. This was also reflected in the institutional provisions which were kept to a bare minimum.

EFTA should be seen more as a defensive response by the European countries which had decided, essentially for political reasons, to stay away from the more ambitious integration projects of the Six. However, with the exception of Portugal which in economic and political terms was clearly an oddity inside EFTA, all the other members of the two rival groups constituted the core of Western Europe. By core, we mean here the most advanced industrialized countries of the region, with pluralist, democratic regimes. Members of the European periphery, as defined at the time, were excluded from those integration efforts, their participation being limited, at best, to the OEEC and the Council of Europe.

Economic Growth, Trade Liberalization, and the Mixed Economy

The establishment of the EEC in 1958 coincided with an important new phase in the international economic system. It was heralded, perhaps unconsciously, by the decision of all member countries, together with the UK and Japan, to restore the external convertibility of their currencies. This also meant that the Bretton Woods agreement could at last be taken off the shelf. However, the international monetary system was in practice to evolve in a very different way from what had been originally envisaged by those gathered in the small resort of New Hampshire, and especially by its American architects.

The US current account progressively deteriorated, and the small surpluses were no longer sufficient to compensate for the large outflows of capital. Meanwhile, European and Japanese payments surpluses grew. This led to the weakening of the dollar in foreign exchange markets and to successive speculative crises. Sterling shared the fate of the dollar, if only in more misery and despair. It usually acted as the soft underbelly of the American currency until the UK government gave way to market pressure by devaluing sterling in 1967. On the other hand, the Six enjoyed healthy surpluses and mounting foreign reserves (Strange, 1976). The 1960s was a decade marked by a significant shift of the economic balance of power from the United States and Britain to continental Europe and Japan, and this was bound to have a positive effect on confidence among the Six and on their integration effort.

Table 2.1. Growth Rates, 1960–1994 (Average annual % change of real GDP at constant prices)

	1960–7	1968–73	1974–9	1980–5	1986–90	1991–4
Belgium	4.6	5.3	2.2	1.4	3.0	1.1
France	5.5	5.2	2.8	1.5	3.0	0.8
Germany	3.8	5.0	2.4	1.4	2.9	1.7
Italy	5.6	4.9	3.7	1.9	3.0	0.7
Luxembourg	2.8	5.5	1.3	2.2	4.7	2.0
Netherlands	4.6	5.1	2.6	1.3	3.1	1.8
Denmark	4.6	4.0	1.9	2.1	1.4	2.0
Ireland	3.6	5.2	4.9	2.6	4.5	4.0
United Kingdom	2.9	3.5	1.5	1.3	3.3	0.9
Greece	5.8	8.4	3.7	1.4	1.7	1.1
Portugal	6.2	7.6	2.9	1.5	5.1	0.7
Spain	7.8	6.7	2.3	1.5	4.5	1.0
EU-12	4.6	4.9	2.6	1.5	3.1	1.2
Austria	4.2	5.7	2.9	1.6	3.0	2.1
Finland	4.1	5.9	2.1	3.2	3.4	−2.0
Sweden	4.5	3.7	1.8	1.7	2.3	−1.7
OECD-Europe	4.6	4.9	2.5	1.6	3.1	1.1
Japan	9.8	9.3	3.6	3.7	4.5	1.4
United States	4.6	3.2	2.5	2.1	2.8	2.4
Total OECD	5.1	4.9	2.7	2.2	3.2	1.6

Note: The total OECD figure includes all the countries that were members of the OECD before 1994.

Source: OECD, *National Accounts.*

The twelve-year transitional period envisaged by the treaty also coincided with what appears with the benefit of hindsight as the last phase of the postwar economic miracle, the Golden Age as it is often referred to (Crafts and Toniolo, 1996). It was a period of high and steady growth and unprecedented levels of employment (Tables 2.1 and 2.2). Although high growth and low unemployment also characterized the large majority of Western European countries, the performance of the Six was significantly better than that of the United States and the UK. The main exceptions were the southern European NICs (newly industrializing countries) which approached the growth rates registered by the emerging economic giant in East Asia. There was only one dark spot, namely the accelerating rate of inflation which was already noticeable towards the end of the 1960s (Table 2.3). But inflation had not yet reached dangerous levels.

Tariffs and quantitative restrictions in intra-EC trade were abolished eighteen months ahead of schedule, and the common external tariff (CET) was adopted by all six member countries. In fact, the CET had already been considerably reduced as a result of the Kennedy Round negotiations within GATT (General Agreement on Tariffs and Trade), in which the Six had participated as a single unit. External negotiations were closely linked to internal developments, as an integral part of the intra-EC package. This is a pattern which was to be regularly repeated in subsequent years. Thus, the mandate given to the Commission to negotiate tariff

Table 2.2. Unemployment Rates, 1960–1995 (Average of annual unemployment rates as % of the labour force)

	1960–7	1968–73	1974–9	1980–5	1986–90	1991–5
Belgium	2.1	2.3	5.7	11.6	10.4	11.6
France	1.5	2.8	4.5	8.3	9.8	11.1
Germany	0.8	0.8	3.5	6.3	7.2	8.5
Italy	4.9	5.7	6.6	7.3	10.0	10.2
Luxembourg[a]	0.0	0.0	0.6	2.8	2.2	2.5
Netherlands	0.7	1.5	4.9	8.2	7.4	6.4
Denmark	1.6	1.0	6.1	9.3	8.6	11.3
Ireland	4.9	5.6	7.6	12.5	15.5	14.6
United Kingdom	1.5	2.4	4.2	9.3	8.1	9.1
Greece	5.2	3.7	1.9	6.1	7.4	9.1
Portugal	2.4	2.5	6.0	8.0	6.3	5.8
Spain	2.3	2.7	5.3	17.0	18.6	20.9
EU-12	2.2	2.7	4.8	8.4	9.1	10.2
Austria	2.0	1.4	1.7	3.1	4.6	5.7
Finland	1.6	2.6	4.4	5.1	4.4	14.8
Sweden	1.6	2.2	1.9	2.9	2.0	6.4
EU-15	2.8	3.4	5.1	8.5	9.2	10.4
Japan	1.3	1.2	1.9	2.4	2.5	2.6
United States	5.0	4.6	6.7	8.1	5.9	6.5
Total OECD	3.1	3.4	5.1	7.3	6.8	7.5

Note: The total OECD figure includes all the countries that were members of the OECD before 1994.

[a] Eurostat.

Source: OECD.

reductions in the Kennedy Round was dependent on an agreement between member countries to proceed with the customs union and the CAP. The Kennedy Round was also the first manifestation of the role and power of the EEC as an international actor, and this had profound effects on the self-perception of the Six and the balance of power on the world economic scene. The EEC successfully challenged the dominant position of the United States which was finally forced to modify substantially its own expectations about the outcome of the trade negotiations (Shonfield, 1976).

At the same time, the Kennedy Round strengthened and confirmed the shift in British policy towards Brussels, a shift which had already led to the first British application for membership in 1961. The EEC was a concrete economic reality, and this was now manifested through a strong presence on the international economic scene. The British who were, according to the architect of European integration, Jean Monnet, unable to understand an idea but supremely good at grasping hard facts, had decided to join. However, two successive applications for membership in 1961 and 1967 were blocked by General de Gaulle's veto.

During the transitional period, trade grew much faster than output, and this was almost entirely due to the growth of intra-EC trade (Fig. 2.1). In other words, the dependence of the six economies on each other grew steadily in relation to

Table 2.3. Consumer Price Indices, 1960–1995 (Average annual % change)

	1960–8	1969–73	1974–9	1980–5	1986–90	1991–5
Belgium	2.5	4.5	8.5	6.9	2.1	3.1
France	3.5	5.8	10.7	10.2	3.1	2.8
Germany	2.5	4.3	4.7	4.2	1.4	4.4
Italy	4.1	5.1	16.1	15.0	5.7	6.4
Luxembourg	2.0	4.3	7.4	7.0	1.7	3.5
Netherlands	3.8	6.4	7.2	4.6	0.7	3.4
Denmark	5.3	6.7	10.8	8.6	3.9	2.5
Ireland	4.0	8.2	15.0	13.3	3.3	3.1
United Kingdom	3.1	7.0	15.6	8.9	5.9	4.3
Greece	2.1	4.7	16.1	21.4	17.4	17.7
Portugal	3.0	7.8	23.7	22.1	11.3	9.1
Spain	6.2	6.7	18.3	12.8	6.5	6.5
EU-12	3.7[a]	5.8	12.3	9.8	4.4	3.9
Austria	3.5	4.8	6.3	5.1	2.2	4.0
Finland	5.6	5.8[b]	12.8	9.7	5.1	2.9
Sweden	4.1	5.3	9.8	9.8	6.2	5.6
EU-15	3.8[a]	6.0	12.8	11.5	6.8	4.1
Japan	5.5	6.8	9.9	3.6	1.3	1.7
United States	1.7	4.9	8.5	6.7	4.0	3.9
Total OECD	2.8	5.6	10.5	8.3	4.8	4.9

Note: The total OECD figure includes all the countries that were members of the OECD before 1994.

[a] 1961–7.

[b] 1968–73.

Source: OECD.

their dependence on the rest of the world. Virtually all empirical studies point to a close link between EC integration and the growth of trade; and by far the largest component of the latter is attributed to trade creation rather than trade diversion (Robson, 1987; Mayes, 1989).[1] The exact magnitude of the integration effect is, of course, impossible to determine, since the rapid growth of intra-EC trade during the transitional period was bound to be influenced by many different factors. The results of empirical studies vary widely, and this should have been expected. Müller and Owen (1989) refer to a 'consensus view' that trade creation in 1970 accounted for 30 per cent of intra-EC trade in manufactures, which may be considered as a rough indicator of the orders of magnitude involved.

There is, however, hardly a 'consensus view' among economists regarding the contribution of increased trade to welfare and growth. On the basis of the static theory of customs union, the only developed part of economic integration theory for many years, the results obtained were meagre: usually, less than 1 per cent of

---

[1] Trade creation and trade diversion are the two main concepts developed by customs union theory. The former arises when domestic production is substituted by cheaper imports from a partner country, and the latter when cheaper imports from a third country are substituted by dearer imports from a partner country. Trade creation represents a shift to a more efficient producer as a result of the establishment of a customs union, while the opposite is true of trade diversion.

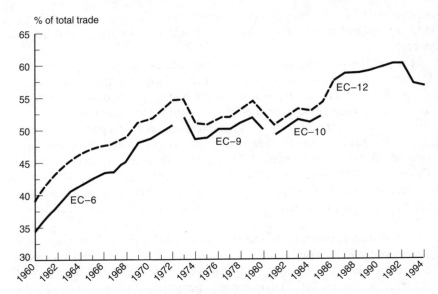

Fig. 2.1. Intra-EU Trade in Goods, 1960–1994

Note: Sum of intra-EU exports and intra-EU imports divided by the sum of all imports and exports.

Source: Eurostat.

the Gross Domestic Product (GDP) of member countries (Robson, 1987). This was hardly the result to match the time and efforts spent, not to mention the expectations associated with European integration. One possible and perhaps obvious conclusion to draw from this empirical finding would therefore be that European integration was taking place for essentially political reasons; the customs union was an economic means to a political end, and this was spectacularly manifested in its marginal economic effects. This does not, however, exclude another possible explanation, namely that the economic theory, on which those econometric studies were based, was in itself highly inadequate and thus unable to capture the effects of integration.

Customs union theory suffers from all the limitations of traditional theories of international trade based on comparative advantage. It concentrates on static effects. It relies on totally unrealistic assumptions such as perfect competition, homogeneous products, full employment of resources, and no adjustment costs. It pretends that the role of the state is only limited to border interventions, thus denying the existence of mixed economies (Pelkmans, 1984). It also ignores, like most neoclassical economics, the fundamental question of distribution. On the other hand, its own inherent logic is totally suspect, since, on the basis of the standard assumptions, the conclusion drawn is that unilateral tariff disarmament is preferable to participation in a customs union. This presumably means that there is something totally irrational in the whole process. Last but not least, customs union theory is unable to explain an important fact which has emerged from empirical studies, namely that the largest part of Community trade is intra-industry and not inter-industry trade, as should have been expected from the theory.

Economists later introduced economies of scale, as part of the dynamic effects. The results obtained are much more significant. Growth in trade has made possible a substantial increase in plant size, and this in turn has led to cost reductions. According to Owen (1983), this could have amounted to some 3–6 per cent of the combined GDP of the Six for 1980. There were also signs of a positive investment effect of integration, both from internal and external sources; US foreign investment in Western Europe being partly attributed to the creation of the EEC (Davenport, 1982; Pelkmans, 1984). Thus economists gradually switched their attention to the more important variables, but their tools of analysis and measurement, despite frequent claims to the contrary, have remained woefully deficient.

The causality between trade and growth is arguably not only one-way, as it is usually implied. The rapid elimination of intra-EEC tariffs and quantitative restrictions between 1958 and 1968 was made possible largely because of the favourable macroeconomic environment, characterized by high rates of growth and low unemployment. Increased exposure to international trade brings with it adjustment costs for both labour and capital. They are much more easily absorbed in times of rapid growth, thus minimizing the resistance from potential losers. This points to a possible virtuous circle: the favourable macroeconomic environment of the late 1950s and the 1960s, attributable to a combination of different factors, such as catching up with the more advanced US technology, and high investment ratios coupled with wage moderation, created the conditions which permitted the signing of the Treaty of Rome and the successful implementation of its trade provisions. Liberalization then led to more trade and this, in turn, contributed to the remarkable growth rates of this period (Boltho, 1982: chs. 1 and 8; Maddison, 1982; for a more recent evaluation of the Golden Age, see Crafts and Toniolo, 1996; Eichengreen, 1996).

There is, however, another major feature of Western European economies during this period, which may appear, at least superficially, in contradiction to the trend towards liberalization. These years were characterized by the continuous strengthening of the mixed economy and the welfare state. At both the micro- and the macroeconomic levels, the role of the state became increasingly pronounced. One clear indication are the figures on government expenditure, which show a steep rise in terms of GDP (Table 2.4). Among the Six, both the Federal Republic and the Netherlands experienced an increase in government expenditure which represents more than 10 per cent of GDP between 1960 and 1974; and the others were not lagging far behind. The figures in this table also show a significant difference between the large majority of Western European countries, including the Six, on the one hand, and the United States and Japan on the other. The Western European experience of the time suggests that high economic growth is not necessarily incompatible with an active economic role for the state. Arguably, domestic institutions played a crucial role in securing the crucial package deal,

Table 2.4. Government Expenditure, 1960–1994 (As a % of GDP)

	1960	1974	1980	1985	1990	1992	1994
Belgium	30.3	39.4	58.6	62.2	54.8	56.2	56.4
France	34.6	39.3	46.1	52.2	49.8	52.2	54.9
Germany	32.4	44.6	47.9	47.0	45.1	48.6	49.0
Italy	30.1	37.9	41.9	50.9	53.2	53.6	53.9
Luxembourg	30.5	35.6	54.8	51.7	51.3[a]	53.0[a]	52.7[a]
Netherlands	33.7	47.9	55.5	56.5	54.0	55.3	54.4
Denmark	24.8	45.9	56.2	59.3	58.6	61.3	63.9
Ireland	28.0	43.0	48.9	52.4	41.2	42.6	43.8
United Kingdom	32.2	44.8	43.0	44.0	39.9	43.1	42.9
Greece[b]	17.4	25.0	29.7	43.3	46.1	44.8	47.9
Portugal	17.0	24.7	25.5	43.1	43.1	49.9	51.5
Spain	—	23.1	32.2	41.1	42.0	44.4	45.6
EU-12	31.8	40.7	45.9	49.7	47.7[a]	50.0	51.0[a]
Austria	35.7	41.9	48.1	50.9	48.6	50.5	51.5
Finland	26.6	32.0	38.1	43.8	45.4	59.1	58.7
Sweden	31.0	48.1	60.1	63.3	59.1	67.3	68.8
OECD-Europe	31.3	40.4	45.9	49.5	48.6	50.2	51.0[c]
Japan	17.5	24.5	32.0	31.6	31.7	32.3	35.8
United States[d]	27.0	32.2	31.8	33.2	33.3	35.0	33.5
Total OECD	28.0	34.8	39.4	40.7	40.7	40.8[e]	40.8[e]

Note: The total OECD figure includes all the countries that were members of the OECD before 1994.

[a] Eurostat.
[b] 1960, 1974 current disbursements only (e.g. gross capital formation excluded).
[c] Except Switzerland, Luxembourg, Turkey, and Iceland.
[d] From 1980 it excludes deposit insurance outlays.
[e] Except Australia, New Zealand, and Turkey.

Source: OECD.

consisting of high investment and wage moderation, which in turn provided the basis for the long period of high growth.

Fiscal policy and, increasingly from the mid-1960s onwards, also monetary policy were actively used by political authorities as a means of influencing aggregate demand. On the other hand, intervention was not limited to the macroeconomic level. Governments also resorted to regional, industrial, and incomes policies, albeit with varying degrees of enthusiasm and with different instruments, in order to influence the domestic allocation of resources and the distribution of income (Boltho, 1982: chs. 10–14).

The promotion of 'national champions',[2] especially in the fields of high

---

[2] This is a term first used by McArthur and Scott (1969) in their study of French industrial planning to refer to large firms which were actively supported by the French government and seen as national representatives in international oligopolistic competition (see also Vernon, 1971 for a study of the relations between big firms and governments in Europe). The promotion of 'national champions' and the need to face the 'American challenge' (Servan-Schreiber, 1967) also explains the rather relaxed view taken by most European governments during this period to the ever-increasing concentration which characterized many industrial sectors.

technology, through active fiscal and credit policies, discriminatory public procurement, and only half-concealed measures of external protection, was just one very important manifestation of the political answer, at the national level, to growing international competition. These were the high days of optimism about the ability of political institutions to guide the 'invisible hand'. The contrast with the economic ideas which have prevailed since the 1980s is, indeed, striking.

Meanwhile, the growing power of trade unions, combined and not unrelated with welfare state provisions and job security legislation, led to the creation of highly regulated labour markets. More generally, it could be argued that the 1960s were characterized by a constant attempt by Western European governments to reduce the incidence of microeconomic as well as macroeconomic risk for both individuals and firms, thus complementing, if not partly negating, the operation of the market mechanism. This was, in turn, a function of social pressures and the existing political balance of power: in other words, the prevalence of social democratic forces and values.

There is, certainly, a strong element of contradiction between the increasing openness of national economies to world competition, closely related to both international and EEC liberalization processes, and the conscious attempt to regulate the market domestically. It was yet another manifestation of 'Keynes at home and Smith abroad' (Mayall quoted in Gilpin, 1987: 355). Both happened simultaneously, and the coincidence may be a surprise only to the economic purists. In fact, it could be argued that both the mixed economy and the welfare state facilitated the process of internationalization and European integration by enabling governments to smooth out and, sometimes, even slow down the necessary adjustment arising from the increased openness of national economies.

It is true that domestic intervention sometimes led to the introduction of non-tariff barriers (NTBs), thus replacing border controls which had been previously negotiated away in the context of the EEC or GATT. But this represents only part of the overall picture. The mixed economy and the welfare state also helped to buy social acceptance of greater international competition by alleviating its effects on potential losers. It may, therefore, have contributed significantly to the process of European integration in the late 1950s and 1960s. The two developments appear to have been closely linked and mutually reinforcing, although the relationship was based on a very delicate equilibrium which was soon to break down. This delicate equilibrium sustained the process of economic integration in Western Europe for many years, based on a symbiosis between external liberalization and the strengthening of the economic role of the state at the domestic level. But this also meant that for years European integration was essentially limited to trade.

The establishment of the customs union in the EEC was coupled with the creation of a CAP relying on three main principles: the unity of the market, based on the instrument of common prices, Community preference, and financial solidarity (Tracy, 1989). This, in turn, led to the progressive liberalization and also rapid expansion of intra-EC trade in agricultural goods, more the result of trade diversion than trade creation. The adoption of a common policy for agricultural products meant the implementation of the original agreement expressed in the

Treaty of Rome and the Stresa conference of 1958; it was also an absolutely integral part of a package deal which included both the intra-EC liberalization of trade in industrial goods and the significant reduction of the CET which resulted from the Kennedy Round negotiations.

The elimination of many border controls and the establishment of the CAP were accompanied by the first steps towards an EEC competition policy. The latter concentrated on restrictive business practices and the 'abuse of dominant position' by private firms, while state aids remained almost untouched. No progress was registered in the field of transport, despite the provisions originally made in the treaty. Economic integration also had little effect on intra-European factor movements. Cross-border labour mobility was limited by cultural and linguistic factors as well as the slow progress in the transferability of social security rights and the mutual recognition of professional qualifications. To the extent that it did take place, it was mainly unskilled labour from the south of Italy and non-member countries of the Mediterranean. As for the liberalization of capital movements, the EEC had virtually no effect during the 1960s; international factors continued to play the decisive role.

No substantial progress was made in the macroeconomic field either. Although there were signs of growing interest in EEC cooperation in this area, the political sensitivity of the issues involved, policy differences, and the inability to reach a common position *vis-à-vis* the United States, and the question of the dollar in particular, prevented the Six from registering any serious progress in macro-economic policy cooperation during the 1960s (Tsoukalis, 1977a). Although growing trade interdependence made policy instruments less effective, the use of the latter remained exclusively in the domain of national discretion. The international environment, and the United States in particular, continued to have a stronger impact on national policies than any half-hearted attempt to coordinate at the EC level.

The external dimension has played a major role in the process of integration, closely linked to the development of internal policies. During the same period, the Six were also involved in numerous bilateral negotiations with third countries. Those negotiations concentrated mainly, but not exclusively, on trade matters, and led to the signing of preferential and non-preferential agreements which were not always reconcilable with the GATT principle of multilateralism. Thus, the EC, through its very nature as a customs union and also through the signing of many association and trade preferential agreements, was often seen as undermining the fragile international trading order.

The creation of a regional bloc in Western Europe was bound to bring about attempts by neighbouring countries to reduce the trade diversion effects arising from the process of regional integration. The Six, very much flattered by the flood of requests for the negotiation of bilateral agreements and in need of international recognition, especially in the early years of the EEC, became involved, almost absent-mindedly, in those negotiations. And sometimes they signed agreements which they were later to regret (Tsoukalis, 1977b).

Largely as a result of the influence of General de Gaulle, who overshadowed the

European scene during the 1960s, the supranationalist element of integration was seriously weakened. But this trend had already become obvious in the first years of the ECSC. The High Authority did not exercise the full powers given to it by the Treaty of Paris. Later on, the EEC treaty confirmed this trend and further reduced the powers enjoyed by the 'supranational' organ, namely the Commission. General de Gaulle then made sure that the high ambitions entertained by the first Commission, and especially its President, Mr Walter Hallstein, were completely squashed. The 'empty chair' crisis and the Luxembourg agreement of 1966, which reintroduced the national veto through the back door, were crucial turning-points on the road towards more intergovernmentalism (Camps, 1967). It took the Brussels executive a long time before it could recover from this shock.

While power was concentrated in the Council of Ministers, as a collective expression of national interests, the Court of Justice was busy building on the foundations of a federal system. And this was done in a very quiet manner, away from the political limelight. According to Weiler (1983), the establishment of the doctrine of direct effect, the doctrine of supremacy, and the doctrine of pre-emption for Community legislation during those years created a constitutional framework for a federal-type political structure. Indeed, the Community legal framework is arguably what most distinguishes the EC, and now the EU, from traditional intergovernmental organizations; and this was bound to have long-term political effects.

No Longer Small and Carefree

At the end of the decade, which also coincided with the end of the twelve-year transitional period envisaged by the Treaty of Rome, the Six were again in search of a new driving force for the process of integration. This was finally provided by the Hague summit which took place in December 1969. The relaunching of European integration took the form of a new package deal. This was described by President Pompidou in terms of a triptych consisting of completion, deepening, and enlargement; and it was based on a, albeit uneasy, Franco-German bilateral agreement, something which was later to become a recurrent phenomenon.

The logic of the new package deal was rather simple: the French green light for the accession of Britain and the other applicant countries required the creation of the Community's 'own resources', a means of strengthening its financial inde-pendence and also providing a more solid revenue basis for the CAP (*l'enfant chéri* of French governments). This, in turn, would require a modest increase in the powers enjoyed by the European Parliament: something which had been vehemently resisted by General de Gaulle only a few years earlier. Deepening meant basically the creation of an intergovernmental system of foreign policy coordination which became known as European Political Cooperation (EPC), and the establishment of an Economic and Monetary Union (EMU). Thus, the relaunching of integration would take place in both the areas of high and low politics, although low politics was clearly a misnomer, at least as far as money was concerned. This became patently obvious during the early stages of the negotiations for the establishment of EMU.

Most of the above ideas had entered the intra-European debate some years earlier. However, it was only at the Hague summit of 1969 that the political environment seemed ripe for their formal adoption. Although partly for different reasons, France and Germany, under their new leadership, were ready to give the Community a new push forward. The positive experience of the 1960s and the fear of the EC being diluted into a free trade area, as a result of British accession, combined to produce extremely ambitious initiatives which went much closer to the heart of national sovereignty than anything which had preceded them. With the benefit of hindsight, it appears that some of those initiatives were taken in a light-hearted fashion.

The first enlargement of the Community took place in January 1973, with the accession of Britain, Denmark, and Ireland. Norway had to drop out at the last minute, when the Treaty of Accession was rejected at a national referendum. Enlargement removed a major issue of contention which had divided the Six for more than a decade. It also marked the final and undisputed victory of the group of countries, led by France, in a division which dated back to the late 1940s and which had led to the creation of two rival organizations in Western Europe, namely the EC and EFTA. The dominant position of the EC was to become even more evident during the next decade, with the further strengthening of Community institutions and the process of integration, which in turn forced most of the remaining members of EFTA to drastically reconsider their relations with the EC, leading to full membership.

The financial independence of the Community was achieved through the introduction of its own sources of revenue, consisting of customs duties, agricultural levies, and a percentage of the value added tax (VAT). In so doing, member countries also adopted a common form of indirect taxation, while the budgetary powers of the European Parliament were extended. The whole process was not, however, completed before the end of the decade, because of long delays in the introduction of VAT in some member countries.

The rest of the overall package of measures agreed at the Hague summit was in the end only very partially implemented. Political resistance to any serious encroachment on national sovereignty was one explanation. Another and, perhaps, the most important explanation is associated with the dramatic change in the political and economic environment which had sustained and protected the process of regional integration until then. Additional difficulties were created by enlargement itself, as full participation in the internal decision-making process enabled the new members to challenge some important aspects of the *acquis communautaire* (the whole body of EC legislation) and thus try to shift the balance of gains and losses in their favour.

The exceptionally long period of high and stable growth, combined with unprecedented levels of employment, gradually came to an end. After 1973, it gave way to a new situation characterized by a rapid deceleration of economic growth, declining rates of investment and productivity, galloping inflation, loss of international competitiveness, and, last but not least, a dramatic increase in unemployment. In terms of unemployment, most EFTA countries fared much better than EC members (see Tables 2.1–2.3).

Numerous explanations have been put forward regarding the end of the Golden Age (Boltho, 1982; Emerson, 1984; Strange, 1985; Lawrence and Schultze, 1987; Crafts and Toniolo, 1996). Some lay the emphasis on external economic shocks and the inappropriate response of European governments, mainly in terms of macroeconomic policies. Such explanations obviously point to the large increase in oil prices, which happened in 1973–4 and then again in 1978–9 and led to a significant worsening of the terms of trade and the transfer of real resources to oil producers. European governments were criticized for excessively restrictive policies which exacerbated the deflationary impact of the oil shocks. Imported inflation from the United States, Washington's policies of 'benign neglect', and the advent of floating exchange rates were also considered as additional destabilizing factors.

Another set of explanations concentrated on internal structural changes and the rigidities associated with the growth of the welfare state. In addition to the loss of cheap energy, European entrepreneurs were also faced with escalating labour costs. This was, in turn, attributed to the gradual exhaustion of labour reserves, both domestic and imported, and the intensification of the political struggle for larger income shares; the latter being also a reflection of the breakdown of the political consensus which had provided the foundation of the economic miracle of the 1950s and the 1960s.

The result was a continuous increase in the share of wages and salaries at the expense of profits, with negative effects on investment. A kind of nemesis theory has been advocated by some economic observers (Giersch, 1983 and 1985; Minford, 1985) arguing that the stagflation (a new term invented to describe the hitherto unthinkable combination of recession and inflation) of the 1970s was the inevitable outcome of the full employment policies of the previous decade and the new bargaining power of European trade unions, itself closely related to the previous high levels of employment. Along similar lines, Mancur Olson (1982) has argued that economic stagnation in pluralist systems is largely attributable to societal immobilism, gradually created during long periods of peace through the proliferation and strengthening of pressure groups which try to defend their entrenched positions and thus resist any form of change.

The real increase in wages and salaries, which regularly exceeded the growth rates in productivity, was one important factor behind the deterioration of the business climate in Western Europe. Another factor was, according to those theories, the rigidities created in the labour market through job security legislation and the growth of the welfare state. Changes in the international economic environment brought about the need for domestic adjustment. But this required a degree of flexibility and mobility on behalf of European labour and the European societies in general, which clearly did not exist. Again according to those theories, which later provided the ideological justification for supply-side measures, the inability of European economies to adjust was a major factor behind the loss of international competitiveness and the continuing high levels of unemployment.

This was a very different argument from the one advocated earlier with respect to the experience of the 1950s and the 1960s. Although the fundamental premise is clearly different, it is also true that the real world had undergone a major transformation in the meantime. The external economic shocks of the 1970s and the gradual disintegration of the internal consensus had brought about a major change in the political economy of Western Europe; and there was also much less scope for catching up. The preconditions for high economic growth were no longer there. In fact, the Golden Age has come to be considered as exceptional, and the period since 1973 as the return to normal (consistent with long-term historical trends). In the words of Crafts and Toniolo, 'the *explanandum* in postwar European economic history appears to be not so much the slowdown of the 1970s as the growth spurt of the previous two decades' (1996: 25).

On the other hand, the deterioration of the international economic environment sparked off different policy responses on the part of individual Western European countries. Broadly speaking, two groups of countries can be distinguished: the first group, consisting of the Federal Republic of Germany, Switzerland, Austria, and, to a lesser extent, the Benelux countries, was characterized by a strong anti-inflationary policy stance; the second group, which included most of the other Western European countries, tried to ride out the storm by accommodating monetary and fiscal policies (Wegner, 1985). Interestingly enough, membership of the EC did not seem to make any difference. The post-1973 recession was accompanied by a widening of economic divergence among national economies, which was manifested both in terms of macroeconomic policies and performances (see, for example, Table 2.3 for the wide divergence in terms of inflation rates). During the period between 1974 and 1979, the inflation differential between Italy and the UK on the one hand, and Germany on the other was more than 10 percentage points a year. An increase in economic disparities between the more and less advanced countries and regions of the Community was another characteristic of the recession, thus reversing the trend of the 1960s when there had been a progressive narrowing of the economic gap.

National economies were affected in different ways by the crisis. Furthermore, nation-states behaved as autonomous political units, and the dialectic of economic, political, and social forces differed considerably from one to another. Under such circumstances, monetary union became a totally infeasible objective. In complete contrast to their verbal commitments, individual member countries showed hardly any interest in using the EC as a framework for an effective coordination of macroeconomic policies. To the extent that an interest in coordination did exist at all, it was more obvious in the context of international fora.

A similar observation can be made with respect to energy matters. Here, the failure of the Nine to coordinate their policies and adopt a common stance in the crisis diplomacy which followed the quadrupling of oil prices in 1973 was particularly striking. Caught between the conflicting pressures and demands emanating from Washington and the capitals of the Arab oil producers, Western European countries offered a sad spectacle of disunity and inaction. The more assertive stance of the United States during this period only served to exacerbate intra-EC divisions (Odell, 1986). The economic crisis and the new international environment appeared to indicate that members of the EC were not yet ready or able to extend cooperation much beyond the area of trade.

Faced with the collapse of the Bretton Woods system, characterized by the end of the dollar–gold convertibility and the abandonment of fixed exchange rates, the EC countries tried to build the foundations of a regional currency bloc in the form of the snake. In a world of generalized floating, which had already become a reality by March 1973, the objective was to maintain bilateral exchange rates within relatively narrow margins. However, the attempt to preserve some of the elements of Bretton Woods at the regional level proved to be a futile exercise. The EC snake was quickly transformed into a Deutschmark zone, after the withdrawal of sterling, the punt, the lira, and the French franc (Kruse, 1980).

This development could be considered as the first clear indication of a new phase in the history of the European Community. One important feature of this new phase was the increasingly dominant economic position of the Federal Republic of Germany and the *Modell Deutschland*, especially in terms of macro-economic management (Markovits, 1982). Another feature was the gradual departure from regional arrangements applying *erga omnes*. The snake, as it gradually developed, was the first important manifestation of a two-tier Community,[3] with some countries outside the EC participating in the exchange rate arrangement. Different variations of the two-tier model were to become increasingly popular in subsequent years, largely in response to the wide economic divergence which characterized the enlarging Community.

On the other hand, the prolonged economic recession and the rapid increase in the numbers of unemployed led to a resurgence of protectionist pressures in Western Europe: a phenomenon which could also be observed in the rest of the industrialized world. This 'new protectionism' mainly took the form of non-tariff measures; it was often of a bilateral nature and directed mostly against Japan and the new Asian NICs. Various forms of indirect protection of domestic production, coupled with 'voluntary export restraints' and 'orderly marketing arrangements' (euphemisms for essentially unilateral restrictions on imports) against third countries, were introduced in an increasing number of sectors (Page, 1981). To all intents and purposes, agriculture, fuel, and textiles had already been taken outside the GATT framework. With the advent of the economic recession in the mid-1970s and the emergence of large surplus capacity, new sectors were added to the above list. They included steel, shipbuilding, cars, chemicals, electronics, and footwear. Meanwhile, protection in high technology sectors, mainly through the promotion of national champions, continued to be stronger than ever.

The common commercial policy was bound to suffer as a result. It was under-

---

[3] This term was first introduced by Chancellor Brandt. It was later taken up by Mr Tindemans in his report on European union (Tindemans, 1975).

mined by the increasing recourse to NTBs which fell largely outside the competence of EC institutions, while being progressively diluted by tariff reductions in the framework of GATT. National measures and bilateral agreements with Japan and Eastern Europe were the most obvious holes in the external armoury of the EC. A common position in international negotiations was sometimes preserved at the expense of free intra-EC trade. Thus, the EC quantitative restrictions on imports, imposed in the context of the various multifibre arrangements (MFAs), were subdivided into national quotas, and this implied the need for controls at national frontiers and the introduction of rules of origin in intra-EC trade.

The Tokyo Round of GATT negotiations (1975–9) was as much a logical continuation and extension of the postwar process of international trade liberalization, concentrating mainly on NTBs, as it was an attempt to resist the reversal of this process because of the new protectionist pressures. Its success in this respect was limited at best (Cline, 1983). On the other hand, the new round confirmed the 'pyramidal style of multilateral negotiation, where issues would first be negotiated bilaterally between the larger powers [the United States and the EC] and then later multilateralized as the negotiations went on' (Winham, 1986: 371). The EC often adopted a defensive stance in view of internal problems and pressures, and this was particularly evident on two important issues, namely agriculture and safeguards against imports supposed to cause injury to domestic producers.

Meanwhile, EC agreements with third parties became increasingly compatible with GATT rules. Largely in response to international criticism, emanating mainly from Washington, the Community tried to conform to the requirements of Article XXIV of GATT, regarding the creation of free trade areas and customs unions, mainly by abandoning its demands for reciprocal trade concessions as far as developing countries were concerned. It was in this spirit that the new Mediterranean agreements were signed in the 1970s. The same principle applied to the successive Lomé conventions signed with a large and ever-growing group of developing countries, the large majority of which were former colonies of different members of the Community. On the other hand, free trade agreements were signed in 1972 with the remaining members of EFTA, thus marking an important step towards the creation of a large free trade area in Western Europe. Regionalism was thus further strengthened at the expense of multilateralism (Hine, 1985).

During this period, the rates of growth of international trade registered a significant decline. However, this decline was in terms of growth rates and not in absolute figures. Thus the experience of the 1970s and the early 1980s was substantially different from that of the interwar period when international trade had declined in absolute terms. Protectionism spilled over into intra-Community trade. There was clear evidence of increasing recourse to state aids and technical barriers, while the number of infringements of treaty articles dealing with the free movement of goods and services multiplied during this period. Protectionism was mainly the result of strong social resistance to economic adjustment, and the emphasis was laid on declining sectors. In 1981 the EC Commissioner for Industry, Etienne Davignon, warned that 'the industrial activism of certain member states ... has become a veritable challenge to the Community' (Noelke and Taylor, 1981: 219). The incomplete customs union of the 1960s did not come crashing down with the advent of the economic recession; and this was, perhaps, a major achievement in itself. The building did, however, suffer a certain degree of damage, and the economic relevance of the EC was considerably reduced as a consequence.

In some cases, in an attempt to preserve the common market and also strengthen the role of the Community, the Commission tried to replace national policies of intervention by common EC policies, thus following the example of agriculture. The sector where it became most active was steel where the Commission, taking advantage of the provisions of the Treaty of Paris and the crisis situation which developed in the European steel industry after 1973, gradually set up the mechanisms for a highly interventionist policy, which included production quotas, minimum prices, and severe import restrictions. It was ironic that the crisis measures in the steel industry, fully implemented in 1980, relied largely on the operation of a cartel of producers (basically a rationalization cartel) created under the guidance and supervision of the EC Commission. One of the main objectives of the Treaty of Paris had been precisely to avoid the reappearance of such a cartel. The latter brought together some prominent national champions from different countries, whose survival, thirty years after the creation of the ECSC, was a perfect illustration of the limitations of the trade model in European integration (Tsoukalis and Strauss, 1985; Messerlin, 1987).

The sun did not shine over European agriculture either; although here the problem was qualitatively different. The CAP, the most developed common policy of the Community, came increasingly under attack in the 1970s. The combination of high guaranteed prices, steady increases in productivity, and stagnant demand led to mounting surpluses which had to be stored or dumped in foreign markets at large expense for the EC taxpayer. The growing financial cost of the CAP, which accounted for approximately two-thirds of total EC expenditure, was coupled with large and persistent income inequalities among the European farming population: inequalities to which the policy itself was contributing. The opposition from member countries with small agricultural sectors, especially the UK, who were the main losers, coupled with ever-growing pressures from third country producers, gradually succeeded in turning the Community's agricultural surpluses into a major political issue. One of the biggest successes of the 1960s was thus transformed into an albatross hanging from the neck of an embattled Community (Rosenblatt *et al.*, 1988).

The earlier trend for intra-EC trade to grow faster than total trade was reversed (see Fig. 2.1). This reversal coincided with the first oil shock and the economic recession and continued until 1981. During this period, there was a decline in relative terms of intra-EC trade for the old members of the Community, which was, however, largely compensated by the increase in intra-EC trade as a result of the 1973 enlargement. But the stagnation of intra-EC trade (as a percentage of total trade) cannot be attributed to protectionist measures. There is no evidence to suggest that such measures were directed exclusively or mainly against other members of the Community. The decline of intra-EC trade, which lasted, with some fluctuations, for approximately ten years, has been attributed instead to the gradual loss of European competitiveness, especially in strong-demand sectors, which led to the growing import penetration of European markets, and the increasing integration of EC firms in the world division of labour (Jacquemin and Sapir, 1988). The oil factor should also not be ignored: the large increase in the price of imported oil led to a shift of European exports to the booming economies of OPEC (Organization of Petroleum Exporting Countries).

While the trade integration model came under increased strain, the Community budget and the distributive impact of EC policies became, for the first time, a major political issue. This was closely related to the economic crisis and the enlargement of the EC. In times of slow growth, the struggle for larger shares of the pie usually intensifies; and this was proved true for the Community as a whole. On the other hand, the 1973 enlargement brought inside the EC two countries with serious regional problems, namely the UK and Ireland; and the former, expecting to be a big loser from its participation in the EC budget, decided to turn this into a major political issue. It was to remain so for many years to come. Last but not least, the question of redistribution was directly linked to the creation of an EMU, since the latter would remove more instruments of national economic policy and thus increase the risks of wider inter-country and inter-regional disparities.

The developments of the 1970s and the accession of the UK in particular brought into question the original package deal which had sustained for years the process of regional integration. The result was serious internal divisions and interminable negotiations which virtually paralysed the Community for a long time. The EC budget and the so-called 'British problem' became the central issue and the focus of intra-EC negotiations (H. Wallace, 1983).

Although fighting over who pays and who gets what and when is the main stuff that politics is made of, and it would be unnatural if Community politics were very different, the amount of time and energy devoted for many years by heads of state and government down to low-ranking officials in Brussels and the various national capitals to EC budgetary disputes was totally out of proportion to the actual amounts of money involved. Disputes over sums which represented only a few decimal points of EC GDP dominated for years the Community agenda; and this was in itself a reflection of the deep political crisis inside the EC. The Regional Fund, established in 1975, was originally conceived as a partial compensation to the UK for the budgetary loss resulting from its participation in the CAP. The progressive increase of expenditure through the Regional Fund was coupled with a similar development with respect to the Social Fund. However, regional and social policies, still representing a small percentage of total EC expenditure, remained the only two policies with an explicit redistributive bias.

The result of all the above developments was a more inward-looking and defensive Community; and also a less important Community in economic terms.

The emphasis was on the preservation of the status quo. The creation of the Regional Fund, together with the introduction of VAT and the establishment of the Community's 'own resources', were the main exceptions to this rule. At the political level, there were three main developments: the creation of European Political Cooperation (EPC), following the initiative taken at the Hague summit of 1969; the transformation of irregular summit conferences into the European Council; and the first direct elections to the European Parliament in 1979. In fact, the first two developments were interpreted, although not very convincingly, by some observers as yet another manifestation of the trend towards more inter-governmentalism (Taylor, 1983).

Despite the internal crisis and the unfavourable economic developments, the Community did not lose its power of attraction, at least with respect to its immediate neighbours. The best illustration was the new applications for membership submitted only a short while after the first enlargement of 1973. The new candidates came from the south of Europe and had only recently emerged from dictatorial rule. The applications of Greece in 1975 and Spain and Portugal in 1977 need to be understood, first and foremost, as an important act of high politics and a search for a *pax Europea* on behalf of the new democratic regimes (Tsoukalis, 1981). Membership of the Community was identified with democratic institutions, economic prosperity, and active participation in the building of a united Europe in countries which had been for long, both literally and figuratively, on the periphery of Europe.

The presence of an economic bloc on the European continent (the EC had always looked stronger from the outside than from the inside), with an obvious political dimension and objectives, left the small and less developed countries of the periphery with little choice in the long term. There were, however, serious doubts as to the ability of those countries to face the economic challenge associated with their integration into the competitive economic environment of the EC. Moreover, at a time when redistribution was a highly divisive issue inside the Community of Nine, the three southern European countries were seen as potential *demandeurs* and a further drain on meagre EC resources.

The result was protracted pre-accession negotiations during which the Nine adopted the time-honoured tradition of postponing the day of reckoning. However, the delay finally seemed to serve some useful purpose. By the time the two Iberian countries were admitted as full members in 1986, Greece having preceded them five years earlier, a whole new package of measures had been agreed for the relaunching of integration. In view of the negative experience of the 1970s, the EC appeared this time determined to combine successfully deepening with enlargement.

3

TREATY REVISIONS AND
THE NEW ECONOMIC ORTHODOXY

The 1980s found Western Europe in the midst of a deep economic malaise. Stagnating output, rapidly rising unemployment, and declining export shares of world markets formed the main elements of a dismal picture in the aftermath of the second oil shock. Community countries were manifestly unable to lift their sights above petty budgetary squabbles and the price of pigs which had absorbed for years an inordinate amount of their time and attention. The trade liberalization model, once the solid basis of regional integration, had apparently reached its limits. True, the EC had survived its first major enlargement and the dramatic deterioration of the international macroeconomic environment; but it was considerably weaker as a result and depressingly unable to adjust to the new economic and political realities.

The efforts to extend integration to new areas of activity, launched at the Hague summit of 1969, had largely failed. The twenty-fifth anniversary of the signing of the Treaty of Rome was greeted on a cover of *The Economist* (20 March 1982) with a tombstone for the EC, carrying a very characteristic epigraph: *capax imperii, nisi imperasset* ('capable of power, if only it had not tried to wield it'). These were the years of 'Euro-pessimism' and 'Euro-sclerosis', terms which became popular in the European and foreign press.

And then things slowly began to change. In the course of the 1980s, the transformation of the economic and political climate was absolutely remarkable. European economies slowly rediscovered their old dynamism; growth rates reached levels that had not been experienced for almost fifteen years, investment picked up rapidly, and many new jobs were created. Meanwhile, regional integration gained an ever-accelerating momentum and Commission proposals, which had been gathering dust for years in ministerial drawers, resurfaced on the Council table and were rapidly turned into Community legislation. European politicians competed in federalist rhetoric, and for once their words were not totally divorced from their actions.

The relaunching of the integration process became centred around the magic number of 1992. Although representing the target date for the completion of the internal market (which was in fact 31 December 1992), it soon came to symbolize the new phase in European integration; and in the end, it was about much more than the internal market. The rapidly expanding agenda of the EC has included redistributive policies, external economic relations, the so-called social space, and, last but not least, a renewed attempt to establish an economic and monetary union. The latter has now become the main issue in the post-1992 phase. Changes in the political and institutional sphere were also bound to follow.

The Rediscovery of Europe and the Market

The 1992 programme was conceived in the depths of the economic crisis. It came to life when economic recovery was still in its early stages, and grew up rapidly at the time of the boom. As a young adolescent, it later had to cope with serious economic adversity; and it seems to have done reasonably well under the circumstances.

Following the second large increase in oil prices in 1978–9, the economies of Western Europe entered into the longest and deepest recession since the end of the Second World War; and unemployment rates registered a meteoric rise (see Tables 2.1 and 2.2; Fig. 3.1). The comparison with other major industrialized economies, notably the United States, Japan, and the countries of EFTA, made the picture even more depressing. While the Europeans had long been used to unfavourable economic comparisons with Japan, since the early 1980s they have also had to reconcile themselves with a performance in terms of growth rates and unemployment which has been generally inferior to that of the United States.

This is particularly true of unemployment. In 1983 for the first time, the EC unemployment rate exceeded that of the United States; and this has continued ever since, while the countries of EFTA were to catch up with the rest of Western Europe some years later (Austria, Finland, and Sweden registered a very rapid increase in unemployment during the 1990s—see Fig. 3.1). It has, of course, been argued that 'persistent poverty is the American equivalent to persistent unemployment in Europe' (Dahrendorf, 1988: 149); and this argument was to become more commonplace in subsequent years. Yet, it could only offer small consolation to the Europeans. Furthermore, the rapid increase in European investment in the United States during the first half of the 1980s, while investment ratios continued their declining trend in Western Europe, was another clear manifestation of business perceptions and the lack of confidence in the future of the European economies.

At the same time, the continuing stagnation of intra-EC trade as a percentage of total trade was coupled with a reduction in EC world market shares in manufactured goods; and this was particularly pronounced in the strong-demand sectors such as electrical and electronic equipment, office machinery, and information technology (Buigues and Goybet, 1989). These were times of major technological advances and rapid industrial restructuring at the global level; and the Europeans increasingly felt that they were losing out in the international race

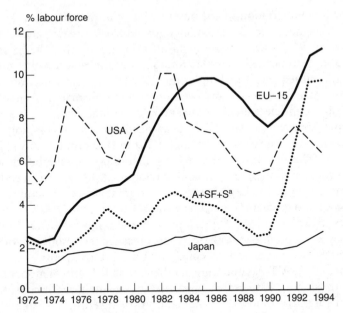

Fig. 3.1. Unemployment Rates in EU-15, the USA, and Japan, 1972–1994

Note: a Austria, Finland, and Sweden.

Source: Commission, 1995a.

for the industries of the future. Serious losses of market shares were also sustained in cars and industrial machinery. These developments were closely interrelated; the gradual loss of international competitiveness of European producers, especially in the rapidly growing sectors, accounted both for the increased penetration of EC markets by third country exporters and the loss of world market shares. The latter was more pronounced than the former, partly due to the protection of European markets.

The next step was to establish a link between the loss of competitiveness and the fragmentation of the European market, due to the existence of NTBs and the policy of national champions pursued by most governments (Albert and Ball, 1983). A consensus view about the existence of such a link gradually developed in the 1980s among key policy-makers and industrialists; and the Commission was highly instrumental in this respect. The emphasis was on high technology sectors where economies of scale and gains associated with learning curves were perceived to be particularly important. After all, these were the sectors where the advantages from the creation of a real common market should have been the greatest; and these were precisely the sectors where the common market did not exist.

Bressand argues that 'the early 1980s marked the limits of the national consolidation process in the larger countries in sectors such as telecommunications, electronics, automobiles, etc.' (1990: 50). But the ground had been prepared earlier for the mobilization of the business lobby in this direction. The role of Viscount Davignon, the Commissioner for industrial affairs since 1979, was absolutely crucial. He was instrumental in bringing together the heads of the twelve leading European firms in electronics in a 'round table' which provided the basis for the subsequent launching of the ESPRIT programme (European Strategic Programme for Research and Development in Information Technology).

The choice of the electronics sector, and information technology in particular, was no coincidence: there was a European obsession with this rapidly growing sector and the perceived danger of being left behind their American and Japanese competitors. The conclusion drawn was that there should be close intra-European collaboration in research and development (R&D) and an early end to the fragmentation of the large European market: that is, a rejection of the old strategies of national champions (Sharp and Shearman, 1987).

The first full phase of the ESPRIT programme ran between 1984 and 1988, followed by a second five-year phase. It was preceded by a modest pilot scheme. The emphasis was on cross-border collaboration in pre-competitive research. The importance of ESPRIT was much greater than the actual sums of money involved, although those sums have grown substantially over the years. It constituted the first major effort to promote close cooperation among European firms which had been until then prominent national champions, starting with R&D and gradually extending into other areas. Cooperation in research meant a sharing of costs and uncertainty; it also facilitated the adoption of common European standards, thus eventually eliminating one of the most important NTBs. Cross-border cooperation among firms, which had been in the past mostly of a transatlantic nature, was consistent with the new corporate search for extensive 'networks' (Bressand, 1990). At the same time, it laid the basis for a powerful lobby militating in favour of a large European market. Yet the logic of increasingly global markets and global competition, combined with the continuing weakness of leading European firms in this sector, imposed serious constraints on the strategy of intra-European cooperation; and those constraints were soon to become apparent.

In the search for intra-European 'networks' and cooperation among firms, the Commission often played the role of a marriage broker. This marked a significant departure from an earlier more interventionist approach in industrial policy which had led absolutely nowhere.[1] The early positive response of European firms to the ESPRIT programme led to the adoption of similar initiatives in other areas such as RACE (Research in Advanced Communications for Europe) and BRITE (Basic Research in Industrial Technologies for Europe) and the proliferation of joint R&D programmes. Following another French proposal, which was a defen-

[1] In September 1983, the French Government submitted a memorandum for the creation of a 'European industrial space' (Pearce and Sutton, 1986). This was the culmination of many efforts made by France to convince its partners about the merits of close cooperation in the industrial field. Although more recent EC policies in the field of high technology bear the marks of French influence, they are, however, both less interventionist and less protectionist in their approach. Thus, they also reflect the conversion which French political élites have undergone as a result of mainly international economic developments.

sive reaction to President Reagan's Strategic Defence Initiative (SDI) and which was appropriately diluted in terms of its supranational character by the British, a new collaborative mechanism was set up in 1985 in the form of EUREKA (European Research Co-ordinating Agency). The membership of EUREKA included all Western European countries. Thus, gradually and in a modest way, European regional cooperation was extending beyond the sphere of trade.

The growing 'Europeanness' of the perceptions and strategies adopted by the large European firms was also manifested through the creation of the Round Table of European Industrialists which has acted both as a powerful lobby behind the scenes and a means of promoting closer ties and cooperation among the heads of some of the largest firms. Such moves were arguably not unrelated to the wave of mergers, acquisitions, and cooperation agreements across national borders, which was to follow some years later. The composition of this Round Table, first led by Mr Gyllenhammar, chairman of Volvo, clearly suggested that the emerging European corporate reality was not much affected by the EC-EFTA frontier. It was, however, abundantly clear to everybody concerned that only the EC could deliver a large European market free from internal barriers. On the other hand, the elimination of intra-European barriers was not always seen as incompatible with higher protection *vis-à-vis* the rest of the world.

The growing perception among business and governments of the large costs of the fragmentation of the European market was conveniently married with the constantly increasing appeal of supply-side programmes and economic deregulation, particularly evident in telecommunications and financial services. Mainly imported from the United States of President Reagan, with Mrs Thatcher acting as the main and highly energetic European agent, those ideas were gradually adopted by other European leaders, although with a mixture of anticipation and embarrassment characteristic of young virgins. The adoption of such ideas, in turn closely associated with the so-called process of globalization, implied at least a partial rejection of old-established notions about the mixed economy and the economic role of the state in Western Europe.

The shift towards supply-side measures, also strongly and consistently supported by the Commission in its annual economic reports, was in turn a reflection of a more general shift to the right in terms of economic policies, evident in most countries of Western Europe during the first half of the 1980s; and this was true almost irrespective of the colour of the political parties in power. A major example of this emerging consensus was the shift of the French Socialist government towards more market- and European-oriented policies in 1983, after the failure of 'Keynesianism in one country' (Sachs and Wyplosz, 1986). This shift marked a decisive defeat for those in the Socialist party who had been advocating protectionist measures and an independent monetary policy. It was also a major turning-point for the Community as a whole, in view of the central role subsequently played by France in the relaunching of the integration process. Economic orthodoxy and a strong market orientation similarly characterized the policies pursued by the Spanish Socialists after their arrival in power in 1981; unlike their comrades in Greece.

The new consensus also found an expression in the area of macroeconomic policy, with an increasing convergence towards restrictive monetary policies and also some degree of budgetary consolidation; and this came with unprecedented levels of unemployment which continued to rise until 1985 (Fig. 3.1). The new consensus meant a collective rush away from the basic Keynesian ideas which had provided the foundation of postwar economic policies in Western Europe; but economic conditions had also changed.

The first important step had been taken back in 1979 with the setting up of the European Monetary System (EMS) and the creation of the ECU (European Currency Unit—a weighted basket of EC currencies), undoubtedly the most important economic event of the 1970s for the Community. It was the crowning act of the close cooperation between Valéry Giscard d'Estaing and Helmut Schmidt, from which Britain had, once again, decided to remain aloof. The main aim was to reduce exchange rate instability among EC currencies and to take another step towards the creation of a regional currency system in a world of generalized floating. The setting up of the EMS also signified the implicit acceptance by France and Italy (the smaller countries never had much choice) of German macroeconomic policy priorities. The emphasis was now clearly on the fight against inflation.

After an early turbulent period, when the EMS came under serious strain due to diverging economic policies (it was the time when the newly elected Socialist government in France adopted an expansionist stance against the general trend), subsequent years were characterized by remarkable exchange rate stability based largely on a convergence of monetary policies. The turning-point was the realignment of March 1983 and France's decision to stay in the exchange rate mechanism. The EMS remained an asymmetrical system, although, arguably, asymmetry was an important element of its success. As with the mini-snake in the 1970s, the Federal Republic was the leader of the system, with the Deutschmark providing the anchor for the other currencies. The existence of this asymmetry was in itself a further manifestation of German success and growing predominance in the economic field.

Although with some exceptions, such as Greece and Italy, there was also a tendency towards budgetary consolidation in Western Europe during this period. Budget deficits were progressively reduced and there was a reversal of an earlier trend towards constantly rising government expenditure as a percentage of GDP. This, however, lasted only until 1989 (Fig. 3.2). The reduction of budget deficits was seen as another sign of the shift in European government priorities during this period.

Supply-side measures, the emphasis on greater flexibility of labour markets and restrictive macroeconomic policies went hand in hand with a weakening of trade union power. This was the product of the adverse economic environment, the large increase in unemployment, and the changing composition of the labour force; thus a very different situation from the one prevailing in the 1960s and early 1970s. The result was a considerable reduction in the share of wages and salaries out of total income and a substantial increase in business profitability.

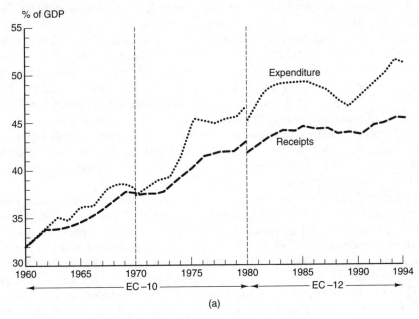

(a)

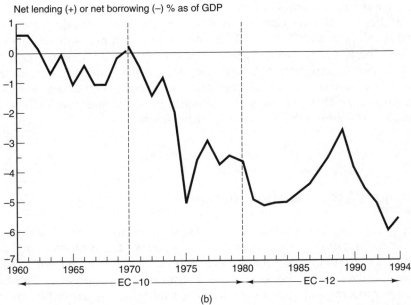

(b)

Fig. 3.2. General Government Expenditure, Receipts, and Net Lending (Borrowing) in the EU, 1960–1994

Note: EC-10; EC-12 excl. Greece and Spain.

Source: Commission.

Interestingly enough, the path followed by some EFTA countries was different for most of the 1980s.

On the other hand, the transformation of the international political scene in the early 1980s also contributed to the collective readiness of Western European countries to proceed further in the field of regional economic integration. It would not be, after all, the first time that essentially economic initiatives were taken at the European level with long-term political objectives in mind. Fears of a revival of the cold war between the two superpowers and a growing divergence of views across the Atlantic increased the uneasiness of Europeans, while exposing yet again the element of schizophrenia which had traditionally characterized their attitude towards the American protector, at least as long as the perception of the need for a protector persisted.

President Reagan's aggressive style of diplomacy and the new arms race strengthened their latent enthusiasm for a stronger European pillar of the alliance; and this would eventually find an expression in attempts to revive the Western European Union (WEU) as well as in new initiatives at the EC level. Paradoxically, some years later the unexpected and rapid dismantlement of the Soviet empire in Eastern Europe also appeared to act as a catalyst for new moves towards further regional integration. But, this time, it was the fear of an eventual withdrawal of US forces from Europe and, even more so, the reappearance of the 'German problem', if only in a different form.

Last but not least, the Community was faced once again with the prospect of further enlargement, this time taking into its fold countries with weaker economies and fragile democratic regimes. The first phase of this new enlargement, with the accession of Greece in 1981, was not particularly smooth; and this was interpreted as a sign of more troubles to come. The accession of new members added considerably to the urgency of strengthening Community institutions and policies, and the objective was to avoid further dilution.

Virtuous Circles are not Forever

The relaunching of the integration process was preceded by long and difficult negotiations regarding the reform of existing policies and institutions and the identification of new areas for common action. The 'British problem' still remained at the centre of the negotiations; but unlike earlier years, when there had been a search for ad hoc arrangements, a general agreement seemed to emerge slowly that a more permanent solution to the 'British problem' should be part of a wider reform.

The successful implementation of new initiatives was predicated on the resolution of two outstanding issues which had plagued the Community for years: budgetary reform and a more effective control of CAP expenditure. The rapid depletion of 'own resources' (customs duties, agricultural levies, and 1 per cent of

VAT), coupled with the continuous increase of CAP expenditure and the legal impossibility of deficit financing, had radically changed the framework for negotiation. It was no longer a question of looking for partial compensation measures to placate the British. New financial resources needed to be found, and this required the revision of the relevant treaty articles and ratification by all national parliaments. On the other hand, the search for new 'own resources' could not be divorced from a thorough discussion of the CAP, which accounted for approximately two-thirds of total EC expenditure, and the prospects for policy reform.

In the 1980s, the need for reform of the CAP became more generally accepted. The policy of price restraint, practised for some years, had not succeeded in eliminating surpluses; nor had it operated as an effective constraint on ever-growing expenditure. Large increases in labour productivity meant that supply continued to grow much faster than domestic demand. The resulting surpluses, combined with tight international markets, led to an ever-increasing financial cost, while farmers' incomes remained stagnant. Attachment to status quo policies thus became increasingly untenable. The rapid approach towards the ceiling of the Community's own resources, used by the UK as a powerful negotiating weapon, combined with growing pressures from third countries and the prospect of further enlargement, which was expected to create new surpluses and thus add considerably to costs, acted as the main catalysts for reform. In fact, it was only in the early 1980s that the very word reform started appearing in official documents. Redistribution also formed an integral part of the wider debate on budgetary reform. Widening intra-EC income disparities and the economic crisis had brought the issue of redistributive policies to the top of the political agenda. The accession of new, economically weaker, members gave this issue even greater prominence.

On the other hand, the extreme slowness of the EC decision-making mechanism, often a euphemism for a complete standstill caused by the search for unanimity in the Council of Ministers, and the prospect of further enlargement, which could only make the situation worse, led to a wide-ranging debate on institutional reform. This also included the problem of the so-called 'democratic deficit' of the Community (which is generally, although perhaps too narrowly, identified with the lack of sufficient democratic control and accountability due to the limited powers of the European Parliament and the inability of national legislatures to perform this role effectively), and the artificial division between normal EC business and foreign policy coordination in the context of EPC. The Genscher–Colombo proposal of 1981 for a new European Act, which would replace the existing treaties, and the draft treaty on European Union (Bieber, Jacqué, and Weiler, 1985) adopted by the European Parliament in 1984 were the most important initiatives in this area. The need to reconcile the growing political and economic heterogeneity of the Community, largely related to its geographical expansion, with further integration also led to the consideration of various models incorporating a degree of diversity in terms of the rules and obligations applying to different members. Hence the proposals for a two-tier Community, 'variable geometry', and 'graduated integration' which became popular at the time.[2]

The Fontainebleau summit of June 1984 was an important turning-point in the long intra-EC negotiations. The package agreed then included new measures to control the growth of agricultural surpluses and the creation of new 'own resources'. The tackling of surpluses would not be based on the pure market solutions advocated by most economists. Instead, the policy of price restraint, as opposed to large price cuts which would have been, of course, wildly unpopular among farmers, was to be combined with an increasing reliance on other measures, such as production quotas and 'co-responsibility levies'. Those measures were intended to limit production and the scale of EC intervention, while also trying to pass on to producers some of the financial cost of storing and disposing of surpluses.

One important aspect of the Fontainebleau agreement was the introduction of a permanent mechanism for a partial compensation to the UK, based on the difference between its VAT contribution and its overall receipts from the Community budget. Special provision was also made for the reduction in the net contribution of the Federal Republic. However, the new agreement, which was heralded at the time as a major breakthrough by all participants, proved to be extremely short-lived. When the new VAT rate of 1.4 per cent was introduced in 1986, the upper limit had already been reached because of the intervening rapid growth in expenditure. Thus, new negotiations on the budget had to start again almost from scratch.

In 1985, a new instrument was created through the Integrated Mediterranean Programmes (IMPs), intended for the less developed regions of France, Italy, and the whole of Greece. The creation of IMPs was a recognition of the special development problems of these regions and the relative bias of the CAP against southern agricultural products. The Iberian enlargement acted as the catalyst: IMPs were, in fact, seen as a compensation to the existing members of the Community of Ten for the expected negative economic effects of the accession of Spain and Portugal.

Meanwhile, a new Commission, under President Delors, had taken office. Looking for a new driving force for the integration process and the main plank of the Commission's strategy for the next four years, President Delors quickly opted for the completion of the internal market as an objective which appeared to have a relatively good chance of gaining the support of member governments. This was announced to the European Parliament in January 1985 when the target date of 1992 was also mentioned for the first time.

---

[2] The idea of a two-tier or two-speed Community could be traced back to Chancellor Brandt and the Tindemans report on European Union (Tindemans, 1975). 'Variable geometry', a French idea, essentially implied variable membership from one issue area to the other (Commissariat du Plan, 1980). Another variation on the same theme was the proposal for 'graduated integration' (*abgestufte Integration*) later put forward by German academics (Grabitz, 1984). There was much more to come in subsequent years.

The elimination of remaining barriers to the free movement of goods, services, persons, and capital, arising mainly out of different national regulatory frameworks, and the creation of conditions approaching as much as possible those in a domestic market was certainly not a new idea. The ground had been prepared in earlier years through various Commission communications to the Council; and there was already a rich collection of parliamentary resolutions and European Council declarations in this respect. Furthermore, an 'internal market' Council had been created in 1983. Interest in the completion of the internal market was a reflection of the negative developments of the previous decade, the stagnation of intra-EC trade, and the growing popularity of supply-side measures and economic deregulation. Yet the decision to adopt the internal market as the first priority of the new Commission and as the principal instrument of European integration for the next eight years was a major strategic decision. It was the Commission that took both the initiative and the risk; and therefore it received justifiable praise for its subsequent success.

Having been given the green light at the Brussels summit of March 1985, the Delors Commission then presented the next European Council in Milan with the White Paper entitled 'Completing the Internal Market' (Commission, 1985*a*). The White Paper spelt out with remorseless logic the consequences of the political commitment to eliminate all remaining intra-EC barriers. It included nearly 300 measures and a timetable for their adoption extending to 31 December 1992. The completion of the internal market provided the unifying concept for a set of very disparate measures, ranging from rules on animal sperm and the right of political asylum to the approximation of indirect taxation rates. Many of the proposed measures had, in fact, been lying on the Council table for years in the form of Commission draft directives and regulations. The implementation of the White Paper would, therefore, depend on the existence of political will which until then had apparently been in short supply.

The White Paper also introduced a new approach to the elimination of NTBs arising from different national rules and regulations. Instead of the old, time-consuming, and highly ineffective attempt to harmonize at the EC level, which had earned the Commission the reputation of specializing in mayonnaise labels and the noise of lawnmowers, the White Paper proposed that the Community should rely as much as possible on the principle of mutual recognition. Whenever harmonization was deemed to be necessary, this should be limited only to essential objectives and requirements, thus leaving the task of defining the technical specifications to private standardization bodies.

The idea was simple but also revolutionary: it built on indications of a more favourable political climate in national capitals and some earlier judgements of the European Court, especially the famous *Cassis de Dijon* which established the general principle that all goods lawfully manufactured and marketed in one member country should be accepted also by the other member countries, while also recognizing the need for some exceptions related to 'the effectiveness of fiscal supervision, the protection of public health, the fairness of commercial transactions and the defence of the consumer' (VerLoren van Themaat, 1988). This new and more flexible approach was considered as the decisive blow against the old Gordian knot of NTBs which had proved the main obstacle in the integration of mixed economies. It was also evident with respect to indirect taxation: the emphasis was now on the approximation and not the harmonization of tax rates.

There are certain characteristics of the White Paper, and the underlying strategy of the Commission, which proved to be crucially important for the eventual success of this new initiative. The first is the supply-side nature of the programme (at least this was the way it was generally perceived) which made it compatible with the prevailing economic and political climate. It received support not only from governments but also, crucially, from the business community; and the support provided by the latter was translated into higher investment. The second is the existence of a clear timetable for the adoption of the different measures, which helped enormously to provide a focus for national politicians and a clear target to aim for. In this respect, the White Paper followed the successful precedent of the Treaty of Rome.

The third and fourth characteristics were also extremely important, although at least partially misleading. The internal market was presented as a programme for the elimination of barriers, hence with no apparent financial cost. As Pelkmans and Winters put it: 'the emphasis is on rules, not money' (1988: 9). Given the long intra-EC budgetary disputes and the strong resistance of many countries to an increase in Community expenditure, this constituted a major attraction of the internal market programme. The subsequent emphasis on redistributive policies suggests that this was not exactly true.

Another characteristic was the technical and low-key nature of the White Paper, considerably aided by the personal style of Lord Cockfield, the Commissioner for the internal market. Only passing reference was made to what later came to be known as flanking policies. Thus, the White Paper, and the concept of the internal market in general, appeared as less threatening to governments, especially in terms of national sovereignty. This was in sharp contrast to EMU as the main economic initiative of the 1970s. A more careful reading of the political implications of some of the measures proposed and, perhaps, a certain prophetic ability to foresee the new momentum in European integration, initiated by the internal market programme and then amply exploited by the Commission, would have made some governments much more reticent about committing themselves to the 1992 target.

The next important step was taken by the European Council in Milan in June 1985. A decision was reached then, against the opposition of Britain, Denmark, and Greece, to convene an intergovernmental conference (IGC) with the task of preparing a revision of the existing treaties. The division inside the Community was centred on the question of institutional reform which included the more extended use of majority voting in the Council of Ministers, the powers of the European Parliament, and the role of the EPC. The division between the six original members of the EC and the latecomers, with Ireland sitting on the fence, had earlier become apparent inside the Dooge Committee which had been asked to prepare a report on institutional reform. Furthermore, the countries with minimalist views on the EC could hardly welcome a new constitutional debate on Europe.

The issue was of major political importance, and the decision of the Italian Presidency to go ahead with a majority vote was both unexpected and without precedent. It thus became clear that the majority of member countries were now determined to push ahead with institutional reform and the relaunching of the integration process (Taylor, 1989). The White Paper and the completion of the internal market had provided the new element which, perhaps, tipped the balance.

The end result was the Single European Act (SEA) signed by the representatives of all twelve members in February 1986. It came into force in July 1987, after the holding of popular referenda in Denmark and Ireland. The political momentum created by the IGC and the fear of being relegated to the second tier forced the three opposing countries to play an active part during the negotiations. In the case of Britain, negative factors were combined with a keen interest in the completion of the internal market which needed to be reconciled with a strong dislike of any institutional changes, especially as regards majority voting in the Council. The final product was in some respects close to the lowest common denominator. In the words of Mrs Thatcher: 'Part of our task the whole time has been to diminish their expectations and draw them down from the clouds to practical matters' (*The Times*, 6 December 1985; see also Colchester and Buchan, 1990; Moravcsik, 1991). The SEA was the result of a compromise among the now twelve members of the Community. It also provided the legal framework for the emerging new package deal in the new phase of regional integration.

A central element of the SEA was the formal adoption of the internal market as an objective to be achieved by 31 December 1992. The internal market was defined as 'an area without internal frontiers in which the free movement of goods, persons, services and capital is ensured' (Article 8*a*), thus adding a political dimension to the 1992 target. On the other hand, in a separate declaration, member governments insisted that the target date 'does not create an automatic legal effect'; this clarification was meant to preclude any such interpretation in the future by the European Court.

The harmonization of national rules and regulations, as part of the implementation of the internal market programme, would be based on qualified majority voting[3] in the Council of Ministers (Article 100*a*). Combined with the new approach towards harmonization and the increasing reliance on mutual recognition, this was intended to break the familiar deadlock in the Council arising from the frustrating search for unanimity. In fact, qualified majority voting was extended to some areas where the unanimity rule used to apply under the old treaties: these included capital liberalization as well as air and sea transport.

On the other hand, there was a certain quid pro quo offered to member countries for abandoning the security of the national veto. A safeguard clause was

---

[3] There is weighted voting in the Council of Ministers and the weights for members range from 10 for the biggest countries (France, Germany, Italy, and the UK) to 2 for Luxembourg. In the Community of Twelve, 54 votes out of a total of 76 were needed for a qualified majority. With the addition of three new members in 1995, 62 votes are now needed out of a total of 87.

introduced which would allow member countries, under special circumstances, to continue applying national provisions after the adoption of new EC rules (Article 100*a*, par. 4). It was meant as an insurance against the lowering of standards for the protection of the environment and working conditions. There were also three important exceptions where unanimity would still be needed, namely fiscal policy, the free movement of persons, and the rights and interests of employees. The exceptions were a reflection of the political sensitivity of the issues involved and the existing divergence of views and actual practices among individual member countries.

In recognition of the heterogeneity of the Community and the different levels of economic development among member countries, Article 8*c* opened the possibility for special provisions and derogations of a temporary nature. This constituted a modest step towards some form of differentiated policies; but certainly not a general acceptance of the two-tier and variable geometry models of integration which had been aired during the negotiations.

There was more to cater for the interests of the weaker economies. Title V, under the heading of 'economic and social cohesion', was an attempt to link the objective of 'harmonious development' and the reduction of regional disparities, objectives which had been mentioned in a very general manner in the original treaties, with specific policy instruments. The reference to economic and social cohesion also constituted a formal recognition of the growing political importance of redistribution. Since then, 'cohesion' has become a key word in the European vocabulary. The new Article 130*d* called for the effective coordination and rationalization of the activities of EC Structural Funds and the Commission was invited to submit proposals in this direction.

The EMS and the ECU became for the first time legitimate children of the Community through a new article included in the SEA. However, this was considered to be a mixed blessing, since Article 102*a* also specified that any institutional change in the field of economic and monetary policy would require a new amendment of the treaties; and this was considered highly unlikely for the foreseeable future. Who could, in fact, anticipate the calling of a new IGC in December 1990 in order to prepare the legal ground for a complete EMU? The SEA also contained provisions extending EC powers in the field of social policy, especially as regards the health and safety of workers, as well as research and technological development, and the environment. Those new provisions were a clear manifestation of the expanding role of the Community in new policy areas.

As a partial answer to the 'democratic deficit' of the Community, a new 'co-operation procedure' was introduced; it was meant to strengthen, albeit in a modest way and only on those issues where qualified majority applied, the input of the European Parliament in the legislative process. The new 'cooperation procedure' also indirectly enhanced the central role of the Commission in decision-making, by reinforcing its powers of mediation between the Parliament and the Council of Ministers. Through the SEA, the European Council acquired for the first time a legal status as an institution of the Community. Similarly, EPC became part of the *acquis communautaire*. The relevant provisions were essentially an official recognition of already existing practices, except that they did add some words on security, thus paving the way for a further extension of EC competences in this highly sensitive area.

The SEA was the culmination of many years of animated discussions and difficult negotiations intended to provide the legal framework for the transformation of the European Communities into a 'European Union' (still a very imprecise concept), in accordance with the solemn declaration of Stuttgart of June 1983. It constituted the biggest ever revision of the original treaties and an indication of the expanding agenda of the EC. Its most important provisions referred to the completion of the internal market and the extension of qualified majority voting. Yet the importance of the latter could only be tested in practice. After all, provisions for qualified majority voting in several areas of decision-making had already existed in the original treaties; but they had been very infrequently applied.

The Luxembourg agreement of 1966 and the subsequent trend towards increasing intergovernmentalism had forced the Council to search continuously for a consensus among its members, even on relatively minor issues. The question, therefore, was whether the political climate had changed sufficiently in order to allow the new rules to have any real effect on decision-making. The first signs of change became evident even before the entry into force of the SEA as member countries started showing greater readiness to resort to voting. Since 1986, the number of votes in the Council of Ministers has increased, even in policy areas totally unaffected by the revision of treaty articles; but voting is still far from the rule.

The SEA was greeted by hardly anybody as a major political event which could change the course of the EC. As *Le Monde* (5 December 1985) put it: 'Ces améliorations ne sont-elles pas de celles qui enthousiasment les foules.' Compared with the ambitious initiatives of previous years—the draft treaty of the European Parliament, and the time and effort put into its preparation—the SEA was generally considered to be a let-down. It was like the mountain giving birth to a mouse. The fact that nationalist leaders, like Mrs Thatcher, did not perceive any serious threat in the revised treaties was seen as yet another proof of the limited political significance of the SEA.

With the benefit of hindsight, it can be argued that the importance of the SEA did not lie so much in the institutional provisions and the new objectives legally enshrined in the new Act, but rather in its somewhat intangible role in the development of a momentum for the deepening and extension of regional integration. It certainly added a great deal to the credibility of the 1992 objective and thus helped to create a virtuous circle, involving both governments and the market-place. The negotiations and the signing of the SEA coincided with a steady improvement in the economic environment. The modest, export-led recovery, which had started in 1983, gradually turned into a self-sustaining process, with a steady increase in investment. The shift towards a more dynamic macroeconomic environment made governments readier to accept the adjustment costs associated with the 1992 target. The political readiness to go ahead with what was basically perceived as a supply-side programme contributed in turn to a further improvement in the economic climate. The necessary ingredients of a virtuous circle were all there; and there was a close similarity with what had happened back in the 1950s and 1960s.

With the internal market, the Community had once again found a *force motrice* for further integration; and this time the economic objective was accompanied by changes in the decision-making process which were meant to facilitate the implementation of the internal market programme. The Commission was very quick in the production of draft legislation submitted to the Council in accordance with the White Paper timetable. Things also started moving at the Council level. The number of decisions taken by qualified majority increased, although this tells only part of the story. The mere knowledge of the possible recourse to voting frequently forced countries to make virtue out of necessity by siding with the majority or simply remaining silent as soon as they realized that they could not command the necessary number of votes in order to block a decision. Schmitt von Sydow has argued that 'the principle of majority voting leads to unanimous decisions, while the principle of unanimity leads to no decisions at all' (1988: 98).

The next crucial step in the credibility game for the internal market programme and the relaunching of the integration process came with the German Presidency during the first half of 1988, and especially with the adoption of the 'Delors package' at the Brussels summit in February of that year. Three important elements were closely linked together, namely the creation of new budgetary resources, CAP reform, and the strengthening of redistributive policies: old issues which, however, remained as preconditions for the successful implementation of the internal market programme. The set of measures finally adopted included an agreement on the growth of EC expenditure until the end of 1992; the introduction of a new source of revenue on a GNP key; a compensation mechanism for the UK and the Federal Republic; a limit on the growth of CAP expenditure; new measures to control agricultural surpluses; the doubling of resources for the so-called Structural Funds; and a major reform in the operation and coordination of the latter. The importance of this package deal can hardly be overstated.

At long last the Community had reached an agreement which could provide a solid basis for the relaunching of the integration process. The broad outlines for the direction of agricultural policy and the budget had been settled for the next few years, thus, it was to be hoped, withdrawing from the negotiating table two main issues of contention. Provisions were made for sizeable side-payments for the economically weaker members. And there was already a specific programme for action with precise timetables which would take the Community well into the 1990s; its feasibility being further strengthened by the institutional changes already introduced. Last but not least, the Twelve were agreed that no further enlargement of the Community would take place before the completion of the internal market programme in 1993 (obviously nobody had ever thought of the German Democratic Republic being a candidate.)

The Brussels package played a crucial role in unblocking the process of integration and thus led to a much faster implementation of the internal market programme. The German Presidency of the first half of 1988 acted like a bulldozer reaching agreements on some difficult and sensitive issues which had remained blocked for many years. The decision to proceed with the complete liberalization of capital movements, after virtually no progress in this area for almost twenty-five years, was of paramount importance: it sent a clear message to markets that European governments actually meant business; and this further boosted the credibility of the internal market programme.

The rapid pace continued in subsequent years. The acceleration in the rate of Council decision-making was sometimes truly impressive: twelve months for the adoption of legislation on the harmonization of technical rules regarding machine safety compared with seventy months in the past for the adoption of a directive on the noise of lawnmowers; less than three years for the mutual recognition of all university degrees compared with eighteen years in the past for an agreement on the freedom of establishment of architects.

This rapid pace in the production of European legislation coincided and apparently also contributed to a very substantial improvement of the macro-economic scene. During the second half of the 1980s, Western Europe experienced a long boom, even though growth rates remained lower than those experienced during the Golden Age of the 1950s and 1960s (Table 2.1). Yet, by the standards of the more recent period, the economic performance was truly spectacular. In the last two years of the decade, the average rate of growth of EC economies approached 4 per cent, while most of the weaker economies grew faster, thus narrowing the intra-EC gap. Growth was largely investment-led. During this period, EC countries became by far the biggest recipients of foreign portfolio and direct investment which registered a sharp increase. There was there something reminiscent of the early years of the EEC.

The rapid increase in investment ratios was accompanied by a process of re-structuring in the manufacturing and services sector. There was a wave of mergers and acquisitions, including an increasing number across national borders. For the first time, European integration was extended to production. Policy measures were consistent with developments at the business level; it was, therefore, only natural that the two processes would become mutually reinforcing. Yet, it was still difficult to separate European from global developments.

During the same period, many new jobs were created and unemployment kept falling until 1990 (Fig. 3.1), while real unit labour costs continued their downward trend, also contributing to a further change in income shares in favour of profits. This was a further confirmation of the important change in political and economic conditions in Western Europe, which was in turn closely linked to the relaunching of the process of integration. Meanwhile, the share of intra-EC trade registered a sharp increase reaching more than 60 per cent for the EC of Twelve (Fig. 2.1); although the Iberian enlargement must also have contributed to this increase in intra-EC trade.

It is clearly impossible to establish a precise link between political initiatives at the European level and the sharp improvement in macroeconomic conditions during the second half of the previous decade. Business confidence was un-doubtedly influenced by exogenous factors which also contributed to the growth of world output during the same period. However, the role played by macro-economic stability and supply-side measures, including the internal market pro-gramme, in shaping business expectations in Western Europe should not be underestimated.

An early business survey, showed that 'the "internal market" is having a not inconsiderable effect on the expectations of firms and, in particular, on their investments' (Commission, 1989a: 183). Although the use of the double negative in the Commission document was, perhaps, a sign of embarrassment on the part of the anonymous economist who could not apply in practice his familiar *ceteris paribus* assumption, there is now little doubt that the 1992 programme had a positive anticipation effect on investment and growth, thus also closing the door to the 'Euro-pessimism' of earlier years. But like all good things, the economic boom was soon to come to an end. The virtuous circle proved short-lived; and political developments were once again to be influenced by the deterioration of the economic environment.

The Post-Maastricht Blues

The political momentum continued, however, for some time, and the agenda kept on expanding. There was certainly an element of the spillover effect on which functionalist theories of integration had so much relied; but there was also a conscious attempt by the Commission and individual member countries to use the internal market and the favourable climate to which it had contributed in order to expand EC activity into new areas (see also Keohane and Hoffmann, 1991; Moravcsik, 1991; W. Wallace, 1990).

The doubling of budgetary resources and the reform of Structural Funds was presented as a precondition for the smoother implementation of the internal market programme and as a means of avoiding a political backlash from potential losers. The new initiatives in the social field had a similar logic; they also con-stituted an attempt to incorporate the trade union movement in the 1992 process. But by far the most important step was taken with the reintroduction of EMU into the European political agenda. It was first linked to capital liberalization agreed upon in June 1988. At the Hanover summit which took place the same month, a high level committee was set up, under the chairmanship of Mr Delors, to reopen the issue. Its report created a new momentum for the establishment of EMU.

Against the strong resistance of the UK government, the European Council which met in Madrid in June 1989 agreed that the first stage of EMU should start in July 1990 and that a new IGC should be called in order to prepare the legal and institutional ground for a complete EMU. This was confirmed at the next meeting of the European Council in Strasbourg which set the date for the beginning of the IGC, only three years after the signing of the SEA.

Meanwhile, the collapse of the political and economic order in Eastern Europe had introduced several new and important factors into the equation. The early celebratory mood caused by the collapse of communist dictatorships was soon followed by anxiety and concern about possible instability in the region and even more so by the re-emergence of the old 'German problem', albeit in a new form. The unification of Germany, which took place in October 1990, would eventually lead to an important shift in the European balance of power; and this prospect certainly unsettled the minds of many politicians and others (for a discussion of Germany's unification and its wider implications, see Garton Ash, 1993; Marsh, 1994). Following the old-established French (and European) logic of '*la fuite en avant*', of which Schuman had been the first teacher, an attempt was made to link German union with the further strengthening of the EC and its federal traits in particular. This lent further support to EMU; but it also helped to bring the subject of political union to the surface.

The term 'political union' was intended to cover institutional reform, the extension of EC powers into new areas, and last but not least, foreign and defence policy. The combined efforts of Messrs Delors, Kohl, and Mitterrand, supported by the large majority of other EC leaders, led to the decision to convene a second IGC which would operate in parallel with the one on EMU. This decision was reached at the Dublin summit in June 1990. Clearly, a long distance had been covered since the 'Euro-pessimism' of the early 1980s. Now, the momentum of economic and political integration appeared to be almost unstoppable and the Europeans were already negotiating the main elements of the new package which would enable the Community to go beyond 1992 and the internal market. At least, this is the way it was seen at the time, with the UK government providing once again the main exception to the rule. This momentum was partly attributable to the success of the internal market programme, but developments in Central and Eastern Europe had also played a major role.

In practice, agreement proved rather difficult to reach, especially as regards the contents of political union. The two intergovernmental conferences started in December 1990 and the new Treaty on European Union was signed in Maastricht in February 1992. Even though Mrs Thatcher had in the meantime been sacrificed by her own party on the altar of European integration, the UK Government offered strong resistance to any extension of Community competencies and the strengthening of common institutions, absolutely consistent in its minimalist line (Pryce, 1994). On many issues, the need for unanimity in the intergovernmental conferences inevitably led to agreements at the lowest common denominator.

Despite the direct link established between EMU and political union in the early stages of the negotiations, the changes introduced under the latter heading were in the end very modest indeed. Supranationality did not appeal much to several European governments, including the French who seemed to have reconciled, at least to their own satisfaction, support for political union with a strong preference for intergovernmental cooperation.

The new treaty established a European Union (EU) resting on three different and very uneven pillars. The three old established Communities, with the EEC having been renamed as the European Community,[4] constitute the most important pillar of the new edifice. It incorporates the traditional *acquis communautaire* as well as the changes introduced under the new treaty with respect to policies and institutions. The other two pillars represent areas of high politics *par excellence*: a Common Foreign and Security Policy (CFSP) and cooperation in the fields of Justice and Home Affairs. Intergovernmental cooperation is the guiding principle for both: the Council and the European Council being almost completely in charge of decision-making.

Institutional reforms for the first pillar were rather modest. They include the extension of qualified majority voting in a few areas and, arguably more important, the granting of new powers to the European Parliament through the system of co-decision (Article 189b). The European legislative process has never been noted for its simplicity or even transparency. With each treaty revision, the process has become more complicated and cumbersome. The new treaty also introduced the concept of the citizenship of the Union which extended the right of movement and residence across member countries to all persons, and not only working people. This includes the right of all citizens of the Union residing in another member state to participate in local and European elections. This concept of citizenship is certainly limited, when compared with the reality of contemporary European countries (see also García, 1993). Citizenship of an idea? Perhaps, but also with a few tangible benefits.

The provisions made for the creation of EMU were by far the most specific and far reaching. The date for entry into the final stage was set as 1 January 1999, or two years earlier if a majority of member countries were deemed by the Council to fulfil the necessary conditions. The final stage will involve the irrevocable fixity of intra-EC exchange rates, the adoption of a common currency, and the establishment of a federal system of central banks (the European System of Central Banks—ESCB), with the European Central Bank (ECB) being responsible for the conduct of monetary policy and exchange rate policy for the union as a whole. Article 107 of the new treaty as well as the accompanying protocol on the statute of the ESCB and the ECB refer in no uncertain terms to the independence of the new institution. Measures in the same direction will also have to be introduced for national central banks which have been until now under the tutelage of their political masters.

There will be no corresponding centralization of budgetary policies. Yet, provisions have been made for the strengthening of coordination, mainly through the introduction of the excessive deficit procedure, which will rely on a mixture of peer and market pressure. The Council of Ministers will issue policy recommendations addressed to individual member countries and, as a measure of last resort, it could even impose fines upon wayward members.

---

[4] As part of the renaming game, the Commission of the European Communities has now become the European Commission.

For the intervening period, the European Monetary Institute (EMI) will be set up in order to help strengthen the cooperation between national central banks and the coordination of monetary policies, thus preparing the ground for the final big step. And it would be, of course, a very big step indeed. Thus, with the new treaty, the Community has acquired for the first time an important macro-economic dimension which will at least match the provisions for the creation of the common market contained in the original Treaty of Rome. The ultimate stage of virtue (read EMU) was defined in great detail in order to satisfy the German demand for common institutions and policies which would match those at home. This was married with the French insistence on a specific date for the final stage which would legally bind the Germans to EMU. By the standards of markets, the road to virtue seemed to be rather long, and the marking on the road left much to be desired. This was soon to become painfully obvious.

Stringent criteria were set for the participation of member countries in the final stage of EMU, which, if strictly applied on the day of reckoning, are almost bound to exclude several countries which would then remain 'in derogation' until they were able to satisfy the criteria. These convergence criteria will also serve to define the 'economically correct' behaviour for members in the final stage of EMU. This part of the treaty is a clear reflection of the new economic orthodoxy: monetary policy will only serve as an anti-inflationary instrument in the hands of independent central bankers, since it is no longer considered to have any long-term effect on output and employment, while fiscal deficits and the accumulated debt will come under strict multilateral control. There was no provision made for an active macroeconomic policy at the European level.

The strong possibility of several member countries being excluded, even temporarily, from the final stage of EMU meant that a further important step would be taken towards the institutionalization of a multi-speed or multi-tier Community. And this was further accentuated by the 'opt-out' clause for the UK which retained the right, confirmed by the treaty, to stay out of the final stage of EMU; a similar clause was also reserved for Denmark. In fact, the differential treatment of member countries was not restricted to monetary affairs. In an even more unconventional agreement, member countries, with the exception again of the UK, decided to proceed further in the field of social policy. They will use Union institutions to legislate as eleven countries with the aim of strengthening the social dimension of economic integration. To this purpose, qualified majority voting among the Eleven was extended to new areas. Thus, the inability to reach a compromise on this highly controversial issue created a legal minefield inside the Union, while also increasing the isolation of the UK, despite the more conciliatory attitude, at least in terms of diplomatic manners, adopted at the time by the government of Mr Major.

EC responsibilities were extended to new areas such as culture, public health, consumer protection, and the development of trans-European networks in the areas of transport, telecommunications, and energy infrastructures. A new Title XIII was added on industry in a very modest attempt to fill the old vacuum in this area. However, the emphasis on open and competitive markets and the retention of the unanimity principle suggest that an active and interventionist industrial policy at the EC level is not on the cards. Community powers in the fields of the environment and research and technology were also strengthened.

On the other hand, this extension of EC powers was coupled with the first explicit reference to the principle of subsidiarity, according to which 'the Community shall take action . . . only if and in so far as the objectives of the proposed action cannot be sufficiently achieved by the Member States and can therefore, by reason of the scale or effects of the proposed action, be better achieved by the Community' (Article 3*b*). Such a general statement can obviously command wide acceptance; it is only when applied to specific cases that disagreement tends to arise.

The new package would have been impossible without some reference to re-distributive measures. The section on economic and social cohesion, together with the separate protocol on this subject, provided for the creation of a new Cohesion Fund for the poorer countries, which would specialize in the fields of environment and trans-European networks in the area of transport. Furthermore, a commitment was undertaken to review the operation of the already existing Structural Funds, leading to the transfer of more resources to the less developed countries and regions of the EU.

The other two pillars were kept separate from traditional EC business, a concession to those who had insisted on intergovernmentalism as the method to be applied to new areas which were dangerously close to the heart of national sovereignty. The twelve countries decided at long last to tackle an old taboo subject, namely defence, which had until then been the preserve of NATO. The signatories resorted to some legal acrobatics in order to try and reconcile the expressed wish for a European common defence policy with continued membership of the Atlantic alliance. However, the inclusion of defence in the new treaty was supposed to be more than symbolic, and it was directly linked to the dramatic developments on the eastern side of the old cold war divide. The WEU would serve as the defence arm of the new Union. All this formed part of the CFSP which would, it was hoped!, develop into something more substantial than the old EPC.

As for the third pillar of the European Union, namely cooperation in the fields of justice and home affairs, this was directly linked to the objective of the free movement of persons inside the Union and the elimination of all intra-EU frontiers. The search for a common asylum and immigration policy *vis-à-vis* the nationals of third countries constituted the main driving force in this area. The constantly increasing number of asylum seekers and potential immigrants had added a great deal to the urgency of this task. There was also the problem of cross-frontier terrorism and drug-trafficking which should be tackled jointly.

Thus, ten months before the target date for the completion of the internal market, which was meanwhile continuing at a steady pace, the Twelve had agreed on a new treaty which mapped out the road for further integration. It was a more radical revision and extension of the old treaties than anything achieved before, including the SEA. The establishment of EMU was the most important and concrete part of the treaty, which meant that the post-1992 phase would be marked by developments in this area. The institutional structure created at Maastricht would certainly not win any prizes for symmetry or even legal refinement and consistency; but this did not seem to cause much concern, at least in the beginning. The highly irregular shape of the overall construction, which also looked rather unstable, was considered as the inevitable price to pay for a difficult political compromise among twelve governments, including some which had been from the very start strongly opposed to the whole exercise; a compromise which nevertheless was meant to bring about a further deepening of the process of integration.

Although very important, the changes introduced at Maastricht fell far short of the expectations entertained by federalists for a significant strengthening of the central institutions of the Community, and especially the executive. But was this any different from the reception accorded to the SEA some years earlier? A window of hope was opened for those who had expected much more in this area: a commitment was undertaken under the new treaty (Article N in the Final Provisions) to call another IGC in 1996. This was largely a concession to the Germans who were clearly dissatisfied with the small progress achieved under political union. The decision to call for another IGC also suggested that the Community, and now the Union, had entered into an almost never-ending process of treaty revisions, starting with the SEA back in the 1980s.

What governments had jointly and rather painfully put together, European societies and international markets were soon to try to pull apart. The ratification of the Maastricht treaty proved an unexpectedly long and agonizing process (Duff, 1994; Franklin, Marsh, and McLaren, 1994). The problems started with the referendum in Denmark, which took place in June 1992 and produced a small 'no' answer, despite the support given to the treaty by all major political parties, business, and trade union leaders as well as most leading newspapers in that country. It looked very much like a popular revolt against decisions taken at the top. This negative result helped to unleash those forces which had remained dormant for years: the opposition movement against the Maastricht treaty grew in several countries, and this opposition often took a more general form against the whole process of integration. Another indication of this change of climate was the decline in popular support for the EU and its institutions, as measured by the Eurobarometer (see Fig 3.3).

This in turn led to a new burst of political activity at the European level in trying to get the treaty past the hurdles of parliamentary ratification and popular referenda. For some, the apparent lack of public enthusiasm for the new treaty could be explained in terms of excessive centralization in the European system; hence the attempt to give a wider and more precise definition to the principle of subsidiarity which soon became the new buzzword in the Community jargon (see, for example, Millon, 1993). There were also attempts to reinterpret imaginatively several sections of the new treaty for the benefit of the Danish voters. The ratification process was finally completed in November 1993, after the holding of referenda in Ireland, France, and a second one in Denmark as well as voting in all twelve national parliaments.

The referendum in France was a close-run thing, with only 51 per cent casting a 'yes' vote. For a country which had all along been at the centre of European integration and which had played a leading role in the negotiation of the Maastricht treaty, this was hardly an encouraging result. On the other hand, popular sentiment was only very partially reflected in the parliamentary debates held in most of the other countries. The UK was one of the very few exceptions: a country in which 'Euro-scepticism' had always found vocal expression at the political level. Judges also had their say on the new treaty: the German Constitutional Court in Karlsruhe, although pronouncing affirmatively on the compatibility of the treaty with the German constitution, questioned the automaticity of the final stage of EMU. This treaty commitment was therefore less solid than it looked.

The lack of popular enthusiasm for the new treaty can be attributed to a number of different factors. It was partly accidental, to the extent that the first Danish referendum, which took place very early in the process of ratification, created a dynamic against the treaty, a dynamic which was not confined to the borders of the Kingdom of Denmark. After all, the population of that country had never shown high rates of support or any kind of fervour for the transfer of political power to European institutions. Thus, arguably, if Danish politicians had waited for other countries to take the lead, things might have turned out differently, although perhaps only marginally.

The problems experienced with the ratification of the Maastricht treaty surely also had to do with the lack of transparency which had characterized the whole negotiation and the highly technocratic and largely incomprehensible nature of the final product. Perhaps also, European élites had taken one step too far in testing the permissive consensus which had always existed with respect to European integration; a permissive consensus which could no longer be taken for granted as the integration process began to affect directly the everyday life of European citizens. This popular reaction had hardly been expected in a period of 'Euro-euphoria', the end of which had, alas, not yet been perceived. On the other hand, the tragic events in Yugoslavia and the apparent inability of the Union to play an effective stabilization role, despite the solemn declarations about a common foreign and security policy, had also played a part.

As it had become evident in earlier periods, Euro-sentiments are closely related to the economic climate. Figure 3.3 plots annual growth rates and popular support for European unification in the twelve member countries for the period 1982–94 (the figure for popular support being derived by adding the percentages of those who express themselves as very much in favour and those to some extent in favour of European unification). There is a strong correlation between the two lines. High rates of economic growth have been closely associated with high rates of support for European unification; and they both declined together in the early 1990s.

Growth rates were steadily declining in the early 1990s, reaching a negative figure in 1993. This led in turn to an upward shift in unemployment which reached a new height at 11 per cent for the EU-12 in 1994. Unemployment kept rising, while capital profitability in the EU countries continued to improve, again

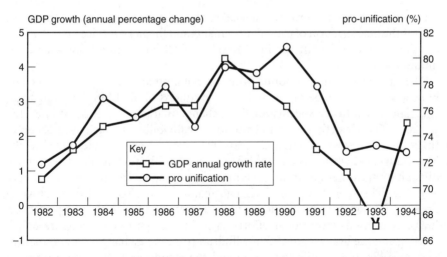

Fig. 3.3. Economic Growth and Popular Support for European Unification, 1982–1994

Notes: Percentage pro-unification includes those who express themselves as very much in favour and those to some extent in favour of European unification; averages of two samples per year.

Source: Eurobarometer (1983–1995), Commission (for GDP figures).

reaching the level of the early 1960s (Commission data). Yet, business confidence remained very low and investment was not forthcoming. Moreover, real economic convergence slowed down during the recession and intra-EU trade suffered a small decline in relative terms (Fig. 2.1).

The deep economic recession also contributed to another increase in budget deficits, despite the commitments previously undertaken by governments in the Maastricht treaty. When the treaty was being negotiated, the average budget deficit in the EU was about 4 per cent of GDP; by 1993, it had gone up to 6 per cent. Part of this increase was due to the working of the so-called automatic stabilizers (tax revenues and welfare spending) at a time of economic recession. Part of it was also due to the servicing of the accumulated public debt which had increased by more than 30 percentage points in relation to GDP between 1978 and 1994, now reaching 70 per cent. The price for this extravaganza would have to be paid by future generations. High interest rates at the time made the burden of the servicing of the debt even heavier. In 1994, interest payments accounted for 11 per cent of total public expenditure in the Twelve (Commission, 1995*b*).

Thus, almost ten years later, European countries were back where they had started: at a very low point of the economic cycle, with an even worse rate of unemployment, business confidence at rock bottom, big deficits and large accumulated public debt, serious structural problems, and a deep concern about the international competitiveness of their economies. With such a negative economic climate, it was therefore no surprise that the target date (31 December 1992) for the completion of the internal market programme went almost unnoticed, despite the fact that the programme had registered a number of major successes, such as the liberalization of capital movements and financial services as well as the decision to proceed with the liberalization of telecommunications—far from unimportant decisions.

The bad news on the economic front was not limited to the real economy. The long period of exchange rate stability in the context of the EMS also came to an end. There was heavy speculation in exchange markets which questioned the sustainability of existing rates and also the sustainability of restrictive policies in times of deep recession. High German interest rates, which were linked to the large budget deficits incurred in the first years of unification, made life extremely difficult for the other European governments; and capital controls were no longer available. The speculation in exchange markets was also fuelled by growing doubts about the survival of the Maastricht treaty and hence also the project on EMU. Concerted government efforts to resist the speculative pressure failed. Sterling and the lira were forced to withdraw from the exchange rate mechanism in September 1992, while the peseta and the escudo went through a series of devaluations.

And then a more systemic crisis followed, which hit some of the core currencies and most notably the French franc. In August 1993, EU governments had to concede defeat. The margins of fluctuation were extended to 15 per cent on either side of the central rates, which was almost tantamount to a floating system, even though participating currencies were to make subsequently only very limited use of the permitted margins (Johnson and Collignon, 1994; Commission, 1994a: 87–104). According to the Maastricht treaty, the second stage of EMU was supposed to start on 1 January 1994; and officially, it did so, even though the old system of fixed but adjustable intra-EU exchange rates, with narrow margins of fluctuation, had suffered a severe blow only a few months earlier. This certainly did not help to restore public confidence in the new treaty and the process of integration in general.

A resurgence of 'Euro-pessimism', like the bad old days? This was true, but still, the Union continued to deliver important policy decisions in several areas. In 1992, a major step was taken in reforming the CAP. This reform centred around a substantial reduction in the price of cereals, which was intended to bring EU support prices close to world prices. It would be followed by compensation in the form of income subsidies to farmers and the adoption of a set-aside programme which should bring about a further cut in production. The 1992 reform constituted the most important step so far in the switch from support prices to income subsidies, a switch which had been called for by many economists for years. Would it also lead eventually to the progressive renationalization of agricultural policies, thus dropping a very important part of the overall package deal which had provided for many years the foundation stone of the European integration process? This question was no longer theoretical (Kjeldahl and Tracy, 1994).

The reform of the CAP made it easier for the Twelve to reach a compromise on agriculture with the Americans in the context of the Uruguay Round, which lasted even longer than earlier rounds of GATT negotiations. The final agreement was signed in Marrakesh in April 1994: it would lead to a further reduction in trade barriers, the extension of common rules and disciplines to agriculture and services, and the replacement of GATT by the World Trade Organization (WTO), which would be endowed with a more permanent structure and also more effective mechanisms for dispute settlement. The strengthening of rules governing international trade did not, however, stem the drive towards regional institutions and arrangements which was manifest in different parts of the world. The Union was not left behind in this area: new agreements were signed with Central and Eastern European countries (CEECs) and the countries of the Mediterranean basin, which had become, undoubtedly, the main focus of attention for the EU's external trade policy.

On the internal front, another very important decision related to the Union budget and redistribution. In December 1992, the European Council held in Edinburgh followed the precedent set by another meeting of the European Council in Brussels back in 1988. An agreement was reached on the main budgetary guidelines until 1999, which included a small further increase in 'own resources', and a substantial boosting of redistribution in favour of the less developed countries and regions of the Union through the Structural Funds and the new Cohesion Fund created by the Maastricht treaty. The interminable budgetary disputes, repeated monotonously year after year and bringing the Community to virtual paralysis, seemed now to be a thing of the past.

In an attempt to recover the high ground of policy initiatives, the Commission presented its White Paper on *Growth, Competitiveness, Employment* (Commission, 1994*b*). The main problems were identified as unemployment and the loss of competitiveness which was, however, never clearly defined or convincingly argued; but after all, the rhetoric of competitiveness had become fashionable for European and American political leaders alike (Krugman, 1994*a*). The Commission proposed a series of measures, ranging from measures to promote the flexibility of labour markets and the reduction of non-wage costs to new versions of Keynesianism with the main emphasis on investment in R&D and the development of trans-European networks. Such measures were deemed necessary in order to create the conditions for sustainable and more labour-intensive growth, while also safeguarding the essential elements of Europe's economic and social model; a model which aimed to combine efficiency with solidarity. The White Paper triggered debate and many more papers and reports, in which competitiveness often figured as a key word; although this activity has so far rarely been translated into actual policy.

Despite the adverse economic environment, the decline in popular support for European integration and the problems experienced with the ratification of the new treaty, the Union seemed hardly to have lost its attraction in the outside world. A further enlargement took place in January 1995, which coincided with the arrival of the new Commission led by Mr Santer. Austria, Finland, and Sweden were the three new members: countries which had apparently decided that their neutrality and highly developed welfare states (which were already suffering from the shock of a recent large increase in unemployment rates—Fig. 3.1) no longer constituted a major obstacle to full membership of the Community/Union. The radical transformation of the European political map, which had resulted from the disintegration of the old communist order in the East, combined with the growing openness of their economies, constituted extremely important variables in the equation facing their policy-makers. Thus, the European Economic Area (EEA) agreements, previously offered to those countries by the EU as a substitute for full membership, no longer made any sense. However, Norway did stay out, when a slightly smaller majority than in 1972 rejected once again the option of joining the EU, despite the strong support given to accession by Norway's political class. It remained in EFTA (and the EEA), together with Iceland and Liechtenstein, while the Swiss voters found even the EEA too much of a constraint on their sovereignty.

This was not apparently the end of the process of widening. One after the other, the CEECs, having already signed association agreements with the EU, presented their applications for full membership. They followed on the steps of Southern European countries which were still outside the Union's fold. The list of actual and potential candidates is very long, and the Fifteen have committed themselves to going ahead with further enlargement which might eventually lead to almost doubling of the membership. There is now a new variation on the old theme/ debate on deepening and widening. It centres around the new IGC which started in March 1996 and the final stage of EMU. We shall return to these issues in subsequent chapters.

4

FROM CUSTOMS UNION TO
THE INTERNAL MARKET

Non-Tariff Barriers and the Mixed Economy

Following a historical overview of the process of European economic integration, this chapter and the next will concentrate on some issues related to the establishment of the internal market. We shall start with a brief examination of the barriers still existing at the time of the publication of the White Paper in 1985: a measure of the incomplete nature of the common market, twenty-seven years after the establishment of the EEC. We shall then go on to examine the strategy behind the internal market programme and the expectations associated with it. This will be followed by a still provisional balance sheet regarding the implementation and enforcement of internal market legislation. Some forty studies were commissioned in 1995 by Brussels to assess the economic effects of the internal market. They were intended to provide the material for a Commission general report regarding the assessment of the internal market effects. The publications arising from the above studies should follow later. Some of the results obtained will be summarized here. The next chapter will venture into the open sea by tackling the question of economic regulation and the interaction between the state and the market as they are affected by the latest phase of European integration.

The list of remaining barriers to the free movement of goods, services, persons, and capital, as contained in the White Paper on the completion of the internal market, was indeed very long, and this could be interpreted as a sign of failure to fulfil the main objectives of the Treaty of Rome. Undoubtedly, many of the remaining barriers were the result of only a partial implementation of treaty provisions and the highly incomplete state of common policies, a situation which had become worse during the prolonged period of the economic recession which preceded the adoption of the White Paper.

For years, most textbooks referred to the five stages of economic integration as defined by Balassa (1961). They include the free trade area, the customs union, the common market, economic policy harmonization, and the complete economic union. The different stages are usually presented in the form of a ladder which can be climbed one step at a time, leading ultimately to the state of eternal bliss, namely complete economic integration. However, this categorization, together with the traditional theory of international trade, has been shown to be very misleading because both basically ignore the reality of mixed economies where state intervention is not limited to border controls or macroeconomic policy (Pelkmans, 1980 and 1984).

In the context of such economies, a complete customs union or a common market can be nothing short of total economic integration; and this has become increasingly apparent in the case of the EU. The long list of remaining barriers contained in the White Paper of 1985 provided perhaps sufficient evidence of earlier failure to achieve a complete common market; but it was also a reminder of the enormity of the task undertaken and a testimony to the omnipresence of the state in European mixed economies and its pervasive role as a regulator of economic activity. This list was long although not exhaustive, and the authors of the White Paper recommended a new determined effort to tackle those barriers, an effort which would rely on a new, more flexible approach and the political will to take the Community to a higher stage of economic integration. However, a number of highly sensitive political issues regarding the choice among different methods of eliminating those barriers and the likely implications for countries, regions, and interest groups were left partially or completely unanswered.

All remaining barriers were divided in the White Paper into three main categories: physical, technical, and fiscal. But with the exception of fiscal barriers, the other two categories have little economic meaning and are only a convenient form of presentation for a mixed bag of disparate issues and measures. This is particularly true of technical barriers which could have been, perhaps more appropriately, referred to as 'other'.

The category of physical barriers contains essentially all frontier controls which had remained despite the establishment of the customs union in July 1968. Some of those controls were the result of gaping holes in the common commercial policy. The most notable example was the survival of national quantitative restrictions on various imports from Japan, which in turn necessitated the application of intra-EC frontier controls in order to establish the origin of goods. Furthermore, EC quantitative restrictions on some imports from third countries, such as textiles and clothing in the context of the various multifibre arrangements (MFAs) and steel products under the crisis measures, were divided into national quotas for individual member countries; and this again brought about the need for intra-EC controls. In all those cases, the EC basically operated like a free trade area and not a customs union; hence the need to apply rules of origin and to preserve frontier controls.

The uncommon nature of the CAP was another important reason for the existence of physical barriers. The system of common prices, expressed in European units of account and later in ECU, did not survive the breakdown of the Bretton Woods system and the frequent changes in intra-EC exchange rates (the problem having been attenuated but not completely resolved after the establishment of the EMS). The myth of unity was kept only through the creation of fictitious exchange rates for agricultural products and the introduction of border taxes, otherwise known under the more neutral name of monetary compensatory amounts (MCAs) which often varied from one product to the other. The elimination of controls would imply the return to real common prices for agricultural goods, a goal which had eluded the Community for many years.

The Treaty of Rome contained provisions for a common policy for transport. But no progress in this area was registered until the adoption of the 1992 target for the completion of the internal market. This meant the perpetuation of licences and national quotas for intra-EC road transport and an effective prohibition on non-resident carriers operating transport services in another member country (the so-called *cabotage*); hence, the need for controls at the frontier, but also higher transport costs. On the other hand, different rates of indirect taxation and the application of the principle of destination (to be discussed in more detail below) raised the need for border tax adjustments and, hence, fiscal controls at the frontier. And so also did different health regulations, especially with respect to food products.

In fact, the task of creating a Europe without frontiers extends much beyond the field of economics; and this was the explicit objective of the White Paper and the Commission's strategy. The elimination of controls for individuals would have to be based on a far-reaching agreement among member governments on issues such as the control of drugs, immigration, and national security more generally; major issues which touch sensitive nerves of national sovereignty. Differences in terms of visa requirements for nationals of non-member countries and the need for intra-EU frontier controls are the political counterpart of the problem created by remaining gaps in the common commercial policy for the intra-EU movement of goods: gaps in the common external policy leading to internal controls.[1]

The proposals for the elimination of technical barriers contained a motley assortment of measures. Different technical regulations, which are legally binding in each country, and standards, which are voluntarily agreed codifications written by national standardization bodies and considered as an indicator of quality, had long been regarded as a major factor behind the fragmentation of the EC market. They also directly added to costs by forcing producers to adjust their products to the requirements of each national market; that is, whenever those barriers could be effectively overcome, which was not always the case.

Different technical regulations and standards were particularly important in specific sectors such as mechanical and electrical equipment as well as transport goods; virtually all high technology sectors were especially affected. That was also true of other sectors such as food and drink, and pharmaceuticals. Different regulations and standards may be the result of legitimate differences between countries regarding the trade-off between economic efficiency on the one hand, and health and environmental considerations on the other. Other factors such as technological development and administrative efficiency also play an important

---

[1] Further steps in this area were later to be taken as a result of the new treaty signed at Maastricht (the so-called third pillar).

role. But regulations and standards can also be a covert, albeit very effective, means of protection against foreign producers. The dividing line between legitimate and illegitimate use of different technical regulations and standards is usually blurred.

The experience of the first twenty-seven years of the EEC had not been very encouraging. Despite the efforts made by the Commission and the Court of Justice, the role of the Community had been effectively limited to slow, rearguard action against the spreading of different technical regulations and standards in individual member countries. Their proliferation reflected growing public concern for the protection of consumers and the environment; but they were also an instrument of external protection in times of recession and growing unemployment. On the other hand, the process of harmonization (or approximation) at the EC level had proved to be both inefficient and ineffective. Its snail's pace compared unfavourably with the speed with which national authorities introduced new laws and regulations (Pelkmans, 1987).

The strategy proposed in the White Paper was, indeed, radical: instead of trying to harmonize everything, the emphasis from now on should be on mutual recognition of technical regulations and standards which should open the way for the unrestricted circulation of goods inside the EC. Recourse to legislative harmonization should be limited only to essential cases. Furthermore, this harmonization, whenever deemed necessary, should be restricted to basic health and safety requirements, while the task of setting detailed technical specifications should be left to specialized European organizations such as CEN (Centre Européen de Normalisation) and CENELEC (Centre Européen de Normalisation Electrotechnique). The task of harmonization was to be made much easier through the subsequent replacement of unanimity by qualified majority voting with the new Article 100a of the SEA.

The strong reliance on mutual recognition, which extends much beyond technical regulations and standards in the general strategy for the establishment of the internal market, is supposed to be compatible with the (quasi-)federal nature of the EU and the so-called principle of subsidiarity. The principle of subsidiarity basically means that only those powers that cannot be efficiently executed at lower levels will be transferred to a higher level of decision-making. The problem is how to apply this principle in practice; and opinions usually differ widely. Mutual recognition was also presented as something compatible with the political, economic, and social diversity inside the EC. But it was certainly not devoid of problems: for example, how does one ensure that mutual recognition and the ensuing 'competition among rules' do not lead to a general erosion of standards? The definition of efficiency and the optimal distribution of power between different levels of political authority are not the kind of issues on which most people easily agree. Can competition and the market determine the optimal level of regulation? This subject will be discussed further in Chapter 5.

Discriminatory public purchasing has been traditionally one of the most powerful and frequently used instruments of industrial policy and an effective means of promoting national champions. Even in the case of the United States, where industrial policy has been almost a dirty word, public purchasing, and defence contracts in particular, have always played such a role. Various EC directives adopted in the past seem to have had virtually no effect on government practices. The comparison of the import content of government purchases (less than 4 per cent for the large member countries according to Commission data) with that of the private and public sectors combined was very revealing of the extent of the discrimination involved.

Public purchasing in general was estimated to account at the time for approximately 16 per cent of Community GDP, and the contractual part of it, what is called public procurement, for 7–10 per cent of GDP. Especially in some sectors with a strong high technology content and sizeable economies of scale, such as telecommunications equipment, the public sector has been by far the biggest client: hence, the inevitable fragmentation of the EC market and the high costs of production. The White Paper aimed at greater transparency and the extension of competition to four sectors which had been excluded from previous EC directives, namely water, energy, transport, and telecommunications.

One important aspect of EC competition policy deals with state aids. Article 92 of the Treaty of Rome contains a general prohibition of such aids, because of the distortions created in intra-EC competition; and this prohibition is then followed by a long list of exceptions. In the past, the Commission had adopted a very cautious (tolerant or passive would be, perhaps, more appropriate terms) approach on this subject in view of the strong resistance of national governments to outside interference. Political realism had thus overridden any desire to attempt a more strict application of treaty provisions. The period of the economic recession saw an increasing resort to state subsidies as a means of covert protection of domestic producers; the example of steel being one of the most prominent. According to the first reports published by the Commission on this subject, the amount of state aids remained quite significant in the 1980s; as a percentage of gross value added in the manufacturing sector, they were highest in the less developed countries and regions of the Community such as Greece, Portugal, Ireland, and South Italy (Commission, 1990a). The White Paper, consequently, pointed to the need for a more rigorous application of Community discipline in this area.

Distortions in intra-EC competition can also arise from different company laws, while also causing major difficulties for cross-border cooperation among firms, including mergers and joint ventures. The creation of a common legal framework, included in an old Commission proposal for a European company statute, would help to deal with this problem. Similarly, the development of a Community trade mark would help to tackle the difficulties arising from different intellectual property laws.

The Treaty of Rome talks about the freedom of establishment and the free movement of services in the context of the common market. Yet reality had remained for many years far short of the full achievement of those objectives. The gap became more noticeable as many services gradually entered the category of 'tradeables', while the size of the whole sector was steadily expanding as a percentage of GDP (around 60 per cent for the EC as a whole). The main barriers resulted from the existence of different regulatory frameworks in the member countries. Thus the cross-border provision of insurance was virtually excluded for this reason. Various restrictions had also survived with respect to the exercise of the freedom of establishment in both banking and insurance. With regard to financial services in general, exchange controls were another major impediment to free intra-EC movement. Road and air transport remained under heavy governmental control: with respect to the former, by imposing restrictions on capacity and access and operating a system of licences for non-national hauliers, and for the latter, through a system of bilateral agreements in which designated carriers provide services whose cost, capacity, and conditions were directly or indirectly regulated. In telecommunications, national monopolies remained the rule. As for new services, such as audiovisual, information, and data processing, government regulations and different standards were the most effective barriers. And the list was almost endless.

Despite the relevant provisions in the Treaty of Rome, the progress made towards the liberalization of capital movements had been extremely slow until the second half of the 1980s. The effect of two directives adopted in the early stages of the EEC was effectively nullified by the extensive use of safeguard clauses, especially during the years of recession and monetary instability, which followed the breakdown of Bretton Woods and the advent of the oil crisis. As for labour, the main restrictions were lifted by July 1968, and considerable progress was also registered with respect to the harmonization of social security legislation. Yet this had little effect on the cross-border movement of many skilled workers and professionals. One, but certainly not the only, reason for this was the lack of harmonization of professional qualifications on which the White Paper laid great emphasis. The Commission proposed to deal with this particular Gordian knot in exactly the same way as with different technical regulations and industrial standards, namely through mutual recognition of university degrees and vocational training.

Distortions arising from different fiscal systems have been an old concern of economic integration theory; and this was duly acknowledged in the relevant provisions made in the Treaty of Rome. The main emphasis has always been on indirect taxation and its effects on the allocation of resources within a customs union or a common market. Taxes on income and capital had received until more recently relatively little attention, because of implicit assumptions about the low mobility of factors of production compared with the movement of goods; and this was also true of the White Paper. However, with the rapidly growing mobility of capital, the validity of such assumptions has become more and more questionable.

The EC had succeeded in replacing different turnover taxes with a single system of indirect taxation, namely the VAT. But the harmonization of the system did not extend to the taxable base and the rates used in the different member countries, despite repeated efforts made by the Commission in the past. The differences in excise taxes were even more dramatic; those taxes are usually levied on tobacco, alcohol, and fuel. In order to avoid discrimination between different national producers, member countries applied the so-called destination principle to both their intra-EC and international trade. This meant that at any consumption point the same tax was levied irrespective of the origin of goods. And this in turn meant that exports were zero rated. The application of the destination principle did, however, raise the need for frontier fiscal controls and border tax adjustments. This was precisely what the White Paper wanted to put an end to: the final aim being to tax sales across borders in exactly the same way as sales within a country.

The abandonment of the destination principle would, however, raise two fundamental problems, namely trade distortions arising from different national rates and a redistribution of revenue among national tax authorities. The way to deal with the former would be, according to the Commission, through the harmonization of the taxable base and the alignment of different rates. Based on the US experience, the Commission argued that a complete harmonization of VAT rates and excise taxes would not be necessary; instead, an approximation within a 5 per cent margin around a target rate (or rates) would be sufficient to avoid large distortions. As for tax revenue, the Commission would aim at the continuation of the status quo through the creation of a 'clearing house'. The differences in rates of indirect taxation reflect different traditions, economic realities as well as political and social preferences. Therefore, resistance to change was expected to remain strong; hence also the insistence on unanimous voting in the Council of Ministers, which survived the treaty revisions introduced through the SEA. We shall return to this subject in the next chapter.

The White Paper referred basically to what are generally known as NTBs: barriers and distortions created by different forms of domestic government intervention. It was largely about services and factors of production, areas in which very little progress in terms of integration had been achieved until then. And the reason was simple: the most effective barriers were not to be found at the border; they were, instead, the result of different regulatory frameworks which created the notorious NTBs. Thus the White Paper signalled a qualitatively new phase in the process of integration.

Domestic government intervention is part and parcel of the established political and economic order in each country. The White Paper was presented as a set of technical measures, presumably intended to assuage nationalist fears. However, a more careful reading of the text and the various measures put forward in the accompanying annex would lead to a different conclusion. Many of those measures touched at the very heart of national economic sovereignty; and modern politics is very much about welfare issues. Fiscal harmonization, monetary policy and capital movements, state subsidies, and even industrial standards are the basic material of which the economic role of the state consists; and also the instruments through which governments can influence the direction of votes. Such issues have become increasingly prominent as the old trade model of European integration reached its limits. As it did so, the contradiction between trade liberalization and the mixed economy, which had been lurking for years in the background, slowly came to the surface.

The White Paper and the internal market programme were an attempt to tackle this problem, and the method adopted reflected the new political consensus in

Western Europe and the shift towards more competition and the market. It could, perhaps, be argued that the main emphasis was on negative integration, following the old distinction drawn by Tinbergen (1954) between negative and positive integration. According to the Dutch economist, negative integration refers to the elimination of obstacles to the free movement of goods and factors of production, while positive integration refers to the harmonization of rules and the adoption of common policies; the latter, therefore, being more consistent with the mixed economy. Would this distinction also apply with respect to NTBs? The elimination of the latter requires, at least in principle, a combination of negative and positive integration measures: deregulation combined with a certain harmonization of national rules and an agreement on new regulatory frameworks for the economic union as a whole. Although the White Paper tried to set some guidelines (would the principle of mutual recognition prove to be a euphemism for negative integration?), the final mixture was impossible to determine in advance. Much would depend on subsequent negotiations in individual areas and the implementation of the measures adopted. This subject will be taken up in Chapter 5.

Supply-Side Economics and the Labours of Implementation

The publication of the White Paper and the adoption of the 1992 target led to the birth of a new, booming industry which was enthusiastically welcomed by the economics profession in all member countries. Its main function has been to analyse the consequences of the internal market and to predict/assess its economic effects. Numerous quantitative estimates (*ex ante* and, more recently, *ex post*) have been produced for individual sectors, national economies, and the EU as a whole, and the range of those estimates is very wide, thus catering for different tastes and expectations.

Among the *ex ante* studies of the likely effects of the internal market, the Commission work on 'The Economics of 1992', otherwise known as the 'Costs of Non-Europe' or the Cecchini report (Commission, 1988a),[2] received wide publicity. It is the most comprehensive work on this subject, and the quantitative assessments contained in it were regularly used in the early years by the Commission and member governments as the scientific support for the internal market programme and as an important instrument to influence market expectations.

The completion of the internal market constitutes yet another phase in the process of integration and the elimination of intra-EC barriers. But since integration is already much beyond the stage of tariff liberalization, the traditional theory of customs union has relatively little to say about it. Surely, there will be further trade creation and trade diversion, leading to even more openness of the EC economies and a further increase of intra-EC trade. More trade should be associated with

---

[2] Its popular version can be found in Cecchini, 1988.

welfare effects, although when dealing with the multiplicity of NTBs, the analysis inevitably becomes much messier. In fact, most studies of the internal market, and the 'Costs of Non-Europe' in particular, point very clearly to the ever-widening gap between traditional theory and the real issues at stake. It is not only the non-tariff nature of the new phase of integration and the central role of services which account for this gap; the emphasis is now clearly on the so-called dynamic effects on which our knowledge still remains rather limited. Thus, faith sometimes substitutes for scientific knowledge.

According to the Commission study (Commission, 1988a), the elimination of the remaining barriers, such as frontier controls and different technical standards, should lead to a reduction of costs, which could then be translated into either a widening of profit margins or a lowering of prices or a combination of both. In fact, the strengthening of competitive forces, through the further opening of frontiers and the pursuit of a vigorous competition policy, should help to turn cost reductions into lower prices. Stronger competition at the EC level should also lead to a further lowering of costs through the reduction of the so-called X-inefficiency (poor allocation of resources inside a firm due to weak external competition). Uncompetitive producers, previously protected through various NTBs, would be pushed out of business, while the more efficient ones would be able to benefit from economies of scale through increased production; hence, even lower costs.

The Commission study laid great emphasis on the scope for further economies of scale as well as learning economies. It referred to the 'minimum efficient technical scale' (METS), and argued that in many sectors the actual firm size is significantly smaller than the estimated METS. Earlier studies on the effects of integration had pointed to sizeable economies of scale (Owen, 1983). A positive relationship was also assumed to exist between stronger competition on the one hand, and technical progress and innovation on the other.

The Commission's views on competition were certainly not those of the old textbook model. The following passage is very illustrative of the approach adopted:

European integration would thus assist the emergence of a virtuous circle of innovation and competition—competition stimulating innovation which in turn would increase competition. This is not to say that the desired form of competition corresponds to the theoretical and simplified model of perfect competition. The relationship between competition and innovation is not linear and indeed there exists an optimal level of competition beyond which competition has an adverse effect on innovation because of the difficulty of allocating gains and the greater risks which obtain in highly competitive markets. *The optimum market structure from the standpoint of innovation ought rather to promote strategic rivalry between a limited number of firms.* [italics added] (Commission, 1988a: 129)

The word 'competition' may crop up all too often in the above quotation. Yet the Commission's approach to it was more akin to the oligopolistic reality of many contemporary markets. 'Strategic rivalry between a limited number of firms' constituted the essence of the Commission's approach; and this did not exclude various forms of inter-firm collaboration as, for example, those promoted by Brussels in various high technology sectors in recent years. They formed part of the new and more flexible approach to industrial policy.

According to the Commission study, a clear indicator of the importance of the remaining barriers, causing the fragmentation of the EC market, were the observed price differentials between member countries. A good example was the financial sector: according to the figures provided by Price Waterhouse, prices in different EC countries often differed by more than 100 per cent and this was attributed largely to the lack of intra-EC competition (Commission, 1988*a*: Table 5.1.4, 91). The next step was to argue that the elimination of barriers and the new competition created would lead to an alignment of prices downwards, which was precisely what the Commission expected or hoped for.

There should also be important macroeconomic effects. Investment was expected to rise because of stronger competition, industrial restructuring, and the lower cost of borrowing resulting from the liberalization of financial services. In this respect, the credibility of the internal market programme should be absolutely crucial in creating favourable expectations among economic agents, which would then be translated into new investment decisions. The Commission seemed to be perfectly aware of the need to keep those expectations well nourished. On the other hand, lower prices should lead to gains in competitiveness and to an improvement of the external trade balance. Gains in competitiveness and in domestic purchasing power, combined with higher investment, should lead to an increase in aggregate demand and higher growth; and this, in turn, to lower public sector deficits and the creation of new jobs. Each step of the argument, however, depended on some crucial assumptions relating to the behaviour of exchange rates and the functioning of labour markets among others.

The 'Costs of Non-Europe' contained seventeen horizontal and vertical studies which provided the basic material for an assessment of the overall effects of the internal market. They were followed by two overall quantitative assessments based on a microeconomic and macroeconomic approach respectively. The results obtained from both were remarkably similar and are summarized in Table 4.1:

Table 4.1. Macroeconomic Consequences of the Completion of the Internal Market

Microeconomic approach	Welfare gains as % of GDP 4.25–6.5				
Macroeconomic approach	GDP as %	Prices as %	Employment in millions	Public balance as % point(s) of GDP	External balance as % point(s) of GDP
Without accompanying economic measures	4.5	–6	1.75	2.25	1
With accompanying economic measures	7	–4.5	5	0.5	–0.5

Note: Margin of error ±30%.

Source: Commission, 1988*a*: 167.

additional growth of 4.5 per cent of GDP, reduction in prices of 6 per cent, creation of 1,750,000 new jobs, reduction of public sector deficits of 2.25 per cent, and improvement of the Community's external balance of 1 per cent of GDP. According to the Commission, the positive effects in terms of GDP and employment could be significantly increased if member governments were to take advantage of the new margin of manoeuvre created by lower inflation, smaller public sector deficits, and the improvement in the external balance by adopting more expansionary macroeconomic policies. This could then lead to additional growth of the order of 7 per cent and 5 million extra jobs. The Commission expressed a strong preference for a more active macroeconomic policy as a means of creating a more favourable environment which would in turn facilitate the implementation of the internal market programme.

With the notable exception of a study by Baldwin (1989), who tried to incorporate the dynamic effects of the internal market on savings and investment, most of the other attempts to measure *ex ante* the effects of the internal market produced significantly smaller net gains (Davis *et al.*, 1989; Jacquemin and Sapir, 1989; Haaland and Norman, 1992; Helm, 1993). In fact, the quantification part of all those studies was, arguably, of little value. In the Commission study, the direct benefits expected from the elimination of frontier controls were relatively small, while on the contrary big expectations were associated with the secondary, so-called dynamic effects, resulting from economies of scale, restructuring, and greater competition, for which it would be extremely difficult to produce anything more than educated guesses.

Some years later, Helm (1993: 4) wrote:

These estimates have been extensively debated. The general conclusion which emerges is unsurprising: the margin of error is extremely large, and depends, sensitively, on the responses of European firms and consumers, as well as the trade effects compared with the counterfactual: what would have happened in the absence of policy. Since the latter is necessarily a theoretical construct, the lack of consensus reflects a more fundamental theoretical disagreement about the nature of microeconomic behaviour in general and models of oligipolistic competition in particular. The only generally accepted conclusion is that the net effects are likely to be positive for Europe as a whole.

In view of the very large degree of uncertainty and the multiplicity of factors involved, *ex ante* (and *ex post*) estimates of the internal market effects should therefore be treated at best as very rough indicators of the direction of those effects and the broad orders of magnitude.

One important question, which was left almost completely unanswered in the 'Costs of Non-Europe' study, was about the likely distribution of costs and benefits associated with the internal market programme. In this respect, the study had little to offer in terms of prediction, apart from acknowledging the problem and expressing the hope that EC redistributive policies would provide adequate means for compensating potential losers or, even better, for helping weaker economies and regions to face the strong winds of competition unleashed through the elimination of barriers.

Modern theories of international trade, with their emphasis on imperfect competition, economies of scale, and the dynamic effects of innovation suggest that a very unequal distribution of gains from integration is a very concrete possibility (Krugman, 1987; Helpman and Krugman, 1985).[3] Comparative advantage is no longer seen as something determined by the particular factor endowments of a country. Instead, comparative advantage is created through deliberate policies directed at investment, education, and research and development. Countries pursue strategic trade policies in order to capture an ever-increasing share of dynamic sectors where demand is growing and where the benefits of scale economies, advantages of experience, and innovation can be reaped; in economic terms, sectors where there are good prospects for 'rent'. In such a world, which is thousands of kilometres apart from the assumptions made by traditional theories of international trade, a highly unequal distribution of gains and losses from integration can by no means be excluded. Krugman (1987: 130), for example, argues that trade based on economies of scale, which seems to be largely the case of intra-EC trade, 'probably involves less conflict of interest *within* countries and more conflict of interest *between* countries'.

After the publication of the 'Costs of Non-Europe', the Commission tried to go further by identifying those industrial sectors which should be more affected by the elimination of remaining barriers (Commission, 1990b). Since the completion of the internal market is largely about NTBs (discriminatory public procurement being one of the most important), it is not entirely surprising that many of the sectors found to be most affected were high technology sectors (telecommunications, computers) and more traditional, capital-intensive sectors (railway equipment, shipbuilding, electrical engineering). But the list of the sectors most sensitive to the 1992 programme also included certain mass-consumer products, such as textiles and clothing, where technical and other barriers continued to have a significant effect on intra-EC trade. While the former category of sectors is more associated with the developed, highly industrialized countries of the Union, textiles and clothing represent a disproportionately large share of industrial employment in the two least developed countries, namely Portugal and Greece.

Those studies also pointed to the inter-industry dimension of intra-EC trade which has grown significantly as a result of successive enlargements. There is a great deal of inter-industry trade between Germany on the one hand and Greece or Portugal on the other (see also Neven, 1990). Economic theory tells us that the adjustment costs from liberalization are expected to be greater in the case of inter-industry trade, which means that adjustment in relation to the internal market should be more painful than what had been experienced in the years following the establishment of the EEC. The elimination of the remaining internal barriers could, for example, accentuate the tendency for geographical concentration of economic activity in high technology sectors for which the availability of skilled

---

[3] There is a close parallel between the new 'paradigm' in international trade theory and the literature on regional economics. Both concentrate on various forms of market failure and try to explain the development of inter-regional and inter-country disparities in the context of free trade. See also Chapter 9.

manpower and proximity to research, administrative, and financial centres can be extremely important; and this can be true of other sectors too. On the other hand, liberalization and deregulation, applied for instance to financial services or telecommunications, should be expected to bring more sizeable benefits to the less developed countries of the periphery. The implicit assumption behind this argument would be that protection and heavy regulation in those countries has been the result of economically irrational policies and thus rationality imported from Brussels should have important beneficial effects: perhaps, not a totally implausible argument.

As mentioned earlier, the first years of the internal market programme coincided with an economic boom to which it did itself, arguably, contribute. The programme enjoyed strong support from the business community, and most notably the large firms represented in the European Round Table. Some important early decisions, such as the decision to liberalize capital movements, accompanied by a very active promotion strategy adopted in Brussels, helped to influence further business expectations which were in turn translated into investment decisions. The rapid increase in cross-frontier mergers and acquisitions and the spectacular growth of foreign direct investment (FDI) were also not unrelated to the prospect of a single European market. Early business surveys pointed to a '1992 effect', which, if true, would be a purely anticipatory effect (Commission, 1989). Similarly, Malinvaud (1991) talked about the 'Schumpeterian' effect of 1992, this effect being generally identified with a boost to entrepreneurship producing in turn a shift in the behaviour of private economic agents; and economists find it difficult to analyse and forecast such an effect.

The internal market should not be seen only as a supply-side programme; it has also been an attempt to influence expectations and strengthen the European orientation of firms: hence, the emphasis on marketing. In this respect, the Commission, and to a lesser extent national governments, were doing an excellent job. The internal market and 1992 were given extraordinary publicity. The hyperbole which characterized many of the official statements originating from Brussels was intended precisely to influence market expectations and thus help to sustain the virtuous economic circle.

Kay (1989: 28) described 1992 as 'the most successful marketing campaign of the decade'. On the other hand, a survey for the Bank of England (1989: 18) identified:

a tendency among some corporate consumers, as well as suppliers, of financial services to feel they ought to be 'in on 1992' . . . This could lead to corporate reorganisations . . . based less on a realistic assessment of opportunities and threats than on concern 'not to miss the boat', or for reasons of 'public profile', or simply out of fear. Some non-EEC . . . institutions also appeared to feel pressure to 'do something' about '1992'.

So much for 'rational' economic behaviour. Unfortunately, the honeymoon period proved to be rather short. It came to an end with the next downswing of the economic cycle, which was made worse by highly restrictive monetary policies in Europe. Thus, the implementation of the internal market programme was to continue in the 1990s in a rapidly deteriorating economic environment; interestingly enough, it did actually continue.

The very large majority of measures contained in the White Paper of 1985 have been adopted, even with some delay in several cases. The most prominent examples of such delays have been with respect to the removal of border controls for the movement of people, the absence of tax harmonization in some fields, the failure to adapt company law to single market requirements, and the slow process of liberalization of certain sectors, such as energy and telecommunications. However, the biggest problem has resulted from delays in the national transposition of Community rules and from differences of interpretation of those rules at national level (Commission, 1995*c*; see also CEPR, 1995*a*).

Since much of Community legislation is in the form of directives, which are binding 'as to the result to be achieved' thus leaving to national authorities 'the choice of form and methods' (Article 189 of the EC Treaty), implementation requires national legislation. This has often been slow, while different national interpretations of the legislation adopted in Brussels have created practical difficulties for the functioning of the internal market. The same observation equally applies to the actual enforcement of Community law, where again the standards seem to differ considerably from one country to the other. Slow or inadequate implementation and enforcement of Community legislation have in turn forced the Commission to resort frequently to legal action against member governments. 'Les institutions européennes sont condamnées à decider—ou ne pas decider—accessoirement à contrôler, mais sont pratiquement interdites de mise en oeuvre' (Mény, 1995: 336). This 'implementation deficit' of European institutions tends to create major problems as Community legislation enters more and more into the 'nooks and crannies' of European markets and societies.

According to Commission data, member countries had by the end of November 1994 adopted 90 per cent of the national measures required for the implementation of the internal market legislation (Commission, 1995*c*). The performance ranged from 96 per cent for Denmark to 85 per cent for Germany and 80 per cent for Greece. The level of national transposition varied considerably from sector to sector. The biggest delays had been experienced with respect to public procurement, where only 51 per cent of the necessary measures had been adopted by that time, the insurance sector, intellectual and industrial property, pharmaceutical products, and veterinary and plant-health controls. The implementation of the internal market legislation has been improving with time. Thus, in May 1996, it was reported that 93 per cent of the relevant legislation had been transposed into domestic legislation. On the other hand, the principle of mutual recognition has proved difficult to apply in practice as a means of eliminating several technical barriers to trade, mainly because of the rather uncooperative attitude adopted by national authorities. Thus, mutual recognition has not proved as effective an instrument as the sword used by Alexander the Great in cutting the famous Gordian knot; perhaps, not surprisingly.

In addition to the latitude which national authorities have *de facto* availed themselves of in the transposition of Community legislation (and even worse sometimes with respect to the actual enforcement of rules), there has also been some *de jure* differentiation between countries in the timetables and the rules applied for the implementation of the internal market programme in recognition of the different levels of economic development, specific sectoral problems, and the particular needs of individual member countries. Sometimes, the three Southern European countries (Greece, Portugal, and Spain) have been given longer timetables and/or greater flexibility in the application of common rules. This has been true, for example, of capital movements liberalization, the adoption of public procurement legislation for sensitive sectors as well as the liberalization of telecommunications which is expected to take place in 1998, with an adjustment period of five additional years being offered to those countries.

Another example of differentiation (variable geometry or multi-speed could be alternative ways to describe it) has been the so-called Schengen agreement for the elimination of all intra-EU border controls for the movement of people. Having failed to reach an agreement at the Union level, despite previous commitments and also despite the highly visible nature of such a measure to European citizens, a group of member countries decided to go ahead separately. In 1995 six countries had taken this important step (Benelux, Germany, Portugal, and Spain); France was still reluctant to open its borders, because of fears of drug-trafficking and terrorism, even though it had signed the agreement; while Greece and Italy were still in the preparatory stage. The new members were to sign the following year, also bringing with them two outsiders, namely Norway and Iceland as associated members, and thus creating an even more complicated case of variable geometry.

The delays in some areas, the difficulties experienced in terms of transposition and enforcement, and the various cases of differentiation do not, however, negate the importance of measures introduced in the context of the internal market programme, measures which have progressively led to the elimination of long-established national barriers. On the other hand, it has become abundantly clear, if such a need still existed, that the road from an incomplete customs union to a truly internal (or single) market will be long. This is certainly true of public procurement with respect to which non-domestic import penetration remains very small, albeit growing, and the scope for unfair treatment of foreign suppliers is large; and it is also true of technical standards. The 1992 programme represents one, albeit very important, part of this journey. Its economic effects were, perhaps consciously, exaggerated in the beginning. Some of those effects will be felt only several years later as the new rules begin to have a concrete effect on markets, and this effect will be strongly influenced by the general economic climate. In view of the steep rise in unemployment in recent years, it would be unkind to remind the reader of early official predictions about the creation of millions of new jobs.

In an OECD study published in 1994, the authors concluded that 'it is difficult to find strong evidence that the single market programme has yet had sizeable effects on aggregate output' (Hoeller and Loupe, 1994:93). They estimated a cumulative gain of 1.5 per cent of GDP so far, although this numerical estimate had, arguably, as much validity as earlier *ex ante* predictions. The new studies commissioned for an *ex post* evaluation of the internal market programme have to deal with the notorious problem of the counterfactual, thus having to isolate the internal market effect from that of many other important developments which took place during the same period, such as globalization trends, the unification of Germany, the Iberian enlargement, and the gradual opening of the economies of the CEECs; with inadequate data which usually do not correspond to the sophisticated techniques developed by economists; and with late implementation in many cases, which in turn means that the period for which the effects of the internal market can be measured is uncomfortably short while the time-lags during which an adequate response of economic agents can be expected in response to institutional changes may be rather long.

The studies commissioned on the internal market effects have produced some interesting results. It appears that there has been significant trade creation, leading to a further increase in intra-EU trade which is now estimated to reach 68 per cent of total trade for the Fifteen. Statistics on intra-EU trade have, however, become less reliable since the elimination of border controls. There is no evidence of substantial trade diversion. On the contrary, import penetration from the rest of the world has grown in most sectors, and this trend has been even more pronounced in the case of several sectors which are considered most sensitive to the internal market programme. Intra-industry trade in products differentiated by price and quality has grown substantially in virtually all sectors since the mid-1980s, although the share of inter-industry trade is still large for Greece, Portugal, Ireland, and (interestingly enough) Denmark. Germany has a comparative advantage in high price quality product ranges, followed by France, while at the other end of the spectrum, Greece and Portugal seem to specialize only in low price products.

The evidence available points to a strong internal market effect on FDI flows, both intra-EU and from outside, which have been growing faster than trade. The EU share of world FDI inflows has grown significantly in recent years, reaching 44 per cent in the early 1990s; but this may also have something to do with early fears about a 'Fortress Europe', which have, however, proved to be unfounded. The big bulk of FDI has gone to services sectors; not only because they have been growing fast, but also presumably because they are less tradable. FDI outflows from Germany and the UK have registered a particularly strong preference for the financial services sector.

The recent period has also been characterized by a very substantial industrial restructuring, although it is not always easy to separate the effect of the internal market from global trends. And this has been accompanied by a significant increase in concentration, especially in technologically intensive industries. Evidence has also been found of increasing concentration in industries which are closely related to public procurement, such as telecommunications and transport, and also in food industries and mass consumer goods. These are sectors which have been particularly affected by the internal market programme and its liberalizing effects. There are still remarkable differences in the average size of firms even among the large economies. Thus, in Germany the average size of gross value added per firm is one-third higher than in France or the UK. Despite the considerable increase in cross-border mergers and acquisitions, concentration has still been taking place mostly within domestic markets: national boundaries inside the EU are therefore still far from irrelevant.

On the other hand, there is little indication that Europe's industrial core has gained at the expense of the periphery. From the second half of the 1980s onwards, three among the least developed economies of the Union, namely Portugal, Spain, and even more so Ireland, have been growing faster than the average. Higher growth rates can be at least partly attributed to large inflows of foreign investment. It is also interesting that, according to business surveys, economic agents in peripheral countries have perceived a stronger effect of the internal market and, broadly speaking, this effect has been deemed to be positive.

The internal market programme was aiming at economies of scale combined with the strengthening of competition which should ensure that cost reductions are being passed on to the consumer. There are several cases of substantial price reductions in sectors which have been progressively opened to competition, such as telecommunications and also segments of air transport and banking; but nothing like the reduction in prices, for example in financial services, which had been expected (or hoped for) in the study on the 'Costs of Non-Europe'. There has also been some price convergence across the EU, which is, of course, an indication of a more integrated European market. It has been more pronounced in the case of consumer and equipment goods. On the contrary, price dispersion for energy, services, and construction remains significant, which in turn suggests that there are still important barriers in those sectors separating different national markets.

In its attempt to assess the effects of the internal market, the Commission has finally succumbed to the temptation of producing numerical estimates of the macroeconomic effects, although, apparently, fully aware of the serious limitations of such an exercise. Perhaps understandably, politicians feel the need for precise figures which they can in turn offer to their electorates, while the wide margins of error to which such figures are usually subject appear only in small footnotes that very few people read. It is often difficult to reconcile scientific rigour and political exigencies, and the European Commission, like other institutions, must have often been caught between the two. Whichever way it is calculated, the macroeconomic impact of the internal market seems to have been rather small; and certainly smaller than expected. According to estimates released by the Commission, the impact of the internal market on GDP has been between 1.1 and 1.5 per cent, with the impact on investment being close to 3 per cent. Between 300,000 and 900,000 jobs have been directly attributed to the internal market, and approximately 1 per cent reduction in prices.

The *ex post* estimates of the macroeconomic impact, for whatever they are worth, are significantly smaller than the *ex ante* estimates which had appeared in the study on the 'Costs of Non-Europe'. But expectations had been deliberately inflated, and the implementation of the internal market programme took place in the highly unfavourable economic climate of the early 1990s. A convenient way out of this problem might therefore be to argue that the effects of the internal market will be long-lasting; a convenient way out and perhaps also an argument which is not too far from the truth.

5

THE POLITICAL ECONOMY OF LIBERALIZATION AND REGULATION

The elimination of the remaining barriers and hence the gradual transformation of an incomplete customs union into a real internal market, which was given a big boost with the 1992 programme, raises some fundamental questions regarding the relationship between the state and the market; in other words, the very nature of economic order and the mixed economy in individual member countries and the Union as a whole.

The gradual opening of public procurement, the liberalization of financial and transport services, the new approach to technical standards, and the renewed attempts at tax harmonization will have a major impact on the role traditionally played by national governments, thus further reducing their ability to influence the allocation of resources within and between countries. The internal market programme was often presented as an essentially deregulatory exercise in which the elimination of the remaining physical, technical, and fiscal barriers would be tantamount to a reduction of the role played by public authorities and, consequently, the erosion of the mixed economy. This aspect of the internal market received different emphasis in individual member countries (compare, for example, the stress on deregulation in Britain with the more subdued approach adopted in this respect by the German government in the domestic debate), depending very much on different traditions, prevailing ideologies, and the political balance of forces.

Given the decision to eliminate the remaining barriers in intra-EU economic transactions, which had been mostly the result of government intervention within the borders of the nation-state, the inevitable question was how much to liberalize and how much to (re-) regulate. At least in some cases, the creation of the internal market has involved the adoption of a new regulatory framework at the EU level and the transfer of new powers to Union institutions. There will be more market in the new economic order, but also more European regulation; and the trade-off between the two is being determined by a combination of economic and political factors, both internal and external to the EU. The growth of European regulation is arguably one of the most important features of the integration process in the 1980s and early 1990s (Majone, 1994; see also Tsoukalis and Rhodes, 1997).

This is what we may call the political economy of liberalization and regulation. It is about the distribution of economic power between different levels of political authority as well as the distribution of economic power between private and public agents. The two are closely interrelated, as we shall try to illustrate below. But it is also, more indirectly, about the allocation of resources; choices between efficiency and stability or between production and the protection of the environment; it is about relations between producers and consumers; and, last but not least, it concerns the ownership and control of the means of production. These are all highly political issues which come under the more general theme of economic order. Thus the internal market programme is part and parcel of *Ordnungspolitik*, as the Germans would call it. This is a vast territory which straddles different disciplines and specializations; and in recent years, it has been visited by an increasing number of researchers largely because of the internal market programme. This chapter will attempt to give tentative answers to some of the questions raised above by concentrating on four case-studies.

The first one will examine the restructuring of European industry and services which has been happening through the large number of mergers, acquisitions, and cooperation agreements. In view of the large share of transnational takeovers and cooperation agreements, national frontiers will no longer be marked by heavy lines on this new corporate map. Are we witnessing the emergence of Euro-champions as a response to a much more competitive international environment and the tendency towards global markets? And what are the policies developed at the European and national level to deal with this phenomenon? We shall be interested not only in the emerging allocation of functions between EU and national institutions but also in the whole approach adopted by public authorities regarding industrial structures and market competition. In recent years, there has been much discussion about the different kinds of capitalism and the effects which European integration and the process of economic internationalization are having on existing national models (see also Albert, 1991).

The second case-study will concentrate on the financial sector, and especially banking. This sector has been traditionally characterized by strong government intervention and different national regulatory frameworks which, precisely because of their difference, have acted in the past as an important barrier to cross-border activity. Liberalization goes together with the adoption of some common rules regarding the supervision of financial markets. But will the competition among different national systems, implied in the principle of mutual recognition, turn liberalization simply into a deregulatory exercise, and what could be the more general effects on the functioning of financial markets?

Tax harmonization is an old issue dating back to the early days of the EEC. Fiscal barriers were among the three main categories of remaining barriers singled out in the White Paper of 1985. On the other hand, fiscal issues are at the very heart of national sovereignty. How important are the distortions created by different tax regimes and how far are national governments prepared to go in relinquishing their fiscal autonomy? In the context of rapidly growing mobility of goods, services, and factors of production, should harmonization be left to the market? Changes in this area can have important effects for the provision of public goods and the internal redistributive function of government budgets. This will be the third case-study on the political economy of liberalization and regulation.

Different technical standards and regulations have an important effect on the allocation of resources within and between countries, even when this does not happen to be the primary objective of governments and private institutions in the use of those policy instruments. The new approach to standards and the emphasis on mutual recognition are intended to deal a decisive blow against an important technical barrier. The last section of this chapter will examine the progress made in this area after the adoption of the White Paper; it will then draw some preliminary conclusions about the wider implications of the choices made.

The relationship between the state and the market is not static. The postwar economic history of Western Europe bears witness to this changing relationship. We have argued earlier that both the internal market initiative and the re-launching of regional integration are, at least partly, a reflection of new economic ideas and, consequently, a conscious attempt to strengthen the market forces in Europe. This chapter is intended as a provisional balance sheet of the movement in this direction, and a snapshot of the changing economic order in Western Europe. It will be complemented by subsequent chapters on the labour market, macroeconomic policies and monetary integration, redistribution, and EU relations with the rest of the world.

Breeding Euro-Champions: Competition or Industrial Policy?

There was a very significant increase in the number of mergers, acquisitions, joint ventures, and other forms of cooperation agreements in European industry and services during the second half of the 1980s. This reached a peak around the end of the decade and then began to decline. Unlike earlier periods of restructuring and concentration, as for example in the 1960s which had seen the emergence of national champions, the merger activity of the previous decade was not confined to national boundaries. The share of cross-border activity went on increasing during the same period, and then it began to fall in the early 1990s, thus following the same trend as merger activity in general.

The accuracy and the comparability of data in this area leave much to be desired; and the same is in fact true of statistics on FDI and capital movements in general. Yet, all the evidence available points in the same direction. Using Commission data, Fig. 5.1 shows the number of mergers and majority acquisitions in industry, involving at least one of the 1,000 largest firms in the Community for the period 1983–92. The corresponding data for services can be found in Fig. 5.2

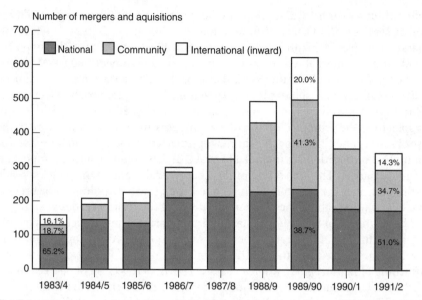

Fig. 5.1. Mergers and Acquisitions of Majority Holdings in Industry, 1983/4 to 1991/2

Note: Operations involving the 1,000 largest firms in the Community or 500 largest firms worldwide.

Source: Commission, Annual Reports on Competition Policy.

for the period 1984–92. The main message is the same for both: there was a wave of mergers which coincided with the economic boom and the early stage of the internal market programme in the second half of the 1980s, and an increasing proportion of those mergers were intra-European and international. In the early 1990s, there was a decline in absolute numbers, coupled with a relative decline in the share of intra-EU and international mergers, although the numbers remained at levels which were still significantly higher than those experienced some ten years earlier. Because the Commission has since changed the database, there are no corresponding figures available after 1992. However, the new data used, which are no longer restricted to the 1,000 largest firms, lead to a similar conclusion as the one drawn above.

Cross-border alliances, ranging from cooperation agreements in R&D to outright mergers and acquisitions of majority holdings, have been prominent for several years; and some have involved household names which used to be considered as national champions *par excellence*. The takeover of Rowntree in the UK by the Swiss multinational Nestlé which was subsequently engaged in a big battle with the Agnelli family over Perrier water; the marriage of Asea and Brown Boveri, the Swedish and Swiss giants in the electricity power plant industry; the purchase of Rover by BMW; the failed attempt to join Volvo with Renault; the takeover bid of Société Générale by the Italian predator Mr de Benedetti, which provoked a nationalist reaction in Belgium and finally sent the Belgian national champion to the arms of the French group Indosuez; the Pirelli and Continental

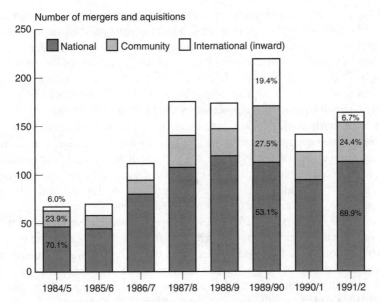

Fig. 5.2. Mergers and Acquisitions of Majority Holdings in Services, 1984/5 to 1991/2

Source: Commission, Annual Reports on Competition Policy.

saga in the tyre sector which exposed some of the peculiarities of industrial cultures and institutions in both Germany and Italy; the alliance between France Télécom and Deutsche Telekom which also acquired an American dimension through the link with Sprint; these are just a few representative examples, some more successful than others, of the process of restructuring which has been taking place in Western Europe and elsewhere.

Corporate behaviour has varied considerably among countries, and there are some interesting observations that can be made in this respect. According to Commission data on mergers and acquisitions for the period 1990–2, French firms were the most active, followed by British firms (Commission, 1994c). The aggressive and outward-looking approach of many French firms, including those under state control, had started in the late 1980s and it could be largely explained as the attempt made by a latecomer to catch up with the others. It was certainly in sharp contrast with past behaviour. Corporate behaviour, therefore, became consistent with the strong 'Europeanization' of French foreign policy in the Mitterrand era and the apparent realization by French politicians and technocrats that the old policy of national champions had reached its limits (Hayward, 1995); and the two trends should not be considered as coincidental in view of the close links between political and industrial élites in France. There was also a strong European orientation in the merger activity of French firms.

On the other hand, German firms apparently showed less willingness to play the game, and they did not frequently venture outside their own country. Thus, the strong presence of German firms in intra-European trade was not matched by a similar level of activity in terms of cross-border mergers and alliances. But in the early 1990s, much of this activity was turned towards what used to be East Germany which was also on the receiving end for a large number of bids from other European firms. Until then, the UK had been the favourite shopping area for predators from other European countries and also from across the Atlantic. Another major target of merger activity were Spanish firms, while the share of Italian firms, both as bidders and targets, remained very small. Among the other countries, the Netherlands, Denmark, and to a lesser extent Belgium were the only active players in the game. In fact, the process of restructuring of production seems to have been accompanied by a process of geographical concentration in terms of ownership and control, with large firms in the economically more developed countries being the most active buyers in the corporate market.

Data on FDI for the period 1986–91 form a picture which overlaps with the one described above (Commission, 1994*d*: 88). France was the biggest exporter of FDI to other EU countries, followed by Germany, while the UK was far ahead of the others as an exporter of FDI to the rest of the world. The same applied to inflows of FDI from third countries: the UK accounted for 45 per cent of the EU total. Those figures confirmed the international rather than European orientation of the British economy. The post-Cecchini exercise, initiated by the Commission in order to assess the effects of the internal market, has produced more recent data on FDI flows. It appears that the peripheral countries, Ireland, Portugal, and Spain, together with the core countries of the Benelux, benefited most from FDI inflows during the early 1990s.

The matching game has not been restricted to the EU. The active participation of firms like Volvo, Asea-Brown Boveri, and Nestlé suggests that the national champions of the EFTA countries were playing an active part even before the accession of some of those countries to the Union. Similarly, the second half of the 1980s was characterized by the rapid growth of US investment in Western Europe and the very active participation of US firms in the mergers and acquisitions game. Strategic alliances and cooperation agreements with US firms formed an integral part of the networking of their European counterparts. The same applies, even though to a lesser extent, in relation to Japanese firms.

In fact, mergers and acquisitions as well as different forms of joint ventures and strategic alliances have been not only a European but an international phenomenon. The two are extremely difficult to disentangle; just as it is equally difficult to disentangle the influence of autonomous market developments from those of policy initiatives: both have been feeding into each other. DeAnne Julius (1990: 36, 40) argues that:

As a means of international economic integration, FDI is in its take-off phase, perhaps in a position comparable to world trade at the end of the 1940s . . . [We] are in the middle of a decade (1985–95) when FDI gains its maturity as a major force in international economic integration. It is in this sense that quantitative increases in FDI flows have reached the threshold where they create a qualitatively different set of linkages among advanced economies.

Growth rates of FDI flows in the second half of the 1980s were a multiple of the growth rates registered for international trade in goods and GDP.

This process of restructuring of the world economy can be linked to the sustained economic recovery which started in the mid-1980s and, even more so, to major technological changes of a more permanent kind. According to Sharp (1990), this is a period characterized by the widespread diffusion of new technologies accompanied by major institutional innovations. Restructuring at the global level also needs to be considered in conjunction with the establishment of wide 'networks' and cooperation agreements among firms, covering the whole range from R&D to marketing and distribution. Production rationalization, specialization, 'customized' services, and improved access to markets and technological skills have been among the primary motives in this respect. Thus economic internationalization rapidly extended beyond trade (Bressand, 1990).

The internal market programme influenced investment behaviour and also the geographical orientation of many European firms; and this is documented in business surveys. There was, undoubtedly, also a strong element of 'herd instinct' (which could be called more politely, fashion) in corporate behaviour linked with the 1992 programme. In addition, there were the various R&D programmes launched by the EC, starting with the first ESPRIT programme in information technology, which created a 'collaboration bandwagon' (Sharp and Shearman, 1987: 60). They concentrated mostly on the pre-competitive stage of research (BRITE for the development of advanced technologies, RACE for telecommunications, HDTV for high definition television, and so on) and they helped to promote cross-border cooperation among European firms. The success of ESPRIT led in turn to the launching of multi-annual framework programmes in science and technology funded by the Commission, the fourth one having started in 1995. Faced with high research costs and uncertainty in increasingly oligopolistic markets, industrial managers saw important advantages in close inter-firm collaboration. The Commission sometimes acted as a marriage broker, also providing part of the dowry for the newly-weds.

However, all this did not lead to a 'Fortress Europe' for the breeding of Euro-champions which would one day be able to compete in increasingly global markets. Many firms did not consider intra-European cooperation as a substitute for strategic alliances (and more) with American or Japanese firms. The takeover of British ICL, a founding member of the old Davignon club, by Fujitsu in 1990 served, even though this could be considered an extreme case, as a reminder of the limitations of a purely European strategy in the electronics sector and the discrepancy between rhetoric and reality. There was no consensus among the European firms nor was there a consensus among the national governments involved. While the French government was thinking of Euro-champions as a modern substitute for the old policy of national champions, the British saw the process of economic globalization as something one should lie back and enjoy. To the industrial activism of the French, they opposed measures of liberalization which would further encourage the process of economic globalization. In this respect, the British seem to have gained the upper hand, judging from the ongoing liberalization in several sectors, even though this has often happened by default rather than by design. It has always proved easier for the Community to agree on the elimination of barriers than the adoption of common measures.

The active participation of US and, to a lesser extent, Japanese subsidiaries in European programmes also seems to suggest that the Commission has reconciled itself with international economic realities and, one should add, the differences in national political perceptions in Europe (see also Wyatt-Walter, 1995). The instruments available at the European level are also very limited both in terms of scope and resources. Without underestimating the importance of European pro- grammes, it should be pointed out that they represent approximately 5 per cent of total R&D spending in all member countries.

The merger and cooperation activity has been generally welcomed, if not actively encouraged, by the Commission and some of the member governments. After all, economies of scale and the efficiency gains from restructuring had received much emphasis in the Cecchini report, and they were considered to be an integral part of the internal market programme. But it is often extremely difficult to decide where efficiency ends and monopoly power begins or even when strategic alliances turn into collusive behaviour. This is the domain of competition policy. The problem has been aptly summarized by McGowan and Seabright (1989: 308), with reference to the boom of inter-firm cooperation agreements and alliances in the airline sector, following the first steps towards liberalization: 'At times it has even seemed as if European airlines would pass directly from the regulated state to a situation of concentration, not bothering to pause for a period of liberalisation in between.'

Modern microeconomic theory has gone beyond simple measurements of market concentration (the definition of the relevant product and geographical market being a difficult task in itself) and, instead, lays the emphasis on the 'con- testability' of markets. Factors such as import penetration, entry barriers, and the elasticity of demand are taken into consideration in deciding the trade-off between efficiency and monopoly power. Obviously, mergers in rapidly growing sectors with strong international competition raise fewer problems in terms of potential monopoly power than those taking place in mature industries with low import penetration. There have been examples of both cases in Europe (Jacquemin, Buigues, and Ilzkovitz, 1989).

The Treaty of Rome laid the basis for a common competition policy to be conducted by the Commission. Article 85 deals with collusive behaviour, Article 86 with the abuse of dominant position, and Article 92 with the problem of state aids, where the general prohibition is followed by a long list of exceptions. No direct powers for an *ex ante* control of mergers were given to the Commission, although provision for such powers had been made in the Treaty of Paris. In view of the long history of cartelization in the steel sector, this was understandable. No such powers were deemed necessary for the EEC and, in fact, the establishment of the latter in 1958 was followed by a process of economic concentration in individual European countries, which saw the birth of many national champions. Member governments and the Commission adopted at the time a relaxed, if not actively supportive, approach on the subject, since large size was generally considered as the way of facing the competition of US-based multinationals. This was, after all, the time of the '*défi américain*' (Servan-Schreiber, 1967).

Britain introduced anti-merger legislation in 1965, and was followed by the Federal Republic of Germany in 1973. This was the year when the Commission also decided to initiate proposals for similar legislation at the Community level. It would have to wait for sixteen years before the Council of Ministers decided to move in this direction. National governments, at least those with legal powers in this area, were not at all enthusiastic about transferring them to the EC. In fact, it is worth noting that by 1989, when Community legislation was adopted in this area, only three countries (Britain, France, and Germany) had effective instruments for the control of mergers; while Ireland and the Netherlands also had some legislation in this respect. If size and the high degree of dependence on international trade might be considered as effective substitutes for domestic rules on market concentration as far as the small and open economies are concerned, this argument would be less valid in the case of Italy and Spain. As a matter of fact, the adoption of EC legislation has triggered, in the meantime, similar responses at the national level.

Three different developments gradually brought about a change of attitudes on behalf of both governments and private firms on the subject of the desirability of EC legislation for an *ex ante* control of mergers. One was the jurisprudence from the European Court of Justice: the decisions issued on the cases of Continental Can in 1973 and Philip Morris–Rothmans in 1987 opened the possibility of using Articles 85 and 86 for an *ex ante* control in some narrowly defined cases. And this immediately brought the Commission into the picture, thus creating a grey area in terms of legal powers between the national and the EC level. On the other hand, the rapidly increasing cross-border activity of European firms in more recent years meant that this activity could be subject to the jurisdiction of many different countries, thereby creating a nightmare for the firms concerned and a very lucrative business for competition lawyers. Hence the yearning for what came to be called the 'one-stop shop' which meant that one single authority, at least within the Community, should be competent to decide on the desirability of a cross-border merger. Thus EC legislation in this area became relevant only when the merger activity started to spill over national frontiers. The third factor which made such legislation politically feasible was the gradual convergence of national attitudes in terms of competition policy.

The long and difficult negotiations revolved around three main issues: the threshold, expressed in terms of the combined turnover of the firms concerned, beyond which Commission powers would be activated; the line of demarcation between EC and national competences; and the criteria to be used when judging whether a proposed merger would be acceptable. On the question of threshold, the division was between big and small countries and, more precisely, between countries which had effective legislation in this area and those which did not. The former, naturally, were in favour of high thresholds which would maximize the catchment area for national bodies. A similar division appeared on whether the

Commission should have the final say on a proposed merger. Thus Britain and Germany fought to restrict as much as possible the powers of the Commission. As for the criteria to be used, the division between countries was a reflection of different traditions and attitudes towards industrial policy. While Germany, with the most developed anti-trust policy among member countries, insisted on the exclusive use of the competition criterion in deciding on the desirability of a proposed merger, countries such as France and Italy wanted to add other considerations related to industrial and regional policy objectives.

The regulation was finally adopted in December 1989, and it has been applicable since September 1990. It set a threshold of 5 billion ECU for the combined worldwide turnover of the firms concerned. Two additional conditions were set for a proposed bid to come under Community jurisdiction, namely that at least 250 million ECU of the combined turnover should be realized within the Community and that less than two-thirds of the combined turnover should be in a single member country. German influence on the new legislation was very strong indeed: Commission decisions should be based primarily on competition grounds, although reference to 'efficiency' criteria in future Commission decisions could not be altogether excluded (George and Jacquemin, 1992). The Germans also succeeded in diluting the objective of 'one-stop shop' by opening the way for joint EC and national decisions in at least some narrowly defined cases. Double control was intended to minimize further the risk of the Commission adopting other than competition criteria in allowing big mergers to go through. There was no reduction of the threshold when the first review of the policy took place in 1994. Two years later, the Commission proposed lower thresholds: 3 billion ECU for the total turnover and 150 million ECU for the turnover inside the Union.

Thus the increasing number of cross-border mergers and acquisitions finally led to the adoption of a new regulatory framework and the transfer of more powers to the Commission. Between the entry into force of the new regulation and the end of 1995, a total of 398 operations were notified to the Commission (Commission, 1995*d*; Commission, 1996*a*). The large majority of them were not seen by the Commission as presenting any problems in terms of competition. A few cases were allowed to go through after the firms concerned had accepted the conditions imposed by the Commission, and four mergers were forbidden. The first was the proposed takeover of de Havilland, a Canadian turboprop aircraft manufacturer, by ATR, a joint venture operated by Alenia (Italy), and Aérospatiale (France). The Commission decision to block it provoked a strong reaction by the French and Italian governments, while the German Commissioner for industrial affairs attacked the 'competition ayatollahs' for not taking into account economic realities (*Financial Times*, 12 February 1992). This was yet another manifestation of the tension sometimes created between competition and industrial policy objectives. The second instance of prohibition under the 1989 merger regulation applied to the MSG Media Service, a proposed multimedia joint venture involving three of Germany's most powerful companies (Bertelsmann, the Kirch group, and Deutsche Telekom). In 1995 there were two more prohibitions by the Commission: they applied to Nordic Satellite Distribution, a proposed joint venture of Danish and Norwegian telecom companies and a Swedish media group; and to the Holland Media Group. Interestingly enough, three out of the four prohibitions up till the end of 1995 concerned media groupings.

In their assessment of how this new instrument of competition policy has been handled, Neven, Nutall, and Seabright (1993) have found the Commission too lenient; and this conclusion seems to be corroborated by the positive assessment of the process made by the firms concerned (the implicit assumption being that if those subject to investigation are satisfied with the process, then there must be something wrong with it). The authors of this study, together with several others concerned with the allegedly soft application of competition rules by the Commission, opt for the creation of an independent regulatory authority, along the lines of the German *Kartellamt*, which would be responsible for the investigations while the final decision would still be left with the Commission. Thus, there would be a clearer separation of tasks and of different stages of decision-making and also greater transparency. Germany has also been pushing in the same direction (Allen, 1996*a*).

The wave of cross-border mergers and acquisitions has given rise to another kind of problem, namely the different conditions applying to hostile takeovers in different member countries; and this has led in turn to pressures for the introduction of Community legislation in order to deal with the distortions created. A disproportionately large number of firms in the UK have been the target of hostile bids. This can be explained in terms of legal and institutional conditions which largely determine the functioning of the 'market for corporate control'; and those conditions vary significantly from one member country to the other.

To start with, the size and role of stock exchanges as providers of finance capital and as a means of correcting managerial failure vary enormously between the different countries of the Union. Furthermore, different regulations with respect to the functioning of stock exchanges as well as differences in competition policy, company law, and labour law can influence decisively the freedom to effect changes in the ownership and control of private firms. The large capitalization of the London Stock Exchange and the active 'market in corporate control' which operates in the UK through the buying and selling of shares in the stock exchange contrasts sharply with the situation prevailing in most other European countries. According to OECD statistics, the market capitalization of listed domestic equity issues for 1994 represented 112 per cent of GDP in the UK, while only 34 per cent in France, 26 per cent in Italy, and 24 per cent in Germany (OECD, 1995*a*). On the other hand, it is not only a question of size. The remaining legal restrictions on hostile bids in France, the importance of family shareholdings and non-voting shares in Italy, the predominant role of German banks, not to mention German legislation on workers' participation in the supervisory boards, all of them impose major restrictions on changes of company ownership and control. It should not be surprising that the most extensive industrial restructuring during the recent period has taken place in the UK. This has much to do with the nature of capital markets and regulatory systems.

British demands for the creation of a 'level playing field' (meaning that similar conditions should apply in all countries) in terms of the takeover of firms does, however, imply that other countries should follow closely the British model which offers the most open 'market for corporate control'; perhaps, on the basis of the same principle that German cartel rules have served as the model for EC legislation for the control of mergers. But here, national practices are still very different, and a considerable distance will need to be covered before anything resembling a 'level playing field' can be achieved. The differences between countries in terms of the relationship between capital markets and corporate control are also a reflection of very different industrial cultures. While the Anglo-American model puts the stress on the 'market for corporate control' as a means of correcting managerial failure, the German model, or what Albert (1991) calls the Rhine model, variations of which can be found in most other European countries and also in Japan, puts the emphasis on long-term relations between investors, managers, and employees. According to Franks and Mayer (1990: 215), 'there is a tradeoff between correcting managerial failure and promoting investment'.

In fact, there is very little evidence to suggest that the Anglo-American model is more efficient in the long term and that the whole of Europe should therefore move in this direction; except, perhaps, for a greater transparency of rules which should be more generally welcome. The increasing internationalization of markets and the growing reliance of firms on equity finance, which also means the need for them to have access to the large stock exchanges of New York and London, may, however, exert pressure on governments and economic systems to converge to the Anglo-American model, albeit very slowly and with much kicking and screaming from the main economic actors. It is precisely this prospect which has provoked the debate on the different kinds of capitalism (OECD, 1995a; for a more popular version, see Albert, 1991). On the other hand, as long as different models persist, the attempt to establish cross-border strategic linkages through corporate acquisitions are bound to raise questions of reciprocity between countries. The Union will not find an easy solution to this problem; 'even playing fields' are not always achieved simply by eliminating barriers.

The Commission has also been flexing its competition muscles in the application of Articles 85, 86, and 92 of the Treaty. Competition policy has evolved as one of the most important common policies and also as a major source of power for the Commission *vis-à-vis* private firms and governments. The record fines imposed on firms for anti-competitive arrangements are one example of the more assertive role played by the Commission in this area in recent years: they include large fines on suppliers of steel beams, manufacturers of cartonboard, and the cement cartel (a fine of 248 million ECU imposed on thirty-three producers and nine cement associations).

The application of Article 92 on state aids has always been extremely difficult and delicate. In more recent years, the Commission has plucked up enough courage to face governments head on in relation to state aids, and this has often led to extremely difficult negotiations with often mixed results. In general, it seems to have been able to impose constraints on government behaviour, even though the Commission has often been forced to make large concessions to political realities (see, for example, the cases of national airlines such as Air France, Olympic Airways, and Iberia, as well as the state rescue of Crédit Lyonnais). In a study of state aids for the period 1981–90, Neven (1994) reaches the conclusion that the role of the EC was still rather minor; but arguably in the ascendant, one might add. On the other hand, the failure to agree on a rescue plan for steel in 1994, which would have linked the Commission's approval for continued subsidies with large capacity cuts, is another illustration of the limitations of the Commission's own power. It was not the first time it faced such a problem with steel producers: for much of the 1980s, the Commission had tried to encourage the restructuring of the steel sector, having gone as far as promoting a cartel of producers to manage this restructuring.

Nationalized firms have continued to present the most awkward problems for both political and practical reasons. How does one distinguish, for example, between investment (which is legitimate) and aid (which may not be)? This distinction is not at all obvious in the public sector. The Commission has been trying to apply the so-called 'market economy investor principle' which consists of asking the question whether a private investor would have made the same investment or not. But if strictly private criteria are to apply in trying to draw the demarcation line between what is legitimate and what is not, what would then be the economic logic of a publicly owned firm? This is obviously not a technical question.

Cross-border cooperation among European firms has been seen as a means of realizing the objective of the single European market and improving international competitiveness. Such cooperation would also help to strengthen the economic and political base for European integration, by gradually shifting political allegiances to the European level and thus cutting the umbilical cord linking large firms to their national governments. The creation of Euro-champions as the first stage towards European political union? It would be a godsend for under-employed Marxists and an excellent case-study of the link between changes in the economic base and the political superstructure.

However, little of that has happened until now.[1] Although many of the large European firms are well past the age of national champion and their presence in or links with several European countries may already be very strong, the Euro-champion is still a rather rare breed. Bressand and Nicolaïdis (1990: 30) have a strong explanation for this:

The importance for European companies of access to Japanese technology and to the US market—as exporters, or increasingly as investors and acquirers—implies, for instance, that Europe is not an intermediate level, half way between the nation-state and the open global environment . . . but rather one dimension in the search for stronger positioning on the global market.

[1] With the benefit of hindsight, it now appears that too much was read into the early wave of intra-European mergers and acquisitions in the first edition of *The New European Economy* (1991). The emergence of Euro-champions appeared then a more realistic proposition than it does now.

Cox and Watson (1995) reach a similar conclusion when they argue that EU policies have promoted not so much the Europeanization as the internationalization of leading market sectors through the adoption of market opening measures.

The policy instruments available at the Union level are still very limited and not of the kind to promote the equivalent of national champions at the European level. Competition policy is not the most powerful instrument to achieve such an objective. As for interventionist instruments, including financial resources, the EU is very short of them; and this situation is not likely to change in the foreseeable future. The new chapter in the Maastricht treaty provides further confirmation of this. There is no consensus for an active industrial policy and the current political environment is very much against it. Furthermore, a weak (European) state implies a weak industrial policy, even if the intention were there.

The 1992 programme, combined with autonomous developments in the market-place, has led to some transfer of powers to Brussels, mostly through the new merger legislation but also through the more strict application of competition rules by the Commission. There is, therefore, some evidence of functional spillover, with economic integration demonstrating a cumulative logic of its own, as had been predicted by earlier functionalist theories (Haas, 1958; Lindberg, 1963). This has been coupled with a process of convergence of national attitudes and policies, even though the national versions of capitalism and the mixed economy are still more than marginally different.

The emphasis has been on anti-trust policy which brings Western Europe closer to US practice. The Commission, and the Union more generally, have often acted as a catalyst for economic liberalization; but this has also meant going along with the international trend. The search for European competitiveness has led to a substantial increase in EU expenditure in science and technology programmes and the active promotion by the Commission of cross-border cooperation and alliances among European firms, which can, however, go so far as the reality of increasingly global markets will allow. In the meantime, national governments have lost much of their ability to influence the allocation of resources; and this loss has not been recovered at the European level.

Deregulation in Financial Services: Efficiency and Stability

The internal market programme was more about services than goods, and the reason is simple: barriers to the cross-border provision of services are mainly the result of government intervention inside the border, intervention which takes many different forms creating barriers which are usually lumped together under the general category of NTBs. Until the publication of the White Paper and the subsequent adoption of the SEA, very limited progress had been registered in this area, thus allowing for little intra-EC competition in most service sectors. Since then, the picture has changed rapidly: the legislation adopted in Brussels, usually in parallel with market developments, has already had significant effects on the behaviour of economic agents.

Financial services occupied a prominent place both in the White Paper and the 'Costs of Non-Europe' study. Remaining barriers were still important; they were the product of exchange controls and different regulatory frameworks in individual member countries, which acted mainly as a barrier to the free cross-border provision of services. The positive effects expected from the liberalization of financial services accounted in the above study for one-third of the overall macroeconomic gains associated with the completion of the internal market; they have now proved to be exaggerated. The large and rapidly growing size of the sector, the closed nature of national markets, manifested through persisting large price differentials, and the indirect effect on investment resulting from the expected lowering of the cost of financial services, and hence on growth through the multiplier effect, are the main explanatory factors for the emphasis laid on the liberalization of this sector in the context of the internal market programme.

On the other hand, the elimination of intra-EC barriers in a heavily regulated sector, such as financial services, can provide an interesting case-study of the link between liberalization and regulation as part of the internal market programme. The effects of liberalization go, in fact, much beyond the functioning of financial markets. They extend to macroeconomic policies and wider issues of economic sovereignty. We shall return to them below. In this section, we shall concentrate on the role of public sector intervention in the new EU regulatory framework and the effects of the change brought about by the 1992 programme on the functioning of financial markets. Since the phenomenon of globalization is most evident in financial markets, what role, if any, has Europe acquired for itself and how much have decisions adopted in Brussels influenced developments in the marketplace? The main emphasis will be on banking where EU legislation has been the most advanced, although reference will also be made to other financial services, especially since the demarcation line between traditional banking on the one hand and a constantly growing range of investment services on the other has become increasingly blurred.

Considerable caution had been expressed in the Treaty of Rome with respect to the objective of capital liberalization, despite the fact that this was supposed to constitute one of the so-called four fundamental freedoms of the EC. Fears about potential instability in the capital markets and balance of payments considerations were behind the cautious attitude expressed by the authors of the treaty. Preserving the autonomy of national monetary policy was the other unspoken reason. Collective caution remained the catchword for many years. Two directives were adopted in 1960 and 1962, marking the first step towards the liberalization of capital movements. They laid the emphasis on transactions related to the movement of goods, the right of establishment, direct investment, and the purchase of listed shares in stock exchanges. They therefore went only slightly further than 'necessary to ensure the proper functioning of the common market' (Article 67 of the Treaty of Rome). No further step was taken in this area for a long time. If anything, the 1970s saw a regression, when an increasing number of countries tightened their system of capital controls, essentially abusing the safeguard clauses included in the above-mentioned directives.

Capital controls were used as a means of preserving some stability in intra-EC exchange rates and widening the margin of independent manoeuvre in terms of monetary policy. National responses in this area were far from uniform: thus while Britain, Germany, and the Netherlands had abolished virtually all restrictions to international capital movements by the end of the 1970s, other countries such as France and the whole of Southern Europe retained for years a heavy armoury of controls directed mainly at short-term capital movements; and these in turn restricted the free flow of financial services.

The financial sector, and banks in particular, have a long history of heavy regulation, with the 1929 Great Crash being a major turning-point in it. Government intervention can be first of all justified with reference to what economists call market failure (Baltensberger and Dermine, 1987). Banks usually borrow short and lend long, and this asymmetry between assets and liabilities depends on a highly volatile element called confidence, that is, the confidence of the depositor. In view of the limited information that the average customer is expected to have of the quality of a bank's asset portfolio, not to mention his or her ability to judge such quality, government regulation is intended to protect the customer and more generally the savings of the population.

On the other hand, because of the potentially unstable nature of public confidence and the ease with which doubts about the liquidity of one particular bank can turn into panic and a general run on banks, governments and/or central banks acting as guardians of the public interest, have felt the need to intervene in order to protect the stability of the whole financial system and at the same time to avoid major negative repercussions for the real economy. The two sides of this intervention are the various forms of deposit insurance schemes and the function of the lender of last resort undertaken by the central bank in times of crisis and illiquidity of the banking sector.

However, protective measures in the form of government guarantees of bank liabilities and the lender of last resort function create the problem of moral hazard. This means that banks may take excessive risks in their lending or over-expose themselves in the search for higher profits, in the knowledge that if things turn out badly, they can always rely on the safety net provided by the central bank. Moral hazard and systemic risk are two sides of the same coin, and they both relate to the intervention role of public authorities. Because of moral hazard in the behaviour of banks, there is the need for direct supervision and control of the activities of the banking sector, which has been translated into numerous prudential and preventive measures.

An additional reason for regulation stems from the role played by banks in the money creation process, the provision of credit, and the financing of public sector deficits, which in turn raises wider issues regarding macroeconomic stability. A wide range of instruments have been used in this respect, such as reserve requirements, deposit rate ceilings, and quantitative credit controls; many of them have been abandoned in recent years. Last but not least, fears of excessive concentration, the close links between banks and industry, and the frequent identification of financial with political power explain many of the restrictions imposed by governments on the activities of banks. Resistance to large mergers and acquisitions, monitoring of the identity of shareholders, and limitations imposed on the degree of control by banks over the non-financial sector have figured prominently among the instruments used by governments.

It is clear that regulation and the various forms of restrictions applied have a negative effect on the efficiency of the banking sector by limiting competition and adding to the costs of operation. Governments have thus always been faced with a trade-off between efficiency and stability, and the choice has varied enormously between countries and time periods. On the other hand, the resulting differences in regulatory frameworks have helped to preserve the high walls separating national markets.

One characteristic which has long distinguished most European countries from the United States and the UK has been the predominance of banks in capital markets: in other words, the relative underdevelopment of non-intermediated finance. Otherwise, the differences between banking structures in individual European countries have been more than substantial (Bisignano, 1992; Dermine, 1990). Those differences manifest themselves in terms of the role of publicly owned banks (mainly in France, Italy, Greece, and Portugal as well as Germany because of the strong position of regional savings banks in the latter country), the openness to foreign competition (particularly strong in the UK, Belgium, and Luxembourg), and the degree of market concentration (not surprisingly, pronounced in some of the smaller countries). Important differences can also be detected in terms of the range of activities undertaken by banks, from the universal bank model, which has mostly been characteristic of Germany, to the more traditional role of banks which used to exclude any direct involvement in the stock exchange.

The decade of the 1980s was marked by a process of deregulation of banking as well as the financial sector more generally, coupled with a further strengthening of the internationalization process, the two being mutually reinforcing (Aglietta, Brender, and Coudert, 1990; O'Brien, 1992; Kapstein, 1994). They were a response to the continuing internationalization of trade and production, the revolution in communications, financial innovation, and the intensified competition among financial centres. The liberalization measures introduced in both London and Paris in the second half of the 1980s need to be understood in that context: a gradual conversion to the market and the growing belief that economic efficiency is promoted by allowing companies (and notably banks) to choose freely their size and product mix were further strengthened by the need to survive in international competition by offering an attractive regulatory framework to private agents. Liberalization measures in individual countries paved the way for the legislation subsequently adopted at the EC level.

The EC strategy for the liberalization of financial services was first expounded in the White Paper of 1985 (see also Commission, 1988*b*; Zavvos, 1988). It started with the complete liberalization of capital movements, as a necessary condition for the creation of a European financial area. A necessary condition but not sufficient: the second plank of the strategy referred to the harmonization of regulatory frameworks. Following the radical innovation introduced in the White Paper, this would be based on the harmonization of only essential rules combined with the application of the principle of mutual recognition (thus using the famous *Cassis de Dijon* decision as the model). As a belated recognition of the dangers of widespread tax evasion and avoidance in a world of unrestricted capital movements, a third plank was later added, aiming at the harmonization of tax rates on savings and investment income. There had been no reference to this subject in the White Paper.

With respect to capital movements, developments were truly spectacular. A new directive was adopted in 1986, which signified the first modest step towards liberalization since the little remembered directives of 1960 and 1962. It was followed by another, much more ambitious directive in 1988 which marked the decision of EC countries to proceed to completely free capital movements, including the abolition of two-tier exchange markets in Belgium and Luxembourg. The decision entailed the elimination of all remaining capital controls in eight member countries by July 1990, while a longer timetable extending until the end of 1992 was offered to the four cohesion countries, with a possibility of a further extension for Greece and Portugal. At the time of writing, virtually all capital controls in the Union have been lifted. The free movement of capital was made a directly applicable right under the Maastricht treaty. The 1988 directive included provisions for emergency measures in case of threat to the monetary or exchange rate policy of a member country; and a similar provision was later introduced in the Maastricht treaty. However, once the armoury of controls has been dismantled, it would be very difficult in practice to start all over again; and increasingly global markets would make such a move extremely costly.

This is, undoubtedly, one of the most important decisions of recent years, after a long period of inaction in this area. The decision to proceed with complete liberalization by countries such as France and Italy, which had a long history of extensive capital controls, represented a search for greater efficiency for national financial sectors in an increasingly more competitive international environment. Undoubtedly, national authorities also decided to make a virtue out of necessity by recognizing the increasing ineffectiveness of capital controls.

The internationalization of financial markets and increased capital mobility, facilitated through the abolition of controls, feed into each other. The 1988 EC directive is part and parcel of this logic. Although liberalization represents an international trend and the new directive made no attempt to discriminate between intra- and extra-EC capital movements (surely a sign of economic realism in a financial world where national or European frontiers have already lost much of their meaning), it is clear that the Community as such did, for the first time in many years, influence decisively national policies and attitudes in this area. And it did send an important message to markets which helped greatly to strengthen the credibility of the internal market programme.

In the case of the banking sector, the harmonization of essential rules and mutual recognition has been combined with the principle of home country control as the three main elements on which the process of EC liberalization has been based. Home country control means that the responsibility for prudential control and supervision of all domestic and foreign branches of a bank rests with the regulatory authorities of the country of origin. This principle had been already adopted in the first banking directive of 1977, although with no concrete effects because of the lack of progress in the area of harmonization. The real breakthrough came only with the adoption of the principle of mutual recognition which reduced the need for harmonization down to essential requirements.

In 1989, the Community adopted three directives which formed the basis for the liberalization of the banking sector, while also serving as a model for the liberalization of financial services as a whole. The directive on own funds was adopted in April 1989; it dealt with some general principles and definitions regarding bank capital. It was followed by the directive on solvency ratios and the second banking directive which were adopted in December of the same year. The former contained an agreement on a weighted risk assessment of bank assets and off-balance sheet items and a harmonized minimum solvency ratio of 8 per cent for all credit institutions.

The second banking directive is the most important in this triad of directives which formed the basis for the new EC regulatory framework for the banking sector. The first main element is the creation of a single banking licence. This enables any bank which has received authorization by the competent authorities of a member country of the EU to provide services across the border and to open branches in any other member country without the need for further authorization. Banks are allowed to engage in any of the activities listed in the annex of the Second Banking Directive; and this list is based on the model of the universal bank, including investment services, but not insurance. The new regulatory framework also includes provisions in terms of minimum capital for authorization and the continuation of business; control of major shareholders and of banks' participation in the non-banking sector; and sound accounting and control mechanisms.

The responsibility for prudential control, including the foreign branches of a bank, is given to the authorities of the country where the parent company is based (home country), while the authorities of the host country will share responsibility for the supervision of the liquidity of branches in their own territory as well as for measures related to the implementation of national monetary policy. The dividing line between home and host country responsibilities would subsequently need some further clarification; and the same would also apply to the concept of 'general good', mentioned in the second banking directive, which allowed some room for the authorities of the host country to impede the provision of cross-border services by credit institutions established in another member country. The directive also contained provisions with respect to reciprocity in relations with third countries. The new EC legislation took effect on 1 January 1993, while the production of new directives, along the lines of minimum common standards, continued: new legislation has been adopted regarding large exposure of credit institutions, deposit guarantee schemes, and money laundering.

Although some parts of the territory were still left uncharted, the significance of the above cannot be easily overestimated. With one stroke, EC countries went further than a federal country such as the United States in creating the legal conditions for an integrated banking sector. Furthermore, in adopting the model of the universal bank, the EC opted for a more liberal approach as regards the permitted activities of banks than either the United States or Japan. This was in recognition of the rapid changes in the traditional role of banks and the process of so called 'securitization', which the new legislation was itself meant to encourage.

The adoption of the single banking licence is intended to eliminate all remaining restrictions and obstacles associated with authorization requirements for the opening of branches in any EU country. The emphasis on home country control is meant to facilitate prudential control on a consolidated basis, thus including the branches of a bank in other EU countries. Through home country control, discrimination by national regulatory authorities against the branches of a bank from another EU country established in their own territory has become extremely difficult. Furthermore, by creating the conditions for regulatory pluralism within each national market (since banks would be subject to prudential control and supervision by different regulatory authorities), the EU also prepared the ground for competition among regulatory systems. The evidence now available suggests that the main barriers have already been eliminated, and this has helped to create a more competitive environment for European banking.

As for the essential requirements for prudential control and supervision, a precondition for the application of the principle of mutual recognition, they were the subject of an interesting and delicate exercise in international financial diplomacy. The main emphasis was laid on minimum capital requirements, and this raised the need for agreement on definitions of bank capital, weighted risk assessments, and solvency ratios. Here, the ground had been prepared by the Basle Committee on banking regulations and supervisory practices of the Group of Ten. Yet, what were only recommendations in the case of the latter, applying to 'internationally active banks', became mandatory rules in the case of all EU-registered banks. A minimum solvency ratio of 8 per cent has been adopted for all EU banks. There were also some differences between the Basle agreement and the directives adopted by the EC in 1989, as, for example, with respect to the definitions of capital.

Reflecting a wider international trend, the EU approach relies heavily on high capital-asset ratios as a means of preventing an overexposure of banks, thus replacing many specific restrictions adopted by regulatory authorities in the past. But there is also an EU-specific explanation for this strong reliance of prudential control on one element. A policy of liberalization based on the harmonization of essential requirements and mutual recognition needs to rely heavily on a few transparent and generally accepted rules and less on the discretionary powers of different national authorities. Hence the emphasis on high capital-asset ratios.

The reciprocity provisions with respect to third countries constituted an important issue of contention. Here, the liberal approach of Britain and Luxembourg, with important international financial centres, clashed with French 'economic nationalism' which now turned into 'European nationalism'. The size of the financial sector as a percentage of GDP in the UK and Luxembourg is more than double that of the average EU country, and this, combined with the strong international orientation of their financial sector, clearly explains the concern of those two countries about any decision which might lead to a loss of business in this area. This may also explain, at least partly, their reluctance to accept any transfer of powers to Brussels, especially as regards policy *vis-à-vis* the rest of the world. The final compromise, included in the second banking directive, was much closer to *laissez-faire* principles, although with some, apparently deliberate, vagueness in the wording used (Kapstein, 1994: 145–9). The reciprocity clause has never been applied until now.

The adoption of minimum common rules in a world where universal banks coexist with specialized financial institutions immediately raised the question whether the same regulatory rules should apply to different activities which may also produce different risks. In other words, should the same capital-asset ratio apply to traditional banking loans and investment brokerage, even though the latter involves little capital risk for the financial institution concerned? This became a major issue of contention precisely because of the different banking structures and regulatory traditions of individual member countries. What was at stake was the search for a formula which would primarily reconcile the interests of investment houses in the City of London with those of universal banks in the Federal Republic. If the same capital-asset ratio were applied to investment activities, it might force many specialized investment firms in London out of business. If, however, a lower ratio were to be adopted, then this would discriminate against large German banks where the whole range of activities comes under one roof. In this respect, the negotiations were not about an optimal rate of regulation, based on some fancy economic theory; they were, instead, a search for a political compromise between different economic interests which are in turn a product of history, economic structures, and regulatory traditions.

A compromise was reached in 1993 with the adoption of the investment services directive and the accompanying capital adequacy directive which came into effect in January 1996. The compromise, which was closer to Anglo-American practice (Coleman and Underhill, 1995), extended the right to the 'European passport', previously granted to European banking institutions, to non-bank investment firms which would therefore be allowed to carry out a wide range of investment business in all member countries. This was expected to lead to the further integration of equity markets.

The progressive elimination of remaining national barriers in banking and financial services in general has been taking place in the context of a rapid liberalization process at the international level. In fact, little, if any, attempt was made to replace national with European barriers, thus recognizing the increasingly global nature of financial markets. The aim was to create a more liberal and competitive environment which would encourage the further restructuring of the industry, thus taking advantage of still unexploited economies of scale and scope which were given much emphasis (arguably too much) in the early Commission documents.

There was strong merger and cooperation activity in the banking sector during the second half of the 1980s, which subsided in the subsequent years of the recession, thus following the same pattern as the manufacturing sector. This activity was closely associated with the anticipation effect of 1992. Here again, perception seemed to be more important than reality. Compared, however, with the experience of non-financial institutions, the merger and cooperation itch was mainly confined within national boundaries. The main aim was the consolidation of a firm's position in the national market in order to face more successfully the expected intensification of international competition resulting both from global developments and EC legislation.

Major changes had been expected in the Southern European countries where EC liberalization was expected to act as a catalyst for the introduction of their banking sectors to the modern era (Commission, 1988a). Some restructuring has indeed already taken place in both Italy and Spain, although with very limited participation by foreign banks. In Spain, for example, where competition from outside was expected to produce a mild storm in the tranquil waters of an oligopolistic, protected, and also lucrative market, a series of mergers between what used to be *las grandes siete* have been actively promoted by the central bank in the role of the undisputed chief of a quarrelsome orchestra. Evidently, national institutions were still far from irrelevant.

In other countries, the targets for majority acquisitions were mostly small banks or specialized investment houses. Thus, several continental banks entered the City of London by purchasing old merchant banks such as S. G. Warburg, Morgan Grenfell, and Kleinwort Benson, and the same happened later to Baring Brothers after its notorious bankruptcy which was caused by big losses in the derivatives market. The large number of state-owned banks, the difficulty of making an effective entry into long-established oligopolistic markets, and the sensitivity of national authorities to transfers of ownership of large banks to foreign hands are likely to continue acting as serious impediments to a surge of mega-merger activity across borders (see also, Collombet, 1995).

Strategic alliances and cooperation agreements have often been used as a means of acquiring access to each other's national networks. The big bulk of retail banking in Europe is still confined within national boundaries and controlled by national banks in conditions of imperfect competition. This explains the term dual economy used to describe the banking sector in several European countries: a wholesale segment, rapidly growing in size, is part of a highly competitive and increasingly global market, while the retail segment is still largely operating under particular national conditions (Bisignano, 1992). Many of the large universal banks operate on both fronts; but this does not prevent the survival of specialized financial institutions.

The creation of an integrated banking structure in Europe is bound to be a very gradual process. The scale and speed of structural changes resulting from EU legislation had been, perhaps consciously, exaggerated. On the other hand, we should bear in mind that the new 'regime'[2] started only very recently: the Second Banking Directive came into effect in 1993 and the Investment Services Directive in 1996. It will take time for the new legislation to work its way through market structures. The completion of monetary union and the adoption of a single currency is also expected to have important long-term effects on the European banking structure.

Unlike competition policy, the new EU regulatory framework for the banking sector and financial services in general does not involve any direct transfer of powers to the Union level. Mutual recognition, coupled with the adoption of minimum common standards, has been the name of the game. The new regime is being constantly tested in the rapidly changing reality of financial markets. The EU liberalization of financial services moves in the same direction as the more general trend towards deregulation and internationalization. However, the experience of the 1980s and the first half of the 1990s does not offer much comfort about the efficiency and inherent stability of financial markets.

Markets have been notoriously unstable. They tend to react late to changes in the economic fundamentals, and their reaction often leads to brutal corrections with major consequences for the real economy, as happened in the case of Mexico. Furthermore, the effects are now being quickly transmitted across national frontiers, hence the growing fears of systemic risk. The Bank for International Settlements has repeatedly expressed serious concern about the instability (read also fragility) of financial markets (Bank for International Settlements, 1995; see also Borio and Filoca, 1994). On the other hand, private institutions have been repeatedly carried away in their lending, always in search of higher profits; and the bigger their size, the less willing have been public authorities to let them go under, thus preventing the market mechanism from performing its customary role.

There have been many examples in recent years: the international debt crisis of the 1980s and the irresponsibly large exposure of some of the world's largest banks; the severe crisis of the US thrift industry; the accumulation of too many bad loans by Scandinavian banks in the early years of deregulation and the accompanying asset price inflation of the second half of the 1980s (Drees and Pazarbasioglu, 1995); and the similar problem, writ large, of many Japanese banks. In all those cases, the taxpayers have been asked to pay a large part of the cost involved. There is, therefore, a real danger that the financial system may be deregulated in its assets and guaranteed in its liabilities; in other words, the privatization of profits and the socialization of risks, a combination which would not necessarily be acceptable to everybody.

---

[2] Regimes became a fashionable concept of international political economy in the late 1970s and 1980s. They were supposed to provide a substitute for hegemonic stability after the decline of the American hegemon. International regimes were defined as 'principles, norms, rules and decision-making procedures around which actor expectations converge in the given issue-area' (Krasner, 1982: 185).

Coleman and Underhill (1995: 510) have argued that the dynamics of regulatory arbitrage are intrinsic to the international political economy of liberalization, as private firms are constantly in search of lower costs and hence cheaper regulation. And they continue: 'Left out of this calculus, unfortunately, is the broader public interest in a stable financial environment, and the importance of this stability to economic development in democratically organized societies.'

The new EU legal framework does not, and perhaps could not on its own, offer an adequate solution to this problem. The appropriate degree and kind of regulation in the new financial environment still remains an open question; and the answer should, ideally, constantly adjust to changes in the market. Where should mutual recognition stop and harmonization begin? What, if any, should be the regulatory role of the future European Central Bank? In view of the increasingly global nature of financial markets, regulation at the national or even the European level will always be subject to severe constraints. If international agreements continue to be so difficult to reach, do we have no other choice but to learn to live with highly unstable markets?

Tax Harmonization: This Side of Eternity?

Tax harmonization issues have figured prominently on the European integration agenda, although there has been little correlation between inputs (man-hours spent in negotiations) and outputs (EC legislation adopted). The subject has been highly controversial, and proposals emanating from Brussels have often provoked strong reactions in national capitals.

Tax matters were dealt with in a general manner in the Treaty of Rome, although the harmonization of indirect tax rates was envisaged in Article 99 of the treaty. Harmonization was seen as necessary only to the extent that different national taxes could create distortions in the free movement of goods, services, persons, and capital. Hence, therefore, the emphasis on indirect and, to a lesser extent, corporate taxation, based on the assumption that goods and capital are more mobile across frontiers and thus more sensitive to different tax conditions applying in the member countries.

When the EEC was set up in 1958, the six member countries had very different systems of taxation. The main achievement of the Community in this area has been the adoption of a uniform system of turnover taxes, based on the French system of VAT. This is a non-cumulative tax levied at each stage of production and/or marketing. It has two main advantages *vis-à-vis* the various forms of 'cascade' taxes previously operating in the other member countries. The VAT system avoids the bias towards vertical integration of firms inside a country, which is inherent in the cumulative nature of different sales taxes. The other advantage is its neutral effect on internationally traded goods. According to the destination principle, generally used in international trade, the tax is levied at the point of consumption and not of production. This means that exports are zero-rated and that tax adjustments (export refunds and payments for imported goods) have to take place at the border. The transparency of the VAT system makes border tax adjustments a straightforward procedure; unlike the experience with other sales taxes which had frequently been used by governments as a means of indirect protection of domestic producers.

The introduction of a common system of turnover taxes by all members of the EC was not, however, accompanied by a harmonization of the base of taxation nor by a harmonization of rates. The second and the sixth VAT directives, adopted in 1967 and 1977 respectively, failed to bring about a completely harmonized base, due to numerous exceptions and derogations included in those two directives; and the wide diversity of VAT rates continued. Any form of differentiated indirect tax creates distortions in the allocation of resources. However, through the application of the destination principle in both international and intra-EC trade, distortions in trade between countries can be minimized (Robson, 1987).

When the White Paper was published in 1985, the diversity of rates was even more true of excise taxes applying mainly to alcohol, cigarettes, and petroleum products. Here diversity reflects different social values, consumption habits, and health considerations, not to mention the financing needs of national governments. On the other hand, it has never been devoid of protectionist impulses which have repeatedly brought both the Commission and the Court of Justice on the heels of member governments. Discrimination against foreign products has usually been achieved through a narrow definition of product categories and the imposition of widely different levies on each one of them. Thus Scotch whisky could be effectively separated from the Italian grappa, ending up with a very different tax burden incorporated in the final consumer price. The different approach to the taxation of beer and wine between Northern and Southern countries is another good illustration of innocent(!) discrimination in the use of excise taxes by national authorities.

A long stalemate also characterized the Commission's efforts to harmonize corporate taxes in an attempt to eliminate distortions in the allocation of direct investment and also as a means of promoting cross-border mergers and alliances. Concern with taxes on investment income is much more recent; it is itself a product of the growing mobility of short-term capital. As for personal taxation and social security payments, they have remained all along beyond the harmonizing ambitions of the Commission.

Despite the frustrations of earlier years, the Commission plucked up enough courage to call for the elimination of fiscal barriers in its White Paper of 1985. The main emphasis was, as before, on indirect taxation. The aim was to do away with frontier fiscal controls which involved a direct cost for companies engaging in cross-border trade. An attempt was made at estimating those costs, which produced a figure of 8–9 billion ECU, representing 0.2–0.4 per cent of Community GDP (Commission, 1988a). In macroeconomic terms, this figure was not very impressive, although surely not insignificant for firms heavily engaged in cross-border trade. But the motives of the Commission were not strictly pecuniary: the elimination of all frontier controls, of which border tax adjustments constituted a substantial part, was expected to have an important psychological effect. Open frontiers would be, after all, the most tangible effect of the 1992 programme for the ordinary citizen.

The Commission came up with detailed proposals in 1987. It called for a shift away from the destination principle for VAT payments (see also Cnossen and Shoup, 1987; Biehl, 1988; Spahn, 1993). This would basically extend the regime applying to transactions within a member country to cross-frontier transactions, which meant that exports would be taxed like any other transaction and that the importer would be able to deduct the VAT payment against the VAT charged on the sale of output in his own or any other member country. Thus sales and purchases across borders would be treated in exactly the same way as similar sales and purchases within a member country. The abandonment of the destination principle would in turn allow the elimination of border tax adjustments. On the other hand, it could also lead to trade distortions as long as the disparity of rates continued. Thus the next logical step, according to the Commission, should be the harmonization of rates. Complete harmonization was not deemed necessary. Instead, the Commission proposed the adoption of two bands of VAT rates within which national VAT rates would be allowed to move. The band for the standard rate would be 14–20 per cent, and 5–9 per cent for the reduced rate. The width of the bands was considered small enough to avoid any serious trade deflection.

But the Commission was not prepared to go all the way along the road of fiscal federalism. Harmonization of rates was one thing, and reallocation of tax revenue another. The replacement of the destination by the origin principle of taxation would lead to a redistribution of tax revenue between member countries. Those with higher tax rates and trade surpluses would gain at the expense of countries with lower tax rates and trade deficits. To avoid such a redistribution, considered to be politically impossible, the Commission proposed the creation of a clearing house system, based on the VAT returns of trading firms (or on aggregate trade statistics according to another proposal), which would enable the preservation of the status quo in terms of tax revenue. The aim was to minimize as much as possible the changes required, without at the same time compromising on the fundamental principle of the unhindered movement of goods and services. As for excise taxes, the single-stage nature of those taxes and the wide differences between rates applying in the various member countries forced the Commission to come up with a proposal for a uniform rate.

The Commission proposals were not popular with most member governments. Opposition was centred on two main issues: the harmonization of rates and the clearing house arrangement for the redistribution of tax revenue among national authorities. The UK led the opposition, finding itself once again in the familiar role of the flag-bearer of those defending national sovereignty against attacks from Brussels. In view of the diversity of rates existing until then, national resistance to change should hardly have been surprising. National sensitivities were at stake; and so were delicate internal political balances which could be upset by tax changes having important sectoral and distributional effects. Asking the British Government to impose even a small VAT rate on food and children's clothing or expecting the Danes to reduce substantially their excise taxes on alcohol and tobacco did not elicit favourable responses from politicians jealous of their power and acutely aware of the sensitivities of their constituents. The harmonization of rates would also restrict considerably the flexibility of governments in the use of fiscal policy for stabilization purposes. On the other hand, changes in indirect tax rates would have important effects in terms of prices, which would then feed into other macroeconomic variables.

Revenue considerations were also very important for some member countries. Although the Commission's proposals were designed to minimize the overall effect, two countries, namely Denmark and Ireland, would be expected to suffer a significant reduction in revenue through the lowering of their VAT rates and excise taxes. The case of Luxembourg was more complicated: the required large increase in rates could be overcompensated in terms of tax revenue by the loss of cross-border purchases from neighbouring countries, since the tax incentive would no longer be there. Tax policies in the Grand Duchy have had an element of the free-rider principle analysed in the literature on public goods: an option open to a small country in the geographical position of Luxembourg. The Commission proposals on tax harmonization were intended to put an end to that situation, thus provoking a negative reaction from an otherwise 'European-minded' country. Last but not least, the proposal for a clearing house crucially depended on the setting up of an effective system for combating fiscal fraud and tax evasion without adding much to the existing administrative burden. This would in turn depend on the close cooperation and mutual trust between national administrations. But neither could be taken for granted, and this soon became obvious through the reactions of several governments.

The Commission's proposals suffered from a strong imbalance between ends and means; the changes required were too big and costly (at least, in terms of loss of national autonomy) for economic gains that were not expected to be very great. Not surprisingly, the Commission was finally forced to concede defeat. This led to the submission of new proposals which were close to the lowest common denominator, thus making agreement at the Council of Ministers easier to reach. The crucial element in the compromise agreement was the idea that the elimination of fiscal frontiers, a crucial part of the internal market programme, could take place without abolition of the destination principle and the harmonization of rates. This miracle(!) was to be achieved by replacing the old system of border controls with a system of regular reporting of cross-frontier transactions by traders to domestic tax authorities, thus partly adopting the system which had already been operating inside the Benelux. However, this also meant that much of the administrative burden had been passed on to the traders.

The new system, considered to be a transitional system, has been in operation since 1 January 1993. Measures have been taken to strengthen the cooperation between national administrations in order to minimize tax fraud, although apparently with limited success. Provisional evaluations of the new system suggest that there have been some net savings by firms engaged in cross-border trade, especially in Southern countries where the costs associated with the previous system had been very high. In a few cases, however, the additional administrative burden imposed on firms engaged in cross-border transactions may have more than compensated for the gains resulting from the elimination of fiscal controls at the frontier (see also, Commission, 1995*c*). In the meantime, an agreement had been reached at the Community level to set a standard minimum VAT rate of 15 per cent and a reduced rate of 5 per cent applying to a limited list of goods and services. Thus, a floor has been set for any competitive harmonization of tax rates downwards (Smith, 1993). Some convergence of VAT rates has, indeed, taken place, although remaining differences are still quite considerable. In 1995, the standard VAT rate ranged from 15 per cent in Germany and Luxembourg to 25 per cent in Denmark and Sweden.

Following the elimination of tax borders under the new system, individuals pay VAT at the point where they purchase the goods. Special provisions had to be made for mail orders across borders and car sales. Cross-border shopping in the context of different national VAT rates is, of course, more of a problem for France, Germany, and the Benelux countries than it is for Greece and Britain, because of geography. This may help to explain, together with ideological reasons, the rather detached attitude adopted by British governments with respect to tax harmonization from above. As regards goods subject to excise taxes, a new system of interconnected bonded warehouses in the different member countries has been introduced in an attempt to reconcile the objective of no frontier controls with the survival of the destination principle and different rates. As with VAT rates, limited progress has been made so far on the harmonization front.

The new system introduced in 1993 was supposed to be a transitional system which would help to prepare the ground for the introduction of the definitive VAT system in 1997. This deadline will not be met. One year before, the Commission put forward a working programme for a gradual passage to the definitive VAT system which extends to 1999, thus meant to coincide with the beginning of the final stage of EMU. It includes further progress in terms of the harmonization of VAT rates, a complete shift to the origin principle, a reallocation of tax revenues among member states on the basis of statistical calculations of total consumption in each country, and what the Commission calls the modernization of the VAT system (see also Keen and Smith, 1996). But some governments still show little sign of being ready to accept such a radical move.

Back in 1975, the Commission had aimed to harmonize corporate taxes, albeit with no success. Trying to make virtue out of necessity, this aim was later abandoned and the Commission emphasized the principle of subsidiarity, pointing to the need to leave as much flexibility as possible to member countries in determining their corporate tax systems. However, the growing mobility of capital imposes greater constraints on national taxation policies, leading to a convergence downwards (CEPR, 1993). The signs of such a downward trend have been there for some time: since the early and mid-1980s, corporate tax rates have come down significantly in several industrialized countries. Corporate taxation has been regularly used as a means of influencing the location of investment; and competition among national authorities will become stronger as Europe moves closer to a real single market. The downward trend of corporate taxes has been the result not only of fiscal competition: supply-side economics has also provided the ideological justification. On the other hand, little progress has been achieved at the EU level in dealing with the problem of double taxation of companies.

The decision to liberalize capital movements has brought to the fore the link between liberalization and the harmonization of taxes on income from interest and dividends. But here again, the belated recognition of the link has proved very difficult to translate into effective action. Repeated attempts to legislate at the EU level have so far led nowhere, despite strong pressures from several countries and most notably Germany, France, and Belgium, which have experienced a reloca- tion of savings and financial activity motivated by a search for fiscal paradises. In the case of Germany, local withholding taxes have led to massive outflows of capital, mostly to neighbouring Luxembourg. The Commission proposed a minimum withholding tax of 15 per cent on all investment income; an exception could be made, however, for member countries which would accept the exchange of information with other fiscal authorities in the Union and would adopt a system of regular reporting of interest paid to all EU residents in an attempt to deal with the problem of tax evasion and tax avoidance.

Both Britain and Luxembourg were strongly opposed, because of fears that tax harmonization and/or the abolition of banking secrecy would lead to the loss of international business to other financial centres outside the EU. After all, the decision to liberalize capital movements would apply *erga omnes* and, therefore, there would be nothing to prevent EU residents from shifting to more attractive locations from the point of view of tax. The spectre of Switzerland and the various small fiscal paradises in Europe (Liechtenstein, Andorra, and the Channel Islands) loomed large in the negotiations.

Given the porous nature of EU frontiers towards the rest of the world in terms of capital movements, the UK and Luxembourg were basically asking their part- ners in the EU to accept the constraints imposed on fiscal sovereignty by free capital movements which were, of course, considered as given. Those constraints have been strongly felt and deeply resented by several member governments whenever they tried to depart from the low tax norms adopted by others. Commission proposals were discussed in 1989 and again in 1993, with the same lack of results (Montagnier, 1995).

It has been argued that the 'liberalization of capital movements stands to turn tax avoidance into a cottage industry' (Giovannini, 1989: 345) Giovannini has argued in favour of the adoption of the so-called worldwide principle of taxation which means that domestic residents are taxed on all their investment income, irrespective of the country where the investments are located. This would be intended to deal with the problem of tax evasion and avoidance in a world of free capital movements. But Giovannini's proposal assumes an effective cooperation among national fiscal authorities, which in turn depends on mutual confidence and the lifting of bank secrecy laws. These assumptions do not appear as yet realistic in the European, not to mention the international, context.

Capital mobility will increase further as the EU moves closer towards monetary union and the elimination of the exchange risk. This may prove to be yet another example of functional spillover. Continued failure to agree on tax harmonization and the means to achieve an effective cooperation among national fiscal authorities is bound to lead to a market-induced harmonization of taxes on interest (and capital more generally?) towards zero. The revenue from taxes on capital income is already very low in most European countries; and this is, surely, not unrelated to the combination of capital mobility and fiscal competition (CEPR, 1993; see also Sørenson, 1993). In contrast to VAT, no minimum rate has yet been adopted; and the mobility of capital is much greater than the mobility of goods.

The unanimity requirement in the Council, which has not changed with Maastricht, persisting differences in national taxation systems, and increasingly international mobility of goods and factors of production have all acted as important constraints on the Commission's tax harmonization efforts until now. Referring to indirect tax rates, Prest (1983: 82) has argued that to expect to achieve an alignment of tax rates 'this side of eternity' would be like 'crying for the moon'. Similar comments have been made in the past about other areas of economic integration, which were subsequently proved wrong. Although, undeniably, considerable progress has been registered in the context of the internal market programme, it seems that national resistance to harmonization and integration on fiscal matters will survive longer than in many other areas. Strict harmonization may, in fact, be unnecessary; what will be needed in many cases is an agreement on minimum rates of taxation as long as they are not always based on the lowest common denominator.

Failure to coordinate at the policy level, implying some pooling of fiscal sovereignty, will inevitably lead to forced harmonization through market forces. The higher the mobility of goods and factors of production, the higher the pressure for tax rates to converge downwards, and in some cases towards zero. Short-term capital movements are the most prominent example. But this will also mean the financial weakening of the nation-state, with negative implications both in terms of the provision of public goods and income redistribution. Can this be politically acceptable in the long run? The preoccupation shown until now by the Union for the resource allocation aspects of taxation has hardly been matched by a similar consideration for stabilization and equity issues.

The Race between National and European Standards

Different technical regulations and standards were identified in the White Paper as one of the most important technical barriers which had to be eliminated in the context of the internal market programme. According to Mattera (1988: 270), they represented approximately 80 per cent of all remaining barriers in intra-EC trade. Their importance was also recognized in the business survey included in the 'Costs of Non-Europe' study where different technical regulations and standards ranked high among different barriers in the answers given by European firms

(Commission, 1988*a*). In fact, according to those answers, a clear distinction could be drawn between Northern and Southern countries in the Community, with representatives of the South (Greece, Italy, Portugal, and Spain) expressing less concern about the negative effects of this technical barrier on trade. The nature of production in those countries and the relatively underdeveloped state of market regulation can largely explain this difference in business attitudes. Technical regulations and standards are after all a feature *par excellence* of the most advanced mixed economies.

While technical regulations are legally binding rules dealing with the health and safety of workers and consumers as well as the protection of the environment, standards are of a voluntary nature. They are written by standardization bodies and are usually an indicator of quality or a means of providing information to consumers and ensuring compatibility between different products or systems. In practice, the distinction between mandatory and voluntary is not always clear. Conformity with 'voluntary' standards is often a necessary precondition for market entry due to the demands of insurance companies, the need for compatibility with other products, or standards specified in public procurement contracts. Conformity assessment, which constitutes the third stage in terms of market regulation, involves tests, inspections, and certification to assess compliance to regulations and standards.

Following the elimination of virtually all tariffs and quantitative restrictions in intra-EC trade by 1968, the Commission and the Council turned their attention to technical regulations and standards as a powerful NTB. Articles 30, 36, and 100 of the Treaty of Rome provided the legal basis for dealing with this problem. Article 30 prohibited quantitative restrictions on imports and 'all measures having equivalent effect', while Article 36 followed with a list of exceptions and the implicit recognition that health and safety provisions, together with the protection of the environment, are ultimately the responsibility of national governments. In an attempt to bridge the gap, Article 100 of the treaty provided for the approximation of national laws and regulations aiming at the elimination of obstacles to the proper functioning of the common market.

The European Court of Justice (ECJ) later gave a broad interpretation to Article 30 in an attempt to erect an effective barrier against the abuse by national authorities of health and environmental considerations for the protection of domestic producers against foreign competition. In the 1974 *Dassonville* ruling, the Court of Justice defined 'measures having equivalent effect' as 'all trading rules enacted by Member States which are capable of hindering, directly or indirectly, actually or potentially, intra-Community trade'. Another landmark ruling was the famous *Cassis de Dijon* decision of 1979 (who would have thought that a court ruling on a relatively unknown liqueur would have revolutionized intra-European trade?). It was followed by similar decisions against the German purity law for beer and its Italian equivalent for pasta (Mattera, 1988, Pelkmans, 1990).

But the problem created by technical regulations and standards could not be completely eliminated by a wide interpretation of Article 30. Derogations still allowed member countries a relatively wide margin of manoeuvre. The next line of defence was, therefore, the harmonization efforts undertaken under Article 100. For many years, the results of this collective effort remained mediocre, at the very best (Dashwood, 1983; Pelkmans, 1987). Bureaucratic resistance, the unanimity requirement in the Council, the excessive emphasis on uniformity, and the technical and complex nature of legislation were the main factors behind the failure of the 'old approach'. There was a big discrepancy between time and effort invested on the one hand, and the amount of directives adopted at the EC level on the other. It took, for example, eleven years before the Council could agree on a directive for mineral water. Furthermore, given the slowness of the decision-making process and the pace of technological change, many of those directives were out of date already by the time they were published. There was also no effective link established between the harmonization of technical regulations at the Community level and the production of new standards by private bodies. Meanwhile, national governments continued on their production spree of new regulations, thus constantly adding to the large number of NTBs in this area.

Frustratingly slow progress in terms of harmonization finally led to the development of a new policy, usually referred to as the 'new approach'. The first step was taken with the mutual information directive of 1983 which called for the notification of draft regulations and standards by governments and private standardization bodies before their enactment. The aim of this directive was to strengthen preventive action against the erection of new barriers, also allowing for a standstill of one year at the request of the Commission, and the promotion of European regulations and standards in priority areas.

The essence of the 'new approach' can be found in a Council resolution adopted one month before the publication of the White Paper in June 1985. There were four main elements:

1. harmonization should be limited to essential safety requirements;
2. the task of drawing up technical specifications in relation to the essential safety requirements established by the Council should be left to European standardization organizations ('reference to standards');
3. the new European standards should be voluntary;
4. but governments would be obliged to presume that products manufactured according to those standards are in conformity with the essential requirements set out in the relevant directives; if producers chose not to manufacture according to European standards, they would need a certificate of conformity from designated bodies.

The 'new approach' was confirmed in the White Paper. The aim was clearly to unblock the legislative process in the Community by transferring the responsibility for technical details to specialized private organizations, while at the same time establishing a direct link (and a division of labour) between legislators and standardizers.

A two-pronged strategy was therefore developed to deal with different technical regulations and standards. On the one hand, there should be heavy reliance on the principle of mutual recognition which means that any good legally manufactured and marketed in one member country should be allowed to circulate freely in the rest of the Community (the *Cassis de Dijon* decision). Any attempt to restrict free movement should be properly justified with reference to health and safety provisions and also be proportionate to the objective. On the other hand, when obstacles created as a result of different national regulations and standards prove insuperable, the 'new approach' to harmonization would be set in motion.

The next important step was taken with the new Article 100*a* of the Single European Act, which replaced unanimity by qualified majority voting. As a counterbalance and in response to the fears expressed about a possible erosion of standards, the new article referred to the need for 'high levels of protection' while also offering a window of escape in the form of a safeguard clause. To complete the picture, new articles in the Single European Act covered health and safety in the working environment and created the legal basis for an EC environmental policy.

Unlike banking and financial services in general, there are no master directives setting out the new regulatory framework in this area. Regulatory provisions are inevitably more specific, varying from one sector to the other, thus rendering more difficult any attempt at generalization. Important directives have been adopted with respect to pressure vessels, toys, building products, and machines. Serious progress has also been registered with respect to 'horizontal' directives in the food sector, dealing with labelling and additives. In conformity with the 'new approach' (seventeen directives have been adopted in total at the time of writing), harmonization has been limited to 'essential requirements', which of course entails a risk, namely that European legal provisions are limited to generalities and some rather anodyne statements based on the lowest common denominator. For example, the machine safety directive, adopted in 1989, packed into seventeen pages almost half of the engineering sector. In order to have a real effect, this directive will therefore need to be complemented by several hundred European standards, and this is bound to take several years.

The production of European standards has been quite impressive in recent years. By 1995, there were more than 5,000 European standards (EN) produced by private organizations such as CEN and CENELEC, as well as the European Tele-communications Standards Institute (ETSI) which was set up in 1988 (Commission data). Membership consists of the national standardization bodies of EU and EFTA countries, although, inevitably, the Union dominates those organizations both in terms of finance and in terms of the standardization process which has so far largely followed the mandates given by the Commission in relation to the harmonization directives adopted in Brussels.

The 'new approach' has helped to eliminate some of the remaining technical barriers in intra-EU trade. Combined with increased cross-border collaboration between firms at the level of production and qualified majority voting in the Council, it has created the foundations for the development of a European doctrine in terms of product safety and the adoption of common European standards. However, this will be a long and arduous process which, although very important for the creation of an internal market, rarely reaches the political limelight because of its highly technical nature.

However, the mission is far from being accomplished. For the large majority of products, the principle of mutual recognition still applies; and in several cases, it has shown its limits, particularly when serious concerns exist about health and safety hazards. National administrations have frequently been unable or unwilling to translate good intentions expressed at the highest political level into concrete action, when faced with specific problems. Many complaints have been registered by traders and manufacturers in particular with regard to motor vehicles, foodstuffs, and pharmaceuticals (Commission, 1995c). In the construction sector, there have been serious difficulties in implementing EC directives and in agreeing on European standards. Delays in the transposition of European directives and standards at the national level have happened in several areas; the delays in the transposition of ETSI standards have, however, been rather extreme.

The production of technical regulations at the national level has not stopped. In fact, the sum total of national regulations is still much bigger than the *acquis communautaire* in this area. The Commission has made use of the mutual information directive in order to minimize the production of mutually incompatible regulations and hence the fragmentation of the internal market. Notification and consultation of other national authorities and the Commission and the provision for standstill have led to frequent amendments as well as the withdrawal of draft regulations. Those countries with the more advanced industrial structures and a strong culture of regulations and standards have remained, as expected, particularly active in this field. Sometimes, the dividing line between safety and environmental concerns on the one hand, and protection from foreign competition on the other, is very thin indeed.

Given the limited resources of European standards organizations, much of the work has been in fact in the hands of the organizations representing the large EU countries, namely Germany, France, and Britain (the Deutsches Institut für Normung (DIN), the Association Française de Normalisation (AFNOR), and the British Standards Institution (BSI)). Those organizations have also continued with the production of national standards which still exceed in number those produced at the European level. European standards sit, sometimes uncomfortably, between national and international standards. On the other hand, producers have become increasingly involved in the process. There is, therefore, a discernible risk that European standard setting may reflect mostly the interests of the economically advanced countries and the large producers at the expense of small and medium-sized enterprises in the weaker countries and regions (and possibly also at the expense of the consumers).

On the other hand, some progress has also been made with respect to the establishment of a decentralized system of testing, certification, and control, even though we are still at the early stages of a long process. The European Organization of Testing and Certification (EOTC) is relatively new, and the resources which have been made available to it are limited. In the absence of common rules for conformity assessment, product safety inspectors in the importing country may have reservations about the reliability of tests performed in the exporting country. They may, therefore, impose a new set of conformity assessment controls, even though the imported good has been manufactured in accordance with the 'essential requirements' of EU legislation and it has already satisfied one series of tests. At the heart of the problem is mutual suspicion about the professionalism and objectivity of testing and certification bodies in partner countries, but also the instinctive desire to protect domestic producers.

German or Danish fears about a possible erosion of consumer safety and environmental protection standards coexist with the understandable apprehension of some of the less developed countries of the Union about the economic costs associated with too high standards, not to mention the implications in terms of certification and testing laboratories. This heterogeneity, which is a characteristic of the Union, also points to the limitations of the mutual recognition principle. Much concern has been expressed about the possible erosion of standards as regards safety and environmental protection resulting from deregulation and the competition among rules introduced by the 'new approach'.

This is part of a much wider debate about regulatory competition versus institutional harmonization which has been sparked off by the internal market programme and the more extensive application of the principle of mutual recognition (see, for example, Héritier *et al.*, 1994; Scharpf, 1995; Siebert and Koop, 1993; Sun and Pelkmans, 1995; Woolcock, 1994). The EU has acquired an important regulatory dimension; and the literature covering many different policy areas has been rapidly expanding. Generalizations may, however, be rather misleading. In the case of technical regulations and standards, there is little sign so far of a race to the bottom, although the jury is still out. The final judgement on this issue may therefore prove to be different from the judgement reached with respect to taxation.

6

SOCIAL POLICIES AND LABOUR MARKETS

One market where state intervention has always been extensive and where conditions in general bear little resemblance to the standard perfect competition model of traditional economic theory is the labour market. Regulations regarding employment and working conditions, remuneration and social security payments have been standard features of the postwar mixed economy and the welfare state in Western Europe. On the other hand, wages and salaries have been largely determined by power relations between employers and organized labour, power relations which do not necessarily reflect supply and demand conditions in the labour market.

The term 'social policy' covers a very wide area, the boundaries of which are usually left undefined. In addition to different forms of regulation of labour markets, intended to guarantee a certain minimum of conditions for the protection of employees, and social security which has both an insurance and a redistributive dimension, social policy also includes education and training, housing and health. There is, of course, hardly any agreement as to where government intervention should begin and where it should end. Concern with equity and industrial democracy is meshed with the pursuit of the objective of economic efficiency. For some, all three are complementary, while others talk in terms of a trade-off which needs to be decided at the political level.

Although different kinds of market failure can provide some justification for government regulation of labour markets, such regulation and social policy more generally have a strong market-correcting and redistributive dimension. T. H. Marshall, for example, defines social policy as the use 'of political power to supersede, supplement or modify operations of the economic system in order to achieve results which the economic system would not achieve on its own . . . guided by values other than those determined by open market forces' (Marshall, 1975: 15; see also Streeck, 1995).

Political views, of course, differ substantially: social policy is at the very centre of the ideological divide between right and left. The historical experiences of individual European countries are also very different in this respect. However, despite those intra-European differences, which are still significant, reference is repeatedly made to the existence of a 'European model' which is contrasted with US and Japanese practices, not to mention those of less developed economies. According to Delors, the European construction, as also the European model of society, rests on three pillars, namely competition, cooperation, and solidarity (Delors, 1994: 232; see also Emerson, 1988; Aubry, 1989). What divides most Western European countries in terms of social policies and the regulation of labour markets appears to be much less important than the wide gap separating them from other advanced industrialized democracies.

This is very much true, for example, of public expenditure on social protection as a percentage of GDP (22 per cent average in EU-15 on the basis of 1990 data, approaching 35 per cent in some Northern European countries, as opposed to 15 per cent in the USA and less than 12 per cent in Japan—Commission, 1995*e*). The difference in the amounts spent by governments is also backed by different popular expectations: a very large majority of Europeans seem to expect their governments to provide a basic income for all, including income support for the unemployed. The corresponding numbers are much smaller in the United States and Australia. The same difference appears as regards popular attitudes on income inequalities (Jacquemin and Wright, 1993: 31–2). Solidarity has become a key word in the political culture of European societies; is it likely to change in the new economic environment characterized by high rates of unemployment and the growing financial pressures on the welfare state?

The early stages of European integration coincided with the rapid expansion of the role of the state in the social policy field, aiming mainly at some internal redistribution and the reduction of what Boltho (1982: 2) calls 'microeconomic risk' (individuals' loss of income arising from unemployment, accident, illness, or old age). Social policies were aimed at the incorporation of the working class in the political and economic system and the achievement of a wider consensus for the growth policies of the 1950s and 1960s. The progressive strengthening of trade union power and the more general acceptance of social democratic values were the logical consequence of this implicit package deal and the long period of prosperity and high levels of employment. With the advent of economic recession, however, the political and social scene changed dramatically. Attention rapidly turned to labour market rigidities and the excesses of the welfare state. 'Euro-sclerosis' then became the fashionable term and the launching board for supply-side economics and the deregulatory wave of the 1980s; and this was coupled with the steady weakening of trade union power and the reversal of earlier trends which had led to a considerably higher share of wages and salaries.

The relaunching of the integration process in the mid-1980s was closely related to the new political trend prevailing in Western Europe. The desire of big business for the elimination of the remaining barriers and the creation of a large European market was coupled with a gradual shift in the political balance of power, from which organized labour was the net loser. The policies which had laid the foundations of the postwar economic miracle in Western Europe were now widely perceived as a heavy liability undermining the prospects of economic growth. The emphasis was more on competition and the market, not on regulation and redistribution. And this was particularly true of the labour market. The internal market programme was born in this political context. Social policies hardly figured at all in the early stages of the 1992 process.

This did not last for long. Pressure soon started to build up for the creation of a European social space as a necessary complement to the establishment of the internal market, and social policy later became one of the most controversial issues of the intergovernmental conferences which led to the treaty revision signed at Maastricht in February 1992. This was further evidence of the continuous expansion of the European agenda. It could also be interpreted as a sign of the resurgence of those political and social forces which had earlier laid the foundations for the development of the mixed economy and the welfare state in individual European countries.

Such efforts have, however, had little effect until now. Despite repeated efforts and large amounts of political capital invested in social charters and protocols, the role of European institutions and legislation in the field of social policy remains limited. The nation-state continues to act as a jealous and effective guardian of its powers and competences in this area; and thus diversity persists. After all, social policy has been traditionally regarded as an important part of state-building; an instrument of statecraft as Banting (1995) calls it. Would national governments easily cede authority to European institutions? The answer is rather obvious. It remains to be seen whether the present division of power will change much in the foreseeable future, although the odds are against it.

On the other hand, the opening of economic frontiers has an impact on the functioning of national labour markets and the effectiveness of social policies. Relations between capital and labour, their respective negotiating power, and the distribution of the pie are all being affected by the division of powers between central and national institutions. In other words, the level of policy-making is directly linked to the contents of policy. This also means that the traditional divisions between left and right at the national level are superimposed on divisions along the federalist/intergovernmental continuum, with much overlapping since those who want a strong European social policy also want strong European institutions.

This chapter will concentrate on the European dimension of social policies and the regulation of labour markets as main themes of the debate on the new economic order. In the first part, we shall discuss intra-European labour mobility and the continuing separation of national labour markets. The second part will deal with the long list of Community initiatives aiming at the creation of a European social space. The provisional balance sheet of those initiatives is very modest indeed. Subsidiarity is the name of the game. This is the main conclusion reached in the third part. Is there a European model to defend and what is the risk of competitive deregulation? Of course, the term risk implies a value judgement.

Free Movement and Little Mobility

The Treaty of Rome was sprinkled with references to several aspects of social action, although a distinction can be drawn between provisions of a more or less binding nature and statements of general intent. Articles 48–51 referred to the free movement of workers, and Articles 52–8 to the freedom of establishment. These two freedoms are an integral part of the customs union, which means that the provisions made in them were of a constraining nature. Articles 117–28 referred specifically to social policy. They included references to the improvement of working conditions, 'equal pay for equal work' between men and women, and paid holidays. There were more specific provisions for the role of the European Social Fund, the main task of which was defined as 'rendering the employment of workers easier and of increasing their geographical and occupational mobility' (Article 123). The ESF was expected to meet 50 per cent of the expenditure of approved programmes for vocational training, the resettlement of workers as well as aid to workers who have been laid off. The origins of such action were to be found in the ECSC Treaty which had made provisions for aid to workers in the coal and steel industries.

The list was long, but it was clear that, with the exception of provisions for the free movement of workers and the freedom of establishment, the authors of the Treaty of Rome did not envisage a major role for European institutions in the field of social policy. The latter remained the preserve of national governments. France had tried hard to secure a commitment to the harmonization of social security payments, because of fears that high social charges would prejudice the competitiveness of French products in the customs union; but the other signatories to the treaty had been adamant. Even the Social Fund was basically seen as an adjunct to the free movement of workers, both offered to Italy and the Mezzogiorno in particular as part of the overall package deal.

During the early years of the EEC, social action at the European level remained low key. The main emphasis was on the achievement of the free movement of labour which proved to be a formidable task in itself. It was not only a question of abolishing frontier controls, restrictive residence permits, and numerous other administrative obstacles for workers and their families. Free movement of labour in the context of mixed economies depends on a much wider set of conditions which need to be fulfilled, including the transferability of social security payments, the mutual recognition of degrees and professional qualifications, and the dissemination of information about jobs through a properly functioning labour exchange.

Not surprisingly, progress in many of those areas proved slow, especially with respect to barriers arising from different national regulations as opposed to physical controls. Despite the continuous efforts made by the Commission and a large number of rulings by the European Court of Justice, several NTBs remained in this area, which were subsequently included in the internal market programme. Pursuing the trade analogy, the Community could have been described as a free trade area in the labour field, because of the lack of a common policy on labour migration from third countries.

Free movement of labour was achieved in 1968; at least, in a formal sense. It was based on the principle of national treatment for workers from other EEC countries in terms of occupational and social benefits. Given the nature of remaining obstacles, this freedom was more relevant to young, unskilled workers rather than older professionals. Labour migration continued to play a significant role in economic growth in Western Europe during the 1960s. It relieved labour shortages in the northern countries and provided additional flexibility in tight labour markets, while at the same time it acted as a safety valve for countries with abundant labour and as a source of much needed foreign exchange through migrant remittances back to the home country. True, it was not an unqualified blessing for either side, and this became gradually more obvious as social tension grew in the host countries with the steady increase of foreign 'guest-workers' who came to stay, while the exporting countries became more aware of the social and economic costs arising from the loss of many of the young and most dynamic members of their labour force.

What is very interesting, however, is that the progressive liberalization of intra-EC labour movements coincided with the steadily diminishing role of these movements as part of total labour migration in Western Europe. The following statistic is quite revealing: intra-EC labour flows represented for the original six members of the Community approximately 60 per cent of total flows at the beginning of the 1960s (Italian workers accounting for a large part of them). The corresponding figure was only 20 per cent one decade later (Straubhaar, 1988); and since then, intra-EC labour flows have declined further.

The transitional period envisaged by the Treaty of Rome coincided with the gradual drying up of the labour pool in Italy. Thus the labour shortages experienced in some of the rapidly growing economies of North-Western Europe were filled with labour immigrants from other Southern European countries. Greece, Portugal, and Spain became the main sources of labour export, and later Yugoslavia, Turkey, and North Africa were added to the list. The next wave of migrants came from the East; and very often, political refugees were hard to distinguish from economic refugees. Economic distress and political instability continue in several parts of the former Soviet empire, while demographic factors and economic stagnation produce an explosive mixture in North Africa. They will continue acting as powerful incentives for emigration towards the much more prosperous and politically stable countries of Western Europe. Stronger pressure from the East and the South has coincided with a steady return flow of early migrants from Southern Europe. By the time Greece, Portugal, and Spain joined the Community in the 1980s, net emigration from those countries had already come to a halt. Thus, intra-EC labour movements have remained small.

The accuracy of statistics on foreign workers and foreign residents leaves much to be desired. Work permits for EU nationals have been abolished, and there has also been a relaxation of rules regarding foreign residence permits. This, therefore, makes it difficult to trace labour movements inside the Union. On the other hand, one important feature of labour migration since the early 1980s has been, precisely, its clandestine nature, and this is particularly true of migration into previously labour-exporting countries in Southern Europe from the other side of the Mediterranean as well as Eastern Europe. According to the official statistics, in 1992 the total number of (registered) foreign residents in the EC of Twelve was about ten million people out of a total population of 344 million. Residents from other Community countries were less than five million (Eurostat data). The bulk of foreign residents were in the Federal Republic, and Turkish migrants constituted the largest group. In percentage terms, Luxembourg and Belgium had the largest number of foreign residents.

Economic 'pull' and 'push' factors, depending on macroeconomic conditions, labour market imbalances, and welfare payments, to which social factors should be added, have been much more important in determining labour movements than any changes in formal or other controls. Rapid economic growth and the raising of the standards of living in Italy during the 1950s and 1960s had a dampening effect on the 'push' factors in a traditional labour exporter; the same later became increasingly true for some of the other Southern European countries. On the other hand, the deterioration of the macroeconomic scene in the mid-1970s and the ensuing prolonged recession, combined with growing social tensions in the host countries, especially as regards the non-European and non-Christian immigrant populations, had a strong negative effect on the 'pull' factors. Special schemes were introduced in some countries for the repatriation of foreign workers. In the Federal Republic, such schemes led to a substantial reduction of the foreign workforce during the first half of the 1980s.

The persistence of high unemployment rates all over Western Europe acts as an important disincentive for intra-EU labour movements. The unemployed in Spain would no longer expect to find jobs easily in Germany or France. And differences in the standards of living are not as wide as they used to be; something which, of course, does not apply to immigrants from outside the Union. The large majority of foreign workers are employed in low-level, unskilled jobs, and are also, frequently, unregistered; this means low wages, no social contributions, and no union rights. Illegal immigration into Europe has strengthened the dichotomy between official and unofficial labour markets.

In fact, it could be argued that the *acquis communautaire* may have had a negative effect on intra-EU movements of labour to the extent that one important advantage of foreign labour from the point of view of employers has been the flexibility and the lower costs associated with the non-application of labour market regulations. Workers from other member countries enjoy the same protection (social security, trade union rights, and so on) as nationals, thus making them less attractive to many employers. At the same time, free circulation inside the EU has influenced the nature of intra-EU flows, therefore encouraging short-term employment and also, increasingly, the movement of professionals. This will become even more true with the progressive elimination of the remaining NTBs in this area.

Indeed, the nature of human flows inside the Union and the whole of Western

Europe in general has been gradually changing. Instead of mass labour movements, European countries have been witnessing the rapid growth of a different kind of human flow, including student exchanges, movements of skilled workers and professionals, changes of residence after retirement, not to mention the explosion of tourism (Romero, 1990). Intra-EU movement of students and professionals has been strongly encouraged by several Community programmes such as ERASMUS (European Community Action Scheme for the Mobility of University Students), COMETT (Community Programme for Education and Training for Technologies), and PETRA (Action Programme for the Vocational Training of Young People and their Preparation for Adult and Working Life). Unlike earlier migratory movements, those flows are two-way in direction and also less permanent.

In absolute numbers, cross-border flows are very small indeed. As an illustration of the continuing importance of national borders in intra-EU labour movements, it may be pointed out that while 1.2 million Italians moved yearly from one Italian city or region to another during the 1980s, the annual emigration of Italians was only 50,000 (CEPR, 1993: 70). Linguistic and cultural factors are very important; and some NTBs still remain. The internal market programme has led to considerable progress with respect to the mutual recognition of degrees and professional qualifications. It has also made the movement of Union citizens easier, even though border controls on people have not yet been completely removed, with the exception of those countries which have signed the Schengen agreement.

The elimination of remaining barriers often touches on very sensitive issues of national sovereignty and different political and economic practices in individual member countries. For example, worker mobility depends very much on the transferability of pensions which has come up against an important obstacle in Germany, namely a system of occupational pensions which has a 'vesting period' of ten years intended to encourage company loyalty by penalizing job-hopping. Should this be simply considered as yet another intra-EU barrier to be eliminated, or an integral part of a particular version of capitalism which should, perhaps, be respected?

The internal market programme seems to have had little effect on intra-EU labour flows which remain very small. Thus, labour mobility should not be expected to play a significant role as a means of economic adjustment in the context of a future monetary union. This subject will be discussed further in Chapter 8. In fact, there is almost a consensus view that large intra-EU labour movements would be politically and socially undesirable. Low labour mobility inside the Union also means that national labour markets will preserve their own separate identity for a long time. The creation of a European labour market is certainly not imminent. The combination of low labour mobility, wide economic diversity, and different traditions and institutions will continue to act as major constraints for the development of social policy at the EU level. The European dimension of industrial relations is also bound to remain underdeveloped for a long time. Labour is much less mobile than capital, and its organizations stand to lose as a result.

On the other hand, labour migratory pressures from outside are likely to persist. Given the low fertility rates in virtually all Western European countries and the projected ageing of the EU population, the entry of young foreign workers into the labour market would help to relieve the strain on European welfare systems. But economic considerations are likely to clash with domestic social pressures as European societies reach a dangerous threshold and racism and xenophobia grow. The persistence of high unemployment rates would make the acceptance of foreign workers even more difficult. This promises to become one of the most sensitive, and potentially explosive issues, for the prosperous countries of Europe.

Charters, Protocols, and White Papers: Battles on the Ideological High Ground

During the period between 1958 and 1973, Community social action was largely limited to the coordination of social security systems for migrant workers. Then came the social action programme adopted in 1974, which reflected the concern of European political leaders with the rapidly deteriorating economic environment and rising unemployment. The social action programme of 1974 included measures relating to the achievement of full employment, the improvement of living and working conditions, the closer participation of social partners in EC decision-making, and the involvement of workers in management decisions.

Good intentions proved difficult to translate into concrete action. The rapid growth of unemployment, combined with the shortage of EC funds and the opposition of most national governments to the transfer of real powers to Brussels, acted as major constraints on the development of EC social policy. This situation continued for many years, with small fragments of EC action here and there as testimony of the Community's subdued role in the social policy field. Collins (1985: 281) argued that European social policy comprised 'a miscellany rather than a social policy informed by a few compelling themes'; and Vogel-Polsky (1989: 179) went even further, talking about a negative consensus in this area: 'le consensus de ne pas faire de politique sociale européenne'.

The miscellany included, however, some important pieces of legislation. One area in which the Community has had a considerable impact is the equality of treatment for men and women. It has played mainly the role of a catalyst, especially after the adoption of the three equality directives in the 1970s which gave the ECJ the legal powers to push national administrations into taking effective action against discrimination between sexes in the labour market. Certainly, discrimination did not completely disappear as a result; but this is another example of the limits of legislation in changing long-established economic and social practices. In the 1970s, some legislation was also adopted in the area of labour law, most notably regarding conditions of collective dismissals. It was mainly an exercise in minimum standard-setting. Furthermore, a series of directives was adopted in the field of health and safety at work. From the mid-1970s onwards, such issues were to appear with increasing frequency on the agenda of the Council of Ministers; they were later given a further boost by the relevant provisions of the SEA.

The ESF has remained all along the main policy instrument in the field of social policy. Expenditure has grown considerably over the years. With the rapid rise in the number of jobless in the 1970s, the emphasis was bound to shift from problems associated with sectoral adjustment in the context of integration and the encouragement of geographical mobility towards measures aimed at the more general problem of unemployment. Thus, the ESF concentrated its efforts on long-term and youth unemployment, relying mainly on vocational training. However, the amounts of money spent remained small, when compared with corresponding expenditures at the national level. The Commission enjoyed little flexibility in the selection of projects, often being limited to a role of rubber-stamping decisions already taken in national capitals. There was also little evidence to suggest that the money spent by the ESF was in addition to social expenditure which would have been undertaken by national governments in its absence. This is the so-called problem of additionality. Like the Regional Fund, the ESF was generally seen by governments as a means of redistribution across national frontiers and not as the instrument of a common social policy (Collins, 1983).

The situation has improved since the reform of the Structural Funds (the ESF being one of them) undertaken in 1988. The amounts of money available have increased substantially. In 1995, expenditure on social policy amounted to 4,547 million ECU, representing 6.7 per cent of total expenditure through the EU budget. The regional bias of ESF expenditure has also been further strengthened, with absolute priority being accorded to the less developed countries and regions of the EU. This increasingly territorial dimension of the ESF and the (not always successful) coordination with the other Structural Funds makes the ESF part and parcel of the EU cohesion policy (Anderson, 1995). Its actions will therefore be examined in this context in Chapter 9.

Social policy did not form part of the White Paper of 1985. Reference was only made to the remaining obstacles to the free circulation of workers in a programme which concentrated almost exclusively on negative integration measures. The sensitivity of national governments in the social policy field was confirmed once again in the SEA where the 'free movement of persons' and 'the rights and interests of employed persons' were two of the three exceptions to the qualified majority principle introduced by Article 100a for the achievement of the internal market. It was clear that many national governments were not ready to take the risk of being overruled in this area. With respect to social policy, only measures related to the health and safety of workers (Article 118a) were made subject to a qualified majority. Reference was also made to 'the dialogue between management and labour at European level which could, if the two sides consider it desirable, lead to relations based on agreement' (Article 118b). Last but not least, economic and social cohesion became an agreed objective of further integration, and this was, in fact, to serve later as the launching board for further action in this area.

The social dimension of the internal market and the development of a so-called European social space soon became important but also highly controversial issues in the European debate. They had not been part of the original package deal. The subject lends itself to ideological confrontation which has, indeed, clearly characterized the European debate; and political rhetoric has been, perhaps unavoidably, associated with it. In fact, words have often seemed to be more important than deeds and the discrepancy between them has sometimes been astounding.

If the free market and competition were the underlying principles of the White Paper of 1985 and the internal market programme, calls for the creation of a European social space were based on very different ideological foundations. True, there is one aspect, at least, in which the social space is directly linked to the establishment of the internal market, namely through the creation of a truly European labour market and the encouragement of mobility as a means of economic adjustment. The elimination of various obstacles to the free circulation of workers and the adoption of positive measures to encourage it are fully consistent with the logic of the internal market. But the main emphasis with respect to the European social space lies elsewhere: it is related to concepts of equity, participation, and consensus which are not necessarily compatible with the 'magic of the market-place', to use a famous expression of President Reagan. They form part of a broader vision in which the social and the economic are inextricably linked; though a vision which is not shared by everybody.

Arguments for the creation of a European social space are, first of all, based on the belief that the market mechanism on its own will not ensure an equitable distribution of gains from the establishment of the internal market. It is both a question of solidarity for those who may suffer from the unleashing of the forces of competition and a form of insurance which may be aimed at the prevention of a political backlash from losers who might be tempted to rally behind the nationalist flag. The elimination of the remaining barriers started taking place at a time when unemployment levels were uncomfortably high. Political concern was further strengthened by the prediction of a J-curve effect on unemployment in the Cecchini report, meaning that unemployment was expected to rise in the first two years after the establishment of the internal market, before it began to fall. Would promises for a better life after death prove convincing to trade union leaders and the large numbers of unemployed in the attempt to secure from them a political endorsement of the internal market programme? Given the actual experience of the first half of the 1990s with the further increase in unemployment rates, such concern for the initial phase of the internal market now seems almost surreal.

Labour markets being highly regulated in all European countries, although the degree and kind of regulation varies enormously from one to the other, there was also the fear that the elimination of the remaining barriers to the free movement of goods, services, persons, and capital would lead to stronger competition among national economic systems and to an excessive deregulation of labour markets at the expense of workers, in terms of both remuneration and working conditions. Repeated references have been made by politicians and trade union leaders to the danger of 'social dumping', meaning some kind of unfair competition based on low wages and poor working conditions. In other words, there was a fear of deliberate underpricing by certain countries through a downward pressure on their labour costs in the search for external competitiveness and the attraction of foreign investment in their economy. The problem of social dumping could therefore be dealt with by creating a floor of basic rights (or minimum common standards) at the European level (Rhodes, 1992).

Calls for a European social space also relate to concepts of industrial democracy, participation, and consensus. They refer to the participation of workers in the running of enterprises, to social dialogue, and the search for consensual forms of politics; that is, forms of collectivism and corporatism in the words of ideological opponents. But whatever the words used to describe them, those practices have marked the postwar experience of several Western European countries. Given the limited role which organized labour had played until then in the process of European integration, which was also true of the launching of the internal market, the addition of the social dimension to the European agenda was intended to integrate the working class more securely in this process and thus avoid the identification of the internal market programme with the 'Europe of businessmen'.

Ideology is closely related to symbols; and symbols have been very important in this debate. The European social space was meant to symbolize a certain European economic and social model: the modern version of Europe's mixed economy which had proved so successful in the 1950s and 1960s. On the other hand, the development of European social policy could help to bring about another reshuffling of cards between national and European institutions. Thus, once again, federalist ambitions are difficult to separate from the intrinsic merits of the proposed policy.

The above discussion of the main motives behind proposals for further European action in the social field suggests that political consensus would not easily be forthcoming. In fact, the battlelines became clear early on. The main pressure in the direction of stronger Community action came from the more economically developed countries, with strong trade unions, high labour costs, and advanced legislation in this field, among which the Federal Republic and France played (as so often in other areas of policy) a leadership role. In Germany, for example, there has been an intense domestic debate (the so-called *Standortdebatte*) about the risks of industrial investment shifting to the south of Europe in search of lower labour costs and more flexible labour legislation, thus risking an increase in unemployment in Germany and the progressive erosion of the many social and other benefits enjoyed by German workers (Adams and Rekittke, 1989; Streeck, 1995; Scharpf, 1995). This has been, for obvious reasons, of particular concern for German Social Democrats.

The sensitivity shown by German governments on this subject needs to be understood in the context of the continuous search for consensus among the social partners on all major economic issues and European integration in particular which has characterized German politics: social policies and the regulation of the labour market being among the keystones of the 'social market economy'. Early on, the implementation of the internal market programme was linked to a Community-wide formulation of minimum social standards. True, the arguments used on this subject have not always been consistent with the liberal economic views generally expressed by German representatives in other areas of EU policy. But consistency is not, after all, the main feature of the political debate in any country.

For ideological reasons, Socialist parties in different European countries have found themselves in the same camp. When those parties happened to be in power in the economically less developed countries of the South, they had to reconcile political ideology and the desire to improve labour standards with the economic constraints imposed by the need to preserve the competitiveness of their national economies. A harmonization upwards of wages, social provisions, and working standards without a corresponding improvement in productivity rates and/or an increase in budgetary transfers across frontiers would seriously damage the ability of their producers to compete in the European internal market. The way out was sometimes to talk much and do little.

In fact, at the level of political rhetoric there seems to be a broad political consensus in Western Europe ranging from left to right of centre regarding welfare policies and employment protection legislation. Most Christian Democratic parties, with close links with the trade union movements in their respective countries, form part of this consensus. When it comes to specific measures, support may, however, become more qualified. Needless to say, the trade union movement has been strongly in favour of EU action in the social policy field, implying an upward harmonization of common standards.

The Commission has, of course, positioned itself on the same side of the battleline, often ahead of the others as a flag-bearer. The desire to secure a wider political acceptance of the internal market programme, through the active participation of the trade unions, was further strengthened by the federalist aspirations of the Brussels executive and the ideological preferences of Mr Delors who played a major role while at the helm of the Commission. Pressure from the European Parliament has also been in the same direction. The left of centre majority of MEPs (Socialists, Greens, and Communists) has acted as an important pressure group in an area where ideological preferences and potential votes have been conveniently married with the Parliament's interest in the further transfer of powers to European institutions.

On the other side, there have been relatively few; small in number but yet a political force to be reckoned with. Helped by the voting procedures in the Council of Ministers, which in most areas of social policy still allow one country to block decisions, and the sometimes ambivalent attitude adopted by supporters of a common policy, they have usually succeeded in imposing a minimalist approach on the Community as a whole. The British Conservatives have acted here again as champions of the opposition against any extension of Community powers. The strong ideological dislike for measures that, according to Mrs Thatcher, smacked of 'social engineering', with socialist and Marxist connotations, has its source in the very nature of the party and in the Conservative interpretation of postwar British history in which market rigidities and powerful trade unions have been identified as the main culprits for the long period of economic decline. Ideological opposition has been reinforced by hostility to any further weakening of national sovereignty and the transfer of powers to European institutions in the field of social policy; in fact, the two have been closely linked together. British Conservatives have found strong support on this issue among European business federations, and especially among their own businessmen. UNICE, the organization representing European employers at the European level, has consistently taken a strong line against any attempt to develop the European social dimension. Thus, UNICE has acted as a close ally of the British Conservatives in this area (and not only here).

In his address to the congress of the European Trade Union Confederation (ETUC) in Stockholm in May 1988, Mr Delors identified three main areas for action in an attempt to give the European social space a concrete meaning. These were the adoption of a European charter of fundamental social rights; legislation on a European company statute with provisions for the participation of workers in the management of firms; and the promotion of dialogue between representatives of business and labour at the European level.

The idea of a social charter was first introduced during Belgium's Presidency of the EC in the first half of 1987. Belgium had recently adopted a similar charter and presumably the idea was that if the charter was good for Belgium, why should it not be for Europe? An alternative explanation could be that if the adoption of the charter implied any economic cost for Belgium, it would be better if the same applied to the other EC partners in order to avoid any loss of competitiveness. The idea was taken up by the Commission, with strong support from France and Germany and the fierce opposition of the UK. Successive Presidencies from countries with socialist governments (Greece, Spain, and France) actively promoted the charter, and this finally led to its adoption by the European Council in Strasbourg in December 1989. It took the form of a solemn political declaration from which the UK abstained; and this became an important precedent for subsequent action taken by the Eleven.

The Community Charter of the Fundamental Rights of Workers (the initial reference to citizens was dropped in order to avoid wider political connotations) built on the existing Social Charter of the Council of Europe, the conventions of the International Labour Organization (ILO), and the various UN instruments. It is a political declaration of a non-binding character, which contains twenty-six provisions under twelve general headings, including freedom of movement, employment and remuneration, living and working conditions, freedom of association and collective bargaining, training, information, consultation and participation, and equal rights for men and women. In an attempt to reconcile economic efficiency with the promotion of the rights of workers, it was stated in the preamble that 'social consensus contributes to the strengthening of the competitiveness of undertakings', thus aptly summarizing the fundamental approach of the majority of Western European countries in the postwar period.

The Charter was followed by a social action programme proposed by the Commission and intended to give legal substance to the social rights enshrined in the declaration. Many of the provisions in the Charter were not at all controversial; and the same could be said of a good part of the legislation proposed by the Commission on the basis of the action programme. In fact, the adoption of several of the proposed measures would require hardly any changes in the existing legislation of member states. The Commission was also very careful in repeatedly stressing the principle of subsidiarity in an attempt to calm any fears about a federalist conspiracy to encroach upon the rights of member governments in the social field.

However, there were also some controversial issues. They included legislation on 'atypical' forms of employment, on the maximum duration of work and holidays, and even on equal opportunities for women, not to mention provisions for the participation and consultation of workers in enterprises. An increasing percentage of the new jobs created in recent years belongs to the category of 'atypical' employment, namely temporary and part-time jobs. Fearing that this would be used to dilute the rights of workers in terms of social security, health and safety protection, holiday and training entitlements, the legislation proposed aimed basically at the establishment of minimum standards. But for some, this constituted another attack on flexible labour markets. Other examples where consensus among member governments would not be easily forthcoming included the setting of statutory limits on overtime work and the protection of pregnant women. Sometimes, the main problem can be found in different national traditions which are difficult to reconcile in a common legal framework, despite the fact that the results are often broadly similar. As an example, we may cite the subject of paid holidays: some countries have legal provisions for the minimum amount of paid holidays, while in others it is a matter which is dealt with through collective bargaining. Under such circumstances, Community legislation becomes extremely difficult, unless it is restricted to rather anodyne statements.

The Charter also referred to an 'equitable wage' which could be interpreted as an attempt to introduce minimum wages in all member countries (they already exist in several of them). This is a highly controversial subject and rarely popular among economists: the creation of an artificial floor is seen as leading to the narrowing of wage dispersion, while also adding an upward pressure on wages and salaries, and eventually leading to an increase in unemployment. Those who are most likely to suffer as a result are new entrants and people with low skills who are gradually pushed out of the labour market (see, for example, CEPR, 1995*b*; and for a more relaxed view about the effects of minimum wages on unemployment, see Dolado *et al.*, 1996).

Thus, the labour market has its own 'outsiders' whose interests are not effectively represented by trade union organizations (see also Saint-Paul, 1996). They become 'outsiders', it is argued, because of excessive regulation and the fact that wages do not reflect supply and demand conditions in the market. More equity at the expense of the unemployed? It is all a question of who is included in the reference group. Of course, the relative bargaining power of 'insiders' and 'outsiders' depends very much on the number of those unemployed; hence the wider political acceptance of deregulation in recent years. The degree and kind of regulation of the labour market is a political question *par excellence.*

In view of the large wage disparities among EU countries, a European minimum wage would make absolutely no sense. This therefore means that legislation in this area can only be limited to general declarations with little concrete effect. However, a minimum wage is not the same as a minimum income which already forms part of the social security system of several member countries. But there can be serious doubts as to whether this is an appropriate area for EU legislation, especially in view of the inability of EU institutions to undertake at least part of the financial cost implied, at least in the foreseeable future.

Information, consultation, and participation of workers is another subject with strong ideological connotations. Participation is, of course, the most controversial, and it has been directly linked to legislation on a European company statute. The latter has a long history: it was initially launched by French legal practitioners in 1959, while the first Commission proposal was submitted as early as 1972. The economic logic behind it has been to produce a legal framework which would facilitate cross-border mergers and cooperation between firms. The enormous differences which still exist between national company laws make such cooperation extremely difficult, thus leaving takeovers as the most practical option. The creation of European companies would also provide a strong fillip for political and economic integration. However, proposals for the creation of a European company statute, which in itself is fairly uncontroversial, have always been linked by the Commission with provisions for workers' participation, this linkage being, arguably, forced upon the Commission by existing national legislation in this area.

As with company law, the situation among different European countries varies enormously, ranging from extensive legislation on employee participation in the Federal Republic—legislation for *Mitbestimmung* (co-determination) was introduced in 1976—and the Netherlands to informal arrangements determined by collective bargaining and no arrangements at all (Pipkorn, 1986). This diversity explains the insurmountable difficulties experienced in the past in reaching a common position on this subject, despite repeated efforts made by the Commission and the Parliament to make the proposals more flexible in order to increase their acceptability by governments which had not yet been convinced of the merits of industrial democracy (the British Conservatives acting, of course, as champions of the undiluted freedom of management). But there were also limits to this flexibility: too much of it and the consequent dilution of the provisions for workers' participation risked the wrath of trade unions and countries with advanced legislation in this area, since this would allow companies to bypass more stringent national rules. The result was a long stalemate within the Council of Ministers.

Earlier experience did not prove sufficiently discouraging for the Commission which submitted new proposals for the adoption of a European company statute in August 1989, presumably trying to take advantage of the more favourable climate of the late 1980s, while also trying to restore the political balance by pushing forward measures with a strong social content. Legislation on industrial democracy was considered as a central plank of this strategy. Once again, provisions for workers' participation were tacked on to the proposed company statute which contained economic sweeteners for business in the form of a favourable tax regime: companies registered under the new legal regime would be able to offset losses in one country against profits in another.

Participation was meant to offer workers a role in supervising the development and strategies of the company registered under the new European statute; participation did not, however, extend to day-to-day executive decisions. Information and consultation of workers would cover a wide range of issues, including the closure and transfer of plants, important changes in the organization of firms, and the substantial reduction or alteration of their activities. The Commission offered three alternative models for workers' participation in an attempt to reconcile the maximalist positions of Germany and the Netherlands, backed by labour organizations, on the one hand, and the minimalist stance of the UK, with the strong support of employers on the other. In the case of the European company statute, there has been an extraordinarily long period of pregnancy. Will anybody be really interested in the offspring, if and when it comes to life?

Proposals concerning the information and consultation of employees in multinational firms were faced with similar problems. It had all started with the so-called Vredeling directive in 1980, named after the Dutch Commissioner in charge. The Commission's proposals had then caused a strong reaction from UNICE and several US multinationals, which found themselves under the political umbrella of the US and the UK governments; and they were consequently buried some years later. They were revived afterwards in the context of the social action programme. Works' councils were meant to provide a channel for the information and consultation of workers of multinational firms on job reductions, new working practices, and the introduction of new technology.

The third area for action, identified by Mr Delors in his address to the ETUC in 1988, was the promotion of a dialogue between representatives of business and labour at the European level. Although the earlier experience had brought few tangible effects, the Commission sought to revive the dialogue mainly as a means of producing common positions which could form the basis for EU legislation in the employment and social fields. After all, the Commission has always been active in trying to associate representatives of business and labour in Community decision-making and in encouraging the creation of European pressure groups as a means of strengthening the political constituency on which the process of European integration is based. There is, however, a precedent which is hardly encouraging. The Treaty of Rome had provided for the setting up of an Economic and Social Committee (ESC) in the good corporatist tradition of some of the founding members. The ESC consists of representatives of the social partners and it acts in a consultative capacity in the Community decision-making process. But it has never really taken off. The various interest groups have worked mostly through national and informal channels.

The serious difficulties experienced in the early stages of the implementation of the social action programme, often although not always due to British threats of using their veto power, forced the proponents of a stronger Community role in this area to seek a way out of this impasse through a revision of the treaty. Thus, social policy became a major issue during the IGC which led to the Maastricht revision. The stakes were high on both sides and in the end only a very un-orthodox compromise could be reached. Faced with the adamant opposition of the UK to any extension of EC legal competences in the social policy field, the other eleven countries decided to proceed separately by signing a protocol and an agreement on social policy (Rhodes, 1995).

This enables the Eleven to extend the use of qualified majority voting to working conditions, the information and consultation of workers (but not participation which remained subject to unanimity), equality between men and women, and the integration of unemployed persons into the labour market. A special role has been reserved for the social partners. Several other important aspects of social policy are included in the above agreement signed by the Eleven, such as social security and the protection of third-country nationals. However, in those cases the unanimity principle has been retained. The eleven countries will therefore be able to have recourse to EU institutions for the adoption of new legislation in the above-mentioned areas, even though this legislation will not form part of the *acquis communautaire*. It is a parting of the ways between the UK and the others; and a further step towards the institutionalization of different tiers and variable geometry. On the other hand, the Protocol and the Agreement on social policy risk creating a legal and political minefield for the Union.

And then came another White Paper which was given almost as much promin-ence as its predecessor on the internal market. The aim was to tackle a dual crisis facing the Union at the time: an economic crisis manifested mainly through the unprecedented levels of unemployment and a political crisis associated with the new wave of Euro-scepticism and the traumas suffered during the ratification process of the Maastricht treaty (hence not very different from the background to the 1985 White Paper). The White Paper on 'Growth, Competitiveness, Employ-ment' was presented by President Delors to the European Council meeting in Brussels in December 1993 (the final version was published the following year: Commission, 1994*b*). It was a political document with which the Commission tried to seize once again the political initiative. The emphasis was on unemploy-ment and much of the White Paper was devoted to social policy and the regulation of labour markets. It tried to preserve some crucial elements of the 'European model', while also making important concessions to the new economic orthodoxy. Noting the manifest failure of European economies to create new jobs, in contrast for example with the US experience, the White Paper recognized the need for greater flexibility in labour markets and the reduction of labour costs.

The stress was on the reduction of the relative cost of unskilled and semi-skilled labour, concentrating mostly on the lowering of non-wage costs.

The problem of unemployment would, of course, be solved through higher rates of growth; but growth should also be more labour-intensive. Considerable emphasis was laid on continuous education and training in order to help workers to adjust to the constantly changing requirements of the market. At the same time, the White Paper repeatedly insisted on the need to preserve and develop further collective solidarity mechanisms. The basis of the European welfare state had to be preserved, even though some adjustments were deemed unavoidable or indeed desirable. Another interesting characteristic of the White Paper was the emphasis on intra-European diversity of labour markets and on subsidiarity as regards policy measures. The role which was implied for the Union was that of a forum for debate, a catalyst for action, and a framework for policy coordination. Evidently, earlier experience with social policy and the more recent setback suffered by European institutions in the course of ratifying the new treaty had left their marks.

There was also a Keynesian element in the White Paper, which was conveniently married with supply-side measures: the emphasis was on the need for higher investment on infrastructure (with strong emphasis on the development of trans-European networks in transport, energy, and telecommunications) as well as education and R&D. However, the Commission did not expect much of this investment to be financed directly through national budgets, given the poor state of public finances. Instead, it called for long-term borrowing through 'Union Bonds' and a greater share of private investment. On the other hand, the White Paper revealed strong shades of green: a reflection of the higher degree of sensitivity in Europe to environmental issues. It called for more environment-friendly policies and a partial shift from labour to environmental taxes, such as the energy tax proposed by the Commission in 1992.

The above were considered by the Commission as key elements of a new development model for Europe which was necessary in order to achieve the goals of growth, competitiveness, and employment in an increasingly globalized economy which left no room for protectionist measures. The White Paper was a highly ambitious document of a kind that national governments and political parties rarely produce. Its ambition was clear: to set the terms of reference for a Europe-wide debate which would eventually lead to concrete measures; and a large part of it was devoted to social and employment issues. Conscious of the need to compromise in politics, the Commission went out of its way to cater for different tastes. In the words of *The Economist* (15 January 1994), the White Paper 'contained enough grand ideas to please French and other *dirigiste* visionaries— and enough stress on labour-market deregulation to silence British and other sceptics'. In the following section, we shall examine the legal and other by-products of the White Paper of 1993 as well as those of the Charter of 1989 and the Maastricht Protocol and Agreement on social policy. How much have those Community initiatives influenced European and national policies?

Subsidiarity and the European Model

Majone (1993) has argued that although there is little scope for EU action in terms of welfare policies, social regulation should offer greater opportunities. The modest treaty revisions introduced through the SEA constituted a step in this direction. Subsequently, the adoption of the Charter and the Maastricht Protocol could be interpreted as an expression of political will by member countries, with the exception of the UK, to proceed further in terms of social regulation at the Community level. The Commission for its part did not stay idle: it produced ideas and papers of different colours, it submitted proposals to the Council of Ministers, and it also tried to make as imaginative use as possible of those treaty articles which allowed for qualified majority voting in order to facilitate decisions at the Council, much to the annoyance of British representatives (see also Rhodes, 1995).

In a few areas, the EU has indeed acted as a catalyst for policy. The result has been an upward harmonization of standards, as hoped for by advocates of a strong European social dimension. One such example has been the creation of equal opportunities for men and women, where Community action has a relatively long history. The directive on the protection of pregnant women is a more recent piece of EU legislation in this area. At the same time, it has become increasingly evident that legislation cannot automatically eliminate the kind of labour market segregation which is the product of deeply rooted cultural norms and values. Hence also a series of projects, measures, and initiatives at the Union level aiming at the promotion of affirmative action. In this context, we should also mention the existence of several EU programmes for the benefit of under-privileged groups of society.

Another example of an important body of EU legislation which has led to the modification and extension of legislation at the national level has been with respect to health and safety at work, although the question of proper implementation has not yet been answered. This has been treated as a fairly uncontroversial issue which should lead to the raising of standards in several countries. On the other hand, the provision for qualified majority voting in the SEA has made agreements at the Council much easier. Article 118*a* has provided the basis for many Commission proposals, as Brussels tried to adopt a very wide definition of the health and safety of workers.

After several years of difficult negotiations, an agreement was finally reached in 1996 regarding legislation on the posting of workers in the context of the free provision of services which thus allowed for qualified majority voting. This directive sets out rules on the rights of employees sent to work in another member country, and it applies mostly to construction workers. The main objective is to avoid undermining local rules regarding minimum wages and paid holidays; a hot issue in a country such as Germany with many 'posted' workers from other EU countries and an even larger pool of illegal labour, especially in the construction industry. On this directive, Portugal and the UK were outvoted.

Otherwise, EU legislation in the social policy field has been rather sparse and the minimum common standards adopted have usually been close to the lowest common denominator. The example of the directive adopted in 1993 on the organization of working time is quite characteristic. It contained several exceptions, especially for the benefit of the UK. On the other hand, Commission proposals for legislation on atypical work have so far had no success. The relative importance of part-time employment varies enormously from one European country to the other, with the highest percentages being registered in the Netherlands, Denmark, and the UK, and mostly among women (Eurostat data). This diversity is partly attributed to different regulatory regimes; and it has rendered agreement at the EU level extremely difficult. Nor has there been any agreement as yet with respect to draft legislation on the European company statute. The flexibility proposed by the Commission as regards workers' participation is still not proving sufficient to overcome resistance and the wide diversity in terms of national practices.

The opposition of the UK can serve as a partial explanation for the limited progress registered in the field of social regulation. Sometimes, British vetos have served as a convenient alibi for other countries who would not be very keen on an upward harmonization of labour standards because of the economic costs implied. The Maastricht Protocol allowed for social legislation which would bypass the walls erected by the British Conservatives. However, almost three years since the coming into force of the Maastricht provisions on social policy, only two directives have been adopted. The explanation is sometimes offered that the Eleven (and now Fourteen) have decided after all to avoid the creation of a wide regulatory gap between themselves and the UK; but this tells only part of the story.

The first directive adopted is a modified version of the old Vredeling directive on information and consultation of workers for large multinational undertakings. It leaves sufficient room for flexibility in allowing management and employees to choose their own form of consultation procedures. Perhaps not surprisingly, multinational firms have not shown any readiness to exclude their British workers from those consultation procedures, despite the fact that this directive does not apply to the UK. More recently, another piece of legislation has been adopted under the Maastricht social chapter. It relates to parental leave and it has been the product of negotiations between the social partners at the European level. Several member countries will have to change their legislation accordingly. As for the UK government, it apparently believes that no such legislation is necessary or indeed desirable; presumably because of a strong belief in traditional values and the preservation of the centuries-old division of labour inside the family! What are the Conservatives for, if not for old family values?

The social dialogue had been an important plank of Mr Delors's strategy for the strengthening of the European social dimension. Here again, this initiative has met with only limited success. A forum for debate and, occasionally, for negotiation—as witnessed, for example, in the case of the legislation on parental leave—has indeed been created (Rhodes, 1995). But it should be remembered that both

UNICE and the ETUC are loose confederations which represent little more than the sum of their parts; that is when those parts decide to act together, which is not always the case. Their membership extends beyond the EU, comprising several other European countries.

The representatives of employers' federations have always resisted a strong EU role in the social field, and the last thing that UNICE wants is European collective agreements. On the other hand, the capacities of trade unions for collective action at the European level are little developed, and the persistent diversity in terms of economic fundamentals acts as another constraining factor for the ability of organized labour to act effectively at the supranational level. Furthermore, trade union power has been steadily weakening in most European countries. Somewhat uncharitably, the European social dialogue could be described as the dialogue of the unwilling and the unable; but perhaps, we should allow more room for symbolism.

The follow-up to the White Paper on 'Growth, Competitiveness, Employment' has been very disappointing. There has been much talk, several committees have been set up at the Union level, more papers have been produced, but virtually nothing concrete has happened until now. At best, some ideas may have filtered down to the national or local level. Otherwise, the discrepancy between words and deeds seems to be characteristic of much of the debate on European social policy.

Judged against early expectations and the political rhetoric which has always accompanied social policy initiatives at the Union level, the achievements have been modest. An EU tier of social policy—in most cases, read regulation—has indeed been created (Leibfried and Pearson, 1995); but social policy is still highly decentralized, the diversity among national systems persists, and subsidiarity remains the name of the game. It could not have been otherwise. Those who express their deep disappointment in the limited progress achieved until now often tend to underestimate the real constraints on the development of the EU social dimension (see, for example, Streeck, 1995; Scharpf, 1995). Union institutions do not have the legitimacy and the financial resources to develop a social policy. Voting procedures at the Council of Ministers do not help either. Furthermore, the diversity in terms of economic conditions and institutions among member countries is still very wide; and there is no European labour market to talk about. Thus, regulation and neo-corporatist arrangements at the European level can only function within very narrow boundaries.

Does it matter? Will subsidiarity make the fears of 'social dumping' come true and what is the political economy of a decentralized system of social policy? Labour costs, both direct and indirect, still differ by large amounts among European countries. In 1992, hourly labour costs in German industry (the old *Länder*) were more than four times those in Portugal. But much of this difference is compensated by different productivity levels. Thus, inter-country differences in terms of unit labour costs are much narrower. On the other hand, the manipulation of labour costs in European democracies, with organized trade unions, is far from obvious; and labour cost considerations only play a limited role in investment decisions. Other factors such as the quality of infrastructure, the availability of skilled labour, and government subsidies are usually more important. Thus, there is little prospect of a massive displacement of production to lower cost locations inside the EU.

It may be different for labour-intensive industries where labour cost considerations are more crucial. But here, EU members have to compete with Tunisia, Morocco, and Turkey, not to mention several countries in Central and Eastern Europe, where labour costs are much lower while access to EU markets has been improving. In a relatively open world trading system, there is, indeed, little scope for social dumping inside the EU. Not surprisingly, several EU countries have called for the introduction of social anti-dumping clauses in international trade: again, a highly controversial issue with little prospect for agreement (see also Chapter 10).

There is also little evidence that the modest achievements in terms of institutional harmonization of labour standards at the European level have led to a race of standards downwards. The pressure for deregulation is certainly there, with strong ideological underpinnings, but it has much more to do with the high level of unemployment in all European countries than with the legislative abstinence of national representatives in Brussels. Numerous theories have been put forward for the steep rise in the number of unemployed; a problem which is really much worse than it appears in official rates of unemployment which do not capture those who have withdrawn themselves from the labour market. European countries have very low participation rates, when compared with those of other industrialized countries. High unemployment is usually attributed to a combination of different factors, including macroeconomic policies, technological change, increased import competition from the developing world, labour market rigidities, and the high relative cost of labour. The emphasis has steadily shifted towards structural factors as the notorious NAIRU (non-accelerating inflation rate of unemployment) continues to go up (Glyn, 1995; Wood, 1994; CEPR, 1995*b*; Commission, 1994*b*).

Heavy regulation of labour markets in terms of hiring and firing rules, minimum wages and the like, combined with generous social protection systems and high taxes on labour, can be at least partly blamed for the high unemployment in Europe, which is particularly high among unskilled workers. The *anti-monde* is provided by the United States where many more jobs have been created in the last twenty years: many more jobs, especially in the low paid categories (the so-called working poor), coupled with rapidly increasing wage disparities and job insecurity (see also Krugman, 1994*b*: 130–50).

Highly regulated labour markets in Europe may therefore be considered as operating at the expense of 'outsiders', namely the increasing number of unemployed; hence the growing pressures for some deregulation which has, indeed, started to happen in several European countries and most notably in the UK which has gone much further along the American road while also experiencing an unprecedented increase in income inequalities (OECD, 1995*b*; Atkinson, 1996). Calls for greater flexibility and the reduction of labour costs have also come from Brussels in recognition of a very real problem. However, there are relatively few signs (at least until now) of a deregulatory race. The American model offers little attraction to most Europeans. Furthermore, many people in employment stand to lose from far-reaching deregulation, while the number of winners would be relatively small and their political power is even smaller (CEPR, 1995*b*). Thus, deregulation has so far proceeded at a slow pace.

High unemployment rates have also begun to undermine the generous welfare systems which have characterized postwar Western Europe. The sky-rocketing of expenditure on unemployment benefits has been added to 'medical inflation' (rapidly rising costs of national health systems) and a similar development with respect to pensions due to higher life expectancy and earlier retirement (Commission, 1995*e*). On the revenue side, developments have also been highly unfavourable. Low growth rates and a steady reduction of taxes on capital, associated with higher mobility and arbitrage between national systems, have led to the draining of resources. VAT rates have also their limits, especially in the context of the internal market; and there is so much income tax that European governments can impose on their blue- and white-collar workers. This is where the main danger for the European social model lies, and not in the competitive deregulation of national systems due to allegedly insufficient legislation and harmonization in Brussels.

Employment and social protection systems now figure prominently on the European agenda; it could not have been otherwise. A European employment strategy was adopted at the European Council meeting at Essen in December 1994; a number of initiatives and proposals have been submitted by the Commission on social protection systems; and the debate on social Europe and the European model has continued unabated. Although the EU can provide a very useful forum for discussion and may occasionally act as a catalyst for action or even as a convenient scapegoat for unpopular measures at the national level, there is still a very conspicuous discrepancy between rhetoric which is addressed to the electorates back home and action which is bound to remain limited at the European level.

The proposal made by President Santer in 1996 for a confidence pact for employment involving national governments and social partners may therefore suffer a similar fate to several other Commission initiatives in the past, initiatives which ventured into areas where real power is divided between national governments and markets, while the margin of manoeuvre available to Union institutions remains extremely limited. There may also be an attempt to strengthen treaty provisions for employment in the new IGC which started in March 1996. But how could this be translated into policy measures?

On the other hand, the persistence of high unemployment and the tendency of losers to rally behind nationalist flags may eventually push the Union into adopting even a small part of the financial responsibility in this area, thus entering with both feet into the sacrosanct territory of social protection. Pressure to move in this direction may grow further with the establishment of EMU; but this would also have major implications for the EU budget. At the same time, EMU will put a premium on the flexibility of labour markets.

The main argument we have tried to develop in this chapter is that social policy and the regulation of labour markets still do not constitute an important part of the core of EU activity; and there are usually good economic reasons for this. Variable geometry, flexible integration, and subsidiarity will remain the key words for some time. Although competitive deregulation is not an immediate issue, at least not in relation to European integration, there is, however, a more fundamental, long-term problem which is usually hidden behind rather simplistic arguments about social dumping. In the context of mixed economies, the distribution of the national pie between capital and labour is the joint product of market processes and power relations. With the rapid opening of economic frontiers, this distribution tends to shift against labour for the very simple reason that capital is more internationally mobile. Precisely the same argument applies to taxation.

In the words of Streeck (1995: 431), 'social policy unbacked by strong state capacities cannot offer groups with limited market power recourse to legal compulsion, so as to change the power balance between them and better-endowed rivals'. The weakening of state power in this area, linked to the weakness of 'the territorial state to control its own boundaries' (Scharpf, 1995: 9), has led to appeals for the transfer of competences to the supranational level; and hence to growing frustration because of the large difficulties encountered.

7

BUILDING A REGIONAL
CURRENCY SYSTEM

Much Ado About Nothing: The Early Years

Although the main emphasis in the Rome Treaty was on the creation of a common market, with the progressive elimination of barriers for the free movement of goods, services, persons, and capital, there was at least some, albeit rather hesitant, recognition of the importance of macroeconomic policies, and monetary policy in particular, in the context of a common market. Article 2 referred to the task of 'progressively approximating the economic policies of Member States'. In Title II of the original treaty, we find references to the main objectives of macroeconomic policy, and the balance of payments in particular. The achievement of those objectives would be facilitated by the coordination of economic policies, the ways and means of which remained to be defined. Specific provisions were made only as regards monetary policy; hence the creation of the Monetary Committee. The treaty also referred to the exchange rate as a matter of common concern. The possibility of mutual aid in the case of balance of payments difficulties was envisaged as well as the progressive elimination of exchange controls to the extent necessary for the proper functioning of the common market.

There was clearly no intention to set up a regional currency bloc. The Bretton Woods system provided the international framework and the US dollar the undisputed monetary standard. On the other hand, limited capital mobility allowed European governments a reasonably wide margin of manoeuvre in terms of monetary policy (hence the caution expressed in the articles of the treaty regarding capital movements). European regional integration was basically about trade in goods. Macroeconomic policies, and monetary policy in particular, remained the concern of national governments subject to the constraints imposed by the international monetary system.

During the 1960s, there was much talk about regional cooperation, but little concrete action. The central country of the Bretton Woods system, namely the United States, proved no longer willing or able to provide the public good of monetary stability, and this led to some discussions between the, by now, much more confident Europeans about alternatives, including closer regional cooperation. There was also some resentment about the asymmetrical nature of the international system, which was, however, combined with different degrees of economic and political vulnerability to US pressure. At best, the intra-European discussions of the 1960s helped to prepare the ground for subsequent plans for regional cooperation, while also leading to the expansion of the small infrastructure of committees at the EEC level. The creation of the CAP, based on common prices, was closely related to the perceived need for exchange rate stability. But this was in little doubt until 1968.

EMU was part of the new package deal agreed at the Hague summit of 1969. Growing trade interpenetration, largely the result of tariff liberalization measures, had reduced the effectiveness of autonomous economic policies; hence the new attraction of coordination procedures and joint action. The Six had proved unable both to insulate themselves from international monetary instability and to pursue a common policy in international fora. The events of 1968–9 provided clear evidence of this failure. This in turn endangered one of the main pillars of the EEC construction, namely the CAP. Thus the political decision to extend and deepen the process of integration led the Six, almost naturally, into the area of macroeconomic activity. And they decided to go all the way, committing themselves to the creation of an EMU which would replace the customs union as the main goal of the new decade. Money was also a means to an end, and the end was political union. This function of monetary union was widely recognized and aptly summarized by the French: 'la voie royale vers l'union politique'.

However, important divisions soon became apparent as regards the priorities and the strategy to be employed in order to achieve the final goal. Those divisions, which had their origins in an earlier debate provoked by the Commission memorandum of 1968 (better known as the first Barre plan) and the alternative proposals put forward at the time by the German Minister of Economics, Mr Schiller, dominated the discussions inside the high-level group which was entrusted with the preparation of a report on the establishment of EMU. This group was chaired by the Prime Minister of Luxembourg, Mr Werner.

The main conflict was between 'economists' and 'monetarists' and was based on the strategy to be adopted during the transitional period in order to achieve a sufficient harmonization of national economic policies which were seen as the main precondition for the elimination of payments imbalances (Tsoukalis, 1977a). More specifically, the crucial difference was whether the Community would move towards the irrevocable fixity of parities and the elimination of margins of fluctuation before the system of economic policy coordination had proved its effectiveness.

The 'monetarists', represented by France, Belgium, and Luxembourg, stressed the importance of the exchange rate discipline and the need to strengthen the 'monetary personality' of the EC in international fora. They also, presumably, would have liked to pass the adjustment burden on to surplus countries and thus face them with the choice of either financing the deficits of others or accepting a higher rate of inflation. This would in turn have largely depended on provisions for the financing of payments imbalances. It was precisely this choice that the potential surplus countries, namely the Federal Republic of Germany and the Netherlands, would have liked to avoid. Hence the insistence of the 'economists' on policy coordination, the results of which were, apparently, expected to be close to their own set of policy preferences, as a necessary condition for progress on the exchange rate front. What the 'economists' in fact implied was the convergence of the inflation rates of other countries to their own. There was a certain degree of ambivalence and confusion on both sides, and also some double-talk.

The debate between 'economists' and 'monetarists' did not touch upon the big question of the economic feasibility of EMU within the relatively short time-scale envisaged. The harmonization of policy preferences was considered as the main precondition for the elimination of payments imbalances, thus basically ignoring the various factors behind different wage and price trends as well as productivity levels between member countries. Turning the realization of EMU into a question of political will, the Community ran the risk of neglecting the possible economic costs associated with the abandonment of a major policy instrument such as the exchange rate. Furthermore, the difference between 'economists' and 'monetarists' was only partly a reflection of fundamentally different approaches to the establishment of EMU. It also served as an ideological cloak for the different short-term interests of individual countries. The 'short-termism' of some governments became clearer through their subsequent actions.

The final report of the Werner group was submitted in October 1970 (Werner Report, 1970). A complete EMU was to be achieved in three stages within an overall period of ten years. The final objective was defined in terms of an irrevocable fixity of exchange rates, the elimination of margins of fluctuation, and the free circulation of goods, services, persons, and capital. The creation of EMU would require the transfer of a wide range of decision-making powers from the national to the EC level. All principal decisions on monetary policy, ranging from questions of internal liquidity and interest rates to exchange rates and the management of reserves, would have to be centralized. Quantitative medium-term objectives would be jointly fixed and projections would be revised periodically. With respect to fiscal policy, the Werner group argued that an agreement would have to be reached on the margins within which the main national budget aggregates would be held and on the method of financing deficits or utilizing surpluses. Fiscal harmonization and cooperation in structural and regional policies were also mentioned as objectives. The creation of two main institutions of the Community was envisaged, namely 'the centre of decision for economic policy' and the 'Community system for the central banks'.

The final report was based on a consensus among its members, regarding the ultimate objective, and a compromise, couched in somewhat vague terms, between 'economists' and 'monetarists' about the intermediate stages. The compromise was embodied in the strategy of parallelism between economic policy coordination and monetary integration, with the Werner group concentrating mainly on the measures to be adopted during the first of three stages before reaching the 'Elysian harmony'[1] of a complete EMU.

The fragility of the compromise and the political commitment of several countries to the final objective was soon to be exposed by the dramatic deterioration of the international economic environment. One of the few concrete decisions was to narrow the intra-EC margins of fluctuation from 1.5 to 1.2 per cent on either side of the parity; a decision, however, which was never implemented. This small, first step on the road towards monetary union took Bretton Woods and fixed exchange rates against the dollar for granted. This proved to be one of the biggest weaknesses of the European strategy. Massive capital inflows and the US policy of 'benign neglect' ('unbenign' would, perhaps, be a more accurate term) showed once again the extreme fragility of EC unity and of only recently concluded agreements. Faced with the Nixon measures of August 1971, the Six suddenly forgot the objective of EMU and produced instead an impressive variety of national exchange rate regimes ranging from independent floating to 'pivot rates' and a two-tier market.

The Smithsonian agreement of December 1971 created only a short-lived illusion of a new international order. The Six hastened to build their regional system on its foundations; and, not very surprisingly, it soon crumbled. The 'snake in the tunnel', created in March 1972, represented a new attempt to narrow intra-EC margins of fluctuation to 2.25 per cent, instead of the 4.5 per cent resulting from the application of the Smithsonian agreement. The snake would therefore consist of the EC currencies jointly moving inside the dollar tunnel, that is the 2.25 per cent bands on either side of their parity against the US currency. Wide margins of fluctuation of intra-EC exchange rates were generally considered as incompatible with the functioning of the common market and the CAP. The birth of the snake was accompanied by rules for joint intervention in the exchange markets and provisions for very short-term credit between central banks for the financing of those interventions. As part of the strategy of parallelism, a steering committee was also set up for the more effective coordination of economic policies.

The continued instability in exchange markets caused the progressive mutilation of the snake, thus creating further unhappiness in the European monetary zoo. Sterling and the punt left the EC exchange rate arrangement in July 1972, soon to be followed by the Danish krone which subsequently returned to the fold. Only a few months after the Paris summit of October 1972, which reiterated the political commitment to a complete EMU by the end of the decade, the lira was floated and then the remaining currencies of the snake decided to make virtue out of necessity by accepting a joint float against the dollar. The snake had, therefore, lost its tunnel and would from then on have to wriggle its way into the open space. The final exit scene was reserved for the French franc which left the snake in January 1974, while a subsequent attempt to return did not last for very long (July 1975–March 1976).

---

[1] This was a term used at the time by Mr Schiller, the German Minister of Economics.

In the following years, the snake was little more than a Deutschmark (DM) zone. The Benelux countries and Denmark remained in it recognizing the importance of stable exchange rates for their small and open economies and the relative weight of their trade relations with the Federal Republic. It was rather ironical (or was it just an illustration of the short-term considerations which had prevailed in national attitudes towards EMU?) that the core countries of the 'economist' group had chosen to remain in the regional exchange rate system, while France, the leader of the 'monetarists', had been forced to leave. The snake was hardly a Community system, with almost half of the EC members staying outside it, while a number of other Western European countries (Austria, Norway, and Sweden) became associate members of the DM zone.

The most common criticism made against any system of fixed exchange rates, with limited amounts of liquidity to finance payments deficits, used to be that the burden of adjustment is likely to fall on the deficit countries, thus creating a deflationary bias in the system. For Germany, the snake helped to contain the appreciation of the DM, at least for a significant part of the country's external trade, while at the same time it did not impose any additional constraints on the conduct of German monetary policy. For the smaller countries, the main attraction was stable exchange rates and the increased credibility of their economic policies. Concentrating on the Danish experience, Thygesen (1979) did not find any convincing evidence of deflationary bias. On the other hand, the snake did not lead to any serious coordination on the external monetary front, except for one-way coordination on the basis of German policies. It was, undoubtedly, an asymmetrical system.

In the attempt to preserve stable intra-EC exchange rates, in the midst of the general upheaval which characterized the early 1970s, Community countries increasingly resorted to capital controls, despite the declared objective of a complete liberalization of capital movements which was supposed to be an integral part of EMU. Furthermore, there was neither uniform action nor even some form of broad agreement on this subject. The question of capital controls produced very different responses on behalf of individual member countries. This continued to be true until the end of the decade when Germany, Britain, and the Netherlands were the only countries of the enlarged EC with virtually no restrictions imposed on international capital flows. On the other hand, no attempt was made to discriminate in favour of intra-EC movements, probably recognizing the futility of such an attempt in view of the permeability of national frontiers.

The combination of an unfavourable international environment, divergent national policies, a half-baked economic strategy, and a very weak political commitment ensured the quick death of EMU. The latter became the biggest non-event of the 1970s. With the benefit of hindsight, it can be argued that the ambitious initiative, originally intended to transform radically the economic and political map of Western Europe, had been taken at the highest level without much thought of its wider implications. It certainly did not survive the test of time and economic adversity.

Monetary Stability and the EMS

Despite the serious setbacks suffered in the attempt to move towards an EMU in the 1970s, interest in the subject never disappeared. The mini-snake was generally considered as only a temporary arrangement which would be improved and extended when the economic conditions became more favourable. Various plans were put forward which served to keep interest alive and also prepare the ground for a new political initiative. The aim of official plans was usually to design a more flexible exchange rate system which would incorporate all EC currencies. On the other hand, many proposals originating from professional economists and academics concentrated on the creation and development of a European parallel currency (Fratianni and Peeters, 1978). Finally, a proposal put forward by the President of the Commission, Mr Jenkins, in October 1977 acted as the catalyst for the relaunching of monetary integration. And this in turn led to the establishment of the EMS in March 1979.

The EMS was the product of an initiative taken by Chancellor Schmidt, against the advice, if not the outright opposition, of his central bank. This was later presented as a joint Franco-German initiative, something which was becoming increasingly regular in EC affairs. It could have been an arrangement among the Big Three to which the other EC countries would have been invited to join. But Britain, once again, decided to stay out (Ludlow, 1982). The setting up of the EMS was a renewed attempt to establish a system of fixed and periodically adjustable exchange rates between EC currencies, operating within relatively narrow margins of fluctuation. Unlike many academic economists who have long remained agnostic about the costs of a floating system, the large majority of European policy-makers and businessmen have always stressed the advantages of fixed (but not necessarily irrevocably fixed) exchange rates. The experience of the 1970s was read as a confirmation of this long-held belief which had been temporarily shaken by new ideas about the alleged efficiency and stability of financial and exchange markets, ideas which were mainly imported from the other side of the Atlantic. Concern about the proper functioning of the common market was combined with the desire to preserve the system of common agricultural prices. On the other hand, the initiative for the creation of the EMS was linked to the expectation that there would be no substantial reform of the international monetary system and hence no prospect of a return to some form of exchange rate stability in the near future. The construction of a regional system was, therefore, seen as a second- or third-best solution.

Exchange rate stability was to be backed by an increased convergence between national economies, with the emphasis clearly placed on inflation rates. The EMS was considered as an important instrument in the fight against inflation, and its creation meant an implicit acceptance of German policy priorities by the other EC countries. The experience of the 1970s was seen as validating the uncompromising anti-inflationary stance combined with the strong currency option adopted by the Federal Republic. The EMS was also intended as a European defensive mechanism against US 'benign neglect' as regards the dollar, and, more generally, what was perceived to be a political vacuum in Washington at the time of the Carter Administration; even though it was never made very clear how the EMS could perform such a role. It was also seen as a means of strengthening Europe economically and politically through closer cooperation at a time when US leadership was seen as waning. Once again, monetary integration was partly used as an instrument for political ends.

One of the novelties of the system was the European Currency Unit (ECU) consisting of fixed amounts of each EC currency, including those not participating in the exchange rate mechanism (ERM). Two revisions of these amounts took place in 1984 and 1989, and they also led to the inclusion of the currencies of the three new Southern members of the EC (Table 7.1). According to the Maastricht treaty, no further changes in the composition of the ECU will take place until the final stage of EMU. The relative weights of each currency are a function of the economic and trade weight of the country concerned, with a clear tilt towards the stronger currencies (see relative weight of the Deutschmark and the Dutch guilder).

Each EC currency has a central rate defined in ECU. Central rates in ECU are then used to establish a grid of bilateral exchange rates. The margins of fluctuation around those bilateral rates were set at 2.25 per cent, with the exception of the lira which was allowed to operate within wider margins of 6 per cent and sterling which stayed out of the ERM completely. Central bank interventions were compulsory and unlimited, when currencies reached the limit of their permitted margins of fluctuation. Central rates could be changed only by common consent.

Against the deposit of 20 per cent of gold and dollar reserves held by participating central banks, which took the form of three-month revolving swaps, the

Table 7.1. Composition of the ECU

Currency	13 March 1979		17 September 1984		21 September 1989	
	1	2	1	2	1	2[a]
Deutschmark	0.828	33.00	0.719	32.00	0.6242	30.53
French franc	1.15	19.80	1.31	19.00	1.332	20.79
Netherlands guilder	0.286	10.50	0.256	10.10	0.2198	10.21
Belgian and Luxembourg franc	3.80	9.50	3.85	8.50	3.301	8.91
Italian lira	109.0	9.50	140.00	10.20	151.8	7.21
Danish krone	0.217	3.00	0.219	2.70	0.1976	2.71
Irish punt	0.00759	1.10	0.008781	1.20	0.008552	1.08
Pound sterling	0.0885	13.60	0.0878	15.00	0.08784	11.17
Greek drachma	—	—	1.15	1.30	1.44	0.49
Spanish peseta	—	—	—	—	6.885	4.24
Portuguese escudo	—	—	—	—	1.393	0.71

Note: Column 1 indicates the number of national currency units in each ECU, while column 2 gives the percentage weight of each country in the ECU basket.

   [a] Weights of component currencies calculated on the basis of current central rates since 6 March 1995.

Source: Eurostat.

European Monetary Cooperation Fund (EMCF) issued ECU in return. Those ECU were therefore intended to serve as an official reserve asset, although they were subject to so many restrictions that they could really be described only as a non-negotiable instrument of credit. ECU were also intended to serve as a denominator for market interventions arising from the operation of the ERM and as a means of settlement between the monetary authorities of the EC. This in turn meant a sharing of the exchange risk between creditor and debtor countries. Exactly the same applied to the credit mechanisms of the EMS.

Another novelty of the EMS was the so-called divergence indicator intended to provide a certain degree of symmetry in the adjustment burden between appreciating and depreciating currencies and an automatic mechanism for triggering consultations before the intervention limits were reached. The device would make it possible to locate the position and the movement of an EMS currency relative to the EC average represented by the ECU. There was a so-called 'presumption to act', when the divergence threshold was reached. In simple terms, the introduction of the divergence indicator implied that average behaviour should constitute good behaviour, although this did not square well with another implicit feature of the EMS, namely a general alignment to Germany's anti-inflation policy. The contradiction was soon to become apparent, and the result was that the divergence indicator was never put into effect.

Very short-term credit facilities, in unlimited amounts, were to be granted to each other by participating central banks, through the EMCF, in order to permit intervention in EC currencies. Provisions were also made for other credit facilities, building on the already existing short-term monetary support and the medium-term financial assistance mechanism of the snake. In principle as a means of fostering economic convergence and in practice as a carrot to lure the economically weaker countries into participating in the ERM, provision was made for the granting of subsidized loans by EC institutions and the European Investment Bank.

Thus the EMS was built on the existing snake with some important novel features intended to ensure the enlargement of its membership and the smoother functioning of the exchange rate mechanism. It was based on a political compromise between Germany which feared the effects of prolonged international monetary instability and an excessive revaluation of the DM, resulting from the continuous sinking of the dollar in exchange markets, and France and Italy which saw their participation in the EMS as an integral part of an anti-inflation strategy. All three also shared the broader political objectives associated with the EMS, namely support for European unification and the strengthening of Europe's identity in relations with the United States. It was clearly a decision of high politics. With tongue-in-cheek, de Cecco (1989: 90) argued that for Italy '[to] be in favour of the EMS meant to be in favour of freedom and of Western civilization'!

The other members of the old snake, countries with small and highly open economies and hence little prospect of independent monetary policies, were only too happy to see an extension of the area in which stable exchange relations applied. As for Ireland, the decision to join the ERM was partly a function of the side-payments offered and the attraction of the external discipline on monetary policy and partly an expression of political independence against Britain. The latter was a totally different case. The fear of deflationary pressures, stemming largely from the traumatic experience with earlier attempts under the Bretton Woods system to keep the exchange rate of sterling fixed, was combined with strong opposition to the political objectives behind the EMS. Thus, Britain stayed out of the ERM for more than eleven years, limiting its participation to the other, much less constraining manifestations of the new system.

The period between 1979 and 1996 can be divided into four distinct phases. The first three phases were characterized by an increasing stability of exchange rates (see also Gros and Thygesen, 1992); that is, until hell was let loose in 1992, which eventually forced member governments to abandon the old narrow margins of fluctuation. During the first thirteen years, the EMS could be described as a zone of monetary stability, and this term applies to both exchange rates and inflation rates. Exchange rate fluctuations were substantially reduced. This is true when a comparison is made with the pre-EMS experience of participating currencies or with the experience of other major currencies, including sterling for the period it stayed outside the system. Stability did not, however, mean absolute rigidity. During the first thirteen years of the EMS, there were twelve realignments, five of which involved more than two currencies (Table 7.2). They soon became a matter of genuinely collective decisions, while the element of drama, which had often accompanied the negotiations leading to the early realignments, gradually disappeared.

Greater stability did not, however, apply to exchange relations with major currencies outside the ERM. This is particularly true of the exchange rate of the ECU against the dollar, which was subject to large fluctuations, both in the short- and medium-term, during this period (see Fig. 7.1). Thus, the EMS did not provide (and how could it?) the insulation against external instability which some Europeans seemed to have hoped for, although the centrifugal effects of the dollar gyrations on intra-ERM exchange rates were reduced in the more recent period. Until the Plaza agreement of 1985, there had been no serious attempt at policy coordination at the international level. The gross overvaluation of the dollar during the first half of the 1980s, seen in the beginning as a sign of national virility by President Reagan and several members of his Administration, and its disastrous effects on the US external trade balance finally brought about a change in US attitudes (Funabashi, 1988). The experience since then suggests that the conversion to the virtues of international economic cooperation and the joint management of exchange rates was neither deep nor long-lasting; but this applies virtually to all parties concerned, which is a further sign of the limitations of international policy coordination.

The greater stability in nominal intra-ERM exchange rates was achieved largely through the gradual convergence of inflation rates downwards; and this convergence, which has survived the exchange crisis of 1992–3, has been, indeed, quite remarkable (see Fig. 7.2). However, it was very slow in the beginning. The first phase of the EMS ended with the realignment of March 1983. It was a

Table 7.2. EMS Realignments: Changes in Central Rates[a] (% change: minus sign (–) denotes a devaluation)

Currency	24 Sept. 1979	30 Nov. 1979	23 Mar. 1981	5 Oct. 1981	22 Feb. 1982	14 June 1982	21 Mar. 1983	22 July 1985	7 Apr. 1986	4 Aug. 1986	12 Jan. 1987	8 Jan.[b] 1990	14 Sept. 1992	16 Sept.[c] 1992	23 Nov. 1992	1 Feb. 1993	13 May 1993	6 Mar. 1995
Deutschmark	2			5.5		4.25	5.5	2.0	3.0		3.0		3.5					
French franc				-3.0		-5.75	-2.5	2.0	-3.0				3.5					
Netherlands guilder				5.5		4.25	3.5	2.0	3.0		3.0		3.5					
Belgian and Luxembourg franc					-8.5		1.5	2.0	1.0		2.0		3.5					
Italian lira						-2.75	-2.5	-6.2				-3.0	-3.5					
Danish krone	-2.9	-4.8		-3.0	-3.0		-2.5	2.0					3.5					
Irish punt							-3.5			-8.0			3.5			-10.0		
Spanish peseta[d]													3.5	-5.0	-6.0		-8.0	-7.0
Pound sterling[e]													3.5					
Portuguese escudo[f]													3.5		-6.0		-6.5	-3.5
Austrian schilling[g]																		
Finnish markka[h]																		

Notes:

a On 2 August 1993 the fluctuation bands in the EMS were widened to ±15% around unchanged central rates, except for the bilateral guilder/mark fluctuation band which remained at ±2.25%.

b The lira reduced its fluctuation bands from ±6% around its central rate to ±2.25%.

c Participation of the pound in the ERM was suspended, and the Italian authorities temporarily abstained from intervening in the exchange rate markets. The lira re-entered the ERM on 25 November 1996, with a fluctuation band of ±15% around its central rates.

d The peseta joined the ERM on 19 June 1989, with a fluctuation band of ±6% around its central rates.

e The pound entered the ERM on 8 October 1990, with a fluctuation band of ±6% around its central rates.

f The escudo entered the ERM on 6 April 1992, with a fluctuation band of ±6% around its central rates.

g The Austrian schilling entered the ERM on 9 January 1995, with a fluctuation band of ±15% around its central rates.

h The Finnish markka entered the ERM on 14 October 1996, with a fluctuation band of ±15% around its central rates.

Source: Eurostat and Bank for International Settlements.

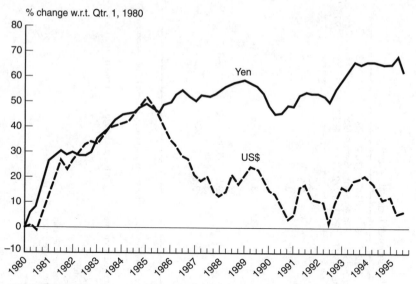

Fig. 7.1. Bilateral Exchange Rates of the US Dollar and the Yen against the ECU, 1980–1995

Source: Eurostat.

turbulent period marked by frequent realignments of exchange rates and wide policy divergence which was reflected in wide inflation differentials. This suggests that the consensus on which the creation of the EMS had been based was in fact rather flimsy. After all, both parents of the EMS (Chancellor Schmidt and President Giscard d'Estaing) had left the political stage before the end of 1982.

The second phase was one of consolidation, and it ended with the realignment of January 1987. There were few realignments during this period, usually involving small changes in the central rates and only a few currencies. It was also the period of increasing price convergence downwards. Following the ill-fated attempt by the French Socialists to apply Keynesianism in one country in 1982–3, exchange rate stability was based on a convergence of economic preferences, which was in turn reinforced by the operation of the system. Several countries participating in the ERM reached the lowest levels in terms of inflation rates between 1986 and 1987; and then there was a small shift upwards linked to the economic boom and, subsequently, in the case of Germany, to the effects of unification.

The third phase was characterized by a remarkable stability of exchange rates, which, with the benefit of hindsight, can be described as rigidity. For more than five years, there was no realignment of exchange rates, with the exception of a small repositioning of the lira, which was announced in January 1990, together with the decision to reduce the margins of fluctuation for the lira to 2.25 per cent. It had been preceded by a major modification of the operating rules of the system (see below, for a discussion of the Basle–Nyborg agreement of 1987). The stability

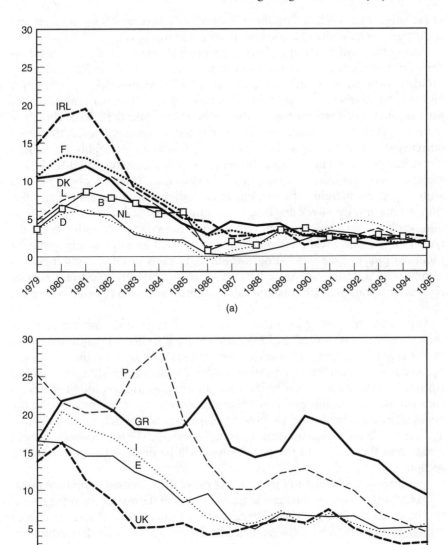

Fig. 7.2. Price Deflator Private Consumption, 1979–1995

Note: Unified Germany since 1992.

Source: Commission.

Key:

B = Belgium	D = Germany	DK = Denmark	E = Spain
F = France	GR = Greece	I = Italy	IRL = Ireland
L = Luxembourg	NL = Netherlands	P = Portugal	UK = United Kingdom

of exchange rates was based on the continued convergence of inflation rates and the increased credibility of the system in exchange markets.

During the third phase, there was also a gradual extension of ERM membership, which was generally seen as a sure sign of the success of the system. Having brought down the rate of inflation and in search of a credible exchange rate target and an external discipline, Spain joined in June 1989, with a 6 per cent margin of fluctuation. Later, it was the turn of the real heretics to take the oath of allegiance to the true faith. After a long internal debate, in which arguments about the petro-currency status of sterling and the role of London as an international financial centre had been used interchangeably with political arguments about the loss of national sovereignty, the UK finally decided to join the ERM in October 1990, also with a 6 per cent margin of fluctuation. It was followed by Portugal in April 1992, thus leaving only the Greek drachma outside the ERM. In all cases, the decision to join was based on a combination of economic and political considerations: the search for a stable anchor for the exchange rate and an external discipline for monetary policy, while at the same time offering further proof of commitment to Europe, and a desire not to be left out of an increasingly important part of regional integration. High inflation rates still prevented Greece from joining the club.

There were three other important events which marked the latter part of the third phase in the history of the EMS. One was the liberalization of capital movements as part of the internal market programme; the second was the decision to proceed to a complete EMU, a decision which led to the Maastricht revision of the treaties; and the third was the unification of Germany, with profound effects on German macroeconomic policy and also indirectly on the other members of the system. The combined effect of those developments was grossly underestimated at the time. This was soon to become painfully obvious. The breakdown of the old system and the entry into the fourth phase will be discussed in the following section.

The growing credibility of the EMS, and hence the increased stability of intra-ERM exchange rates, during the first thirteen years of the operation of the system was based on the downward convergence of inflation rates. In this respect, three groups of countries can be distinguished; and there is a close correlation between inflation rates and participation in the ERM. The first group comprises the seven original members of the narrow band of the ERM, which experienced the highest degree of convergence and the lowest rates of inflation (see Fig.7.2(*a*)). This has been particularly true since 1983. The second group consists of those countries which had long remained in the wider band of the ERM or completely outside it, namely Italy, Portugal, Spain, and the UK (see Fig.7.2(*b*)). They had higher inflation rates for most of the period (with the UK being on the margin between the two groups) and they were also the first to suffer from the crisis which hit exchange markets in 1992. Greece constitutes a category of its own, with significantly higher inflation rates (even though declining rapidly in recent years) which have prevented it from ever joining the ERM.

How much can this convergence of inflation rates be attributed to the operation

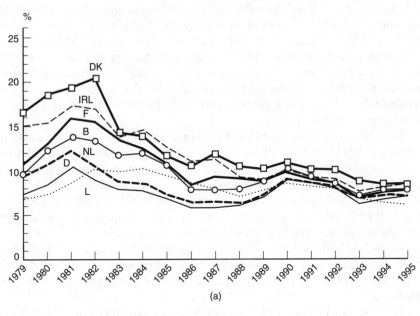

(a)

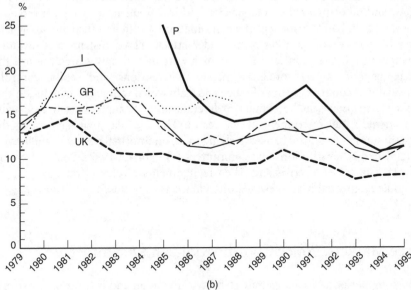

(b)

Fig. 7.3. Nominal Long-Term Interest Rates, 1979–1995

Note: For Greece, no data are available after 1988.

Source: Commission.

Key:

B = Belgium	D = Germany	DK = Denmark	E = Spain
F = France	GR = Greece	I = Italy	IRL = Ireland
L = Luxembourg	NL = Netherlands	P = Portugal	UK = United Kingdom

of the ERM? After all, inflation rates in most industrialized countries, including the other countries in Western Europe, followed a similar trend during the same period. The link is virtually impossible to prove econometrically, although there is more than circumstantial evidence to indicate that participation in the ERM served, at least for a large part of the period under consideration, as an important additional instrument in the fight against inflation. This is, for example, true of France, Italy, and Ireland. Participation in the ERM acted as an external constraint on domestic monetary policies.

Price convergence and intra-ERM exchange rate stability relied basically on monetary policies and the almost exclusive use of short-term interest rates for exchange rate stabilization purposes. Price convergence also brought with it the gradual convergence of nominal long-term interest rates. This is clearly shown in Fig. 7.3. Here again, a distinction can be drawn between the seven original members of the narrow band and the rest, with the UK once again falling in between the two groups. The convergence of long-term interest rates was very strong in 1995–6 as financial markets became increasingly convinced of the political commitment to EMU; and the convergence of long-term interest rates was directly linked to expectations about which currencies would be admitted to EMU and which not.

The ERM operated for many years as a system of fixed but adjustable exchange rates; and adjustments became smaller and less frequent as price convergence grew. Central banks made use of a combination of different instruments whenever bilateral exchange rates came under attack. Those instruments included changes in short-term interest rates (which were increasingly geared towards the exchange rate target), foreign exchange interventions, and capital controls, especially in countries such as France and Italy which were later to abandon this policy instrument in the context of liberalization. Realignments were usually considered as an instrument of last resort. The everyday management of the system was left to central bankers, relying more on informal networks and less on established EC institutions and committees (Goodman, 1992). Politicians were involved in times of crisis and when realignments of central rates were to be negotiated, invariably at weekends when markets were closed.

Free Markets, Policy Coordination, and Asymmetry

The long period of exchange rate stability came to an end in 1992 under strong market pressure. Speculation against the existing bilateral rates began during that year; it rapidly gathered momentum, leading to unprecedented transfers of funds across frontiers and currencies. Repeated changes in interest rates and heavy central bank intervention in exchange markets proved grossly inadequate to deal with the problem. The result was a series of realignments, the withdrawal of two currencies from the ERM, and finally the abandonment of the old narrow bands of fluctuation in August 1993; not to mention the big losses incurred by central banks, and most notably the Bank of England, as well as the negative effects for the real economy and the process of European integration (see also Commission, 1994*a*: 87–104; de Grauwe, 1994; and the country case-studies in Johnson and Collignon, 1994).

It was highly unfortunate, although not unrelated, that all this happened at a time when EC governments were going through the ratification process of the Maastricht treaty, the most important element of which was precisely the construction of a complete EMU with deadlines and detailed provisions, especially for the final stage which was planned to happen before the end of the decade. The small 'no' majority in the first Danish referendum in June 1992 acted as a catalyst for a new wave of 'Euro-scepticism', and the ratification process of the new treaty became both long and painful. This in turn added fuel to speculative attacks against the existing central rates in the ERM. European societies and international markets clearly took a very sceptical view of commitments solemnly undertaken by government leaders.

The entry into the new phase of the EMS, which happened violently and was forced upon unwilling governments, was caused by a combination of different factors. One such factor was the progressive overvaluation of some currencies. Exchange rate realignments until then had not fully compensated for inflation differentials. There was a deliberate attempt by governments and central banks to use the exchange rate as an anti-inflationary instrument; hence the resistance to devaluation in countries with higher inflation rates. High nominal (and real) short-term interest rates were used by Italy and Spain to make their currencies more attractive to holders of mobile capital; and this policy seemed to work for a time leading some analysts (Giavazzi and Spaventa, 1990) to argue that in the 'new EMS' the monetary standard would be effectively set by the weaker members. The other side of the coin was that the currencies concerned became progressively overvalued, with a loss of external competitiveness, which was in turn translated into growing trade deficits.

Measurements of competitiveness of the different ERM currencies vary depending on the indicator used (consumer prices, unit labour costs, and so on). Figure 7.4 shows the development of real effective exchange rates (trade-weighted nominal exchange rates adjusted in terms of inflation) for ten currencies (excluding Greece and Luxembourg). It takes 1979 as the starting-point, although this does not, of course, imply that the exchange rates at the beginning of the EMS should be considered as equilibrium rates, whatever that may mean. Figure 7.4(*a*) traces the development of real effective exchange rates for the old members of the narrow band, and Fig. 7.4(*b*) does the same for the weaker members of the family. The message is clear: EMS realignments until 1992 had not compensated fully for inflation differentials.

Figure 7.4(*b*) shows a steady appreciation of the lira in real terms, which had reached more than 30 per cent before the crisis of 1992 broke out. A similar trend can be observed with respect to the escudo and the peseta, although in the case of the latter the problem appears to be less pronounced because of the earlier depreciation of the currency in real terms between 1979 and 1983. The entry of

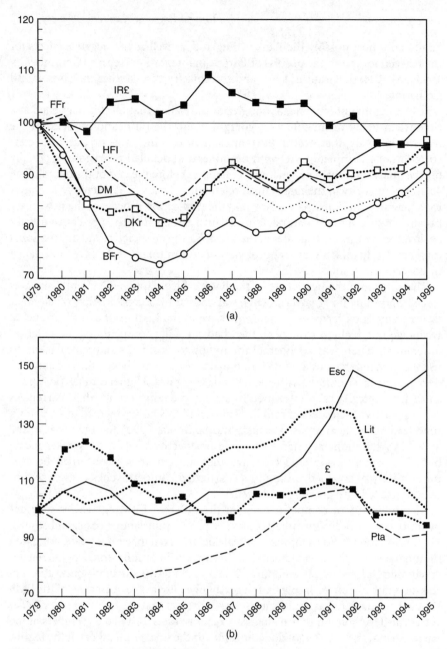

Fig. 7.4. Real Effective Exchange Rates, 1979–1995

Note: Relative to nineteen other industrialized countries, 1979 = 100.

Source: Commission.

Key:

BFr = Belgian franc	DM = Deutschmark	Dkr = Danish krone
Esc = Portuguese escudo	FFr = French franc	HFl = Dutch guilder
IR£ = Irish punt	Lit = Italian lira	Pta = Spanish peseta
£ = sterling		

the two Iberian currencies in the ERM in 1989 and 1992 respectively had been preceded by a period of shadowing of the ERM marked by restrictive monetary policies and a rapid decline of inflation rates. During the whole period, the exchange rate was deliberately used as an important anti-inflationary instrument. The counterpart to the resulting overvaluation of the currencies of Southern countries was the gain in competitiveness for countries with low inflation rates, notably Germany, France, and the Benelux countries, a gain which lasted as long as the credibility of exchange rates lasted. Although always a member of the narrow band, Ireland suffered a loss of competitiveness as long as its inflation rate remained high, for precisely the same reasons as the three above-mentioned Southern countries (Fig. 7.4(*a*)).

But good things (and stable markets) do not last for ever, especially when the economic fundamentals are wrong. The crisis of September of 1992 was largely a crisis of confidence affecting the weaker currencies which were widely perceived as being overvalued. The three Southern currencies in the ERM were the first to be hit by speculative attacks, together with sterling which was also considered by market operators as overvalued, although it had not experienced anything like the real appreciation of the other three currencies (Fig. 7.4(*b*)). The governments concerned were soon forced to concede defeat: sterling and the lira withdrew from the ERM in September 1992, while the peseta and the escudo went through a series of devaluations in order to remain inside (see also Table 7.2).

Market instability did, however, continue and more currencies came under attack. Credibility had gone out with a bang, and the herd instinct (of Anglo-Saxon speculators as repeatedly denounced by French politicians!) led to ever-growing market pressure. According to an IMF study published at the time: 'The discipline exerted by capital markets is neither infallible nor is it always applied smoothly and consistently. Nevertheless, the markets eventually decide on what are unsustainable situations, and when they do, their size alone increasingly allows them to force adjustments' (IMF, 1993).

National authorities had deprived themselves of a policy instrument to which they had frequently resorted in the past in the defence of exchange rates. Capital controls were no longer available when the massive transfers of funds began to take place, although they were temporarily reintroduced in some countries after the September 1992 crisis. Reacting to the crisis, some economists called for the introduction of measures which would be intended to 'throw sand in the wheels of international finance': a tax on foreign exchange transactions or non-interest bearing deposit requirements on banks taking open positions in foreign exchange (see, for example, Eichengreen and Wyplosz, 1993). But such proposals went against the trend. It was not always clear whether people objected to such measures because they were undesirable (market distorting) or impractical (in the name of globalization), or perhaps both. The role of international financial markets seemed to be accepted as a fact of life, even though not always a pleasant one. But going against it was generally considered as politically incorrect.

There were also problems of policy coordination in an asymmetrical system. During the crisis of 1992–3, markets increasingly challenged the sustainability of restrictive monetary policies in a period of deep economic recession and rapidly growing unemployment. German unification had brought about large increases in public expenditure in the new *Länder*, which were not matched by corresponding increases in taxation; hence growing budget deficits in Germany which were accompanied by an acceleration of inflation. The burden of the stabilization effort thus fell almost entirely on monetary policy: the Bundesbank drove short-term interest rates upwards and kept them high, while unemployment was rising fast in the whole of Western Europe.

What was good (perhaps unavoidable under the circumstances) for Germany was not good for the rest of Europe. The system of fixed exchange rates, combined with the continuing central role of the DM, meant that other countries could not lower their own interest rates, unless, of course, they were ready to opt for a more general realignment of central rates or leave the system. The resistance to a general realignment—basically a euphemism for a devaluation of the other currencies against the DM—was justified in terms of the so-called economic fundamentals (after all, several countries participating in the narrow band of the ERM were running lower inflation rates than Germany, as shown in Fig. 7.2). There was, in fact, much more at stake, namely the prestige and credibility of governments; and this was apparently more strongly felt in France where governments had been since 1983 seeking 'competitiveness through disinflation' at a high cost in terms of unemployment (Blanchard and Muet, 1993). There was a clear policy conflict between Germany and the other countries and there was no mechanism in the EMS to resolve it. German (and European) interest rates remained too high in a period of recession, the domestic opposition to deflationary policies kept on growing in several countries, while market operators placed ever larger bets on a general realignment of currencies, thus questioning the sustainability of existing exchange rates and/or policies.

The problem was also part and parcel of the fundamental asymmetry in the EMS, which was, of course, not a new phenomenon. Asymmetry had been for several years a dirty word, mainly because of German embarrassment with such politically loaded terms, until the evidence became too glaring to ignore. Despite special provisions, such as the creation of the divergence indicator, the EMS has operated throughout its history in an asymmetrical fashion, thus following the earlier example of the snake. The degree and nature of the asymmetry have, however, changed over time and so has the assessment of its effects, which has also been a function of the economic paradigm used to analyse those effects. After all, this is hardly a topic on which economists would be expected to agree.

The asymmetry relates to the central role of the Deutschmark, which in more recent years has been explicitly referred to, even in official documents, as the 'anchor' of the system (see, for example, Delors Report, 1989: 12). The source of the asymmetry is dual: the German low propensity to inflate (the period following unification has proved both rather short and exceptional, thus adding in the end to the credibility enjoyed by the Bundesbank) and the international role of the DM. The former, combined with the economic weight of the country and the priority attached by the other EU partners to exchange rate stability and

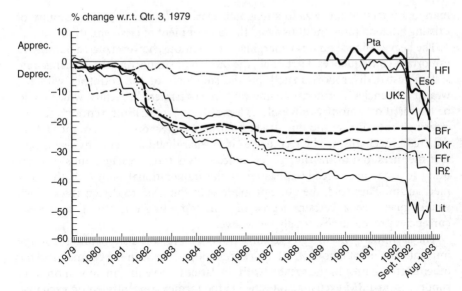

Fig. 7.5. Bilateral DM Rates of ERM Currencies, Mar. 1979–Aug. 1993

Note: Price of each ERM currency in terms of the DM; the exchange rates are monthly averages.

Source: Deutsche Bundesbank, Monthly Reports.

Key:
BFr = Belgian franc   Dkr = Danish krone   Esc = Portuguese escudo
FFr = French franc   HFl = Dutch guilder   IR£ = Irish punt
Lit = Italian lira   Pta = Spanish peseta   £ = sterling

the fight against inflation, enabled Germany to set the monetary standard for the other countries. On the other hand, the increasingly important role of the DM as an international reserve currency has placed the German central bank in a key position with respect to the external monetary policy of the EMS as a whole.

No realignment of ERM central parities has ever involved a depreciation of the DM in relation to any other currency. Figure 7.5 shows the evolution of bilateral rates of the ERM currencies against the DM between March 1979 and August 1993 when the narrow margins of fluctuation in the ERM were abandoned. Figure 7.5 gives an indication of the margin of manoeuvre used by other members *vis-à-vis* Germany, ranging from the Netherlands on the one extreme, with an almost complete alignment with German monetary policy, to Italy on the other, which had repeatedly resorted to devaluations (and capital controls), without even being able to compensate fully for its higher inflation rates.

Asymmetry in a system of fixed (even if periodically adjustable) exchange rates is manifested in terms of an unequal distribution of the burden of intervention and adjustment and also of influence in the setting of policy priorities. Central bank interventions in the exchange markets had from the early years of the EMS begun to take place inside the permitted margins of fluctuation. The aim of intra-marginal interventions was to strengthen market confidence in the stability of existing bilateral rates and thus avoid the development of crisis situations.

The heavy reliance on intra-marginal interventions, however, had a number of important consequences. First of all, the burden of supporting the exchange rate system rested disproportionately on the shoulders of the countries with the weaker currencies. Furthermore, the very short-term credit facility, which could be triggered off automatically only as a result of marginal interventions, fell increasingly into disuse; and this also had a negative effect on the use of the ECU in the credit mechanism. The recourse to intra-marginal interventions also meant that the threshold of the divergence indicator was rarely reached, thus contributing to what had already appeared as the inoperational nature of this new mechanism. Therefore, the attempt made with the EMS to design rules which would guarantee a certain degree of symmetry between strong and weak currencies proved almost totally ineffective.

The asymmetry in foreign exchange interventions was also manifested in the implicit division of labour which quickly developed between the German and the other central banks in the system, with the latter intervening mainly in order to support intra-ERM exchange rates, while the former concentrated on exchange relations with third currencies, and most notably the US dollar. This division of labour was also reflected in the holding of foreign currencies by EU central banks; the Bundesbank holding only relatively small amounts of other EU currencies.

Another manifestation of asymmetry in the EMS was through the interdependence of interest rates in different national markets. Short-term interest rates have been consistently used as a key instrument in the exchange rate policy of participating countries. In times of crisis during the earlier phases of the EMS, the burden of adjustment was borne mainly by France, Italy, and the smaller countries, with capital controls often being used to insulate domestic interest rates from the effects of foreign exchange speculation. Giavazzi and Giovannini wrote in 1989: 'the data on interest rates suggest that only Germany sets monetary policy independently. Italy and France can either accommodate German monetary policies perfectly or decouple domestic and foreign interest rates, at least temporarily, by resorting to capital controls' (Giavazzi and Giovannini, 1989: 75).

The Basle–Nyborg agreement of September 1987 was an attempt to correct, at least partially, the asymmetrical nature of the system. It referred to a 'presumption' that loans of EC currencies would from then on be available through the EMCF for the financing of intra-marginal interventions. It also announced the extension of the very short-term credit facility and the use of ECU for the settlement of debts as well as the intention of central bankers to achieve a closer coordination of interest rates. Those measures were intended to achieve a more equitable distribution of the burden of intervention and adjustment between different countries. As a counterpart to the extension of credit facilities, participating countries also expressed the intention to make realignments of central parities as infrequent and as small as possible, while also making explicit their intention not to compensate fully for inflation differentials.

In subsequent years, the system did become less asymmetrical, but also more rigid. The realignment of central rates was strongly resisted by most members; in fact, asymmetry had never meant that Germany could force exchange rate realignments on the other members. The ERM finally exploded during the exchange crisis of 1992–3, despite massive foreign exchange interventions by all central banks, including this time the Bundesbank. One thing has, however, hardly changed throughout the whole period, namely the leadership role of the German central bank. This has been repeatedly confirmed when interest rate changes initiated by the latter have been immediately followed by central banks in other European countries. There is little doubt among central bankers as to who is the leader in the European game.

Is asymmetry necessarily bad, at least from an economic point of view? Giavazzi and Giovannini (1989: 63), for example, argued that 'the EMS reproduces the historical experiences of fixed exchange rate regimes'. The literature on fixed exchange rates refers to the so-called N–1 problem which means that in a group of N countries (and currencies) there can only be N–1 exchange rates. One solution to this problem is that the Nth country sets its monetary policy independently, while the others peg to its currency and use their monetary policy to defend the exchange rate. Another solution would be that all N countries agree collectively on the thrust of monetary policy and are also equally responsible for defending the exchange rates. In the EMS, as with the Bretton Woods system earlier, reality has always been much closer to the former than the latter solution.

There are two sides to the asymmetrical nature of the EMS. On the one hand, it can be argued that countries with a higher propensity to inflation, such as Italy for example, borrowed credibility by pegging their currencies to the DM and they consequently reduced the output loss resulting from disinflationary policies. This is the alleged advantage of 'tying one's hands' to the DM mast, like Ulysses had done to protect himself from the Sirens (see also Giavazzi and Pagano, 1988). Participation in the ERM is also supposed to have reinforced the commitment of national authorities to non-inflationary policies by introducing an external discipline and thus strengthening the hand of institutions and interest groups inside the country fighting for less inflationary policies. This largely explains the popularity of the system with most central bankers, which is contrary to their earlier expectations. The Banca d'Italia is the best example in this respect. However, faced with the profligacy of the domestic political class and an inflexible labour market, the Italian central bank has also experienced the serious limitations of an anti-inflation strategy based almost entirely on the exchange rate and monetary policy (Micossi and Padoan, 1994).

But as with most arguments in economics, there is also the other hand. The asymmetry of the EMS has also been seen as leading to a deflationary bias in the system which becomes particularly important in times of recession and growing unemployment (Wyplosz, 1990; de Grauwe, 1994). This was true in the early and mid-1980s and was again painfully true in the early 1990s when economic adversity and growing social pressure forced the other European countries to take a less benign view of German leadership.

The deflationary bias of the system relates basically to the one-way coordination of monetary policies as the main instrument used to achieve both internal and external stability. On the other hand, there is precious little evidence of effective coordination and convergence of budgetary policies. To the extent that such convergence did take place during the earlier phases of the EMS, it was the result of autonomous decisions leading to the reduction of public deficits in several member countries (for a large part of the 1980s) and not the product of an effective coordination of national fiscal policies within the EU. In fact, the old mechanism for the coordination of policies never worked properly: it was strong on procedure and weak on implementation (Mortensen, 1990). Co-ordination of fiscal policies has acquired new teeth with the excessive deficit procedure adopted at Maastricht. This subject will be discussed further in Chapter 8.

The vicious circle created during the exchange crisis of 1992–3 by growing internal resistance to the continuation of the link with the DM in several countries and market speculation regarding the sustainability of existing policies could have been broken either by a substantial reduction of German interest rates or a revaluation of the DM against the other currencies. The rejection of both those options finally led to a major change in the existing rules of the system. In August 1993, EC governments announced the widening of the margins of fluctuation of the ERM to 15 per cent, with the old 2.25 per cent margin being kept only between the DM and the guilder. The widening of the margins was an ingenuous way of conceding defeat to the enemy (in this case, the market). Markets had won because they had become more powerful and also because governments had shown themselves unable to make use of the flexibility offered by the system they had themselves designed. During the crisis of 1992–3, policy coordination at the European level showed its limitations.

The widening of the bands was followed soon afterwards by successive cuts in German short-term interest rates, which in turn contributed to improvements on the European macroeconomic scene. Coupled with continued policy convergence, this combination of factors helped gradually to restore stability in the exchange markets. The nine countries which remained in the ERM plus Austria which joined in January 1995 and Finland in October 1996 (followed by Italy one month later), chose not to take advantage of the wider margins of fluctuation in their monetary policy. Inflation convergence continued downwards and most currencies of the ERM returned quickly within the old narrow bands.

The new margins of fluctuation were, however, kept: they helped to make market speculation more costly while they also served as a protective shield in times of crisis. Another realignment involving the two Iberian currencies in March 1995 confirmed the new-found flexibility. Thus, necessity was gradually (and genuinely) changed into virtue. Participating countries came to like the new ERM with the wider bands, and more members joined or contemplated joining. Following the entry of the Finnish markka in the ERM in October 1996, the lira came back to the fold in November. As for the other three currencies (of Greece, Sweden, and the UK), there was no prospect of joining the ERM at least in the foreseeable future. On the other hand, entry into the new phase of the EMS did not put an end to the asymmetrical nature of the system. If anything, it seemed to reinforce the ability of the Bundesbank to set the monetary standard.

Like the snake in the 1970s, the EMS has not produced a regional currency system with universal membership. It has become once again a prominent example of a two- (or multi-) tier model of integration, or perhaps more correctly, a model of variable speed since most countries outside it aspire to come in one day. Meanwhile, the new flexibility imposed by the markets has led in some cases to big changes in nominal exchange rates. Figure 7.6 shows the evolution of DM rates between September 1992 and January 1996 for the lira and pound sterling, which had left the ERM, as well as for the peseta and the escudo, which went through successive devaluations while remaining within the wider bands of the new system. During the first two and a half years after the crisis of September 1992, the lira and the peseta lost approximately 35 and 25 per cent, respectively, of their value against the DM. The depreciation of sterling and the escudo against the DM was significantly smaller during the same period. Both the lira and the peseta recovered some of the ground lost subsequently.

It was partly a question of overshooting; but there was more. The depreciation of weaker currencies can largely be explained as a way of compensating for the accumulated loss of external competitiveness during the earlier period (see also Fig. 7.3). It did, however, cause considerable tension inside the Community, because other countries treated this depreciation as an unacceptable form of 'beggar thy

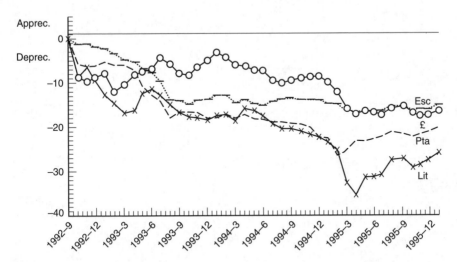

Fig. 7.6. Depreciation of Currencies against the DM, Sept. 1992–Jan. 1996

Note: Price of each ERM currency in terms of the DM; the exchange rates are monthly averages.

Source: Deutsche Bundesbank, Monthly Reports.

Key:
Esc = Portuguese escudo   Lit = Italian lira
Pta = Spanish peseta   £ = sterling

neighbour' policies. In times of low economic growth and unprecedented levels of unemployment, this situation threatened to become politically explosive. At the same time, it served as a useful reminder of the dangers inherent in independent monetary and exchange rate policies in a context of high economic interdependence. Was this worse than a system of rigid exchange rates without the necessary convergence in terms of the economic fundamentals? If only real choices would include some more attractive alternatives. Meanwhile, the Community was preparing for the final stage of EMU.

8

TOWARDS MONETARY UNION

Since the late 1980s, EMU has been back on the European agenda and it is almost certain to occupy the most prominent place for several years to come. It has had a long and chequered history which now goes back almost thirty years starting with the early plans on monetary union.

There is already a huge and still rapidly growing literature on the pros and cons of EMU, the necessary preconditions to be fulfilled before the adoption of a single currency, and the requirements for its successful operation. This should not be surprising; after all, the creation of a monetary union which will bring together some of the oldest and most advanced industrialized economies provides a real world laboratory for the testing of modern economic theories. Economists were bound to rise to the challenge. However, most writings on the subject are of a highly technical nature. Thus, the initiated are separated by high fences and impenetrable jargon from the ordinary folk. This has not always helped economic arguments to enter the political debate. Furthermore, the creation of an EMU has never been treated as a narrow economic issue; and contemporary economists are usually ill at ease with questions of power and prestige which do not lend themselves to quantification.

EMU is a major political issue, because of its wider economic ramifications and also because it touches the very heart of national sovereignty. Without exaggeration, it can be argued that developments in this area will largely determine the future course of European integration and hence also the shape of the emerging new European architecture. Money has frequently been used as an instrument of wider political objectives, even though markets and economic fundamentals have not always obliged by adjusting themselves to the exigencies of high politics.

This chapter will examine the course of negotiations leading to the Maastricht revision of the treaty of which EMU constitutes the most important and concrete part; the interests and the policies of the parties involved; and the main issues at stake ranging from high politics to economic competitiveness and adjustment. Maastricht has provided the general framework, and there is still a great deal to be decided and to be done in preparation for the final stage which is scheduled to begin before the end of the decade. The second part of this chapter will discuss the transitional period and the main obstacles on the road towards a complete EMU. The long-term issues of political and economic viability of EMU will be dealt with in the final part which will also examine the main contributions of economic theory. It will end with some general conclusions about the place of EMU in the process of European integration.

Negotiating EMU: The Primacy of High Politics

The subject of EMU initially came back via the internal market, although no binding commitment had been undertaken in the SEA. An attempt was made, mostly by the Commission, to present EMU as the logical continuation of the internal market programme and exchange rates as another NTB to be eliminated. In the late 1980s, the EMS was still remarkably stable and Euro-euphoria was at its peak; hence the urgency for a political commitment to the next stage of integration while the conditions remained favourable.

Monetary union would be the final and irrevocable confirmation of the reality of the single European market and the European economy. A common currency was seen as the means of welding national economies together, and also the means of accelerating the movement towards political union. And then came the breakdown of the old political division of the European continent, bringing down with it the communist regimes in Central and Eastern Europe and the disintegration of the Soviet Union. It also brought with it the unification of Germany, which acted as a powerful driving force for EMU. The change of the European political scene called for a stronger Community and also a Community which would provide a stable and secure framework for a larger Germany; and money once again served as the main instrument.

Earlier initiatives in the field of European monetary integration had been largely motivated by external preoccupations; the instability of the dollar and US policies of 'unbenign neglect' had served as powerful federalizing factors in Europe. This was not true of the various initiatives which finally led to the new treaty provisions adopted at Maastricht for the establishment of EMU—or, at least, not to the same extent as in the past. True, the reform of the monetary system was not on the cards and the lack of unity among European countries remained an important factor behind the asymmetry in the international system. But this asymmetry was now less evident, the US Administration did not adopt the aggressive stance of its predecessors, and intra-ERM exchange rates appeared at the time less vulnerable to the gyrations of the dollar. Perhaps less preoccupation with external factors was also a sign of the new collective confidence of the Europeans.

The decision to liberalize capital movements provided the catalyst. Padoa-Schioppa (1994: ch.6) talked about the 'inconsistent quartet' of economic objectives. This includes free trade, free capital movements, fixed exchange rates, and monetary autonomy. His conclusion was simple and straightforward: since the EU countries had already committed themselves to the first three objectives, through the internal market, the EMS, and the decision to liberalize capital movements, monetary autonomy would have to give way, moving gradually from an effective coordination of national policies to the centralization of monetary policy at EU level. This is also the main argument on which the Commission strategy was later based: another example of the Commission trying to make full use of functional spillover.

In June 1988 the European Council of Hanover set up the 'Committee for the Study of Economic and Monetary Union', under the chairmanship of the President of the Commission, Mr Delors. This decision was taken only a few months after the adoption of the directive on capital liberalization, and the two were directly linked. The committee included all governors or presidents of EC central banks, an additional member of the Commission plus a small number of independent experts. Its unanimous report was submitted in April 1989 (Delors Report, 1989). There were many similarities with the Werner report which had appeared almost twenty years earlier, something which should come as no surprise since the briefs of the two committees were virtually identical. The final objective in terms of monetary union remained the same, namely the complete liberalization of capital movements, the irrevocable fixity of intra-EC exchange rates, coupled with the elimination of margins of fluctuation (and the eventual replacement of national currencies by a single currency), and the centralization of monetary policy.

The Delors Report was, however, more explicit about the necessary transfer of powers to the level of the union at the final stage and put more emphasis on the institutional changes required. In fact, the central bankers, constituting a large majority in the committee, appeared only too keen to stress the full economic and institutional implications of EMU to their political masters. Much emphasis was placed on the independence of the new institution which would be in charge of monetary policy for the union. This consensus on the question of the independence of the future European central bank reflected not only the composition of the committee but also the leadership and prestige enjoyed by the Deutsche Bundesbank which had provided the role model.

The Delors Report also called for a system of binding rules governing the size and the financing of national budget deficits and referred to the need to determine the overall stance of fiscal policy at the EC level, with decisions taken on a majority basis. The disciplinary influence of market forces on national budgetary policies was not deemed to be sufficient on its own. It did not, however, call for any kind of centralization of budgetary policies nor did it call for the setting up of a new institution at the European level. Subsidiarity, coupled with some constraints on national fiscal autonomy, was the name of the game (Gros and Thygesen, 1992: 311–27; Padoa-Schioppa, 1994: 1–9).

As for the intermediate stages, the strategy of parallelism seemed to have survived the long period separating the publication of the Werner and the Delors reports. In the latter, the major institutional changes were reserved for the second stage of EMU, while the real transfer of powers from the national to the European level would only take place at the final stage. On the other hand, the report stressed that 'the decision to enter upon the first stage should be a decision to embark on the entire process' (p. 31); certainly, not the right message for the faint-hearted.

The Delors Report set the EMU ball rolling; and it did roll very fast indeed. On the basis of the report, a decision was taken at the Madrid European Council of June 1989 to proceed to the first stage of EMU on 1 July 1990 which coincided with the complete liberalization of capital movements in eight members of the Community. This was followed by the decision reached at the European Council in Strasbourg in December of the same year to call for a new IGC to prepare the necessary treaty revisions for a complete EMU. Both decisions were taken unanimously, despite the expressed opposition of the UK and the persisting differences on important aspects of EMU and the nature of the transitional period among the other members.

In a subsequent meeting of the European Council, the date for the second stage of EMU was fixed for January 1994, that is one year after the expected completion of the internal market. Before the official opening of the new IGC in December 1990, a great deal of the preparatory work had already been done in the context of the Committee of the Governors of Central Banks and the Monetary Committee, following closely in the steps of the Delors committee. This included the draft statutes of the European Central Bank. The Commission had also published a major study of the potential costs and benefits of EMU, very much along the lines of the Cecchini report (Commission, 1990c).

Thus, money was once again at the centre of European high politics and commitment to monetary union was almost indistinguishable from the more general commitment to European unification. The second IGC on political union, called in June 1990, was, at least initially, seen as an adjunct to the EMU project. During the negotiations, the economic and political desirability of EMU was not seriously put in question. This matter was supposed to have been already settled. The political decision had been taken at the highest political level, and only the British were ready to express their doubts in public. The other doubters, and they did exist in the other countries, kept a low profile and they preferred to concentrate on specific problems instead of challenging the main principles and objectives. After all, much of the work had already been done by committees of experts. There was very little public debate on the subject of EMU prior to the signing of the treaty, and one important reason was that it was still considered a matter for the *cognoscenti*.

The negotiations revolved around three categories of issues: the institutional framework of EMU; the balance between the monetary and the fiscal arm of the union; and the nature and length of the transitional period leading to a complete EMU, including the criteria for participating in the final stage. The negotiation on the contents and length of the intermediate stages was reminiscent of the old debate between 'economists' and 'monetarists'. The final package deal included in the new treaty contained detailed provisions for the final stage and relatively little on the intermediate stages. Considerations of economic convergence, as a pre-condition for monetary union, were happily married with the natural instinct of politicians and lesser mortals to postpone difficult decisions: 'God, give me virtue (and EMU), but not yet'.

The articles of the new treaty and the related protocols attached to it made provisions for the centralization of monetary and exchange rate policy at the final stage. The European System of Central Banks (ESCB) will be based on a federal structure, composed of the European Central Bank (ECB) and the national central banks, although the precise relationship between the ECB and national central banks still remains to be defined. The latter will operate in accordance with the guidelines and instructions of the ECB. The primary objective of the new institution will be to maintain price stability and it will take no instructions from political authorities. Arrangements for accountability to EU institutions are made, but they are accompanied by strict guarantees of independence from political interference.

The ESCB will define and implement monetary policy for the union as a whole, it will conduct foreign exchange operations, and it will hold and manage the official foreign reserves of member countries. As regards the exchange rate policy of the union, the new treaty allows ECOFIN (Council of Economic and Finance Ministers) a role, notably in the negotiation of international agreements and the formulation of 'general orientations', thus leaving the formulation of exchange rate policy and the division of responsibilities between the ECB and ECOFIN somewhat unclear. The ECB will have the exclusive right to authorize the issue of money. It will not be permitted to lend to governments: any form of 'monetary financing' of governments is prohibited and so is any 'bailing out' of indebted governments and other public institutions. Provision is also made for a future role of the ECB with respect to the prudential supervision of financial institutions, although this will have to be authorized eventually by the Council.

The ECB will be governed by a six-member executive board, including a president and a vice-president, appointed for an eight-year, non-renewable term by the European Council; and a governing council consisting of the members of the executive board and the governors of the national central banks. In order to further ensure the independence of the ESCB, national legislation regulating the operation of national central banks will also have to be changed accordingly. Thus, entry into the third and final stage of EMU will imply not only the transfer of monetary powers from the national to the European level, but also a very significant change in relations between political authorities and central banks. The Bundesbank has provided the example to follow.

The Maastricht treaty did not create any new institution for the conduct of fiscal policies, which will remain a national responsibility, nor was there any mention of fiscal federalism which might lead to the creation of a much bigger EU budget. The treaty did, however, make provisions for the strengthening of existing mechanisms of multilateral surveillance, while also attempting to define in some detail what constitutes 'economically correct' behaviour. On the basis of a recommendation made by the Commission, ECOFIN will draft each year 'the broad guidelines of the economic policies of the Member States and of the Community' (Article 103); but these guidelines could easily remain a list of pious wishes. There are, however, much stricter provisions for the profligate members, which are introduced through the so-called excessive deficit procedure (Article 104*c* and the attached protocol). The ceilings of 3 per cent for public deficits and

60 per cent for public debt in terms of GDP, adopted as part of the convergence criteria for admission to the final stage of EMU (see below), will also be used as reference values for the assessment of national budgetary policies.

On the basis of reports prepared by the Commission, which is thereby given the role of a watchdog, ECOFIN will decide by qualified majority whether a situation of excessive deficit exists in a member country. A whole range of measures will then be available to the Council, from public recommendations to the imposition of fines. In between, the Council may resort to other measures such as requiring the EIB to reconsider its lending policy to the particular member country and asking the latter to make non-interest bearing deposits with the Community.

This is certainly not 'soft' coordination; but is it politically realistic? Except for extreme cases, the excessive deficit procedure should be expected to rely mostly on a combination of peer and market pressure, the two being usually mutually reinforcing. Small countries which also happen to be major beneficiaries of the Structural Funds (there is, in fact, an explicit link in the treaty between transfers from the new Cohesion Fund and macroeconomic policy) will undoubtedly prove more vulnerable to collective pressure than others. On the other hand, since the reference values for public deficits and debts are also part of the convergence criteria which will determine a country's participation in the final stage of EMU, the actual constraints on national budgetary policies should prove tighter during the intermediate period rather than after the establishment of a complete EMU. Hence the worries expressed by defenders of financial orthodoxy.

The new treaty provides for the establishment of EMU in three stages. The first stage, which had already started in July 1990, was meant as a consolidation of the status quo. It was supposed to include the liberalization of capital movements and the inclusion of all currencies in the narrow band of the ERM. Unfortunately, markets did not share this view; thus, instead of consolidation, there has been a breakdown of the old ERM.

The second stage started as planned on 1 January 1994. The main purpose of this intermediate stage is to secure the economic convergence of member countries in preparation for the complete EMU. The Committee of Governors of Central Banks has been replaced by the European Monetary Institute (EMI) with its seat in Frankfurt (which is also expected to be the seat of the future ECB) and Mr Lamfalussy, a highly respected Belgian economist and banker, as its first president. The EMI has several tasks, including the strengthening of the co-ordination of monetary policies, which remain during the second stage a national responsibility, the monitoring of the EMS, the execution of tasks previously assigned to the EMCF which is now dissolved, and, most importantly, the technical preparations for the third stage. Its life-span will be rather short: it will be replaced by the ECB at the beginning of the third stage.

The most crucial part of the transitional arrangements relates to the conditions to be fulfilled at the beginning of the third and final stage. The latter will start with the irrevocable fixity of the exchange rates of those currencies participating in it, to be followed by the 'rapid introduction' of the single currency which will thus replace national currencies. The definition of speed, moving from irrevocably fixed exchange rates to a single currency, was to be decided later. According to the treaty, the European Council would decide on the basis of reports from the Commission and the EMI whether each individual country fulfils the conditions for admission to the final stage. The third stage would begin on 1 January 1997 only if the majority of member countries were found to fulfil those conditions. A qualified majority decision about whether there is a majority fit to enjoy the fruits of paradise (and EMU): this would be a rather uncommon case in international and even domestic politics.

In fact, the authors of the new treaty went further. It was stipulated that the third stage would start on 1 January 1999 at the latest, irrespective of how many member countries were found to fulfil the necessary conditions at the time; again the European Council was to decide on each case on the basis of qualified majority. Those failing the test would remain in 'derogation' and, to all intents and purposes, they would be excluded from the new institutional framework. Their case would, however, be examined at least every two years. Voluntary 'opt-outs' were added to provisions for temporary derogations, thus turning EMU into a new kind of experiment with variable speed and multi-tier forms of integration. Because the UK refused to commit itself in advance to participating in the final stage of EMU, it secured an 'opt-out' protocol which left the decision for a future government and parliament. Denmark chose a softer version of 'opting out': in this case, the relevant protocol referred to the possibility of a referendum prior to Denmark's participation in the final stage.

The conditions for admission to the final stage, otherwise known as convergence criteria, are quite explicit and they concentrate exclusively on monetary variables. The first convergence criterion refers to a sustainable price performance, defined in the attached protocol as a rate of inflation which does not exceed that of the best performing member countries by more than 1.5 percentage points. The second relates to the sustainability of the government financial position: the actual or planned deficit should not exceed 3 per cent of GDP, while the accumulated public debt should not be above 60 per cent of GDP. With respect to this criterion, the wording of the new Article 104c of the treaty leaves some margin for manoeuvre: it allows for higher deficits as long as they have been declining 'substantially and continuously' or are considered to be 'exceptional and temporary'; and it also allows for higher government debt on the condition that the latter is 'sufficiently diminishing and approaching the reference value at a satisfactory pace'. The wording is thus vague enough to allow room for interpretation.

Exchange rate stability is the third criterion: the national currency must have remained within the 'normal' fluctuation margins of the ERM for at least two years prior to the decision about the final stage, without any devaluation and without any severe tension. Since the widening of the bands in August 1993, 'normal' is expected to be defined as the existing margins of the ERM. The fourth criterion refers to the durability of the convergence: the average nominal interest rate on long-term government bonds has been chosen as the appropriate indicator and it should not exceed that of the three best performing member states by more than two percentage points.

Thus, the Maastricht treaty went into considerable detail (arguably excessive for a document which serves as the constitution of the emerging European political system) in describing the final stage of EMU and the criteria for what should constitute 'economically correct' behaviour as a precondition for entry; the rest was more flexible and less precise. It was a typical Community compromise. The French got a clear commitment enshrined in the treaty as well as a specific date. The Germans made sure that the date would be distant, with little happening in between, and that the new European model would be as close as possible to their own. The British, followed by the Danes, secured an 'opt-out' for themselves, while the poor countries obtained a more or less explicit link with redistribution.

The driving force for the relaunching of monetary union came from Brussels and Paris, with EMU representing the flagship of the European strategy of both the Commission (Mr Delors in particular) and the French government. The Commission saw in EMU the consolidation of the internal market and the further strengthening of European political construction. It was the inevitable next step in the process of integration. As for France, it had always been in favour of fixed exchange rates. Its politicians had never believed in the stability or efficiency of financial markets which were often caricatured as a den of Anglo-Saxon speculators. For France, the move towards a complete EMU would help to end the asymmetrical nature of the existing system and would therefore secure for the country a stronger say in the conduct of European monetary policy. Last but not least, money provided the instrument for integrating the German giant more tightly into the Community system.

Initially, Germany showed very little enthusiasm: the government and the central bank were happy with the status quo and any move towards monetary union was perceived, quite rightly, as leading to the erosion of Germany's independence in the monetary field. In purely economic terms, there was in fact precious little advantage for the Germans in a monetary union; assuming, of course, that some kind of a regional currency arrangement which helps to contain the overvaluation of the DM can be taken for granted. The main gain for the Germans for most of the period of the EMS was the stability of exchange rates for much of German trade and the gain in competitiveness; and this has always been a very important consideration, arguably more important for politicians and industrialists than for central bankers (see also Fig. 7.4(*a*); and CEPR, 1995*a*). On the other hand, there is no doubt that an EMS in which Germany sets the monetary standard is infinitely better for the Germans than a monetary union in which they will have to share with others the power to run monetary policy.

What finally tipped the balance was the perceived need to reaffirm the country's commitment to European integration in the wake of German unification. This is how the matter was presented in Brussels and Paris. Thus, the German decision (Chancellor Kohl's to be precise) to proceed with EMU was highly political (see also Garrett, 1994; Woolley, 1994). Mr Kohl spoke of economic and monetary integration as a matter 'of war and peace in the 21st century' (quoted in *Financial Times*, 19 October 1995); and this statement is highly indicative of his approach to the subject. His predecessor, Mr Schmidt, would almost certainly have subscribed to it; and so would Presidents Mitterrand and Giscard d'Estaing. The stakes were very high; or so was the perception of political leaders in both Germany and France. The strong link established between EMU and political union made German policy more internally consistent than that of many of its partners, although the link may also occasionally have served as an excuse for keeping the EMU project on the shelf forever.

The combination of different factors, namely the relative weight of the country, its high reputation in terms of monetary stability, especially among European central bankers, and its strong preference for the status quo, has enormously strengthened the negotiating power of Germany, thus enabling it in most cases to impose its own terms with respect to the transition and the contents of the final stage of EMU. The arrangements for the final stage are very much along German lines, even though Germany would have liked even more strict rules with respect to the excessive deficit procedure. Not surprisingly, German representatives have been pushing in this direction subsequent to the ratification of the Maastricht treaty. The convergence criteria also strongly reflect German preferences. Although arguably they may make little economic sense, they will help to restrict, at least for some time, the number of countries allowed into the final stage; and Germany would have ideally liked to have a veto on this issue (de Grauwe, 1994).

A monetary union without Germany makes no sense; and Germany will not have a monetary union unless it is on its own terms. Until now this has been the bottom line; and it has been recognized as such by the other countries. The bargaining power of Germany has also been evident in many decisions taken since the treaty on European Union has come into force: the choice of seat for the EMI, the renaming of the single currency which will be called the Euro (the ECU having been identified in Germany with a relatively weak currency), as well as the timetable for the introduction of the single currency which will extend over a period of more than three years. The monetary area is where German power has been most pronounced; and this is likely to change after the entry into the final phase, hence the attempt made by the Germans to exact as high a price as possible for allowing this to happen. They would argue that they only want to make sure that the new European currency is at least as stable and strong as the Deutschmark, and the German public seems to wholeheartedly support this argument.

Once a Franco-German agreement had been reached on the subject of EMU, the process appeared almost unstoppable, thus repeating earlier patterns of European decision-making. The Dutch shared much of the economic scepticism of the Germans, but their margin of manoeuvre was extremely limited. Belgium and Luxembourg were fervent supporters, although Belgium was at the same time extremely concerned in case a strict application of the convergence criteria kept it outside the privileged group, because of its very high public debt. Denmark felt almost like a natural member of the European currency area, although its politicians were not at all sure whether they would be able to carry the population with them into a monetary union; hence the 'opt-out' protocol.

The main concern of the Southern countries was to link EMU to more substantial budgetary transfers and also to avoid an institutionalization of two or more tiers in the Community: they were only partially successful, more with the former than with the latter. Ireland benefited from the transfers and felt more secure than its Southern brethren that it would be among the first to obtain an entry ticket into the final stage. It would, however, have preferred that the other island separating it from the continent would also join since so much of its trade is still done with it.

As for Britain, it remained the only country to question in public the desirability and feasibility of EMU, on both economic and political grounds. The situation had apparently changed little since 1979. Realizing its isolation, the Conservative government made a conscious effort to remain in the negotiating table. In the end, it reconciled itself to an 'opt-out' provision in the treaty. The exchange crisis of September 1992 forced sterling out of the ERM, while also inflicting heavy financial losses on the Bank of England. At the same time, this constituted a heavy blow for the prestige of the Conservative government. Thus, it further reduced the chances of Britain being among the first to enter the final stage (see also Taylor, 1995).

In terms of decision-making, the negotiation on EMU during the Maastricht IGC bears considerable resemblance to earlier European initiatives and especially the one which had previously led to the adoption of the internal market programme. The gradual build-up of momentum, the steady expansion of the political support base through coalition building, and the isolation of opponents were combined with an effective marketing campaign orchestrated by the Commission and addressed primarily towards opinion leaders and the business community (the wider public was destined to enjoy the fruits of such a campaign later, when Brussels discovered that the attractions of EMU were not so obvious to everybody). Functional spillover was also successfully mixed with high politics and the appeal to 'Euro-sentiment'—a recipe which had proved quite powerful in the past.

Central bankers, who are absolutely crucial for the successful implementation of the EMU project, have been closely involved from an early stage, notably through their participation in the Delors committee and subsequently in the drafting of the ECB statutes. They have also been responsible for the everyday running of the EMS. In contrast, domestic interest groups and the wider public have played hardly any role during the negotiations. EMU became a political issue only after the signing of the treaty; and popular reactions came as an unpleasant surprise to most politicians. EMU has since become identified with deflationary policies at times of high unemployment; and this hardly helps to make it an object of love for European citizens.

A Long and Bumpy Road Leading to Narrow Gates

The Maastricht treaty met with little applause from European societies and international markets alike. What proved to be an agonizing process of ratification of the treaty coincided with the turmoil in the exchange markets, and the two became mutually reinforcing. The treaty (and the part on EMU) survived in the end, while the EMS suffered serious damage. The withdrawal of currencies and the widening of the margins of fluctuation to 15 per cent for those remaining in the system was not the most auspicious way to start the journey towards the irrevocable fixity of exchange rates and the introduction of a single currency. It did not sound at all promising, although the more flexible ERM, created as a consequence of the crisis, may in the end prove to be a vehicle with much greater endurance for the long and bumpy road leading to the final stage of EMU.

A short time later, the return to higher rates of growth, coupled with the greater stability in exchange markets, helped to bring the EMU project back on the agenda, thus confirming once again the strong sensitivity of the process of European integration in general to the economic state of affairs. The process soon gathered new momentum and thus the establishment of a complete EMU before the end of the decade became once again a credible proposition. The creation of the EMI in 1994, which happened with entry into the second stage, made a real difference in terms of the analytical work and the technical preparations needed for the final stage. In addition to the publication of annual reports and the monitoring of the economic performance of member countries, the EMI has started work on the operation of a common monetary and exchange rate policy, on statistics and payments systems, on the design of new banknotes and coins, on harmonization of the accounting rules of participating national banks and information on communications systems, on banking supervision, and on a host of legal questions.

A number of important decisions were taken at the European Council meeting in Madrid in December 1995. It was first of all agreed that the final stage of EMU would start on 1 January 1999, thus officially dropping the option of 1997 mentioned in the treaty. The crucial and highly sensitive decision about which countries fulfil the convergence criteria will need to be taken early in 1998 on the basis of the relevant data for the previous year. The final stage will start with the irrevocable fixing of conversion rates among participating currencies and against the Euro, which is the name finally adopted for the single currency instead of the hapless ECU. At the same time, the ECB and the ESCB should also be in operation.

The Madrid Council adopted the scenario for the changeover to the single currency, following the introduction of the final stage. It veered on the cautious side, which was also the attitude previously adopted by the Bundesbank and the EMI. Thus, the withdrawal of national currencies will be very gradual after the entry into the final stage. According to this decision, the Euro and those national currencies participating in the final stage of EMU will coexist, with conversion rates established (and protected against speculation?) by law, until July 2002 when the Euro is planned to become the only legal tender. Banknotes and coins in Euro will begin to circulate at the latest by 1 January 2002. In the meantime, private economic agents will be able to use the Euro in their financial transactions, while public authorities will gradually shift from national currencies to the new European currency in the issuing of new public debt.

Following earlier discussions which had taken place in ECOFIN, the Madrid Council identified two major outstanding questions which would require answers before the beginning of the third stage. The first question relates to the kind of arrangements needed to ensure budgetary discipline in the context of monetary union, thus implicitly accepting that the provisions made in the Maastricht treaty were not sufficient, or at least that they would need further elaboration. The Germans were already pressing for the adoption of a 'stability pact' which would go further than the excessive deficit procedure mentioned in the treaty.

The second question is about relations between the 'ins' and the 'outs' (or the 'pre-ins', as those more optimistic prefer to call them) after entry into the final stage. Would the 'outs' participate in a new kind of ERM, would the ECB intervene in exchange markets to influence the exchange rate of those currencies, and what kind of coordination of policies and budgetary discipline should apply to countries in 'derogation' or with an 'opt-out'? Fearing competitive devaluations, France was keen on establishing a mechanism which would impose some discipline on the 'outs'. Typically, Britain was fervently arguing in favour of a complete freedom in the conduct of economic policy and exchange rate policy.

In the context of an internal market, should participation in a system of stable exchange rates, involving also a close coordination of monetary policies, constitute a minimum requirement for all member countries? This is the view expressed by the authors of a CEPR report, who argue that 'attempts to improve competitiveness through the discretionary use of monetary policy, or through policies that merely reallocate production across countries' could cause serious disruption (CEPR, 1995a: 98–9). This view is shared by the large majority of member governments; but will they be able to impose it on everybody?

The Union has been preparing for the crucial meeting scheduled for the early months of 1998 when the select few(?) will be chosen for the final stage of EMU. Experience tells us that in the meantime anything could happen. In many respects, the best transitional period is the shortest one. The Community has opted instead for a rather long transitional period; for economic reasons which are, however, hotly debated among economists and for political reasons which are, perhaps, more understandable. In fact, the transitional period, and the uncertainty associated with it, will not completely end with the selection of the first countries to participate in the final stage. There will be another short, but potentially dangerous, period between this decision and the irrevocable fixing of exchange rates, which is expected to happen in January 1999. And then, there will be more than three years until the Euro takes over completely as the single currency. This is more than enough time for markets to undo the plans designed by politicians.

The journey to EMU will therefore be dangerously long and prone to many accidents. The credibility of the project will depend on the continuous interaction between governments, societies, and markets. With very few exceptions, EU governments seem to be committed to the objective of a complete EMU and to the pursuit of policies aimed at fulfilling the convergence criteria, thus ensuring their early participation in the final stage. This does, however, imply the pursuit of restrictive policies, especially in order to meet the convergence criterion relating to public deficits and debts. Will the electorates go along with these in times of high unemployment?

In the late months of 1995, EMU was fought in the streets of Paris, when mass demonstrations took place against the cuts in welfare expenditure announced by the French government. And there may be more to come in France and elsewhere. Markets will also be constantly judging the credibility of the project as well as the credibility of existing exchange rates. Markets are far from infallible; but they have the power to turn their collective perceptions into reality. On the other hand, the wider margins of fluctuation adopted in August 1993 should provide a greater margin of manoeuvre for governments during the transitional period leading to the irrevocable fixing of exchange rates. And assuming that they manage to get there, what would then happen, if the markets decided to test the meaning of 'irrevocable'? With this dangerous prospect in mind, the EU may in the end experiment with legal measures intended to shield those irrevocably fixed exchange rates against market speculators.

The remaining part of the journey to EMU will be highly sensitive to changes in the political and the economic weather. A prolonged period of economic recovery would greatly facilitate the journey; but such a recovery will not be helped by the kind of budgetary policies which need to be pursued in conformity with the convergence criteria. The political climate, especially in the two most important countries, namely France and Germany, is another unknown variable. The credibility of EMU will also be influenced by the progress, if not the outcome, of the new IGC which started in March 1996. Although EMU does not figure on the agenda, the outcome of the negotiations is bound to influence the political climate in the EU and hence the prospects for monetary union.

The convergence criteria, on the basis of which admission to the final stage will be decided by qualified majority in the European Council, following reports by the Commission and the EMI, can be criticized on many grounds (de Grauwe, 1994; CEPR, 1995a). They are mechanistic, some of them are arbitrary and, perhaps, also superfluous. Worst of all, they may actually do serious damage by contributing to a deterioration in the macroeconomic environment and thus undermining the political and social acceptability of the EMU project.

How much convergence in terms of inflation rates is needed before the adoption of a new monetary regime? Does it really matter so much what the inflation rate is in, say, Italy prior to the establishment of a complete EMU, when the latter implies the creation of a new currency and the transfer of power in terms of monetary policy from the Banca d'Italia to the ECB? Such questions relate to the old controversy between 'economists' and 'monetarists'.

The absolute numbers adopted in terms of public deficits and debts are totally arbitrary. No provision has been made for cyclical adjustment in terms of public deficits, and this problem became very clear during the recession of the early 1990s when almost all member countries exceeded the ceiling adopted at Maastricht. The 60 per cent rule for public debt says very little indeed about the sustainability of a country's financial position. Compare, for example, the case of Belgium on the one hand, where a very large public debt has coexisted for years with low inflation and nominal interest rates, both short- and long-term, and also low current deficits, with the case of Italy and Greece on the other, where the situation has been very different. The Maastricht criteria will largely determine the macroeconomic policies pursued by member countries during the transitional period; and they will be highly restrictive policies in most member countries.

The exchange rate criterion is no longer very stringent, since the 'normal' bands are now very wide making membership of the ERM easier. But will the two-year rule be enforced? The haste of the Finns and the Italians to join the ERM before the end of 1996 needs to be understood in this context. Furthermore, the choice of long-term nominal interest rates as an indicator of the credibility of inflation convergence in the market-place, is indeed highly questionable and the two-percentage point differential allowed for in the treaty is arguably too wide.

Last but not least, the convergence criteria adopted do not refer to any real economic variables. For example, can a temporary fall in inflation achieved at the expense of high unemployment be sustainable, since the disinflationary policy is apparently not credible in labour markets (Gros and Thygesen, 1992)? The convergence criteria are based on the assumption that there is no real trade-off between price stability on the one hand and growth and employment on the other. According to the Commission: 'The old theory that there is a trade-off between high inflation and low unemployment is now unsupported as a matter of theory or empirical analysis, except for short-run periods' (Commission, 1990c: 22). Although the short run may be a long time in politics, this statement is, in fact, consistent with the economic paradigm prevailing at the time.

Arguably, adjustment for countries with higher inflation rates and/or higher public deficits and debts would be easier in a monetary union than during a rather long transitional period leading to it, as long as the appropriate rules were adopted to ensure the credibility of the new monetary regime. Several proposals have been made in this direction to try to shift the focus away from the convergence criteria as a precondition for entry into the EMU and towards the adoption of tighter constraints in the conduct of national budgetary policies in the context of a monetary union (see, for example, the proposals made by Paul de Grauwe, *Financial Times*, 17 October 1995; Barry Eichengreen, Jürgen von Hagen, and Ian Harden, *Financial Times*, 28 November 1995). Thus, the transitional period could be made shorter, the risk of destabilizing speculation during this period could be reduced, and the admission of countries to the final stage would be made easier. The price to pay would be further constraints in terms of national budgetary autonomy, including heavier sanctions, during the final stage.

In economic terms, the convergence criteria could be viewed at best as a very rough (and also ephemeral) indicator of the stability orientation of countries to be admitted into the final stage. This could, arguably, influence the credibility of EMU and the new monetary institution which will be entrusted with the management of the common monetary and exchange rate policy. In other words, the credibility of the ECB could be seen as a function not only of the rules governing

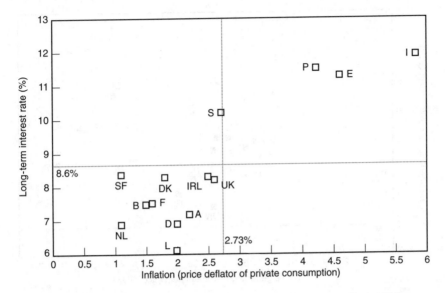

Fig. 8.1. Convergence Criteria: Inflation and Long-Term Interest Rates, 1995

Note: For Greece, no data were available for long-term interest rates; the inflation rate was 9.3%.

Source: Commission

Key:
A = Austria   B = Belgium   D = Germany   DK = Denmark
E = Spain   F = France   IRL = Ireland   I = Italy
L = Luxembourg   NL = Netherlands   P = Portugal   S = Sweden
SF = Finland   UK = United Kingdom

its behaviour but also of the recent history of countries allowed to participate in the monetary union and hence also in the ECB (through independent and largely unaccountable technocrats). This would, therefore, call for economic convergence as a precondition for EMU, which is the old 'economist' argument and which also happens to receive very wide support in a country like Germany. This is the other side of the coin. Winkler has tried to reconcile the above two arguments: 'Gradualism is the enemy of the credibility of stage two, while gradualism is the friend of credibility in stage three (1995: 18). Economics is an inexact science, and politics the art of the possible; hence the very imperfect product of Maastricht.

The transition to a complete EMU will make no sense without Germany and France. Thus, the beginning of the final stage depends on whether those two countries are able to meet the criteria set out at Maastricht, with the possibility that some of those criteria may need to be interpreted in a rather loose manner. On the basis of 1995 data, neither country fulfilled all criteria, both failing to meet the public deficit criterion (Figs. 8.1 and 8.2). It is possible, although far from easy, that they will succeed in doing so before 1998. Certainly, the budgetary plans of both the French and German governments for 1997 aim in this direction; and so do the budgetary plans of the large majority of other member governments,

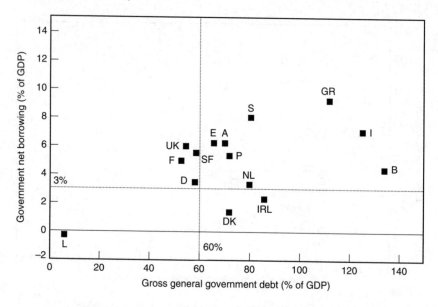

Fig. 8.2. Convergence Criteria: Government Net Borrowing and Gross General Government Debt, 1995

Source: Commission.
Key:

A = Austria	B = Belgium	D = Germany	DK = Denmark
E = Spain	F = France	IRL = Ireland	I = Italy
L = Luxembourg	NL = Netherlands	P = Portugal	S = Sweden
SF = Finland	UK = United Kingdom		

even though sometimes resorting to dubious accounting practices in order to satisfy the 3 per cent budgetary criterion.

The decision about which countries qualify for entry into the final stage, which should be taken during the first half of 1998, promises to be one of the most difficult and politically loaded decisions, given that the convergence criteria allow some room for interpretation. Any predictions are therefore extremely hazardous. Assuming that France and Germany do qualify, the most likely candidates to join them in the first group of countries to be admitted to the final stage are the countries whose currencies have been operating without interruption within the 'normal' fluctuation bands, both old and new, of the ERM. Figures 8.1 and 8.2 as well as the predictions made for 1997 suggest that they are all fairly close to meeting the criteria. In fact, Luxembourg already did in 1995, and so did Ireland and Denmark with a more flexible interpretation of the debt criterion which has already been applied by ECOFIN in both cases.

In this group of 'stability-minded' countries, there are, however, two problem cases. Denmark may in the end be able but unwilling. Its politicians and central bankers seem to appreciate the benefits of the ERM and may also be keen to join; but will they be allowed by the Danish population which seems to attach great importance to national independence and sovereignty, even though these may be very relative concepts in the case of a small and open economy? On the other hand, Belgium will present a difficult political dilemma: a country which has participated all along in European currency arrangements, with a stable currency, a low inflation rate, and a relatively small public deficit, but also with the highest public debt as a percentage of GDP among all members of the Union. Should Belgium be allowed in and what kind of precedent would such a decision set for other countries?

In 1995, the UK met some of the convergence criteria. But public deficit was significantly above the reference value and the exchange rate criterion was also not met since sterling had left the ERM in September 1992. The UK could be part of the group of those able to join, but would it be willing even with a Labour government? Two new members of the Union, namely Austria and Finland, stand a good chance of meeting all the criteria before 1998. Austria joined the new ERM in January 1995, and Finland followed it in October 1996. As for Sweden, the question is as much economic as it is political.

The Southern countries are among the least likely candidates for early membership. On the basis of 1995 data, they met none of the criteria. Greece has already reconciled itself to the hard reality of being a willing but unable candidate for the 1998 selection, thus aiming for the next round. The other Southern countries are likely to strive hard to meet the criteria on time, although this will be a difficult task. Italy is likely to present the most difficult problem. Its exclusion, even though temporary, from the select group participating in the final stage would be politically loaded: it is after all a founding member of the Community and also a big country which has always supported moves towards further integration. In economic terms, however, its participation may be difficult to reconcile with the need to strengthen the credibility of EMU, especially in its early stages, because of Italy's large public debt and its poor record in terms of stability-minded policies.

Thus, the application of the convergence criteria may involve some difficult political decisions and the haggling which usually accompanies such decisions. The strong possibility that at least several EU members will be excluded from the first selection, coupled with the economic, political, and institutional importance of EMU, means that a major, new step will have been taken in the direction of a multi-tier and multi-speed Community. The rights and obligations of those who stay out, willingly or otherwise, still remain to be defined.

Living in an EMU

There has been a rapidly growing literature on the economics of EMU. In general, economists have expressed considerable scepticism about the project, although they have quickly seized the opportunity to undertake (well-paid) research on its various aspects. True, several economists, among the most reputable and also among the most prolific, have argued in favour of EMU; but the arguments put forward have often been political rather than economic. European institutions, and the Commission in particular, have invested much money and mental energy in order to influence informed opinion; and the effect has not been insignificant.

The benefits of monetary union are first of all linked to savings in currency conversion and other transaction costs. These are, however, estimated to be very small (Commission, 1990c; see also de Grauwe, 1992; Gros and Thygesen, 1992; Taylor, 1995). There are also the gains associated with the elimination of exchange rate variability and uncertainty. In this respect, the dynamic gains could be considerable, but also impossible to quantify. For precisely this reason, economists have generally tended to underestimate those gains. On the other hand, the creation of a single currency would improve the transparency of prices and would secure further the credibility of the internal market and the gains associated with its completion; 'one market' and now 'one money'.

Another important argument presented in favour of EMU is the achievement of price stability. This does, however, depend on assumptions about the policy stance and the credibility of the new European Central Bank; and the expected gains would vary enormously from Germany to Italy and Greece. Given their inflation record, it is not at all surprising that EMU has always enjoyed wide popular support in the latter two countries. On the other hand, the adoption of a single European currency is supposed to bring seigniorage gains resulting from the readiness of outsiders to hold the new currency. An international currency would also be accompanied by gains in prestige and political power, associated with the pursuit of a common monetary policy *vis-à-vis* the rest of the world. But here again, there is a host of implicit assumptions (Goodhart, 1993); and would there be anything for the Germans who already enjoy the benefits, real or imaginary, of an international currency? The implications of EMU for the rest of the world and the role of the Euro as an international means of payment and reserve are bound to become hotly debated issues.

As for the expected costs of a monetary union, they are directly related to the scope and the effectiveness of an independent monetary policy, including the use of interest rates and the exchange rate, which will have to be abandoned in a monetary union. How effective are those policy instruments and how frequently would national monetary authorities need to make use of them? On this question, there is a wide variety of views among economists.

Very few would argue that the EU is an optimum currency area. This is a concept which became very popular in the literature during the 1960s when economists looked for factors which could act as near substitutes for the exchange rate instrument; such factors also being, usually, good indicators of the degree of economic integration inside the potential currency area (Mundell, 1961; McKinnon, 1963; see also Krugman, 1990). That means that economic integration inside the EU has not yet reached the level where capital and especially labour mobility could act as near substitutes for changes in the exchange rate; or that wages and prices in different countries are sufficiently flexible so as to make exchange rate realignments redundant; or even that the EU economy is sufficiently homogeneous so that different countries and regions are not frequently subject to asymmetric external shocks. But is this true of the United States or even Italy, and if not, are those countries optimum currency areas? It is largely a matter of degree.

Of course, some differentiation is needed with respect to individual countries. The attachment to stable, although not necessarily irrevocably fixed, exchange rates is usually closely related to the openness of an economy to international trade. In the case of the EU, the readiness of individual countries to accept the implications of a monetary union should also be a function of the relative importance of intra-regional trade. A broad distinction can be drawn between small and big countries in the EU as regards their openness to international trade (Table 8.1). The Benelux countries and Ireland on the one hand and the Big Four (France, Germany, Italy, and the UK) on the other fit nicely into those two categories. By comparison, Greece and Spain are still relatively closed economies (at least in terms of trade in goods, since the inclusion of services would significantly modify this picture), while Denmark and Portugal find themselves in between the two groups; and this also applies to the three new members.

As for the importance of intra-EU trade, this is relatively more pronounced in the case of the Benelux countries and Ireland, although differences between member countries have gradually diminished over the years. Intra-EU trade represented on average approximately 60 per cent of total trade before the 1995 enlargement; it has risen further as a result of the latter. Interestingly enough, the corresponding percentages for Austria, Finland, and Sweden were similar even before they joined the EU; economic (and, of course, geographic) realities often precede political institutions and treaties.

Views on the relative effectiveness of the exchange rate instrument and the desirable margin of manoeuvre for monetary policy depend very much on whether a Keynesian or a rational expectations model is adopted. Rejecting the existence of a trade-off between inflation and unemployment, except in the very short term, the latter puts the emphasis on policy credibility and its advocates generally aim at tying the hands of policy-makers (Taylor, 1995; Winkler, 1995).

Only a small minority of economists (including the so-called global monetarists) would go as far as arguing the complete ineffectiveness of the exchange rate as an instrument of adjustment, even for a small and open economy such as Belgium. Yet, the EU countries have increasingly found themselves in the uncomfortable state in which, while national wages and prices still have a life of their own, being a function of history, political institutions, social traditions, and labour power among other factors, and while the need for adjustment differs considerably from one country to the other and from one period to the next, the effectiveness of the exchange rate has become progressively curtailed, even before the instrument is politically banished. Matters will, of course, become even more uncomfortable if the move towards monetary union is not accompanied by a corresponding convergence in some of the economic fundamentals. The loss of the exchange rate instrument, while the need for real adjustment continues to exist and labour mobility as well as wage and price flexibility remain too weak to

Table 8.1. Openness of EU Economies, 1960–1994 (Average of imports and exports of goods as a percentage of GDP[a]; intra-EU trade is given as a % of total trade)

	1960–7		1968–72		1973–9		1980–4		1985–90		1991–4	
	World	Intra-EU	World	Intra-EU	World	Intra-EU	World	Intra-EU	World	Intra-EU	World	Intra-EU
Belgium and Luxembourg	37.5	64.8	42.8	71.2	48.9	71.2	61.5	67.0	60.8	71.7	53.3	70.0
Denmark	27.0	52.3	23.4	46.7	25.3	48.2	29.1	49.1	26.7	50.8	25.4	53.0
Germany	15.9	44.8	17.6	50.9	20.4	50.3	24.8	50.5	24.9	53.1	20.7	52.2
Greece	12.7	50.6	12.7	53.4	17.6	47.3	19.5	48.1	20.8	60.5	17.0	59.2
Spain	8.1	47.8	9.2	44.4	11.2	41.3	14.4	39.3	14.4	56.0	15.2	62.9
France	11.0	45.8	12.5	57.2	16.6	55.0	18.9	53.9	18.6	61.9	18.7	63.3
Ireland	33.6	72.2	35.3	71.6	45.8	74.3	50.1	73.1	52.0	72.2	50.3	68.8
Italy	11.7	42.9	13.1	49.5	18.4	48.7	19.4	46.1	16.9	55.0	15.9	56.4
Netherlands	37.7	62.7	36.4	67.8	40.6	65.9	47.8	64.1	49.0	67.8	43.9	65.9
Portugal	19.8	48.3	20.3	49.6	22.2	50.2	30.1	50.1	32.5	65.1	28.5	73.3
United Kingdom	16.0	26.7	16.7	31.2	22.3	37.9	21.6	44.1	21.0	49.9	20.2	52.1
EU-12	8.8	45.0	8.3	51.0	10.2	52.6	11.5	52.2	9.8	59.8	8.9	58.6
Austria	—	—	—	—	—	—	—	—	—	—	25.6	66.1
Finland	—	—	—	—	—	—	—	—	—	—	22.4	46.7
Sweden	—	—	—	—	—	—	—	—	—	—	23.6	54.9

Note:

[a] Figures for world trade as a % of GDP have been calculated by inserting country data for imports and exports of goods (SITC categories 0–9) in the formula:

$$\frac{\frac{1}{2}\sum(x+m)}{GDP} \times 100.$$

For the Member States, these figures include intra-Union trade; for EU-12, intra-Union trade has been excluded.

Source: Eurostat.

act as effective substitutes, could turn whole countries into depressed regions. This is what most of the economic argument boils down to.

The scepticism with respect to EMU shown by many academic economists (and central bankers, until they began to discover with considerable delight that participation in the EMS and the future EMU went hand in hand with greater independence for themselves *vis-à-vis* elected representatives) does not, however, mean they are in favour of free floating. Exchange markets, and all financial markets, have shown repeatedly their inherent instability. Economic fundamentals play little role in the short term, and the herd instinct leads to so-called overshooting. There is also the real danger of competitive devaluations engineered by national authorities in the pursuit of international competitiveness.

For those reasons, many economists (although certainly not those whose admiration for the magic of the market remains undiluted) would therefore be in favour of a system of fixed but periodically adjustable exchange rates for a group of countries with a high degree of economic interdependence, such as the members of the EU. Such a system would have to be based on a close coordination of monetary policies. But they would also be wary of the apparent tendency of governments to forget progressively the adjustable part of the arrangement. The experience of the third phase of the EMS is quite indicative. There is certainly no agreement among economists about the costs of exchange rate instability on the real economy nor is there any consensus about the ability of governments to manage the exchange rate. Recognizing in the end that the decision to set up a complete EMU is essentially a political decision, many economists have in recent years concentrated more on the necessary conditions to make EMU viable. Long debates about economic optimality had not after all led anywhere.

A very important factor which acts as an effective instrument of stabilization in existing monetary unions are the automatic transfers taking place through the budgetary process. Here, a distinction needs to be drawn between the stabilization function of a budget, which is intended to deal with fluctuations in economic activity, and the redistribution function which has a more permanent character. In the words of Goodhart and Smith (1993: 419): 'Differences in the level of fiscal variables that are functions of the level of economic activity are essentially redistributive, whilst differences in fiscal variables that are a function of the rate of change of economic activity constitute stabilization'. In real life, there is, of course, a considerable overlap between the two. Inter-regional transfers are very sizeable in all federal systems, be they Germany or the United States (Eichengreen, 1990; CEPR, 1993; see also several country studies in Commission, 1993*b*). In contrast, the EU budget, at least in its present size and form, cannot perform a stabilization role; and its redistributive dimension, although growing, still remains rather limited (see also Chapter 9). Thus, inter-regional budgetary transfers cannot be relied upon to take much of the adjustment burden in a future EMU.

A comparison has sometimes been drawn between EMU at the European level and monetary union between West and East Germany (Siebert, 1991; Gros and Thygesen, 1992). German monetary union was accompanied in the early years by a major decline in production in the Eastern *Länder* and a correspondingly large increase in unemployment. The state of the former centrally planned economy and the artificially high exchange rate adopted for political reasons have made the scale of economic adjustment very large. Wage convergence has proceeded much faster than convergence in productivity rates. On the other hand, labour mobility from the new *Länder* to the West has been very high. But the shock of economic unification in the East has been mostly absorbed by large budgetary transfers and, to a lesser extent, private investment flows. In 1994, annual budgetary transfers to the new *Länder* reached the amount of DM 180 billion (Deutsches Institut für Wirtschaftsforschung, 1995: 18) which was significantly bigger than the entire budget of the EU. They corresponded to more than 50 per cent(!) of the *per capita* income in the new *Länder*, the percentage figure having been even higher in earlier years. Thus, there can simply be no comparison with the EU.

The Maastricht treaty provides for a centralized system of monetary policy which will be entrusted to a new independent institution. The provisions made for its political accountability may in practice mean even less than they were intended to, because of the lack of a corresponding political system at the European level. And this is a crucial point. Unless the IGC of 1996 produces spectacular results, which is rather unlikely, a future European monetary union will operate within a highly decentralized political system with a highly decentralized fiscal policy. The latter will remain essentially a national responsibility, with a further high degree of decentralization in the case of federal political systems within the Union, while a system of constraints and economic sanctions has been provided for in order to deal with large national deficits. We shall discuss below some of the issues relating to the political and economic viability of the Maastricht arrangements.

Since the ECB will have no history and reputation to rely upon, its credibility will have to depend, at least in the beginning, on strict rules, thus allowing less room for discretion. Arguably, the credibility of the ECB will also depend on the past record of participating countries in terms of stability-minded policies; hence the adoption of strict convergence criteria. Although hardly anybody would doubt the value of price stability (the real question is how much and what, if any, is the trade-off), the greater emphasis placed on it in recent years may also have something to do with demography and more precisely with the increasingly ageing populations in Europe and the rentier culture associated with this phenomenon. Retired people need stable prices more than others in order to protect their savings and their pensions. Price stability is in turn linked directly to the independence of monetary institutions, which means independence from political control. For many countries, EMU will imply a double transfer of power: from the national to the European level and from politicians to technocrats, thus following the precedent set by the Bundesbank, although actually going even further because of the weakness of the European political system.

Here lie some fundamental political questions. How much economic policy-making should remain in the hands of elected representatives? This question is very familiar to all students of European integration, and not only them. There is a further question that requires an answer: can there be a central bank without a corresponding political authority? There is hardly any historical precedent for that (see also Cohen, 1994). And will this central bank be able to take decisions which will be widely perceived (even erroneously, according to some economists) as having a direct impact on unemployment in Lille, Andalusia, or Attica? It is all a question of legitimacy which may not be for sale in the European market-place. A newly independent Banque de France, for example, can draw on the reservoir of legitimacy of the French state in its conduct of national monetary policy. But there is no such equivalent, at least as yet, at the European level. The Germans are therefore entirely logical when they link monetary union to political union.

The link between economic and monetary union has been the subject of a long debate among economists. Several study groups consisting of prominent policy-makers and professional economists have attempted in the past to tackle this issue (see, for example, MacDougall Report, 1977; Padoa-Schioppa Report, 1987). It is, of course, not surprising that the members of both the Werner and the Delors committees experienced serious difficulties in reaching a compromise on this sensitive subject; and the political negotiations which ensued were even more difficult.

In a monetary union, there are strong arguments for greater flexibility of fiscal policy which could serve as an instrument of adjustment at the national and regional level. In fact, fiscal policy should also be more effective in the context of a monetary union. On the other hand, there is the risk of free-riding by national or even regional governments operating under the shield of the Union, assuming, of course, that markets cannot be relied upon to provide an effective restraint in terms of government overspending (and undertaxing). They usually react too slowly and they then tend to overshoot.

The long experience of fiscal laxity in some countries and the evident inability of financial markets (see, for example, the international debt crisis of the early 1980s) to act as effective and efficient constraints on sovereign actors can be used as arguments in favour of some central discipline on national deficit financing. The treaty provisions are aimed essentially against 'free-riders' in the future monetary union. Their effectiveness, however, remains to be tested, although some countries should be expected to be more vulnerable to collective pressure than others.

But this cannot be the whole story. What is at stake is who will determine the macroeconomic priorities for the EU as a whole and how. And there is as yet no mechanism for this. The EU budget is still very small and with no provision for a stabilization function. On the other hand, the present system of national policy coordination cannot be expected to deliver the goods. The broad guidelines adopted by ECOFIN every year are likely to remain too broad to have any real effect on national economic policies. In the words of Lamfalussy (1989: 101):

The combination of a small Community budget with large, independently determined national budgets leads to the conclusion that, in the absence of fiscal coordination, the global fiscal policy of the EMU would be the accidental outcome of decisions taken by the Member States. There would simply be no Community-wide macroeconomic fiscal policy.

This also means that the future European economic system will tend to be 'under-stabilized' against both common and asymmetric shocks (Allsop *et al.*, 1995). The same will apply with respect to inter-regional redistribution. Of course, such arguments will sound heretical for those preaching the new 'economic orthodoxy'.

The decentralized nature of EU fiscal policy will also have implications for the representation of EU interests in international fora. Until now, the Big Four of the EU, plus the Commission, have participated in the Group of Seven (G-7) within which the leading industrialized countries have tried, albeit with very limited success, to coordinate their economic policies. In a future EMU, the President of the ECB will be able to speak on behalf of the Union with respect to monetary policy; but what about fiscal policy? The problems experienced by US Administrations in the past in terms of being able to commit themselves and eventually deliver the goods in international policy coordination will pale into insignificance compared with those to be faced by Union representatives in the future.

The pressures for a less decentralized system of fiscal policy are therefore bound to grow with EMU. There will be pressures for a more effective coordination of fiscal policies at the European level and there will also be pressures for a bigger EU budget with a much stronger role in terms of redistribution and stabilization. There is certainly no question of the EU budget acquiring anything like the size of national budgets. An effective role in terms of stabilization and redistribution could be performed even with a relatively small budget.[1] But still, important changes in the area of European public finance would be required in order to make EMU an economically viable proposition; and such changes would presuppose the development of a political system which is much closer to a federation than a system of intergovernmental cooperation.

With the decision to proceed to a complete EMU, European political leaders have decided to play with very high stakes. EMU could divide the EU; it could destabilize it politically, if the new institutions do not enjoy the legitimacy which is necessary to carry their policies through; and it could create economically depressed countries and regions. These are the main risks. On the other hand, if it works (and it remains a big 'if'), it will much accelerate the process of economic integration, thus giving a much more concrete and stable form to the internal market; and it is also bound to create a new momentum for political integration as a necessary corollary to monetary union.

---

[1] A classic on this subject, if the use of this term could be stretched to apply to European integration, is MacDougall Report, 1977. See also Padoa-Schioppa Report, 1987; Commission, 1993*a* and 1993*b*; and Issing, 1996.

9

COHESION AND REDISTRIBUTION

Traditional economic theory concentrates on questions of efficiency and the maximization of global welfare, while considerations about equity and the distribution of the economic pie are usually left to more 'normative' disciplines; alternatively, they are simply assumed away as problems. The theory of customs union is a good example of this eclectic approach. But everyday politics is largely about the distribution of gains and losses among participants in any system. Depending on the nature of the latter, the relevant participants can be countries, regions, different social groups and classes, or even individuals.

A relatively equitable distribution of the gains and losses, or at least a perception of such an equitable distribution, can be a determining factor for the continuation of the integration process. Regional integration schemes in other parts of the world have often foundered precisely because of the failure to deal effectively with this problem. It would have been surprising if distributional politics had not entered the European scene. Indeed, its absence could have been interpreted as an unmistakable sign of the irrelevance of the EU as an economic and political system. But there should be no cause for alarm among 'Euro-enthusiasts'. The distributional impact of integration has been paramount in the minds of national politicians and representatives of various pressure groups; and it has strongly influenced negotiations within the common institutions from a very early stage. This was already evident in the first package deals on which the Paris and Rome treaties were based. Yet those package deals made very few provisions for explicitly redistributive instruments. This is a more recent development brought about by the international economic recession of the 1970s, the increased internal divergence of the EU, caused mainly by successive rounds of enlargement, and, last but not least, the progressive deepening of the process of integration.

Redistribution is one of the central elements of the European mixed economy at the national level; and this has become increasingly true of the EU as well, although there is still a very large difference between the two. Redistribution can also be considered as an index of the political and social cohesion of a new system; large transfers of funds, as a very tangible expression of solidarity, presuppose the existence of a developed sense of *Gemeinschaft* (a community based on common values) which is, of course, not a feature of international organizations. The objective of the EU now extends beyond a balanced distribution of gains and losses associated with integration. The explicit objective enshrined in the treaty is the reduction of existing disparities between regions.

This chapter will examine the nature and scale of the regional problem inside the Union and the development of redistributive instruments at the European level. The EU has indeed travelled a long way in the collective recognition of the concepts of cohesion and redistribution as key elements of the European package deal. Particular emphasis will be paid to the operation of the Structural Funds, and the more recent Cohesion Fund, which now serve as the main instruments of cohesion policy at the European level. The chapter will end with a section devoted to public finance: the main functions currently performed by the EU budget, with particular emphasis on redistribution, and the forces of change which point, however, in opposite directions. Important decisions will need to be taken with respect to structural policy and the budget before the end of the decade. They will be absolutely crucial decisions for the future course of European integration, especially as regards EMU and further enlargement.

The Regional Problem

'Regional problems are difficult to define but easy to recognise' (Robson, 1987: 168). Perhaps the main difficulty does not lie so much with the identification and definition of those problems as with their explanation and even more so with the ways of solving them. Regional problems refer to the persistence of large disparities among different regions of the same country in terms of income, productivity, and levels of employment. To understand the nature of these problems, one usually needs to go beyond neoclassical economic theory and the host of simplifying assumptions on which it is founded, including perfect competition, full employment, constant returns to scale, and perfect mobility of factors of production.

The literature on regional economics concentrates, precisely, on various forms of market failure which constitute a radical departure from the strong assumptions of neoclassical models. It stresses the existence of economies of scale and learning curves for individual firms. It points to external economies such as location advantages associated with easy access to large markets, centres of administration and finance, and sources of skilled labour and technological knowledge. It argues that the imperfect nature of labour markets can lead to situations in which money wages in different regions do not necessarily reflect differences in productivity rates. This is referred to in the literature as differences in 'efficiency wages', defined as money wages over productivity. Furthermore, inter-regional mobility of labour, which is certainly far from perfect, can have perverse effects in terms of regional disparities to the extent that migration to fast-developing areas is usually led by the most dynamic and highly skilled members of the labour force in the lagging regions (Myrdal, 1957; Robson, 1987; Prud'homme, 1993).

Under these conditions, initial differences in productivity and economic development or simply an autonomous shift in demand for the goods produced by a particular region can lead to 'circular and cumulative causation' and thus growing polarization between different regions; hence the creation and perpetuation of regional problems. This is what Myrdal calls the 'backwash' effects. On the other hand, the growth of dynamic regions will also have 'spread' effects arising from an increased demand for imports and the diffusion of technology from those regions, and eventually also from diseconomies of location associated with over-congestion in the rapidly growing centres. The relative importance of 'backwash' and 'spread' effects will determine the development of regional disparities within a country.

The main message from regional economic theories is that there are no strong reasons to expect the elimination of regional problems through the free interplay of market forces. On the contrary, such problems could be aggravated without the countervailing influence of government intervention. Interestingly enough, there is a close similarity between the literature on regional economics and the new theories of international trade which also place the emphasis on the role of economies of scale, imperfect competition, differentiated products, and innovation. Comparative advantage is no longer seen as the result of different factor endowments. Instead, the reasons for the large intra-industry trade which characterizes relations among industrialized countries, including members of the EU, seem to lie 'in the advantages of large-scale production, which lead to an essentially random division of labour among countries, in the cumulative advantages of experience which sometimes perpetuate accidental initial advantages, in the temporary advantages conveyed by innovation' (Krugman, 1986: 8).

Although the new theories do not reject completely the old Ricardian premise regarding the welfare-improving effects of free trade, associated in those theories mainly with economies of scale and increased competition, this conclusion is now hedged with many 'ifs' and 'buts'. The gains and losses from trade liberalization are most unlikely to be distributed evenly among different countries and regions. Tariffs, subsidies, and strategic trade policies can make perfect economic sense from the point of view of an individual country, although the risks of market failure need to be set against the risks of government failure, which are also very real. Furthermore, such policies would have a disastrous effect if pursued by all countries concerned.

The dividing line between regional and international economics becomes blurred as economic interdependence among different countries increases. After all, what basically distinguishes an intra-country from an inter-country problem in terms of economic disparities is the higher degree of labour mobility within a country and the automatic transfer of resources through the central budget, factors which are meant to compensate for the lack of independent trade, monetary, and exchange rate policies for individual regions. It is those factors which differentiate the problem of the Mezzogiorno inside Italy and the Eastern *Länder* in unified Germany from the problem of Portugal or Greece inside the EU.

However, with the progressive deepening of European integration, and especially with the establishment of the internal market and later EMU, this

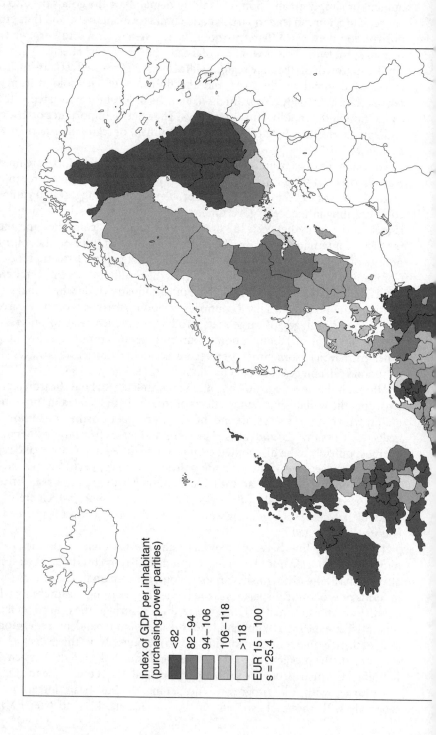

Index of GDP per inhabitant
(purchasing power parities)

<82
82–94
94–106
106–118
>118

EUR 15 = 100
s = 25.4

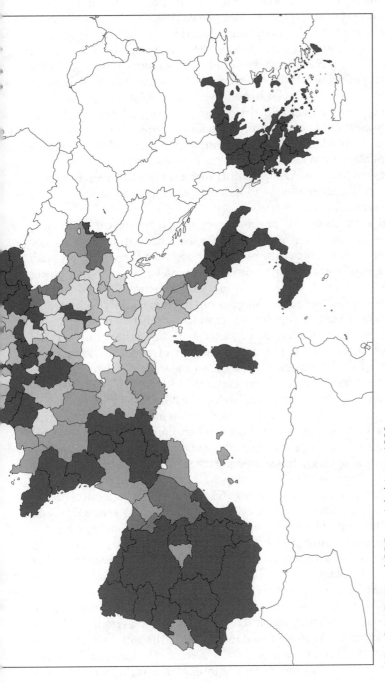

Map 9.1. Regional GDP per Inhabitant, 1993

Note: EU-15 = 100, PPS.

Source: Commission, 1996b.

distinction will become increasingly less obvious, particularly with respect to policy instruments aimed at influencing relative prices and, ultimately, the inter-country allocation of resources. Independent trade policies have long since been merged in the context of the common commercial policy of the EU. Monetary policy and the exchange rate will also need to be sacrificed at the altar of monetary union in which case intra-EU trade will be determined by absolute and not comparative advantage; thus effectively turning inter-country disparities in the EU into regional problems. On the other hand, linguistic and cultural frontiers are likely to remain for long a major barrier to labour mobility inside the EU. In fact, it would not even be politically desirable for labour mobility to act as an important adjustment mechanism among member countries. Thus the avoidance of serious regional problems inside an increasingly integrated Union would have to depend essentially on two factors, namely the flexibility of product and factor markets on the one hand and compensating measures on the other. Compensating measures could either attempt to influence the allocation of resources or act as a form of redistribution.

International comparisons of income levels should be treated with some caution, because of the distortions created by exchange rates which do not adequately reflect relative purchasing power over goods and services, a problem which is only partially dealt with by attempts to establish purchasing power standards (PPSs), and also because of considerable differences in the size of the unrecorded sector of each economy. Comparisons of cross-country regional data are even less reliable given the large differences which exist between the territorial units within individual countries; the existence of those territorial units being usually the product of history. For the production of regional statistics, the Statistical Office of the EC has established the so-called nomenclature of territorial units for statistics at three different levels (NUTS 1, NUTS 2, and NUTS 3). For practical reasons to do with data availability, the NUTS nomenclature has to be based, however, on the existing institutional divisions inside member countries.

The EU of Fifteen is characterized by large economic disparities among countries and regions, which greatly exceed those inside the United States (Boltho, 1994). The maps and figures in this section are taken from the Commission's first cohesion report (Commission, 1996*b*). Map 9.1 is based on GDP per capita by region (NUTS 2, with a total of 206 regions). GDP figures have been calculated on the basis of purchasing power standards (PPSs). It should come as no surprise to anybody at all familiar with the European economic scene that regional disparities have a strong centre–periphery dimension, the poorest regions being concentrated on the southern, western, and eastern periphery (the incorporation of the new German *Länder* and the accession of Finland having added an eastern dimension to the periphery of less developed regions of the EU).

Inter-country disparities are quite significant. Figure 9.1 shows that on the basis of 1993 data Luxembourg was at the top reaching 160 per cent of the EU average, while Greece and Portugal found themselves at the bottom of the ladder with approximately 65–70 per cent of the EU average. The German figure has been adjusted downwards as a result of unification, thus bringing it closer to the

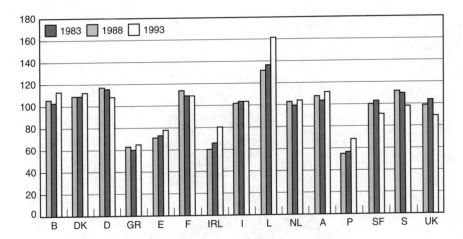

Fig. 9.1. GDP per Inhabitant by Member Country, 1983–1993

Note: EU-15 = 100, PPS.

Source: Commission, 1996b.

average. In the period between 1983 and 1993, the four poorest members of the Union, namely Greece, Ireland, Portugal, and Spain, have experienced an improvement in their relative position. Exactly the opposite has happened in the case of Finland and Sweden in the years prior to their accession to the EU; and also with the UK.

As expected, inter-regional disparities are much wider. Figure 9.2 shows regional disparities in GDP per capita by member country of the EU of Fifteen on the basis of data for NUTS 2 regions. In some countries, those disparities are extremely wide (Germany being the most prominent example of a dual economy following unification, with a difference of more than 3.5:1 between the most and the least prosperous region). For the Union as a whole, the difference in terms of GDP between the most prosperous (Hamburg) and the least prosperous (Açores and Alentejo) regions is of the order of 4.5:1. The ten poorest regions in the EU of Fifteen are all found in Germany, Greece, and Portugal, if we exclude the overseas territories of France (Commission, 1996b).

Regional disparities are due to a combination of productivity differentials as well as differentials in the employment rate. The former reflect differences in physical productivity, prices, and earnings which may result from differences within a single sector or from differences in sectoral and functional specialization. Differences in the employment rate reflect the capacity of an economic system to mobilize its human potential. The employment rate is a function of demography, social, and political factors as well as the scale of unemployment (Smith and Tsoukalis, 1997).

Greece and Portugal have very low productivity rates and near average employment rates. The combination is quite different in the case of Ireland and

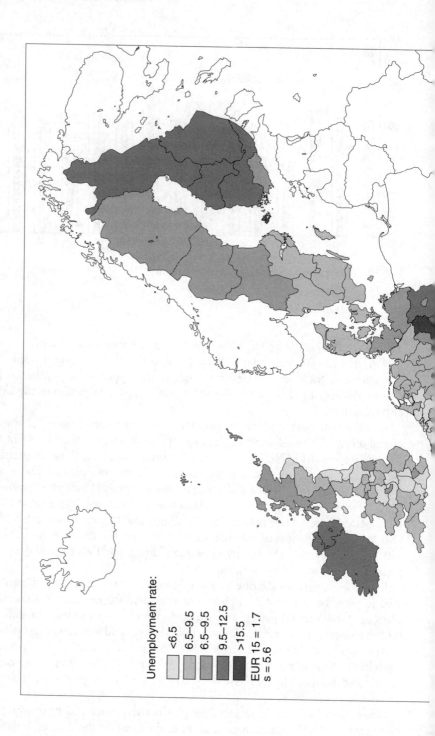

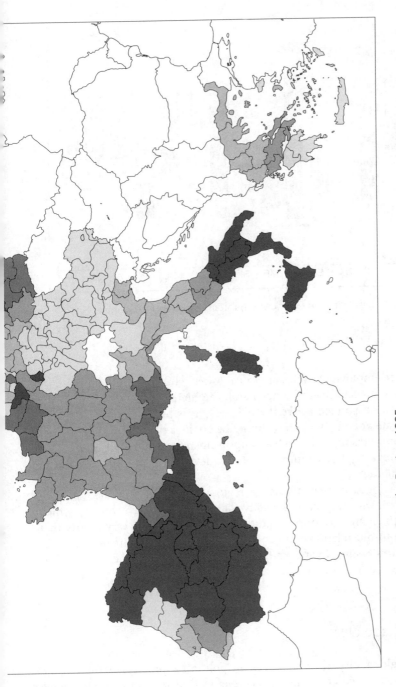

Map 9.2. Unemployment Rates by Region, 1995

Source: Commission, 1996b.

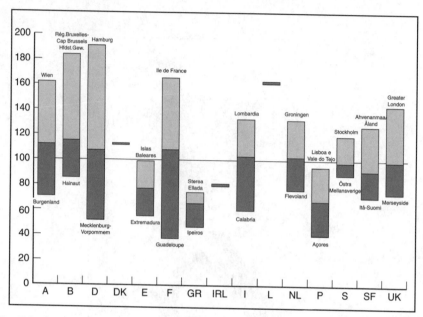

Fig. 9.2. Regional Disparities in GDP per Inhabitant by Member Country, 1993

Note: EU-15 = 100, PPS.

Source: Commission, 1996b.

Spain where the employment rates are much lower, while the productivity rates are substantially higher. On the other hand, the high productivity rate in the Netherlands, which is much above the EU average, is partly compensated by a relatively low rate of employment. It should be obvious that regional disparities cannot be eliminated simply through an improvement in productivity rates in the less developed regions, if this improvement is achieved solely through a decline in the employment rate.

Map 9.2 shows unemployment rates by region (unemployment rates being, of course, measured with respect to the active labour force in each country, which changes with time and economic conditions). Map 9.2 shows very clearly that there is no one-to-one relation between income disparities and differences in unemployment rates. Spain, Finland, and southern Italy have the highest rates of unemployment, while Greece and Portugal have a better than average performance.

A New Package Deal

The scale of regional disparities as well as the political approach and the specific policy instruments used at the European level to deal with this problem have changed very much over the years. The original six members of the EC constituted a relatively homogeneous economic group, with the exception of the south of Italy; a problem which was, in fact, recognized in the protocol for the Mezzogiorno, attached to the Treaty of Rome. Article 2 of the treaty referred to the objective of a 'harmonious development of economic activities, a continuous and balanced expansion', while in the preamble the contracting parties went even further by calling for a reduction of 'the differences existing between the various regions and the backwardness of the less favoured regions'.

There were, however, only a few provisions made in the treaty for the creation of instruments which could contribute towards this 'harmonious development' and the reduction of regional disparities. The European Investment Bank (EIB) was intended as a source of relatively cheap interest loans and guarantees for the less developed regions of the Community. Provisions for the free movement of labour also had an indirect regional dimension in the sense that labour mobility would help to deal with the problem of high unemployment in a less developed region such as the Mezzogiorno. Last but not least, the setting up of the CAP was expected to contribute towards the reduction of disparities, since farm incomes were generally much below the national or EC of Six average, while economic backwardness was most often identified with a heavy regional concentration on agriculture.

There was no explicit reference to regional policy, albeit in the form of derogations from general provisions in the different policy areas dealt with by the treaty. This is true of social, transport, and agricultural policies. The best known derogation which bears upon the regional dimension can be found in Article 92 of the original treaty, which has remained almost intact. It indirectly accepts state aids for intra-country regional development purposes, thus making a big exception to the application of the common competition policy. The various derogations, together with the lack of any separate chapter on a common regional policy, suggest that the authors of the Treaty of Rome, while recognizing the regional problem and the need to employ special instruments to deal with it, had decided to leave the main responsibility in the hands of national authorities. The role of the Community would remain marginal in this respect, while the common institutions were asked to show some flexibility in the development of other common policies in order to accommodate the regional policy objectives of national authorities.

Regional disparities were not as yet generally recognized as a major policy concern at the time of the signing of the treaty. On the other hand, large transfers of money across frontiers were considered as politically impossible. Since the redistributive mechanisms could only be very modest, the six signatories tried to 'control and distribute the gains and losses which might arise in the particular sectors involved in such a way as to determine beforehand the extent to which the national interest of each party to the agreement would be satisfied' (Milward, 1984: 498).[1] This explains the complicated and perhaps economically 'irrational'

---

[1] This comment by Milward was in fact made with reference to the Paris Treaty of 1951. It can equally well apply to the EEC treaty signed six years later.

nature of some of the treaty provisions. On the other hand, equitable distribution of gains and losses basically referred to the distribution among countries.

Although regional policy had its heyday in most Western European countries during the 1960s and the early 1970s, with large sums of money spent in this direction (Nicol and Yuill, 1982), very little happened at the EC level. The EIB did, as originally envisaged, orient its lending activities mainly towards the less developed regions of the Six, and the south of Italy in particular. However, the sums of money involved were relatively small and the attraction of EIB loans consisted entirely of the relatively low rates charged on loans, which was made possible because of the high credit rating which the EIB enjoyed in international capital markets and which therefore enabled it to borrow at the lowest possible rates. The majority of loans went for energy and infrastructural investment. The EIB could not, according to its statutes, offer any capital grants or subsidies to inputs.

The ESF also played a modest redistributive role. As for the EAGGF (European Agricultural Guidance and Guarantee Fund), which accounted for the biggest part of the EC budget, it surely acted as an important redistributive mechanism in favour of European farmers, although its general impact on regional disparities was rather mixed (see below). The first serious attempt towards the coordination of national regional policies was made as late as 1971, with the aim of preventing an 'overbidding' between regions, which almost always worked at the expense of the poorer ones.

Distributional issues in general did not become a serious political problem in the early years of European economic integration. But this was the Golden Age of the Western European economies, characterized by rapid economic growth, high employment rates, and relative monetary stability. The overall size of the cake grew constantly bigger and European integration continued to be perceived as a positive-sum game in which there were gains to be made by all the countries involved. The reduction of inter-country income disparities among the Six during the same period helped to allay earlier fears about the effects of trade liberalization on the weaker economies. On the other hand, national governments pursued active regional and redistributive policies inside their borders aiming at a reduction of income disparities. At the time of prosperity and the rise of social democracy, equality became a widely respected political objective, while the rise of autonomist movements in several European countries surely strengthened the political will for an effective reduction of regional inequalities.

Interest at the Community level grew as a result of the first enlargement of the EC and the rapid deterioration of the international economic environment, both coinciding in the early 1970s. The accession of three new members brought countries with serious regional problems inside the EC. On the other hand, clearly dissatisfied with the overall economic package which had taken shape prior to the UK's accession to the Community, the government in London searched for other mechanisms which would partly compensate for the budgetary loss arising from the operation of the CAP. The creation of the European Regional Development Fund (ERDF) soon became the spearhead of this effort (H. Wallace,

1983). Regional policy and redistribution have been used almost interchangeably ever since.

The ERDF was set up in 1975. Its birth signalled the growing concern with intra-EC disparities, although, strangely enough, this growth of interest in EC regional policy has more or less coincided with the noticeable decline in the popularity of regional policies at the national level. This is an interesting contradiction which cannot, however, be explained by any conscious decision to transfer powers and responsibilities to the emerging European centre. The ERDF started with small sums of money which were initially distributed among member countries on the basis of quota allocations determined by the Council of Ministers. This therefore meant a wide dispersal of limited funds. A 5 per cent, non-quota element, allocated at the discretion of the Commission, was first introduced in 1979, while, with the 1984 reform of the ERDF, quotas were replaced by indicative ranges for each country's allocation of funds.

Funds available through the ERDF grew steadily over the years. Disbursements were in the form of matching grants for the financing of investment projects, with almost exclusive emphasis on infrastructural investment (approximately 85 per cent of total expenditure for projects for the period 1975–88). There was also an increasing concentration of resources on the least developed countries and regions. However, the total sums of money remained very small, when compared with expenditures in terms of regional policy at the national level or even with EC expenditure on agriculture.

On the other hand, while EC regional expenditure increased, there was little evidence until the 1988 reform to suggest that the money spent by the ERDF was in addition to regional aid which would have been given by national governments in its absence. This is the so-called problem of additionality. It is highly indicative that for years the overwhelming majority of projects receiving ERDF assistance had begun before application for funds was made by the national governments. For the sake of high absorption rates of the funds allocated by the Commission, national and regional administrations were often tempted to sacrifice economic efficiency. Regional aid by the EC was generally viewed by national governments as a means of fiscal redistribution across national boundaries, with little effect on actual regional policies or the total sums of money involved. This led a member of the European Parliament to argue that 'there never was a regional policy at all, it was a Regional Fund operated on a Red Cross basis, with handouts here and there' (quoted in Shackleton, 1990: 44). Nor was there any serious coordination with other instruments of EC policy, and this further reduced the effectiveness of ERDF assistance as a means of tackling regional problems in the Community.

A new approach to regional policy was introduced in 1985 with the Integrated Mediterranean Programmes (IMPs), intended for the Mediterranean regions of France, Italy, and the whole of Greece. The creation of IMPs was in recognition of the special development problems of these regions and the relative bias of the CAP against southern agricultural products (Yannopoulos, 1989). In political terms, those programmes could be seen as a compensation for regions which were expected to lose from the accession of Spain and Portugal, because of the close similarity in their production structures. The main innovation of IMPs was that funding was based on medium-term development programmes, instead of a project by project basis, and that those programmes involved a close coordination of different EC instruments. The Integrated Mediterranean Programmes were the precursor of more general reforms which followed in 1988.

The crucial turning-point was the signing of the Single European Act which inserted a new Title V to the Treaty of Rome. Article 130*a* linked the strengthening of 'economic and social cohesion', which also served as the general title of this new section, with the reduction of regional disparities, while Article 130*b* referred to specific EC instruments which should be used for that purpose, namely the ERDF, the ESF, and the EAGGF-Guidance Section (all three now referred to as Structural Funds, to which a fourth one was added in 1993, namely the Financial Instrument for Fisheries Guidance—FIFG), as well as the EIB. The ERDF was entrusted with the principal task of redressing intra-EC regional imbalances. The new articles called for the effective coordination and rationalization of the activities of Structural Funds and the Commission was invited to submit proposals in this direction. Through the SEA, cohesion thus became a key word of the European vocabulary, while redistribution acquired a new political dimension. Furthermore, a clear intention was expressed to obtain better value for the European taxpayer's money.

The next step was taken with the decision of the European Council in February 1988, following a Commission proposal (the so-called first Delors package, since a second one was to follow some years later) to combine a substantial reform of the Structural Funds with the doubling of the resources available for the period until 1993. This was a major political decision and part of a bigger package deal which was meant to ensure the successful implementation of the internal market programme. Thus, the concept of cohesion, which had been introduced earlier through the SEA, was now being translated into considerable sums of money (see also Allen, 1996*b*). Should this be understood as some form of compensation for potential losers from further market integration or should it be interpreted, perhaps more positively, as a means of enabling economically weaker countries and regions to take better advantage of the new liberalization measures? The real motivations may be irrelevant; the result is what really counts.

The doubling of resources went hand in hand with an effort to improve the effectiveness of EC action through the adoption of clearer objectives, a higher concentration in the use of resources, an improved coordination of different financial instruments, and a close monitoring of jointly financed programmes. Another important feature of the 1988 reform was the emphasis on multi-annual programming as a means of identifying and quantifying priorities over a period of five years, thus following the precedent set by the IMPs.

Through the SEA and the subsequent decision of the European Council in 1988, the Structural Funds and redistribution in general have become an integral part of the European construction. The role played by Germany in this context is worth stressing. Being by far the biggest contributor, both in terms of its gross and net contribution to the EC budget, Germany played an absolutely decisive role in the agreement which led to the reform of the Structural Funds and the doubling of the resources available. The Community's 'paymaster' was apparently ready to dig into the pockets of its taxpayers in order to pay for the necessary lubricant for the smooth functioning of the Community's engine.

The Maastricht revision of the treaties and the provision made in it for the establishment of an EMU offered almost a repetition of the same story, thus reinforcing the link between further economic integration on the one hand and cohesion and redistribution on the other. The strengthening of economic and social cohesion is listed as one of the three main objectives of the Union, alongside the internal market and EMU, in Article B of Title I (common provisions for the EU). A new addition to the institutional set-up of the Union is the Committee of the Regions. The separate section devoted to economic and social cohesion (Article 130) calls for a further reform of the Funds and also provides for the setting up of a Cohesion Fund which will make financial contributions in the field of environment and trans-European transport networks. The Commission is also invited to submit a report every three years on the progress made towards achieving economic and social cohesion. The first cohesion report was submitted in the end of 1996.[2]

According to the separate protocol attached to the new treaty, the beneficiaries of this new Fund could only be countries with a per capita GNP of less than 90 per cent of the Union average: Greece, Ireland, Portugal, and Spain, which are now often referred to as the Cohesion Four. A new element of conditionality was introduced with respect to the Cohesion Fund: the countries benefiting from it would need to pursue economic policies which lead to the fulfilment of the convergence criteria. Thus, the link with EMU was very clearly established.

Side-payments and redistribution constituted very important elements of the Maastricht negotiation. With the protocol on economic and social cohesion, the treaty signatories went far beyond general declarations, thus trying to give a fairly concrete shape to the new package deal which also included detailed provisions with respect to EMU. Spain had led the negotiation on behalf of the poorer countries. And as a result, the new Cohesion Fund had a distinct Spanish flavour both in terms of the priorities adopted and the distribution of funds among the beneficiaries.

Following on the steps of the Delors package of 1988, which had contributed so much to the budgetary peace and the successful implementation of the internal market programme during the intervening years, the Commission submitted a new set of proposals in February 1992. In a somewhat diluted form, the Commission proposals were adopted by the European Council in Edinburgh in December 1992; and a further revision of the rules governing the Structural Funds followed in July 1993. The key elements of the Edinburgh agreement were: a further small increase in the Community's 'own resources' until 1999, a slight revision of the system of revenue raising to take account of the 'contributive capacity' of each

---

2 The first cohesion report also draws on an in-depth examination of the cohesion impact of different EC policies (Smith and Tsoukalis, 1997; see also below).

member country, and most importantly, a very substantial further increase in the share of the Structural Funds, which, together with the Cohesion Fund, should reach 35 per cent of total EU expenditure by 1999 (see also the section on the EU budget; Laffan and Shackleton, 1996). Undoubtedly, the EU had travelled a very long way since the 1970s when member governments were involved in interminable negotiations about very small sums of money. And in the process, the link between the internal market and EMU on the one hand and redistribution on the other had become firmly established.

Structural Funds: Development Policies in Europe's Periphery

In 1988 the reform of the Structural Funds came with a rich dowry. Another, albeit less radical, reform was introduced in 1993, while the dowry became even richer. Furthermore, it was guaranteed to last at least until 1999. Thus, the Union has acquired powerful policy instruments to assist the development of economically weaker countries and regions. In 1993, 21 billion ECU were devoted to structural policies. For the sake of comparison, it should be noted that the same year a total of approximately one billion was spent on economic assistance to all the countries of Central and Eastern Europe: another illustration of the importance of being in. By 1999, total annual expenditure on structural policies will have reached 30 billion ECU (in 1992 prices), including 2.6 billion through the Cohesion Fund. The total amount is expected to represent approximately 35 per cent of the EU budget.

One important feature of the reform has been the increased concentration of resources on areas most in need. Six priority objectives have been assigned to the Funds.

- *Objective 1*: economic growth and adjustment of less developed regions; the main economic indicator being a GDP per capita of less than 75 per cent of the EU average (at NUTS 2 level).
- *Objective 2*: economic reconversion of declining industrial areas; the main indicators being the rate of unemployment and the industrial employment rate.
- *Objectives 3 and 4*: combating long-term unemployment, promoting the adaptation of workers to changes in industry and systems of production, and facilitating the integration of young people in the labour market.
- *Objective 5a*: adaptation of structures in the agricultural and fisheries sectors in line with the reform of the CAP; and *Objective 5b*: diversification and development of rural areas.
- *Objective 6*: dealing with the special problems of sparsely populated regions in the Nordic countries; having been added as a result of the 1995 enlargement.

Objectives 1, 2, 5*b*, and 6 have a regional dimension and they absorb 85 per cent of total funding, while Objectives 3, 4, and 5*a* are Union-wide. Objective 1 absorbs the biggest share of the resources: almost 65 per cent of total expenditure for the period 1989–93, a figure which is expected to reach 74 per cent by 1999. Objective 1 includes the whole of Greece, the Republic of Ireland and Portugal, the greater part of Spain, Mezzogiorno, Northern Ireland, as well as Corsica and the overseas territories of France. Germany's Eastern *Länder* were later added as a result of unification; and the list of beneficiaries became even longer in 1993 when a few more regions managed to sneak in, usually with a rather flexible application of the GDP (75 per cent) criterion. The attraction of Objective 1 (and the funds it represents) is clearly too strong for anybody to resist; hence the inevitable haggling to be included in the list of beneficiaries and the allocation of resources among them.

Financing through the Structural Funds, in the form of matching grants with EU participation often reaching a very high percentage of total expenditure, is done on the basis of Community Support Frameworks (CSFs) for each country. These are in turn the product of negotiations between the Commission and the member governments concerned, which submit their regional development plans to Brussels. The CSFs set the main guidelines for expenditure on a multi-annual basis (1989–93 for the first period and 1994–9 for the second). Thus, the emphasis is on programmes of economic development which involve the setting of policy priorities for a longer period and for more than one region. In an attempt to streamline the process, which had proved rather heavy and slow, the 1993 reform introduced the possibility for member governments of submitting single programming documents. Several member governments have taken advantage of this possibility.

There are two other main principles of the new approach to EU structural policies. One is the principle of partnership which means that the programming and setting of priorities as well as the implementation stage of the CSFs should involve a close and continuous cooperation between the Commission and the appropriate authorities at national, regional, and local level; in other words, national governments are no longer the only interlocutors of Brussels. The other is the principle of additionality which is meant to guarantee that EU funds complement rather than replace national funding for regional development.

We shall concentrate here on the effects of Structural Funds on the four poorest countries of the EU, which now receive more than half of the total amount spent on structural policies, including the operations of the new Cohesion Fund which has been specially designed for those four countries. In macroeconomic terms, the annual transfer of resources is now significant, although it is still low when compared with inter-regional transfers in countries such as Germany and Italy. Annual transfers through EU structural policies represent more than 3 per cent of Gross National Product (GNP) for Greece and Portugal; and more than 2 per cent for Ireland and Spain (Commission, 1996*c*). On the other hand, stronger demand for investment goods also means more imports. Between 30 and 40 per cent of the total amounts transferred to cohesion countries through the Structural Funds is being translated into imports from the other more developed countries of the EU (Commission, 1996*b*).

The operation of the Structural Funds has a clear redistributive effect: total transfers which represent 0.45 per cent of EU GDP for the period 1994–9 are estimated to have an income equalization effect of 5 per cent (Commission, 1996*b*). The importance of those transfers seems to be very well understood by the populations of the countries concerned. There is surely some correlation between the large amounts of transfers and the relatively strong popular support registered in those countries for European integration, even though transfers, as the most tangible benefit of EU membership, cannot be the only explanatory variable for 'Euro-enthusiasm'. For the three young democracies of Southern Europe, membership of the EU has been generally identified with democracy and modernization; and it has often served as an instrument and even as an excuse for measures of administrative reform and economic liberalization (Tsoukalis, 1981; Maravall, 1993). In this respect, some useful lessons may be drawn for the candidate countries in Central and Eastern Europe.

Economic priorities differ from one country to the other, and so does the distribution of resources made available through the Structural Funds. For instance, almost 50 per cent of the Greek CSF for 1994–9 will go to infrastructural investment, compared with only 20 per cent in the Irish CSF (Commission, 1996*b*). In general, the latter is a clear reflection of the higher level of economic development of Ireland in relation to the other cohesion countries and its more efficient and sophisticated administrative structure. Despite considerable differences among the cohesion countries, there are important elements in common: a large part of total expenditure for Objective 1 regions goes to infrastructural investment and investment in human capital. This also reflects the Commission's approach to economic development in the weaker regions, an approach the Commission has attempted to justify also with reference to economic theories of endogenous growth (Commission, 1994*d*; Begg, Gudgin, and Morris, 1995). In a study on Spain, de la Fuente and Vives (1995) have found that disparities in human and public capital account for a third of observed regional inequality. They have also found that ERDF transfers to Spain have had a clear redistributive impact among different regions.

There are, of course, many other factors which influence the economic development of a particular country or region. The effects of EU structural policies on economic growth and employment creation are very difficult to calculate *ex post*. There is the usual problem of constructing an *anti-monde* and thus the results depend very much on the assumptions fed into the econometric model. It has been estimated that EU structural policies added almost 1 per cent to annual GDP growth in Greece, Portugal, and Ireland during the period of the first Delors package (Commission, 1996*b*; see also Goybet and Bertoldi, 1994). During the same period (1989–93), Ireland, Portugal, and Spain grew faster than the EC average, thus also contributing to greater economic cohesion. Greece's performance was close to the average (the growth figures in Table 2.1 are not exactly compatible with the Eurostat estimates in Fig. 9.1), while Southern Italy and Northern Ireland fared less well.

This difference in economic performance needs to be explained in terms of domestic economic policies as well as a host of other variables. For example, Ireland, which has experienced for several years the highest rates of economic growth in the EU, has been able to attract during the same period large flows of FDI, because of a combination of low corporate taxes, generous incentives, a highly skilled and abundant labour force at relatively low wages, and the English language. A stable macroeconomic environment must have also played a role. Thus, for the period between 1986 and 1991, the gross inflow of FDI into Ireland was more than three times larger than transfers through the Structural Funds. The experience of Greece was very different during the same period: transfers from the Structural Funds were more than twice the value of FDI flows (European Commission, 1994*d*: 90–1). In Greece, much needed economic reform and adjustment were unduly late and this had a strong negative effect on growth (Tsoukalis, 1993*b*; Alogoskoufis, 1995).

Experience seems to suggest that there is a positive correlation between economic growth and the reduction of inter-country income disparities in the EU. They were reduced during the boom years of the 1960s and early 1970s. The trend was reversed during the long recession, and then again growth rates in the less developed countries picked up during the second half of the 1980s. This is a rather broad generalization which may, however, indicate that the 'spread' effects of economic growth are stronger than the 'backwash' effects; assuming, of course, that the local conditions are right, and those conditions may include the existence of the necessary 'civic values' in the words of Putnam *et al.* (1993), who have studied the north–south problem in Italy.

During the period 1989–93, the rate of absorption in the recipient countries with respect to commitments made through the Structural Funds was generally high, although there had been problems especially during the early years. Some of the cohesion countries have registered the highest absorption rates, while Italy has consistently fallen behind leaving large sums of money unspent (Commission, 1996*c*). In several cases, the failure to spend the money committed in EU-approved programmes has been the result of an unwillingness by national governments to come up with the matching sums. In other cases, it has been the product of administrative inefficiency at the national, regional, or local level. On the other hand, high absorption does not always imply a cost-effective use of resources. After all, both the recipients and the administration in Brussels have an interest in achieving high rates of absorption for different reasons in each case. There is an element of moral hazard in this interaction.

In the case of the Greek CSF (1989–93), for example, there is evidence of shifting expenditure to smaller and thus more easily realizable projects, with lower expected economic returns, in order to reach higher rates of absorption (for the evaluation of the Greek CSFs, see Synthesis, 1996); and there have been similar instances in the other countries. There have also been reports of considerable waste and fraud in several countries with respect to the operations of the ESF; the very large number of small individual projects on training being perhaps an important explanation, because of the difficulties involved in securing effective monitoring. On the other hand, the actual coordination of different financial instruments has left much to be desired. After all, the Commission is not famous for the internal coordination between the different directorates-general.

Having said that, there is, however, little doubt about the overall positive impact of structural policies on the less developed countries and regions of the Union. Despite a very large increase in the amounts spent on structural policies, both the Commission and the recipient countries and regions have coped reasonably well. The effects on infrastructure, and perhaps to a lesser extent on human capital, are very important. And all parties concerned have been learning from experience, which should lead to a more efficient use of resources during the second period (1994–9).

Subsidiarity remains, of course, a major issue. The division of competences between Brussels and national or regional authorities has always been a moot point. Why should Brussels know better than national capitals and regional authorities about their own development needs and priorities? This is not only a question of principle; it is also linked to the serious administrative limitations of the EC executive. The small staff and the internal organization of the Commission do not always match the large sums of money which it has been asked to administer. There are, however, powerful counter-arguments which can be used. First of all, the objective of additionality, namely that EU expenditure should represent a net increase in the amounts spent on development and should not therefore be used to subsidize current consumption, militates in favour of some central control, even though such control can never be absolutely effective. For this reason alone, structural policies could never be substituted by a simple form of fiscal redistribution through the EU budget, with no strings attached; at least as long as the Union insists on the principle of additionality.

Experience also suggests that the efficiency of some national and regional administrations leaves much to be desired, thus making the Commission look almost like a model of efficiency. After all, low levels of development are not only manifested in income statistics. Administrative inefficiency is often compounded by short-term political considerations which are not always consistent with long-term development needs. Thus, the Commission has often been forced to navigate dangerously between the Scylla of national sovereignty and the Charybdis of administrative inefficiency and political short-termism (or corruption). How much of the responsibility for the planning and the implementation stages, including the monitoring of programmes, could be given to outside experts in order to fill the gap left by weak administrations? This will remain an awkward question for the future.

In the meantime, the operation of the Structural Funds has in some cases forced much-needed reforms upon recalcitrant governments and administrations. In such cases, the EU has indeed fulfilled expectations by acting as a catalyst of modernization, especially in the countries of Southern Europe where the effects of EU membership have been felt perhaps more strongly than anywhere else and where popular judgement of those effects seems to be overwhelmingly positive. The CSFs provide for technical assistance to the recipient countries in order to enable them to make more efficient use of the resources available. The operation of Structural Funds has also introduced more transparency and accountability through the spreading, among other things, of the 'evaluation culture' imported from the Anglo-Americans via Brussels. Successive evaluations (*ex ante*, ongoing, and *ex post*) of all programmes financed by the Commission are now an integral part of EU structural policies.

The influence exercised by the Commission with respect to the formulation and implementation of programmes financed through the Structural Funds seems to be a function of the amounts involved and the relative power of its interlocutors. There has been, for example, a big difference in the handling of the Greek and the German CSFs; the German government having allowed the Commission virtually no room for manoeuvre in the setting of priorities and the implementation of the CSF for the Eastern *Länder*, presumably because some of the common rules are considered to be appropriate only for the lesser mortals.

In general, the Cohesion Four have been obliged to accept stronger interference from Brussels as the inevitable price for the large amounts of transfers. In many other cases, the influence of the Commission has been more questionable. Despite the effort to concentrate resources, slightly more than half of the total population of the Union is covered by the Structural Funds, which means a large number of small projects. Does it really make sense to spread the benefits of EU structural policies so thin, thus also stretching to the limit the administrative capacity of the Commission? This may be, arguably, one way of making the Union's presence felt to as many citizens as possible; and also a way for regional and local authorities in several countries to escape even occasionally from the stranglehold of central governments. Local authorities in the UK, and not only there, seem to greatly appreciate their direct access to Brussels (and the money it can dispense). The influence of the Commission is strongest with respect to the Community Initiatives which represent approximately 9 per cent of the total budget of Structural Funds. Community Initiatives are directly administered by the Commission and some of them involve cross-border and transnational co-operation.

Through the principle of partnership, the Commission has tried to obtain direct access to regional and local administrations in the member countries. We are certainly not yet in the Europe of regions. National governments remain the dominant actors: they are the ones who set the priorities and the ones who negotiate in Brussels. It is highly indicative that although, for example, the eligibility criteria for Objective 1 operate on a regional basis, the allocation of resources decided by national representatives in the Council has been among countries and not regions. Furthermore, the more recent addition to the range of financial instruments, through the creation of the Cohesion Fund, seems, if anything, to confirm this political reality: the eligibility criteria are now on a country basis

(Hooghe and Keating, 1994; Allen, 1996*b*; for a series of studies on the role of sub-national institutions, see also Leonardi, 1993).

Generalizations usually hide a very complex reality. It is true, of course, that in countries such as Germany, Spain, and more recently Belgium, regional governments wield considerable power and they increasingly insist on active participation in the formulation of European policies in their respective countries and on direct contact with the Commission. On the other hand, it seems that the operation of Structural Funds may in some cases have acted as a catalyst for the devolution of power within member countries and the strengthening of regional administrations in order to be able to cope with the demands made in Brussels. One can go even further: European integration may indeed strengthen in the long term the centrifugal tendencies inside some member states. But this will have little to do with the principle of partnership or other such ideas which have often been blown completely out of proportion in the literature.

Although things have changed very much since the days when the ERDF operated 'on a Red Cross basis', or as a thin camouflage for simple fiscal redistribution, it would still be rather misleading to talk of a European development (or regional) policy. As with most other areas, EU policy remains a highly decentralized process of decision-making and implementation, while the power of the Commission is still relatively limited. This also explains why, for example, the German *Länder* and the Mezzogiorno receive much more money in the form of regional aid than Alentejo. Political power, and the financial resources which go with it, is still very much concentrated in national capitals. Such are the limitations of European regional policy; a policy which does, however, produce a significant transfer of resources in favour of the poorer countries.

The basic operating rules of the Structural Funds, the total sums of money involved, and their distribution have been decided for the period extending until the end of the decade. Important decisions will therefore need to be taken before 1999 about the future direction of EU structural policies; and those decisions will have a decisive effect for EMU and further enlargement. What kind of redistributive mechanisms, and of what size, will be needed in the context of a monetary union; and what kind of structural policies in an enlarged Union where the new members will have income levels which are only a fraction of that of the poorest member of the EU of Fifteen? The data available for the candidate countries are still very incomplete and they should therefore be treated with considerable caution. Yet, all calculations made by Eurostat and several international organizations suggest that, with the exception of Slovenia and the Czech Republic, for which GDP per capita is estimated to be around 50 per cent of the EU of Fifteen average (and even higher in the case of Cyprus), for all the other countries GDP per capita is estimated to be much lower and in some cases below 20 per cent of the EU average.

Will there be a further large increase in the total amounts spent or will the present beneficiaries accept a substantial reduction of EU transfers in order to allow a reallocation of funds in favour of the new members? Will the goalposts (for example, the 75 per cent GDP indicator for Objective 1) be shifted in order to adjust for the increased number of players? Here there is also a problem of moral hazard: should the least successful among the existing players be allowed to stay in the game, while the better performers (such as Ireland) are taken out of the field? Should more emphasis be placed on innovative policies rather than simply throwing money at problems, which is the way EU structural policies are viewed by some of the net contributors to the budget? And should conditionality be strengthened, not only in terms of the macroeconomic policies pursued by the recipient countries but also in terms of efficiency in the use of the resources made available to them through the Structural Funds? These are some of the questions which will require political answers before the EU enters into a new phase of integration.

The Budget: Small and Beautiful?

In the early years of European integration, the common budget remained completely in the background. Unlike national budgets, which represent the main economic policy statement of the government, EC budgets were the end-product of decisions taken almost independently and in an uncoordinated fashion by different Councils of Ministers in Brussels in the context of EC action in separate policy areas. The overall expenditure, arising from those decisions, was then financed through national contributions, and the keys for those contributions had been established by the treaty. As explained earlier, the common budget was not seen as an instrument of redistributing resources across national frontiers, since equity in terms of the distribution of benefits from integration was to be achieved essentially through the package of different policies which had been agreed upon in advance.

The creation of own resources for the EC and the extension of the powers of the European Parliament in this area were major items in the Commission's proposals of 1965 which led to the first serious constitutional crisis inside the Community. But the real dispute at the time, provoked by General de Gaulle, was about questions of national sovereignty and the division of power between Brussels and the national institutions. The budgetary questions were of only secondary importance. Both proposals were to be adopted some years later. Through the treaty revisions of 1970 and 1975, the system of 'own resources' was introduced, consisting of customs duties, agricultural levies, and VAT contributions calculated on a harmonized base; the European Parliament acquired significant powers especially as regards the so-called non-compulsory expenditure, defined as expenditure other than that necessarily resulting from the treaty; and a new institution was created, namely the Court of Auditors, with the aim of strengthening accountability in the management of EC taxpayers' money.

The financial independence of the Community has in fact had a much longer history. The Paris Treaty of 1951 gave the High Authority of the ECSC the right to raise levies on coal and steel production. The creation of own resources was envisaged in Article 201 of the Treaty of Rome. This has always been a very important subject for the Commission and European federalists more generally for both practical and symbolic reasons. The financial independence of EC policies and institutions has been considered as a source of political power and an unmistakable sign of the qualitative difference of the Community from other international organizations (Strasser, 1992).

The 1973 enlargement, the economic recession, and the plans for the creation of an EMU combined to usher budgetary issues to the forefront of Community politics. The efforts of the UK to reduce its own net budgetary contribution opened the Pandora's box by turning net national contributions to the budget for the first time into an important, and also explosive, political issue, and thus raising alarm in Brussels about the negative consequences on further integration of a possible entrenchment of the *juste retour* principle (meaning that each country would strive for at least a zero balance in its net budgetary contribution and thus risk the transformation of the integration process into a zero-sum game). Gains and losses through the budget are much more easily identifiable by politicians and the public at large than, say, the trade effects of the customs union and the CAP, which are, however, more important in economic terms. Furthermore, with the gradual swing to the right in European politics in the early 1980s and the strong emphasis on budgetary consolidation, an ideological factor was later added to the intra-EC debates about the budget.

The bargaining position of the UK was progressively strengthened as the EC budget approached the limits imposed by the 1970 treaty revision in terms of own resources, because of the rapid increase in agricultural expenditure. A new revision required a unanimous decision by the Council and the subsequent ratification by all national parliaments. It thus provided an excellent opportunity to strive for a more wide-ranging restructuring of the EC budget as part of the general reform of common policies in which the Community became gradually engaged. The new political climate was also more propitious to such an attempt.

The first important step was taken at the Fontainebleau summit of June 1984. The package agreed then included new measures to control the growth of agricultural surpluses, an increase of the VAT rate (as part of the Community's own resources) to 1.4 per cent, and the introduction of a permanent mechanism for the partial compensation of the UK based on the difference between its VAT contribution and its overall receipts from the budget. Special provision was also made for the reduction of the net contribution of the Federal Republic. Thus, the objective of a certain degree of equity (not the same as redistribution) in terms of net national contributions to the EC budget was in the end officially recognized. It had taken a great deal of pressure on other members by the then British Prime Minister, Mrs Thatcher, for this principle to be accepted, albeit reluctantly. It was a very important turning-point.

The Fontainebleau agreement did not, however, succeed in imposing an effective control over agricultural expenditure. Thus, the new own resources were exhausted even before the increase in the VAT rate could be implemented; and this led to the opening of new negotiations on a subject which had deeply divided

EC countries for years. But this time, the negotiations took place in a much more favourable political environment in the aftermath of the signing of the SEA and the adoption of the internal market goal. Furthermore, the new budget negotiations could build on earlier agreements, especially as regards the UK compensation.

Then came the agreement reached by the European Council in Brussels in February 1988. It included an increase in financial resources, reaching a ceiling of 1.2 per cent of Community GNP by 1992; the creation of a new, fourth resource, which would consist of national contributions calculated on the basis of GNP, and intended to bring the system of Community financing closer to the 'ability to pay' principle; much tougher measures to contain CAP expenditure; and a considerable strengthening of redistributive policies through the Structural Funds. The agreement also incorporated provisions for the UK compensation basically along the lines established earlier at Fontainebleau. The European Council decision was followed in June of the same year by an inter-institutional agreement on the budget between the Commission, the Council of Ministers, and the European Parliament. It was an agreement on the financial perspectives which referred to the six main categories of expenditure in the EC budget for the period extending to 1992 (Laffan and Shackleton, 1996). It was unprecedented, and the ensuing budgetary peace contributed significantly to the new momentum of integration.

This successful experiment was repeated once again following the decision reached in Edinburgh in December 1992. The European Council established maximum levels of revenue and expenditure for the budget, with the revenue ceiling set to rise to 1.27 per cent of Community GNP by 1999; it decided that a bigger proportion of EC revenue should come progressively from the fourth resource created back in 1988 and based on a GNP key, while the uniform VAT rate should come down to 1 per cent by 1999 and the VAT base should be cut to a maximum of 50 per cent of GNP; it agreed on the total amounts of expenditure by main category for the period 1993–9, including the very substantial increase for the Structural Funds and, to a smaller extent, external actions undertaken by the Community; and it also decided to continue with the system of national rebates, despite the opposition earlier expressed by several member countries. It was followed by a new inter-institutional agreement in October 1993, thus creating the conditions for budgetary peace to extend at least until the end of the decade. Relatively small adjustments were subsequently introduced in relation to the 1995 enlargement.

Two basic characteristics of the EU budget are its very small size, compared with national budgets, and the legal requirement for zero balance between revenue and expenditure. This means a limited role in terms of allocation and redistribution, while the stabilization function of the budget for individual countries or regions as well as for the EU economy as a whole has so far been completely excluded. As shown in Fig. 9.3, total EU expenditure according to the 1996 budget was expected to reach 83 billion ECU, including expenditure through the ECSC and the European Development Fund (EDF), which are not part of the general budget. The latter also does not include the borrowing and

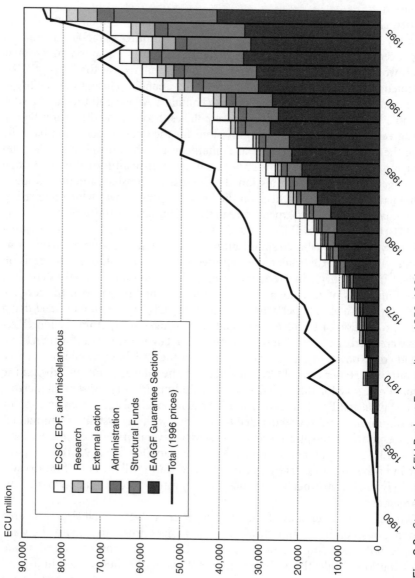

Fig. 9.3. Structure of EU Budget Expenditure, 1958–1996

Source: Commission, 1996d: 29.

lending activities of EU institutions such as the EIB. In absolute terms, EU expenditure has been steadily rising over the years; in real terms, it has more than doubled since 1985. Yet, it still represents approximately 1.2 per cent of EU GNP and 2.5 per cent of public expenditure in member countries.

Figure 9.3 shows the predominance of the EAGGF-Guarantee Section in EU expenditure; agricultural spending (excluding expenditure on agricultural structures, which is relatively small and comes under the Structural Funds) still represents approximately half of total EU spending, although its share has been steadily declining since 1988 and this trend should continue at least until the end of the decade when the CAP is expected to account for 45 per cent of EU budgetary expenditure. Of course, the most spectacular change in recent years has been the growth of structural policies which is shown in Fig. 9.3. Smaller increases have also been registered in expenditure related to research and external policies.

The Common Agricultural Policy (CAP) has involved large transfers of income from consumers and taxpayers to producers of agricultural products in the Union by maintaining a wedge between EU and world market prices. Thus, the budgetary cost of the CAP has been mostly a function of this difference in prices, resulting from purchases of agricultural products at high intervention prices and the payment of export subsidies. The 1992 reform of the CAP has brought about a partial shift from price to income support, thus also leading to a similar shift of the burden of supporting European farmers from consumers to taxpayers.

Transfers through the EU budget are only part of the overall redistribution of income generated by the CAP. The budgetary effect is relatively easy to calculate, being the difference between direct payments through the EAGGF-Guarantee Section to farmers in a particular country (or region) and transfers from taxpayers in the same country (or region) to finance the share of the agricultural budget which is equal to the share of the national (or regional) contribution to the general budget. Thus, it is essentially a transfer from taxpayers to producers, which also involves inter-country and inter-regional transfers. On the other hand, the trade effect cannot be calculated on the basis of budgetary data, because it involves a different kind of transfer, namely from consumers to producers. The trade effect measures the benefits and losses arising from intra- and extra-EU trade in agricultural goods at prices which are different from world market prices. As long as EU prices have been higher than world prices, imports have implied a transfer from consumers in the importing country or region to producers in the exporting country or region. The overall benefit or loss from the CAP for a particular country or region (budgetary plus trade effect) should be mainly a function of the relative size of agricultural production and the product mix (some agricultural products enjoy a higher rate of support than others).

According to calculations made by Tarditi and Zanias (1997), it appears that three cohesion countries, namely Greece, Ireland, and Spain, have a net benefit from the application of the CAP, Spain having joined the group of net beneficiaries only in recent years. Denmark, and, to a lesser extent, France (depending on the year) also have a net benefit, while all the other member countries (data are only available for the EU-12) appear to be net losers. Thus, Portugal, one of the four cohesion countries, is also among the net losers. In absolute terms, the biggest loser is Germany, followed by Italy and the UK. On a per capita basis, Danish farmers enjoy the biggest transfers from the CAP, followed by the Irish and the Greek.

Within countries, the CAP has a positive redistributive impact because on average it is transferring income from richer, urbanized, and industrialized regions towards poorer regions where agriculture accounts for a relatively large share of regional production. In contrast, the overall impact of the CAP on social cohesion (interpersonal income disparities) appears to be negative. Higher food prices have a regressive effect on consumers, because lower income households spend a higher share of their budget on food. On the other hand, a policy which operates on the basis of guaranteed prices favours mostly the better-off farmers, the amount of subsidy being a function of the total size of production. This explains, for example, why Danish farmers benefit much more than the Spanish: they have larger and more efficient farms. Furthermore, meat and dairy products enjoy a much higher rate of protection than most Mediterranean products which are characteristic of a very large part of Spanish agriculture.

Thus, the cohesion impact of the CAP, which still accounts for the biggest part of EU expenditure while also having very important allocation effects, is rather mixed. On an inter-country and inter-regional basis, the redistributive impact is broadly positive, although with important exceptions as in the case of Denmark and Portugal. On an interpersonal basis, the impact of the CAP is regressive. In this respect, the 1992 reform seems to have moved the CAP in the right direction: by shifting the burden of price support from consumers to taxpayers for some basic commodities such as cereals and oilseeds, it has had a positive effect in terms of cohesion.

The second biggest item of EU expenditure comes under the heading of structural policies. They constitute the most important redistributive instrument the impact of which has been examined in the section above. The CAP and the Structural Funds together now account for almost 80 per cent of total EU expenditure. If we add to this figure the cost of administration and external policies, there is very little left to spend. Clearly, there is an enormous difference from the budget of a typical member country where the large bulk of budgetary expenditure goes on defence and social security.

The only other item of EU expenditure which may be worth mentioning in terms of its redistributive impact are the amounts spent on research and technological development (RTD) under successive framework programmes. They now represent approximately 4 per cent of the EU budget and 5 per cent of the total research effort in the member countries; hence relatively small sums. The main objective of European RTD policy is to strengthen the science and technology capabilities of Union industry and to promote competitiveness. It also tends to act as a catalyst for inter-firm and inter-institute collaboration, particularly on a cross-country basis. Perhaps not surprisingly, the analysis of the available data suggests that the richest countries and their high technology regions tend to profit most from EU programmes (Sharp, 1997). Thus, the allocation of contracts tends

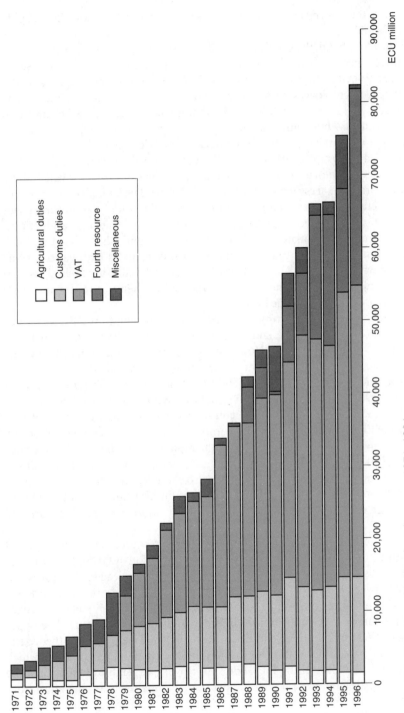

Fig. 9.4. Structure of EU Budget Revenue, 1971–1996

Source: Commission, 1996d: 40.

to reinforce the existing concentration of research activity in the so-called 'islands of innovation'.

On the other hand, the distribution of RTD expenditure must be related to the absorptive capacity of individual countries and regions; indicators of the absorptive capacity being the total amounts of RTD expenditure per capita and the percentage of employees involved in research activity. If EU expenditure is calculated by RTD employees, it appears that the poorer countries benefit more than the others. Thus, European RTD programmes may be helping to reduce disparities in research capacities in the weaker countries and regions.

Figure 9.4 shows the breakdown of EU revenue for the period between 1971, when the system of own resources began to take effect, and 1996 for which there were only provisional estimates at the time of writing. The Union's own resources consist of customs duties on imports from outside the Union, agricultural levies (variable taxes on imports plus sugar and isoglucose levies on production), VAT contributions calculated on a harmonized base, and GNP-related national contributions since 1988. The item 'miscellaneous' includes national contributions of new members during the transitional period, following their accession, and intergovernmental advances for the years 1984–6 when ad hoc measures were needed in order to balance the books.

Customs duties and agricultural levies naturally belong to the EU system of own resources. They are the end-product of common policies in the fields of agriculture and external trade. However, their contribution to total EU revenue has been steadily declining and they now represent only a small fraction of the total amounts needed to finance expenditure. Due to the growing importance of intra-EU trade as a percentage of the total external trade of member countries and the progressive lowering of the common external tariff, as a result of successive GATT negotiations, the relative importance of customs duties was bound to decline over time. On the other hand, the rapid increase in EU self-sufficiency in agricultural products largely explains the declining importance of agricultural levies as a source of revenue; declining but also variable, since those levies depend on the difference between world and EU prices for agricultural goods, and thus also on the exchange rate of the dollar in which most farm products are still quoted.

The declining importance of the traditional own resources should be expected to continue in the future because of the further reduction of tariffs, following the Uruguay Round, and the CAP reform which is intended to lead to a narrowing of the gap between ECU and world prices. For several years, the structural weakness of the above sources of revenue forced the Community to rely on a constantly growing share of VAT contributions in order to finance expenditure. The upper ceiling of VAT contributions had been set in 1970 at 1 per cent of a theoretical harmonized base, while waiting for the harmonization of indirect taxation, which may prove to be like waiting for Godot. As growing expenditure hit against the VAT ceiling, the latter was raised to 1.4 per cent at Fontainebleau, with effect from 1986.

As expenditure continued to grow, a new fourth resource was introduced in

1988. This consists of national financial contributions, based on a GNP key, which cover the difference between total expenditure, within the limits defined by the 1988 and the 1992 agreements, and the revenue raised by traditional own resources and the VAT contribution. In 1992, it was also decided to bring the VAT rate gradually back to 1 per cent, while also setting a lower limit for the VAT base as a percentage of GNP (50 instead of 55 per cent). This means that the fourth resource will have an increasing share of total revenue; and this is already obvious in the 1996 budget.

Before the introduction of the fourth resource, any redistributive impact of the EC system of revenue had been totally haphazard: the distribution of tax revenue among countries depending on their propensity to import from third countries (customs duties and agricultural levies), their propensity to consume (there is no VAT on investment), and the efficiency of their tax collection systems and hence the size of the unrecorded sector of the economy which is not subject to taxation. Important steps towards the application of the ability to pay principle, which still does not contain any form of progressivity in terms of the tax burden, were made with the 1988 and 1992 decisions which led to the creation of the fourth resource and the reduced share of VAT contributions. The fourth resource, as a function of GNP, is more closely related to the ability to pay than any other source of EU revenue; VAT contributions being slightly regressive since the propensity to consume is generally inversely related to levels of income. The fourth resource also has the advantage of flexibility in order to meet further increases in expenditure, although traditional federalists may view with some apprehension this increasing reliance on national contributions. But does this really endanger the Union's financial independence and the development of common policies?

The EC Court of Auditors undertakes painstaking work every year in an attempt to trace receipts and payments through the budget. This in turn makes possible the calculation of net national contributions for a large percentage of total expenditure (the amounts spent on external policies, for example, cannot be apportioned among the member countries). Those calculations are subject to the usual qualifications about accuracy, including the so-called Rotterdam–Antwerp effect.[3] Table 9.1 shows the net transfers effected through the EU budget for the period 1980–94. The Federal Republic has remained all along the biggest net contributor to the budget, thus justifying the popular image of Germany as the paymaster of Europe. The overall sums are, however, still relatively small (net contributions being less than 1 per cent of GDP). In recent years, the Netherlands has joined the club of net contributors, to which Belgium, France, Italy, and the UK also belong. Given the small net figures for the UK, one is presumably led to conclude that the old 'British problem', which had caused so much aggravation back in the 1970s and 1980s, has been essentially solved.

Greece and Ireland have become important beneficiaries, with net inflows

[3] This refers to the general problem created by large transit trade in calculating net national contributions to the EU budget. Should the revenue raised from imports through a Dutch port, with Germany as the final destination, be attributed to the Netherlands or the Federal Republic? A substantial amount of trade in Northern Europe goes through the ports of Antwerp and Rotterdam.

Table 9.1. Net Transfers through the EU Budget, 1980–1994 (Receipts minus contributions expressed in ECU m. and as % of national GDP)

	1980		1984		1988		1992[a]		1994[a]	
	ECU m.	%	ECU m.	%	ECU m.	%	ECU m.	%	ECU m.	%
Belgium	−273.4	−0.32	−398.2	−0.41	−995.0	−0.79	−21.3	0.01	−307.4	−0.16
Denmark	333.9	0.70	487.2	0.70	350.9	0.38	234.7	0.21	188.1	0.15
Germany	−1670.0	−0.28	−3033.1	−0.39	−6107.1	−0.60	−9309.2	−0.67	−13834.1	−0.90
Greece	—	—	1008.2	2.34	1491.6	3.30	3512.9	4.65	3812.6	4.62
Spain	—	—	—	—	1334.3	0.46	2535.9	0.57	3006.0	0.74
France	380.4	0.08	−459.8	−0.07	−1780.9	−0.22	−2140.4	−0.21	−2801.0	−0.25
Ireland	687.2	5.00	924.1	4.01	1159.3	4.30	2131.9	5.49	1726.9	3.94
Italy	681.2	0.21	1519.0	0.29	124.2	0.02	−813.3	−0.09	−2805.7	−0.58
Luxembourg	−5.1	−0.15	−40.1	−0.93	−67.4	−1.20	179.1	1.87	249.8	2.12
Netherlands	394.5	0.32	434.8	0.27	1150.0	0.60	−738.7	−0.30	−1811.1	−0.64
Portugal	—	—	—	—	514.9	1.45	2173.7	2.96	1880.9	2.55
United Kingdom	−1364.6	−0.35	−1337.0	−0.24	−2070.0	−0.30	−3076.6	−0.38	−1585.4	−0.18

Note: Approximately 10% of all expenditure is absorbed by administrative costs or is used for development aid. These outlays cannot be apportioned among the member states and consequently the aggregate of member states' contributions to the EU budget exceeds the total for receipts.

[a] For 1992 and 1994 administrative costs have been apportioned among member states. Therefore, for those countries with European institutions, namely Belgium, Luxembourg, and to a lesser extent France, results are biased.

Source: Court of Auditors, Annual Reports; and Commission (for GDP data).

through the budget, excluding loans, accounting now for 4–6 per cent of GDP, a figure which is expected to increase further until the end of the decade. Both countries benefit from the Structural Funds and the CAP, although in the case of Greece the net budgetary gain from the CAP is partly compensated by a trade loss. Portugal follows behind as the third most important net beneficiary; the operation of the CAP accounting mainly for the difference with the other two cohesion countries. The net budgetary benefit for Spain is much lower. This has to do with the large size of the country and its relatively higher level of economic development; although not different from Ireland's which, however, has an unbeatable combination: small size, the right mix in terms of agricultural products, and a highly capable political class (and administration) which have learned to play with great skill the Brussels game.

Thus, the redistributive function of the EU budget is already a reality; certainly limited, when compared with the size of inter-regional redistribution of resources inside member countries and federal systems outside the EU, but no longer negligible. Net inflows for at least three out of the four cohesion countries now have a significant macroeconomic effect, and the gradual shift of emphasis from the CAP to the Structural Funds, which also means a shift from consumption to investment, makes those inflows even more beneficial in the long run. On the other hand, the position of Denmark as a net beneficiary, while also being one of the richer countries of the Union, constitutes an anomaly which is the product of financial arrangements in the agricultural sector. The other obvious problem, which is likely to acquire a major political dimension before the next big budgetary negotiation, is the large net contribution of Germany, which has continued rising despite the very large economic cost of unification. Germany's share of the financial burden is disproportionately large.

Income statistics have acquired a very important economic meaning which is often translated into large sums of money through the operations of the Structural Funds and the EU budget in general; and they will also be crucial when the convergence criterion on budget deficits and debts comes to be applied before entry into the final stage of EMU. Pity the statisticians who will have to define purchasing power parities and produce guestimates of the unrecorded sector of national economies. Statistics is thus becoming a profession for the politically brave! Italy has already paid a high price through the EU budget for the upward revision of its income statistics, and other countries may have to follow in the future.

The battles waged by the UK for many years helped to bring budgetary issues to the forefront of public attention. UK representatives waved the flag of equity which for some Europeans was almost indistinguishable from the banner of *juste retour*, associated with infidels. In more recent years, the battleline has shifted considerably: the poorer countries of the Union have been fighting for ever bigger budgets, waving the flag of redistribution. Redistribution has been part and parcel of bigger and restructured budgets; and also of complex package deals which have allowed the implementation of the internal market programme and the adoption of the EMU project. The two major budgetary deals, which were struck in 1988 and 1992, had a very important characteristic in common: they were of long duration (five and seven years respectively) and they were accepted by all the EU institutions concerned. Those budgetary deals have been a major success for the EU and a sign of the strength of the European integration process. The Commission, under the Presidency of Mr Delors, played a decisive role by identifying the main ingredients of the package deals; the Germans acted as a catalyst by adopting a dynamic interpretation of their role as the largest contributor; and the European Parliament gave its approval while also securing an expansion of its own budgetary powers.

There is, of course, no shortage of problems. Many of them are associated with the management of EU financial resources as well as with accountability and transparency, which in turn have to do with the weaknesses of the EU decision-making system, the many failings of the administration in Brussels, and the fragmentation of responsibility in the implementation of common policies and the execution of the common budget. Numerous cases of fraud have been reported by the Court of Auditors in its annual reports, often involving large sums of the European taxpayers' money. The Santer Commission and the Council have begun to take some action in order to deal with those problems which seriously risk to undermine any future attempt to go beyond the existing narrow boundaries of the EU budget (Laffan and Shackleton, 1996).

Both EMU and further enlargement will be pushing in the direction of an expanded role for the EU budget in the future. Back in 1977, the MacDougall group (MacDougall Report, 1977) had stressed the redistributive role of the central budget in existing federations such as the United States and Germany, which accounted for a substantial reduction of inter-state income disparities (for more recent studies, see also Eichengreen, 1990; Sala-i-Martin and Sachs, 1992). This was due to the differential impact of taxation and expenditure policies and the specific and general purpose grants from the federation to the states. The German system of fiscal equalization (*Länderfinanzausgleich*) is a good example of how relatively small amounts of horizontal transfers can have a large effect in terms of the tax revenue of each individual *Land* and the reduction of disparities.

Aware of the political constraints in what it then called the pre-federal state of European integration, the MacDougall study group had proposed a relatively small and high-powered budget. An EC budget accounting for 2–2.5 per cent of GDP (compared with approximately 1.2 per cent at present), with heavy concentration on structural, cyclical, unemployment, and regional policies as well as external aid, and coupled with progressive taxation, could result in a 10 per cent reduction of inter-regional disparities inside the Community, while also providing an effective insurance policy against short-term economic fluctuations. True enough, the MacDougall group had written about the EC of Nine; the task would be, of course, much bigger for the EU of Fifteen. Those proposals stood, however, little chance of being adopted in the political climate of the late 1970s and early 1980s; and they still sound over-ambitious today. In the words of Goodhart and Smith (1993: 443), '[T]he fact that the Report has been pigeon-holed, with none of its recommendations implemented, is not a commentary on its economic analysis'. This failure to implement the recommendations of the MacDougall report has entirely to do with the resistance of several member governments to any further transfer of fiscal powers to Brussels.

Some years later, following in the steps of MacDougall, another study group argued in favour of a long-term social contract between the Community and its member states based on competitive markets, monetary stability, redistribution, and growth (Padoa-Schioppa Report, 1987). According to this group, redistribution through the budget should become virtually automatic. Thus, net national contributions should be progressively related to national income per capita. The Community has already partially moved in this direction with the introduction of the fourth resource, even though there is still no progressivity in national contributions to the EU budget. The need for stronger redistribution in the context of EMU was again reiterated in the Delors report (Delors Report, 1989), while during the Maastricht negotiations the Commission (and especially the Directorate-General for Economic and Financial Affairs as the apostle of financial orthodoxy in Brussels) made an effort to dissociate EMU as much as possible from redistribution, fearing that the demands from the poorer countries could kill the EMU project (Commission, 1990c).

The creation of EMU raises issues of stabilization and redistribution. Redistribution through the EU budget is already there, although it may be deemed insufficient when the exchange rate instrument is no longer available. This redistribution is certainly small when compared with the redistributive impact of national budgets within member states. But still, it may be close to what is politically feasible given the *sui generis* (and rather underdeveloped) nature of the European political system. On the other hand, the stabilization function of the EU budget is still non-existent. A distinction needs to be drawn between stabilization in relation to asymmetric shocks affecting individual countries and regions within an EMU, and stabilization with respect to symmetric shocks affecting the European economy as a whole. The former could be undertaken at a relatively low cost and with a small EU budget (Goodhart and Smith, 1993; Pisani-Ferry *et al.*, 1993). As for the latter, it will most probably have to rely on the close coordination of national fiscal policies, although this is easier said than done. Otherwise, we would have to assume a much bigger EU budget which is not on the cards in the foreseeable future.

The so-called automatic stabilizers in national budgets, which perform the traditional stabilization role, operate mainly through progressive taxation and social security systems. It is through those mechanisms that a substantial reduction of interpersonal disparities is also achieved. The redistributive mechanisms of the EU have so far put the emphasis on inter-country and inter-regional transfers, while interpersonal inequalities (social cohesion in the EC jargon) have been left to national governments to deal with. In a world of growing unemployment, where those who are being pushed out of the market also show signs of turning against Europe and where national systems face increasing difficulties in coping with the new problems, there will be pressures for the Union to shift, at least partially, the direction of its own redistributive instruments. Such a shift could also include a stabilization dimension. It would be an act of political self-defence; but it would also require considerable changes in the whole area of European public finance.

Where and how could the extra money be raised? Should there be an element of progressivity in national contributions as a function of GDP per capita or could we even envisage an EU progressive surcharge on national income taxes? On the other hand, greater reliance on the VAT, as a source of EU revenue, would very much depend on further progress towards harmonization and the shift to the origin principle (see also Chapter 5; and Spahn, 1993). Should there be new EU taxes and of what kind? The Commission has proposed the introduction of an energy tax which would also have an environment-friendly dimension; but with little success so far. On the other hand, the Union could make a more extensive use of its capacity to borrow in international capital markets in order to finance investment expenditure. The development of trans-European networks offers a very good example.

Any further strengthening of the EU budget and its redistributive/stabilization functions would inevitably raise more general questions regarding efficiency in the use of scarce resources, transparency, and democratic accountability. These are the inevitable questions faced by a fledgling political system, which have not been answered adequately by Maastricht. It remains to be seen whether the new IGC which started in 1996 will deliver anything more substantial in this respect.

The demands on the EU budget are bound to multiply as a result of future enlargements. Almost all candidate countries (and the list is very long) have much lower income levels than the existing members of the EU and also large agricultural sectors. Even though the financial cost has sometimes been exaggerated, assuming unchanged EU policies and unlimited absorptive capacity on the part of the future members, there is no doubt that further enlargement will entail an important additional burden on the EU budget (see also Chapter 10). The new budgetary deal will have to be struck before 1999. It will have to take both EMU and further enlargement into account, with perhaps more emphasis on the former rather than the latter, since the accession of new members is not envisaged to take place before the early years of the new century, followed by long(?) transitional periods. Even if the EU of Fifteen decides to buy time with respect to further enlargement, this will inevitably cost money; and so too will a more active international role in the context of the CFSP. Small may be beautiful for some, but the pressures on the EU budget are bound to grow stronger, assuming of course that the ambitions enshrined in treaties are meant to be taken seriously.

10

EUROPEAN OR GLOBAL POWER?

European economic integration does not take place in an international vacuum. The countries of the EU are open economies, with close interaction with the rest of the world. Therefore, intra-EU developments are bound to be seriously affected by economic events and political decisions taken outside the Union boundaries. On the other hand, the combined size of EU countries makes them a major economic actor on the world scene, an actor whose actions have a significant impact on the international economic system. The small country assumption frequently employed in economics textbooks hardly applies to several EU member countries taken separately; it makes absolutely no sense for the regional bloc as a whole.

The early stages of European regional integration were directly linked to the postwar process of international liberalization, and both in turn contributed to the remarkable growth of international interdependence. Later, the internal market programme was largely a response to world market forces; and it is now very difficult to separate the effect of political decisions at the European level from the effect of autonomous economic forces which transcend political frontiers. Much of the literature on globalization in fact goes much further by arguing that in (already?) global markets there is very little that governments can do to influence economic outcomes, and that the transfer of power from the national to the European level would make little difference. What, if any, is the specificity of Europe, who should define it, where should the external frontier be, and by what means should it be defended? These are old questions which acquire new significance during the current phase of deepening of regional integration. A group of people usually defines itself collectively with reference to outsiders, and the same applies to political and economic systems. There is little reason to assume that the new regional economic system in Europe will behave differently.

The EC started basically as an incomplete customs union, which meant that the common external tariff constituted the building block of its fledgling international role. With the gradual deepening of integration, new common instruments have been created. It has happened with the internal market programme; and the same will happen in the future with EMU. The division of power between different levels of authority has been constantly changing, and in some cases it has remained, perhaps intentionally, ambiguous. The picture is further complicated by the wide discrepancy between political objectives and economic instruments at the Union level, which has often made it difficult to understand and even more difficult to evaluate EU policies in terms of purely economic criteria. Duchêne (1973) coined the term 'civilian power' to describe the reality of a powerful economic bloc which was heavily constrained in the traditional area of foreign and defence policy, in other words in what is generally referred to in the academic literature as high politics. The Community/Union has frequently resorted in the past to economic instruments for the pursuit of wider political objectives. The concept of the 'civilian power' could therefore be considered, at least partly, as an *ex post* rationalization of the constraints imposed by an underdeveloped political system and the international balance of power; and sometimes as an attempt to make virtue out of necessity, by offering this as a new model of international political behaviour.

Things seemed to change with the decision reached at Maastricht to create a second pillar on common foreign and security policy. Some years later, the assessment made of the CFSP by most political analysts was hardly encouraging. Hill (1993: 306) had already stressed the capability–expectations gap in terms of Europe's international role. The experience of the first few years of the CFSP has provided ample confirmation of the existence of such a gap. Forster and Wallace (1996: 433) write:

The twenty-five years since the launch of EPC have moved west European foreign policy-making from independent diplomacy to information-sharing, limited common analysis, extensive interpenetration of governments, and the beginnings of integrated west European defence. The policy networks are in place, constituting a powerful interest in maintaining the momentum. The symbol of sovereignty, however, hampers movement; and the ambivalence of political leaders and publics about the desirability of the declared objective slows it further.

In stronger terms, it could perhaps be added that the functional and territorial division of tasks in the formulation and implementation of European foreign policy/external relations almost ensures the political emasculation of this new and rather *sui generis* international actor. The artificial distinction between the two pillars created at Maastricht (in the area of high politics, the emphasis is still on intergovernmental cooperation) and the division of responsibilities in the external relations of the Community pillar among three Commissioners and three different directorates-general, coupled with poor internal coordination in the Commission, allow little room for the development of a coherent and effective European role in the international system. Thus, many of the frustrations of the political dwarf seem to have remained until now. What kind of solutions will the new IGC provide to this problem?

This chapter will concentrate on European external economic policies, although always bearing in mind that economic policy instruments usually have wider political effects in the same way that political means often serve economic ends. The first section will discuss the Union's position in the international division of labour and the policy instruments created at the European level. These policy instruments enable the Union to influence market outcomes and also to play an active part in the management of international economic interdependence, at least in some areas. The first section will also critically assess some of the conclusions drawn in the globalization literature. The next one will concentrate on trade policies where the competences of EU institutions are most clearly defined and also effectively exercised. It will examine the link between European integration and international trade liberalization, and more specifically the link between the internal market programme and the Uruguay Round. Are regionalism and internationalization/globalization compatible, and what role does the EU play in this context? The World Trade Organization (WTO) will have a long and difficult agenda; and it will also be expected to manage the entry of new and important actors in the international trading system.

Multilateralism, of course; but not without preferences. The EU's preferential relations with an impressively long list of countries will be examined in the third section. This will inevitably lead us to the discussion of wider economic and political aspects, the choice of privileged partners, the effectiveness of the instruments used, and the changing context within which preferences have been granted. Full membership of the club is the ultimate preference that can be accorded to outsiders. The spectacular change of the European political scene brought about by the breakdown of the old communist order on the eastern side of the Iron Curtain has placed once again the issue of further enlargement at the top of the Union's agenda. The list of candidate countries is very long. The entry of new members will require important reforms of both institutions and internal policies, and the IGC which started in 1996 is supposed to prepare the ground for both widening and deepening; in other words, a new variation on an old and familiar theme. The preparations for the new enlargement will be discussed in the final section of this chapter.

The EU and International Economic Interdependence

Excluding intra-EU trade, the EU accounts for more than 20 per cent of world exports, a share which is significantly bigger than that of the United States and even more so in respect of Japan. The three together, the Triad as it is frequently referred to in the press and the academic literature, represent approximately one-half of total world trade, which is, of course, more than reflected in the relative power and influence they exercise in international trade negotiations. In terms of exports and imports of goods as a percentage of GDP, the openness of the EU as a whole is very much comparable to that of the United States and Japan; the former country having registered a substantial increase since the early 1970s (Fig. 10.1; see also Commission, 1993*c*). Averages can sometimes be very misleading. Thus, the average of exports and imports in the case of Japan conceals very large surpluses and a still relatively closed economy, if one looks at import penetration ratios in the manufacturing sector.

The figures for the EU of Twelve show considerable fluctuations, especially during the last two decades, which have been largely due to changes in commodity

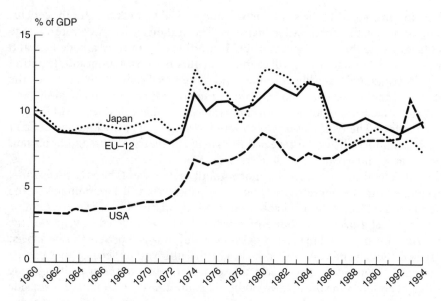

Fig. 10.1. Exports and Imports of Goods of EU-12, USA, and Japan, 1960–1994

Source: Eurostat.

Table 10.1. Breakdown of EU Trade by Trading Partners (Imports and exports as % of extra-EU trade)

Trading partner	1970			1980		
	% of imports	% of exports	exports/ imports	% of imports	% of exports	exports/ imports
Western industrialized countries (non-EU)	54.6	59.3	0.85	46.1	49.6	0.83
EFTA countries	17.4	25.1	1.28	17.0	25.5	1.15
United States	21.7	18.0	0.73	16.9	12.8	0.58
Japan	3.4	2.6	0.68	4.9	2.2	0.34
Central and Eastern Europe and former USSR[a]	8.4	7.3	1.00	7.3	8.0	0.84
CIS	—	—	—	—	—	—
Developing countries	38.0	31.0	0.71	45.7	41.2	0.69
ACP countries[b]	8.9	7.6	0.75	7.3	7.9	0.82
Mediterranean basin[c]	9.4	10.3	0.96	8.3	13.4	1.23
OPEC countries[d]	16.3	7.5	0.40	27.2	18.1	0.51
Asian NICs[e]	1.5	2.1	1.19	3.5	2.7	0.58
China	0.5	0.9	1.32	0.7	0.8	0.90

Notes:

[a] Soviet Union, German Democratic Republic (until 1990), Poland, Czechoslovakia, Hungary, Romania, Bulgaria, and Albania.

[b] This group includes sixty-nine African, Caribbean, and Pacific countries (signatories of the Lomé convention at the end of 1994).

[c] Malta, Yugoslavia, Turkey, Albania, Morocco, Algeria, Tunisia, Libya, Egypt, Cyprus, Lebanon, Syria, Israel, and Jordan. Gibraltar, Ceuta, and Melilla are also included.

prices and most notably oil. What is, however, rather surprising, especially for those who have been brought up in the interdependence and now globalization cults, is that EU external trade as a percentage of GDP is now virtually the same as it used to be more than thirty years ago, namely around 10 per cent. What is true of the EU as a whole is certainly not true for individual member countries which have experienced a very substantial increase in their trade openness due to the increase in intra-EU trade as a percentage of GDP, which after the 1995 enlargement represents more than 60 per cent of total trade for the average EU country (see also Table 8.1). As long as important macroeconomic policy instruments remain in the hands of national governments, national trade statistics will continue to be relevant and Greece will be very different from Arizona (at least in policy terms). This will, of course, change radically with EMU.

The strong regional concentration of the external trade of individual member countries of the EU becomes even more pronounced if trade figures with other European countries are added to those of intra-EU trade. Table 10.1 gives the geographical breakdown of EU external trade. Before the accession of Austria, Finland, and Sweden, EFTA as a group was the biggest trading partner of the Union. Since the 1995 enlargement, more than one-half of the share of EFTA countries has been added to intra-EU trade. For an average EU country (and the same is broadly true of the remaining EFTA countries), approximately three-quarters of its total trade takes place within the wider European area. Regional

Table 10.1. (cont.)

1984			1988			1994		
% of imports	% of exports	exports/ imports	% of imports	% of exports	exports/ imports	% of imports	% of exports	exports/ imports
51.0	55.0	0.97	61.6	61.2	0.83	58.1	53.3	0.96
19.4	21.8	1.01	23.4	26.6	1.06	22.9	22.2	0.97
17.2	21.0	1.10	17.6	19.8	1.05	17.3	17.6	1.02
6.6	2.7	0.36	10.7	4.7	0.41	9.0	4.9	0.54
9.2	6.3	0.62	6.4	5.7	0.83	9.1	8.1	0.99
—	—	—	—	—	—	3.2	3.0	0.75
38.9	37.4	0.86	30.1	31.3	0.97	29.7	34.2	1.15
7.2	5.2	0.66	4.5	4.3	0.89	3.4	2.8	0.80
10.2	12.3	1.09	7.8	9.8	1.17	7.9	10.2	1.29
18.5	15.6	0.76	8.2	8.8	0.98	7.5	6.9	0.91
3.6	3.3	0.82	6.3	5.4	0.80	5.5	5.2	0.93
0.9	1.1	1.13	1.8	1.6	0.83	4.2	2.3	0.56

Notes (cont.):
   d There is an overlap between the Mediterranean and OPEC countries since Algeria and Libya are members of both groups.
   e Hong Kong, South Korea, Singapore, and Taiwan.

Source: Eurostat.

Table 10.2. Sectoral Breakdown of EU External Trade, 1970–1994a (As % of total extra-EU imports or exports in each year)

Commodity type	1970			1980		
	% of EU imports	% of EU exports	exports/ imports	% of EU imports	% of EU exports	exports/ imports
Food products, beverages, and oils (SITC 0+1+4)	18.7	8.2	0.39	9.9	8.7	0.67
Crude materials (SITC 2)	18.8	2.4	0.11	10.6	1.8	0.13
Fuel products (SITC 3)	17.1	3.0	0.15	34.4	4.5	0.10
Chemicals (SITC 5)	5.0	10.6	1.84	4.2	10.3	1.89
Manufactured goods (SITC 6)	18.3	23.0	1.10	12.7	21.8	1.32
Textile and Fabrics (SITC 65)	2.0	5.1	2.27	2.1	3.2	1.20
Iron and Steel (SITC 67)	3.3	6.5	1.70	1.8	5.7	2.51
Machinery and transport equipment (SITC 7)	14.2	40.4	2.50	13.6	37.1	2.10
Office machines and data processors (SITC 75)b	1.7	1.5	0.75	1.9	1.4	0.59
Telecommunications equipment (SITC 76)c	0.7	2.0	2.45	1.7	1.9	0.87
Miscellaneous manufactured articles (SITC 8)	5.0	10.3	1.79	7.4	9.9	1.02
Apparel and clothing accessories (SITC 84)	1.2	1.9	1.36	2.4	1.7	0.53
Goods not classified elsewhere (SITC 9)	2.8	2.2	0.68	7.2	5.9	0.63

Notes:
 a All figures for EU-12. Columns headed 'exports/imports' give the value of EU exports divided by the value of EU imports.
 b For 1970, subcategory 714 of the SITC system as of that time.
 c For 1970, subcategory 724 of the SITC system as of that time.

self-sufficiency is most likely to increase further with the progressive integration of Central and Eastern European countries (CEECs) in the European economic system, starting with trade liberalization and continuing with further enlargement. Thus, regionalism has real meaning in Europe, at least in trade terms.

The share of developing countries has registered a big decline since the 1970s, which is very largely due to the fall in oil prices and the dwindling share of OPEC countries. Among the EU's privileged partners, who have been enjoying preferential treatment as discussed below, the Mediterranean countries have experienced a small reduction in their share of EU external trade, especially as regards their exports, while the ACP (African, Caribbean, and Pacific countries) have suffered a much bigger loss in terms of both exports and imports. On the contrary, the Asian NICs, despite negative preferences, have been steadily increasing their share; and the increase in China's share of the EU external trade, and especially imports in 1994, is really spectacular. These developments further confirm an old prejudice that some countries trade and others sign preferential trade agreements.

Table 10.2 shows the sectoral breakdown of EU external trade for the period between 1970 and 1994. The big bulk of EU external trade has always been intra-industry trade in manufactured goods, although some important changes have

Table 10.2. (*cont.*)

1984			1988			1994		
% of EU imports	% of EU exports	exports/ imports	% of EU imports	% of EU exports	exports/ imports	% of EU imports	% of EU exports	exports/ imports
10.2	8.5	0.75	9.3	7.4	0.75	8.2	7.5	0.78
10.0	1.9	0.17	9.2	2.1	0.21	6.9	1.9	0.27
30.6	5.0	0.15	12.3	2.3	0.17	11.6	2.6	0.22
5.2	10.8	1.89	6.5	12.3	1.77	7.5	13.3	1.77
11.8	19.5	1.49	15.1	18.1	1.13	15.6	16.5	1.05
2.0	3.1	1.40	2.5	3.0	1.12	2.5	3.1	1.24
1.5	5.2	3.18	2.0	4.1	1.96	1.9	3.1	1.62
17.6	35.8	1.83	27.5	38.9	1.32	31.3	43.2	1.38
3.6	2.0	0.50	5.3	2.5	0.44	5.6	2.8	0.50
2.0	1.6	0.74	3.5	1.7	0.44	3.5	2.3	0.66
8.5	11.7	1.24	12.9	13.4	0.97	15.9	13.4	0.84
2.6	2.0	0.67	4.1	2.4	0.55	5.5	2.3	0.42
6.2	6.8	0.99	7.3	5.5	0.71	3.0	1.8	0.60

Sources: Eurostat, External Trade Statistics. Figures for subcategories 65, 67, 75, 76, and 84 for years 1970 and 1980 have been calculated using the OECD, Statistics of Foreign Trade, Series C (Trade by Commodities).

taken place in the position occupied by the EU in the international division of labour over the years. Machinery and transport equipment which has always accounted for a large percentage of EU exports shows a steadily increasing import penetration. This is true of motor vehicles; but it is also true of several dynamic sectors, with a high technology content and very rapid rates of growth, such as telecommunications equipment, office machines, and data processing. With respect to those sectors, the decline of the EU export/import ratio has been substantial. The Union has remained a big net exporter of chemicals and steel; and it has retained a strong presence in the up-market end of what are generally considered as traditional sectors such as textiles and clothing, although the overall export/import ratio for those sectors has been steadily declining. It has increased its self-sufficiency in food products, beverages, and oil, largely due to the operation of the CAP, while it always remains a big net importer of raw materials and fuel products.

Several studies have pointed to the unfavourable pattern of export specialization for the EU, the poor geographical spread because of heavy reliance on slow-growing economies in the developing world, and increasing import penetration (Buigues and Goybet, 1989; Lafay *et al.*, 1989). Growing concern with the progressive loss of competitiveness in high technology sectors had been an important factor for the launching of the internal market programme. Some years later, there were hardly any signs of improvement in this respect. According to the Commission (1993c: 1), the EC had moved from a 5 billion ECU surplus in high technology products in 1982 to a 23 billion ECU deficit in 1990.

Although the above observations are generally true of the EU as a whole, generalizations of this nature conceal enormous differences among the member countries. Obviously, the commodity structure of external trade for a country such as Portugal or Greece is closer to that of some developing countries than the commodity structure of Germany's external trade (Germany accounting for approximately 30 per cent of total EU exports of manufactured goods). The same observation is true of the geographical orientation of trade. Central and Eastern European countries are much more important for the Federal Republic, UK exports to the United States represent a much higher than average share of total exports, while the presence of Spain, the UK, and France is relatively more pronounced in the developing world. This explains why member countries have tended to squint in different directions.

Statistics on merchandise trade are, of course, not the only indicator of economic interdependence. In recent years, trade in services has been growing faster than trade in goods, although still accounting for approximately one-fifth of total world trade. FDI flows have also been growing faster than world trade, mostly during the boom years of the second half of the 1980s, thus leading to a significant restructuring of world production, especially in services and high technology products (see also, Greenaway, 1993; Commission, 1993d). This has been the phase of widespread and rapid diffusion of new technologies accompanied by major institutional innovations. Restructuring at the global level also needs to be considered in conjunction with the establishment of wide networks and co-operation agreements among firms, covering the whole range from R&D to marketing and distribution. The rapid growth of trade in intermediate products and intra-company trade is also consistent with the trend towards an increasing internationalization of production.

A similar, and indeed much more pronounced, trend can be observed with respect to financial markets (O'Brien, 1992). And this is directly linked to technological developments and the rapid liberalization of all capital movements. Capital is much more mobile than either goods or labour. In terms of foreign exchange and to a lesser extent bonds, we can perhaps already talk about 'global' markets; although certainly not yet about stocks and even less so about retail finance where international integration takes place at a more modest pace and mainly through the increasing interconnection of what are still national markets. In this respect, global networks are a more common phenomenon than global actors.

Increasing economic internationalization is an undeniable fact, and there has been considerable acceleration of this process during the recent period. Yet, references to the 'global' economy seem premature and can only be made under poetic licence (for opposing views on this subject, see Ohmae, 1990; Hirst and

Thompson, 1996). The big bulk of production and economic exchange still takes place within national boundaries; the mobility of capital experienced in recent years is still not greater than it was at the beginning of this century; only a small number of multinational companies can be accurately described as global actors; and last but not least, governments continue to form an integral part of the overall economic picture. In other words, political boundaries are far from irrelevant, and this also applies to the EU which has reached the highest stage of integration of national economies.

In recent years, the growth of unemployment and earnings differentials in Western industrialized countries—developments which seem to be like two sides of the same coin—have sparked off a vigorous debate about causes in academic circles and elsewhere. Some writers have attributed much of the increase in unemployment in the EU (and falling relative wages of unskilled workers in the USA) to the rapid growth of imports of manufactured goods from developing countries (see, for example, Wood, 1994; and for a survey of the literature, see Hine and Padoan, 1997). Others argue that technological change has played the dominant part in modifying labour markets (Cooper, 1994). Since unemployment and/or income inequalities are a major political problem, the establishment of a direct link with international trade could have important consequences in terms of protectionist measures; assuming, of course, that the process of liberalization and internationalization is not treated as irreversible.

The EU's position in the international division of labour and the international economic system in general has been the joint product of autonomous economic forces and government policies. Gilpin (1987: 223) has argued that '[in] a world where who produces what is a crucial concern of states and powerful groups, few are willing to leave the determination of trading patterns solely up to the market'. European countries have certainly not been innocent of such intentions and practices, although the policy instruments used have not always been mutually consistent. Although hardly anybody could accuse national governments of internal consistency in their policies, the performance of the Union has usually been worse because of the highly decentralized nature of political power.

The common external tariff (CET) forms an integral part of the customs union, and it has therefore provided the basis for the Community's common commercial policy (CCP) and its role as an international actor. This was, indeed, enshrined in the Treaty of Rome where Articles 110–16 referred to the progressive establishment of the CCP during the twelve-year transitional period; unlike its predecessor, the Paris treaty, which had made no provisions for a common external policy in the sectors of coal and steel. Article 113 provides the legal basis for the common policy which is conducted by the Commission on the basis of mandates agreed upon by the Council of Ministers. But a commercial policy does not only rely on the use of tariffs, and this is explicitly recognized in Article 113 which also refers to other instruments such as liberalization measures (mainly quotas), export policy (credits), anti-dumping, and countervailing measures against subsidies. The EC started as a trading bloc, and it has continued acting as such for a long time.

As regional integration has been progressively moving beyond trade in goods, with the internal market programme acting as an important catalyst in this respect, new issues have entered the agenda of European external economic policy and this has in turn forced member countries to negotiate as a group in international fora, although the Commission's legal right to act as single representative of the Community is still limited to trade in goods. European moves in this direction have more or less coincided with similar developments at the international level as witnessed, for example, by the agenda of the Uruguay Round and the newborn WTO (see also below). The 1992 programme ushered in new issues, such as public procurement and technical standards. It also brought services into the picture. The adoption of new 'regimes' at the European level therefore required a common stance/policy *vis-à-vis* the rest of the world.

Interestingly enough, financial integration as the most advanced form of international economic interdependence is precisely the area where the EU had virtually no role to play until recently. And when it did acquire such a role, through the implementation of the internal market programme, liberalization measures were extended *urbi et orbi*, arguably on the grounds that a common European frontier would be neither desirable nor indeed feasible in view of the high degree of internationalization of economic forces in this area. The same is not, of course, true with respect to labour movements. EU countries have always kept high fences in order to protect their domestic labour markets from large migratory flows from outside, even though the height and the deterrent effect of those fences have varied considerably from one EU country to the other.

Money can buy influence and power. The amounts of money spent through the EU budget on foreign aid have substantially increased in recent years, although they still remain a relatively small fraction of bilateral aid granted by individual member countries. The main beneficiaries have been the Union's privileged partners in its immediate neighbourhood and in parts of the developing world, aid usually being combined with trade preferences. The overall effect, for better or worse, has often fallen much short of expectations, largely because of the difficulties experienced in pursuing a coherent EU policy *vis-à-vis* third countries and the inhibitions often shown by the Commission in the exercise of power on the international stage.

The lack of provisions in the original treaty for a common macroeconomic policy meant, unavoidably, the lack of an EC international presence in this area. This situation has not changed very much after the setting up of regional currency arrangements, first with the snake and later with the EMS. There has been little effective coordination of national policies inside the IMF, and the same has been true of other international fora, including the Group of Seven (G-7) despite its highly selective membership. In the words of Cohen (1995: 256), 'international monetary cooperation, like passionate love, is a good thing but difficult to sustain'. The lack of constancy in the collaborative efforts of the members of the Triad has been coupled with the absence of an EU interlocutor; the Big Four in Europe having always insisted on preserving their own privileges and independence. Things will have to change with the establishment of EMU, although it is not at all clear how the Union will be able to reconcile a single voice in terms of monetary policy with a plurality of (uncoordinated) voices in the area of fiscal policy. Only time will tell.

Trade Policies and the World Trade Organization

Successive GATT negotiations have contributed to the liberalization of international trade mainly through the reduction of tariff levels and the elimination of quantitative restrictions (QRs). This is particularly true of goods, since services have only recently started figuring on the agenda of multilateral negotiations. The EC/EU has played an active part in all those negotiations on the basis of common positions which have usually been the result of long and painful intra-EC bargaining; and the role of the Commission has been very important in this respect. The advantages of a single voice in multilateral trade negotiations soon became evident to EC members; and the emergence of the European regional bloc helped to change the balance of power within GATT.

The CET has been progressively reduced, reaching an average of about 6 per cent for trade in manufactured goods after the Tokyo Round; and it will be further reduced after the implementation of the Uruguay Round agreement. Of course, wide differences in tariff rates lie hidden behind the low average; higher tariff rates have survived in some sensitive sectors such as textiles and clothing, paper products, and consumer electronics. Furthermore, effective rates of protection calculated on the basis of value added are almost invariably higher than nominal rates because of low or even zero rates for the import of raw materials.

However, the internal experience of the Community suggests that tariff barriers are only one part of the story, while the rest is usually much more complicated. Different forms of government intervention, either inside or at the border, create NTBs which play an important role in terms of international economic exchange. Over the years, the attention of GATT has shifted progressively towards NTBs, both because of the reduction in tariff levels and the growth of what used to be called 'new protectionism' in the 1970s. The Tokyo Round was mainly about NTBs, although subsequent experience seems to suggest that the adoption of various codes on technical regulations and standards, customs valuation, import licensing procedures, anti-dumping duties, subsidies and countervailing duties, and public procurement among others, had only a very limited effect on national practices. The same issues figured again prominently on the agenda of the Uruguay Round.

Two broad categories of products can be distinguished which are still subject to relatively high protective barriers in Europe (Jacquemin and Sapir, 1990), with agriculture perhaps forming a third category of its own. On the one hand, there are the labour-intensive products, with low R&D intensity, such as textiles and clothing, leather and footwear, which are characterized by growing import penetration from the developing countries. In these cases, international trade is close to the old Heckscher–Ohlin paradigm of comparative advantage based on different factor endowments. European protection has been aimed mainly at resisting and/or slowing down the process of adjustment imposed by the loss of comparative advantage.

On the other hand, there are products with high R&D, large economies of scale and learning curves, such as telecommunications, consumer electronics, and office equipment, where the steady loss of market shares by European producers has been mainly due to competition from the United States and Japan, and more recently the rapidly industrializing countries of Asia, starting with the so-called Gang of Four (Hong Kong, Singapore, South Korea, and Taiwan). Modern strategic trade theories seem to be more relevant to these products. The new theories of international trade put the emphasis on economies of scale and imperfect competition. Comparative advantage is not given; it is largely created, and governments can play an active role through policies directed at investment, education, and R&D. If there is market failure, then the most relevant question to ask is about the probability of government failure (limited information, vulnerability to interest group pressure, and so on) and the danger of retaliation from other countries. But the answer is no longer clear cut as in the good old days of Ricardo.

In the words of Krugman (1987: 132), a pioneer of the new theories of international trade, 'free trade is not *passé*, but it is an idea which has irretrievably lost its innocence. Its status has shifted from optimum to reasonable rule of thumb'. Strategic trade theories have gained growing popularity among policy-makers in the United States, who often exhibit the enthusiasm of new converts; several of them having gained their reputation as academics before turning to policy-making (see, for example, Tyson, 1992; and for another influential view running along similar lines, see Thurow, 1992). As for most Europeans, a more sceptical (or shall we say agnostic?) view of free trade has a much longer history.

The EU has a variety of policy instruments which can be used as means of influencing the allocation of resources between itself and the rest of the world. They are mostly of a defensive character, since European institutions have neither the instruments nor the legitimacy to pursue an active industrial policy (see also Strange, 1988); and the nature of the European political system does not allow them to adopt the aggressive stance which often characterizes American policies. Strategic trade interaction is hardly an option for the Europeans, and this is, of course, considered as a blessing by those who are liberally minded.

Industrial and trade policy are, of course, intimately linked. If EU industrial policy, even in the very low-key form it has developed in recent years, is intended to strengthen European companies in the struggle for world market shares, a struggle in which both private firms and governments are supposed to play an active role according to the advocates of strategic trade policies, what should be the treatment of foreign subsidiaries? For example, is IBM-France more or less French (and European) than Bull? The increasing participation of US, and to a lesser extent, Japanese subsidiaries in European research programmes suggests that the question has been in fact already answered by deferring not only to international economic realities but also to the large differences in perceptions among member countries (Wyatt-Walter, 1995).

Agriculture was left outside the GATT framework from the very beginning, largely because of the insistence of the United States which had been granted a waiver in 1955 allowing it to keep its domestic agricultural policies outside international control. The subsequent development of the Community's CAP made the Americans bitterly regret the early reluctance to submit to international rules in this area. In turn, Western European protectionism in agriculture has a very long history: it dates back to the end of the previous century and is associated with the loss of comparative advantage in extensive farming to the New World and the political pressure from large landowners. It was further strengthened during the Great Depression (Tracy, 1989).

Community preference, as one of the main principles of the CAP laid down between the Stresa conference of 1958 and 1962, works through a system of variable import levies and export restitutions. The former are calculated as the difference between threshold prices and the price offered by low-cost third country suppliers.[1] They ensure that imports cannot sell below domestically produced goods. This is clearly the most effective form of protection. Tariffs and QRs also form part of the EU armoury. Export restitutions are the other side of the coin of Community preference. They are meant to cover the difference between EU and world prices; and this difference has sometimes been very big indeed. The 1992 reform of the CAP, leading to a substantial reduction in intervention prices, opened the way for an EU–US agreement which in turn eliminated one of the main stumbling blocks of the Uruguay Round. And for most of 1996, as a result of a large increase in world prices, Community preference worked in reverse: subsidizing imports and taxing exports. But until then, this had been very much the exception and not the rule.

Many QRs have been eliminated in recent years, both as a result of the internal market programme, which led to the phasing out of some residual national quotas, and the progressive liberalization of trade with the CEECs. They are still used as an important instrument of protection for textiles and clothing: another sector where protectionism in industrialized countries has a long history. The so-called Long Term Arrangement, dating since 1962, was replaced by four successive Multifibre Arrangements (MFAs) which provided the framework for bilateral agreements between importing and exporting countries for quantitative restrictions on low-cost traded products originating from the developing world. The protectionism of industrialized countries (the EU is certainly not alone in this area) has not prevented the steady increase of import penetration from developing countries; but it has, undoubtedly, slowed down the process. The Uruguay Round has reached an agreement for the progressive phasing out of QRs for textiles and clothing.

---

[1] Although market organizations vary from one product to the other (and they have become increasingly complex over the years), there are some basic principles which are common to most of them. The unity of the market relies on a system of price support which usually includes a target price, as the upper end of the range within which producer prices are left to fluctuate, and an intervention price which operates like a floor (a minimum guaranteed price at which producers can sell their products to intervention). Threshold prices are set between the target and the intervention price.

The EU (and also in some cases, individual member states and producer organizations) have resorted to voluntary export restraints (VERs) in order to slow down the growth of import penetration of their markets. One important advantage of VERs in general is that they offer a certain predictability in terms of trade outcomes, including import ceilings and sometimes also some form of 'price discipline'. Being 'voluntary' and informal agreements, they also provide importing countries with a cloak of legality. From a purely economic point of view, tariffs would be preferable, since these 'voluntary' agreements usually imply some form of cartelization on the side of exporters who also benefit from the higher prices. But tariffs are 'bound' in GATT; hence the recourse to economically second- or third-best solutions.

VERs were an integral part of the policy developed by the EC in order to deal with the deepening crisis of the steel sector which began in the mid-1970s (Tsoukalis and Strauss, 1985). Bilateral agreements were reached with the main suppliers of steel to the Community; and they were renewed annually for several years. Some labour-intensive products such as footwear have also been subject to VERs. They have been applied to more sophisticated goods as well, such as motor cars and electronic equipment, thus being directed mostly against Japan and other Asian countries.

Before the implementation of the internal market programme, the European car industry had been protected mainly through QRs and VERs set on a national basis; external protection being complemented with generous state subsidies (Smith and Venables, 1990). While some EC countries resorted to highly restrictive measures (the Japanese share of the Italian car market being for many years less than 1 per cent), other countries, and most notably the UK, were only too happy to act as a gateway for the Japanese leading to the large European market for cars. Different national measures of protection meant that the EC operated with respect to this sector as a free trade area and not a customs union, which in turn led to long intra-EC disputes about rules of origin and minimum local content as Japanese 'transplants' in the UK tried to export to the rest of the EC. National VERs gave their place to an agreement reached between the EC and Japan in 1991, also in the form of a 'voluntary' ceiling on Japanese car exports, an agreement which, however, does away with the problem of different national restrictions and thus the need to control intra-EU trade in this sector.

Both the EU and the United States have made active use of the anti-dumping instrument in order to protect themselves from 'unfair trade practices' in third countries. Views on what constitutes legitimate protection in this respect vary widely among countries, depending almost entirely on which side of the fence they find themselves on each particular occasion. Neither economic theory nor international legislation offer clear guidance on this issue, and the resulting gap is filled with an explosive mixture of unilateralism and arbitrary action. Such luxury items can usually be afforded by large countries which are less concerned with the threat of retaliation.

Anti-dumping action by the EU needs to be based on evidence of discriminatory pricing by exporters and injury caused to domestic producers. In many cases, however, especially in the context of oligopolistic competition and economies of scale, differential pricing can constitute a perfectly rational and legitimate form of economic behaviour which has little to do with predatory pricing. The line of distinction between the two is virtually impossible to define. On the other hand, the definition of injury is again largely arbitrary.

Anti-dumping action by the EU has been directed mostly at imports of iron and steel products from the CEECs, processed materials and chemical products from China and other low wage economies, textile yarns and fabrics from Turkey and Asian countries, and electronic products from Japan and the Asian NICs. Anti-dumping duties are frequently a multiple of the relevant CET, and they therefore have a large effect on imported quantities. Even the threat of anti-dumping action, which becomes increasingly credible through the cumulative effect of earlier action, can sometimes lead to voluntary restraint both in terms of prices and quantities exported to the European market. In addition to acting as a deterrent, anti-dumping investigations have sometimes also led to the conclusion of 'voluntary export restraint' agreements (Messerlin, 1989; Schuknecht, 1992).

The launching of the internal market programme back in the mid-1980s had been the cause of much speculation and genuine fears about the building of a 'Fortress Europe'. One remarkable feature of the White Paper of 1985 was its apparent introspection manifested through the absence of any serious consideration of the external dimension of the internal market. To a large extent, there was a deliberate attempt to sidestep a potentially controversial issue at a delicate stage of intra-EC negotiations. One step at a time, following popular wisdom.

The US initiative for a new round of multilateral trade negotiations launched in November 1982 had met with very little enthusiasm from the Europeans. In the depths of the recession and 'Euro-pessimism', the EC was hardly in the mood to contemplate measures of international trade liberalization, especially since agriculture and high technology were among the priority items on the American agenda. On the contrary, external protectionism seemed to be the name of the game, at least in some European countries. The French were keen on promoting European champions and therefore argued that the elimination of intra-EC barriers should be accompanied by the raising of the external wall as European producers set about '*la reconquête du marché intérieur*' (Pearce and Sutton, 1986). Such ideas were finally swept aside by the big deregulation waves originating from the other side of the Atlantic and coming to the European shores mostly through the Channel.

'Fortress Europe' proved in the end a false alarm. The internal market programme has not led to higher levels of external protection; if anything, it has contributed to further international liberalization through the essentially deregulatory character of the internal market and also by facilitating an international agreement in the context of the Uruguay Round. In some cases, such as capital movements, internal liberalization has been extended to third countries. In others, the issue of reciprocity became a hot issue, even though it was subsequently heavily diluted as happened with European legislation on banking (Bisignano, 1992); and it has never been applied until now. The legislation for the opening of public procurement in utilities, namely water, energy, telecommunications, and transport, envisaged a 3 per cent premium for EU suppliers. This preference has in fact been waived for those countries which have subscribed to the relevant GATT code.

As regards technical standards, there are no signs that the work of organizations such as CEN, CENELEC, and ETSI has had a protectionist bias, or at least no more protectionist *vis-à-vis* the rest of the world than the work of their national counterparts. The Union has also been negotiating mutual recognition agreements on health and safety tests and certification with several countries. On the other hand, the benefits from the elimination of intra-EU customs and fiscal formalities are reaped by all firms, European or not. And the replacement of national by European quotas, as in the case of Japanese exports of motor cars, has had at least a small liberalizing effect. Hundreds of national quotas for different products have been replaced by a handful of EU quotas.

Competition policy is directly affected by the increasing internationalization of production and economic exchange; and the EU is now even more involved in view of the important powers exercised by the Commission in this area. The growing integration of the world economy, coupled with the inadequacy of international rules, inevitably leads to unilateral actions and the attempt to give an extra-territorial dimension to national laws and decisions. The US courts have acted as pioneers in this respect, especially as regards anti-trust laws and also taxation; and in several cases, the Union has taken action against companies based outside the EU (Rosenthal, 1990). Unilateralism and extra-territoriality are indeed the privilege of the strong. The bilateral agreement on competition policy signed between the EC and the United States in 1991 is meant precisely to avoid conflict between two parties which are more likely than any other to resort to unilateral action with extra-territorial effects.

The further deepening of European integration has also acted as a catalyst for the more recent round of multilateral trade negotiations, following a rather familiar pattern: the Community's partners, first of all, trying to anticipate and minimize the trade diversion effects of internal EC decisions, and then the Community's involvement in the negotiations helping to bring about a shift, albeit reluctant, in the attitudes of the less liberal-minded members. Given their collective experience, it is not altogether surprising that the Europeans have shown greater enthusiasm than the Americans for more effective international institutions and the strengthening of multilateral rules, as witnessed, for example, in their support for the WTO, for stronger multilateral dispute-settlement procedures, and their support for the extension of multilateral rules to services, investment, and intellectual property rights. The main qualification needs to be made with respect to EU resistance to agricultural trade liberalization and tighter discipline over anti-dumping action (Woolcock and Hodges, 1996). While acknowledging the slow-moving nature of the Union decision-making system and also that the relative efficiency in the formulation of common EU positions is often achieved at the expense of transparency and accountability (a familiar problem of the European political system), Woolcock and Hodges (1996: 323) argue that 'in some cases there may be more checks and balances against protectionism [in the EU] than within an individual country'.

The Uruguay Round started officially in September 1986 and the final agreement was signed by 119 countries in Marrakesh in April 1994: nearly eight years to which another four years of preliminary negotiations (1982–6) should be added. The final product arguably does not match the collective effort invested in this latest round of multilateral trade negotiations; but such are the real constraints imposed by a wide diversity of interests, the consensual character of decision-making, and the large number of participants, even though in most cases, the final stages of the negotiation only involve a very small number of countries, and more specifically the countries of the Triad.

There has been a close similarity between the European internal market programme and much of the agenda of the Uruguay Round, dealing with the multitude of NTBs and the extension of jurisdiction to new areas and most notably services. The final result was, however, bound to be very different, with European regional integration going much further than international liberalization. This can be explained by the considerable similarity of economic and social values, the long history of cooperation, the existence of an elaborate institutional machinery, a well-established legal order, and common long-term political goals. The EU is not yet another international 'regime'.

The achievements of the Uruguay Round should not, however, be underestimated (for a general evaluation, see Messerlin, 1995; Hoekman and Kostecki, 1995; Cline, 1995). An agreement has been reached for a further reduction in tariffs, although going down from an average of 6 to 4 per cent for the industrialized countries as far as trade in manufactures is concerned is unlikely to have earth-shattering effects on international trade. More importantly, developing countries have decided to 'bind' a much larger proportion of their own tariffs, while also lowering them significantly.

The successful conclusion of the Uruguay Round had for years hinged around an agreement between the EU and the United States for the liberalization of agricultural trade. The European decision to proceed with the CAP reform in 1992, which will lead to a substantial reduction in intervention prices (and a corresponding reduction in export subsidies), while shifting the burden of support towards income subsidies, opened the way for such an agreement which is not likely to require any additional measures at the EU level. The progressive reduction of export subsidies will be coupled with the conversion of QRs and other NTBs into tariffs, thus helping to reinsert agriculture into the multilateral trading system. A new round of negotiations for a further liberalization of agricultural trade is scheduled to start in 1999. Another sensitive sector was textiles and clothing: here a decision was reached to phase out the MFA quotas over a period of ten years. Although this phasing out will be backloaded and tariffs will remain higher than for most other manufactured goods, the agreement to eliminate quotas in this sector should be seen as an important concession by industrialized to developing countries.

On anti-dumping, there was relatively little progress made to constrain the action of individual countries, mainly because of the resistance of the EU and the United States. In fact, some observers fear that in the future countries will be tempted to resort more to anti-dumping action in order to compensate for liberalization through tariffs and quotas (Messerlin, 1995). The provisions for the control of subsidies have been strengthened, while the Tokyo code on public procurement has been extended. It is, however, difficult to predict the real effect of such measures which can only be tested in practice. Services have also come under multilateral trading rules through the General Agreement on Trade in Services (GATS). But this is basically a framework for negotiations on the liberalization of trade in services, and early experience of such negotiations which started in 1995 was not very encouraging. The Agreement on Trade-Related Intellectual Property Rights (TRIPs) went slightly further, while the Agreement on Trade-Related Investment Measures (TRIMs) was too limited to deal with the host of problems associated with foreign investment. Perhaps in a new round?

Last but not least, the Uruguay Round led to the creation of a new international organization, the WTO, which has replaced the old GATT Secretariat, also putting an end to the provisional character of the GATT agreement (after all, it had only lasted forty-seven years!). The WTO, itself the product of an EU initiative, will be responsible for administering the multilateral trade agreements negotiated by its members; a code of conduct, but perhaps more importantly, a negotiating forum where decisions will continue to be reached by consensus (Hoekman and Kostecki, 1995: 3). In comparison with its predecessor, the WTO has been strengthened with regard to dispute-settlement and surveillance mechanisms. The growing use made of the dispute-settlement procedures of the WTO during the first year of its operation is a good indication of the change in this area. The Uruguay Round agreement is also intended to reduce the possibilities of free-riding and *à la carte* participation (Cline, 1995).

The international economic and political context has changed radically in recent years: the rapidly growing service intensity of production and consumption; the communications revolution; extensive deregulation in the industrialized world; the transition of CEECs as well the New Independent States (NIS) of the former USSR to market economies; the wave of economic liberalization in many parts of the developing world, including most notably the gradual opening of the economies of China and India; and the proliferation of regional integration arrangements. The decline of US hegemony is not such a recent phenomenon. The postwar international economic order had been based on a *Pax Americana* which gradually (and inevitably?) weakened as the world economy returned to a multipolar structure. There is, however, little doubt that among the members of the Triad, which occupy a dominant position in international economic relations, the United States still has a leadership role, arguably because trade negotiations have never been completely unrelated to political power.

The growth in number and scope of regional arrangements, usually on the model of free trade areas with a variable number of exceptions, may be, at least on the surface, difficult to reconcile with increasing globalization and the strengthening of multilateral rules. Regional integration arrangements had been allowed under Article XXIV of the original GATT treaty, with a very liberal interpretation of this article being subsequently made in order to allow for regional preferential agreements which often fell far short of free trade areas or customs unions. For years, the EC used to be the main culprit because of its frequent resort to preferential agreements with its privileged partners. The rules have not been tightened very much as a result of the Uruguay Round.

On the other hand, regional integration arrangements are not necessarily incompatible with international liberalization. On the contrary, many of them, especially in more recent years, seem to be part and parcel of the international liberalization process; and they go into areas where WTO rules cannot reach, thus representing deeper forms of integration (Lawrence, 1996). The North American Free Trade Agreement (NAFTA), the common market of the countries of the southern cone (MERCOSUR), and the Association of South-East Asian Nations (ASEAN) among others point in the same direction. Some have, of course, been more successful than others. Regional integration efforts in Africa and the Arab world, for example, have met with little success. But broadly speaking, regional arrangements are no longer perceived as a serious threat to the multilateral trading system, or at least not so much as in the past. The EU experience, although still very much unique in terms of the breadth and width of economic integration (and not in this respect alone), has contributed to this change of attitude. The limits of an effective joint management of international economic interdependence are still rather narrow, and regional arrangements often allow like-minded countries to proceed further in this direction.

The Changing World of Preferences

Multilateralism, based on the Most Favoured Nation (MFN) treatment, is a principle that the Americans fought very hard to establish as one of the foundations of the postwar international economic order. Yet, important exceptions to this principle soon became unavoidable. Article XXIV of GATT served to legitimize the Community (and the EEC in particular). On the other hand, the Treaty of Rome also made provisions for trade and association agreements with non-member countries and international organizations. The founding fathers thus expressed their intention to make a much wider use of Article XXIV, and this intention was soon to be confirmed. Historical legacies, pressures from outside, the shortage of other policy instruments to bind a privileged relationship, and, shall we say, a rather half-hearted commitment to the principle of multilateralism imported from the other side to the Atlantic, led the EC to rely for many years on trade preferences as an important instrument of its external policy. The conditions have now changed radically.

The attitude adopted by the EC towards preferential agreements, and the actual contents of those agreements, used to be influenced mostly by two main variables, namely the level of economic development of the EC partner and its eligibility as a future member of the Community. In most cases, the two conveniently co-incided, since countries with a higher level of economic development were also, with very few exceptions, those which were considered as potential members (the ultimate test being the European status of a country). For the latter group of countries, preferential agreements were characterized by reciprocal concessions and thus the agreements could be considered as a preparatory stage to full membership. This approach to preferential agreements remains valid and it applies to a significant number of European countries. For the others, who may be considered as the Community's privileged partners in the developing world, there used to be limited or no reciprocity at all in the agreements signed with the EC, although things have now begun to change.

EFTA started as a rival organization to the EEC in Western Europe and as an alternative for countries which opted for the intergovernmental model of cooperation. For the few countries which have remained, its main function is now to manage their relations with the ever-enlarging EU. In 1972, on the eve of the Community's first enlargement, when the first two EFTA countries decided to join the other camp, the remaining members signed individual but similar agreements with the EC. They were free trade agreements covering most industrial goods, while the agricultural sector was virtually excluded. They were accompanied by the usual safeguard clauses and provisions for the application of the rules of origin, the latter being necessary in order to deal with the problem of trade deflection. Through these agreements, a large free trade area for industrial goods was therefore created in Western Europe within which the EC constituted the hard core. Cooperation with the EC was gradually extended to many other areas. The need to secure their access to the large European market often forced the members of EFTA to conform unilaterally with EC rules. For small and very open economies, with a high degree of trade dependence on the EC, there was very little choice. This explains Nell's phrase: 'EFTA countries have reacted against marginalization, but at the inevitable price of satellization' (1990: 352).

The Community's internal market programme presented EFTA countries with a new challenge, and the result was in the end an agreement for the creation of a European Economic Area (EEA) which came into effect on 1 January 1994. The EEA agreement implies the acceptance by the EFTA countries of a very large part of the *acquis communautaire*, concentrating on the free movement of goods, services, persons, and capital, with some transitional arrangements for sensitive areas. It also includes the application of EU competition rules to the whole area of the EEA as well as rules applying with respect to social policy, consumer protection, the environment, and R&D. Regulatory issues are therefore a very important part of the EEA agreement. Provision was also made for a relatively small EFTA contribution in terms of soft loans and grants destined for the less developed members of the EU. On the other hand, agriculture and tax harmonization were left out of the EEA agreement.

In the words of Mortimer (*Financial Times*, 23 October 1991): 'the EEA is a kind of second-class citizenship, which allows you to be governed by rules you do not make, but does not exempt you from contributing to the cost of helping other people, poorer than yourself, to conform to them.' At best, it could be seen as an intermediate stage leading to EU membership. And this is precisely what happened in the case of Austria, Finland, and Sweden, which joined the Union in 1995, thus cutting the duration of this intermediate stage to the absolute minimum. Economic and political conditions have changed radically: the acceleration of the process of internationalization in terms of production and economic exchange, coupled with the deregulatory wave of recent years, not to mention the rapid growth of unemployment, have all seriously undermined the economic and social model which used to characterize most EFTA countries; and neutrality in terms of foreign policy has also lost much of its meaning after the end of the cold war. The time had therefore come for 'peace-loving social democrats' to join the EC/EU.

Small and highly sovereignty-conscious Norway finally stayed out, when the population rejected the proposed treaty of accession by a small majority; it was the second time in slightly more than twenty years. It opted instead for membership of the EEA, together with Iceland, which is particularly sensitive to the fisheries policy of the EU, and Liechtenstein, a small tax paradise in the centre of Europe. For the population of Switzerland, even the EEA agreement proved to be too much of a constraint on national autonomy; it was rejected in a popular referendum. As a result, the Swiss have been negotiating a bilateral agreement with the EU; free movement of labour and transport being among the most difficult items on the agenda. How long will this intermediate stage last? On the economic front, the close integration of the remaining EFTA countries in the wider European system has been a reality for a long time.

There has always been a clear hierarchy of treatment accorded to the Community's partners in the developing world. Although different kinds of agreements have been signed with the large majority of developing countries, either individually or with regional groups, a number of countries have been singled out for special treatment by the EC. One such group can be found on the shores of the Mediterranean. Bilateral agreements with Mediterranean countries started soon after the establishment of the EEC in 1958. Most of them were renewed and extended in the context of the so-called global Mediterranean policy during the 1970s. The term global was essentially a euphemism. Bilateralism still characterized relations between the EC and individual Mediterranean countries. Separate, if virtually identical in some cases, agreements were signed with several countries as a result. The Mediterranean mosaic which emerged had two distinct patterns: one for the European non-member countries which had accepted reciprocity in the agreements signed as part of the package which also included the prospect of membership in the future, and another for the Arab countries of the Mediterranean which involved no reciprocity. The agreement with Israel belonged to the first category, because of the relatively high level of economic development of that country, although there was, of course, no prospect of EC membership.

Three of the existing members of the Union, namely Greece, Portugal, and Spain, had concluded different kinds of preferential agreements with the EC prior to their accession. These agreements served as a preparatory stage for full membership. Three other Mediterranean countries (Cyprus, Malta, and Turkey) have also subsequently applied for membership. All three have association agreements with the EU, centred on the much-delayed objective of customs union, and accompanied with provisions for financial aid and political dialogue (Redmond, 1993; see also below). Very different from one another, they were once referred to by Mr Delors as the 'orphans of Europe', because they remained outside the main economic blocs. Since the dissolution of the Council of Mutual Economic Assistance (CMEA), better known as Comecon, the number of European orphans has increased enormously, and the EU is now the only credible candidate to adopt them.

The typical cooperation agreement with the countries of North Africa and the Middle East provided for free access to the European market for the industrial products of these countries, without any reciprocity on their part (with the exception of Israel), and some special concessions for their agricultural exports as well as technical and financial assistance. The northern members of the EU have been traditionally more favourable to trade concessions, while the southern countries, which would mostly have to pay the price of those concessions because of the existence of competitive products, have naturally been more in favour of aid to which they themselves would have to contribute relatively little. It has all been very predictable.

The old generation of Mediterranean agreements were comprehensive in their coverage and at least superficially generous in the treatment accorded to the Community's partners. But free access for industrial exports does not mean a great deal if there is little to export. The economic and political conditions prevailing in the countries of the southern shores of the Mediterranean were not propitious to development; and this is to put it mildly. The very low levels of FDI are another indication of a more general problem. The economic gap between the north and the south of the Mediterranean has been steadily widening because of economic and also demographic factors. The gap between the EU and the countries of North Africa in terms of nominal GDP per capita is now of the order of 10:1. Will the Mediterranean prove a more effective barrier to population flows from the south than the Rio Grande has been for the United States?

On the other hand, the application of rules of origin, together with restrictions imposed on exports of textiles and clothing and the progressive reduction of the CET, have significantly reduced the value of EU trade concessions to the Mediterranean non-member countries. Most of these countries are mainly agricultural producers whose entry to the European market is heavily restricted through the application of CAP rules. The accession of Greece, Portugal, and Spain to the EC has further reduced the export possibilities of other Mediterranean countries to European markets by substantially increasing the EC self-sufficiency ratio in typical Mediterranean products such as fruit and vegetables. It should not be surprising therefore that, despite trade preferences, the share of Mediterranean countries in the EU's external trade has hardly changed at all between 1970 and 1994 (Table 10.1; see also Bensidoun and Chevallier, 1996). Two countries, Israel and Turkey, now account for approximately one-half of total Mediterranean exports to the EU.

Driven mostly by fears of political instability in their southern backyard, coupled with the growth of Islamic fundamentalism, the presence of large communities of migrants from North Africa in some European countries, and the threat of large new waves of migrants from the area, European countries have long since been searching for a way of exercising a stabilization role in the region. This need has, of course, been felt more strongly by the southern members of the Union. The opening of the economies of the CEECs and the prospect of a new EU enlargement eastwards has added a new dimension, namely the need to strike a balance between the East and the South in the Union's external policy. This is in turn directly related to the internal balance inside the EU. In simple terms, and without underestimating the importance of Italy or Spain, it is about striking a balance between the interests of Germany and the interests of France. In their search for a more effective Mediterranean policy, EU countries have faced the old dilemma of how to reconcile essentially political and security objectives with limited trade and financial instruments. Admittedly, even with a wider range of instruments, the achievement of those objectives would not have been at all easy. Economic development and political stability in many of the Mediterranean non-member countries require major internal reforms which simply cannot be imposed from outside.

There are, however, signs that the 'new' Mediterranean policy is moving, albeit by small steps, precisely in this direction. The emphasis is now on internal structural reforms, reciprocal free trade, and financial aid (Rhein, 1996). The Barcelona conference of November 1995, which brought together the foreign ministers of the EU of Fifteen and the non-member countries of the Mediterranean, with the exception of Libya, adopted some very ambitious objectives. They include the creation of a free trade area comprising all European and Mediterranean countries by 2010 (which is a conveniently distant target). New bilateral agreements are being negotiated which will also attempt to tackle some of the old problems, such as rules of origin and the variety of NTBs. And the hope is expressed that trade liberalization measures will soon be adopted by non-member countries.

The EU has committed the amount of 4.7 billion ECU as financial assistance for the period 1995–9, which constitutes a large increase compared with the amounts spent in the past; and there will be more as loans through the EIB. Yet, the total amounts involved are still significantly smaller than those committed for the CEECs, even more so when compared on a *per capita* basis, which is an indication of relative priorities. Financial assistance will no longer be tied to individual projects, thus following the example set by internal structural policies. And by refusing to establish an *ex ante* allocation of funds among recipient countries, the EU will be able to reward those who undertake internal reforms. The respect of human rights, the strengthening of civil society, and the development of links at the non-governmental level are important features of the new approach adopted by the EU in its Mediterranean policy. They may, however, prove difficult to apply in some cases. Yet, there is little doubt that the new approach is more sophisticated and has a better chance of having a tangible effect.

The ACP are the other important group among the Union's privileged partners.

This group includes some of the poorest countries in the world, and it consists almost entirely of former colonies and dependent territories of EU member countries in Africa plus a few island states in the Caribbean and the Pacific. It does not, however, comprise former colonies in Asia, essentially because of their higher level of economic development and export possibilities. The number of ACP countries has been steadily rising with successive enlargements of the EC, the first enlargement having led to the transition from the Yaoundé to the Lomé conventions. Lomé IV, which was signed in December 1989, is an agreement of ten-year duration between (now) fifteen European countries and seventy countries of the Third World. Tariff-free access applies to virtually all exports of ACP countries, without any reciprocity obligations from their side. This is coupled with preferential rules of origin, complex arrangements for sugar exports, a scheme for the stabilization of export earnings for several commodities (Stabex) and minerals (Sysmin), as well as financial and technical aid.

A mid-term revision of the Lomé IV convention was signed in November 1995, together with a new financial protocol which raised the total sum of financial aid to 14.6 billion ECU for the whole period. Financial assistance to the ACP countries is provided by the European Development Fund (EDF) which is financed through national contributions from member states and not through the EU budget. Other important features of the 1995 revision include improved access for ACP agricultural exports, greater flexibility in the application of the rules of origin, the establishment of a link between economic cooperation and respect for human rights, emphasis on structural adjustment policies, and the allocation of some money to support administrative reforms in the ACP countries. There is clearly some similarity with the new approach adopted as regards the EU's Mediterranean policy.

The Lomé conventions have often been hailed in the past as a model of economic relations between the North and the South. Even allowing for an element of exaggeration, or indeed propaganda, such statements would be completely unthinkable now. In the old days, the combination of preferential access for exports without reciprocity, export stabilization schemes, and relatively generous financial aid were considered as meeting at least some of the demands made by Third World countries in the context of the New International Economic Order (NIEO), which reached its peak during the 1970s, only to sink into oblivion some years later when it became clear that the demands made by the developing countries had been based on a clear misjudgement of both the internal cohesion of the Group of 77 and the international balance of power.

Later, it also became evident that EC concessions could not on their own bring about a fundamental change in economic structures and hence also in international trade. The very large majority of ACP countries are a very good illustration of this. Despite trade preferences, the share of ACP countries in EU total imports from the rest of the world declined from 8.9 per cent in 1970 to 3.4 per cent in 1994 (Table 10.1). What lies behind those figures is the disastrous economic performance of most ACP countries during the last twenty and more years, although the gradual erosion of preferences has also played a part (Davenport *et al.*, 1995;

Cosgrove, 1994). Financial transfers are now by far the most important element of these agreements; and here again, they will become more effective if directly linked to internal structural reforms. Although often criticized as insufficiently generous, the Lomé conventions have been judged positively by governments in the ACP countries; and this is also witnessed by the steadily growing number of participants and the interest of other developing countries in joining.

Outsiders have sometimes levelled accusations of neocolonialism and have seen in European policies a deliberate attempt to divide the Third World; but the assistance of Europeans in this respect would hardly have been essential. Assuming that the EC/EU has indeed tried through the Lomé and the Mediterranean agreements to create its own spheres of influence, it has clearly not chosen the most dynamic countries in the world, at least from an economic point of view. The contrast with developing countries in Asia could not have been starker. A recent study (Commission and UNCTAD, 1996) has pointed to the relatively small attention paid by European companies to the booming economies of Asia. Perhaps, to be more accurate, history and geography seem to have chosen for the Europeans. The policies pursued have been subject to many constraints and have not always shown much internal coherence: a familiar story, after all, in international politics.

Trade preferences have gradually lost much of their economic importance, both because of the declining level of the CET, resulting from successive GATT rounds, and the proliferation of preferences. Too many preferences mean no preferences at all. With respect to developing countries, the economic significance of the preferential concessions offered to the Union's privileged partners has been further reduced by the application of the Generalized System of Preferences (GSP) offered to all developing countries, including in more recent years the CEECs. Under the GSP, tariff-free access has been offered to the industrial exports of all developing countries, although subject to quantitative restrictions beyond which the CET applies as normal. This has sometimes led to absurd situations: Hine (1985), for example, referred to seven different tariff rates for canned sprats and frozen prawns, with marginal differences between them, presumably as an example of bureaucratic paranoia.

The Union seems to have slowly but surely learnt some lessons, although it has not abandoned the idea of privileged partners. The CEECs are the most obvious example of countries which have since 1989 climbed from the bottom to the top of the Community's pyramid of privilege. But here, preferential trade relations, involving progressive liberalization and delayed reciprocity from the other side, are considered as an intermediate stage leading eventually to full membership (see below). And this is not the end of the story: free trade agreements, depending on what operational definition is adopted of the 'substantial' part of trade which is required in order to qualify as such according to GATT (and now WTO) rules, have become fashionable in recent years. They form part of a more general trend of international trade liberalization moves. They also provide good photo opportunities for Commissioners and national politicians on both sides, even when the economic substance of such agreements is sometimes in doubt. Among the more ambitious ideas is that of a transatlantic free trade area which would further strengthen the economic ties between the two sides of the Atlantic. Bilateralism and regionalism seem to prosper, albeit in a more liberal international economic context and with stronger multilateral rules; and the motivations are not always purely economic.

Preparing for a New Enlargement

The cold war had been an important catalyst for the integration process in Western Europe. Its unexpected end, with the breakdown of the communist order in Central and Eastern Europe and the former Soviet Union, created a totally new situation which caught the EC and its member countries totally unprepared. They were certainly not alone. Ways and means had to be found to support the process of political and economic reform. After all, a smooth and peaceful transition to parliamentary democracy and the market economy for countries which had no experience of either for at least several decades was not only an important end in itself; it was also seen as a major investment in peace and stability on the old continent. Not surprisingly, the Community's first response was to employ the policy instruments with which it had been most familiar, namely trade and aid. More instruments were to be employed later (Sedelmeier and Wallace, 1996; de la Serre *et al.*, 1994).

Trade and cooperation agreements, otherwise known as first generation agreements, were signed with individual CEECs. They aimed at the progressive elimination of quotas and the application of MFN treatment, since most CEECs had suffered until then from negative preferences. A new financial instrument was created in 1989 in order to provide technical assistance for the restructuring of the old command economies. The PHARE programme was initially set up for Poland and Hungary, and it was subsequently extended to all other CEECs. The Community also played a central role in the development and coordination of policies for Western countries as a whole. Thus, the European Bank for Reconstruction and Development (EBRD) was set up in London as a result of a French initiative; the aim of EBRD being to foster the transition to market-oriented economies through the provision of loans primarily to the private sector. The EC took 51 per cent of the shares (this figure includes the shares of individual member countries), while a small percentage of shares was allotted to the beneficiary countries. And following a US initiative, the Commission was entrusted with the responsibility to coordinate Western aid to the CEECs channelled through the Group of Twenty-Four (G-24).

The first generation agreements were very quickly overtaken by events; and this led to the conclusion of a new form of association agreements, otherwise known as second generation agreements or Europe Agreements (EAs). They were also subsequently modified and extended. The first negotiations started in December 1990, and by the middle of 1996 Europe Agreements had been signed with ten

CEECs. The Czech Republic, Hungary, Poland, and Slovakia (otherwise known as the Visegrad Four), and the two Balkan countries, Bulgaria and Romania, acquired the status of associates in the first round. They were followed by more difficult cases, namely the three Baltic states, Estonia, Latvia and Lithuania, which had previously been part of the USSR, and later by Slovenia, the only republic from former Yugoslavia to have signed an EA. The pattern was set in the early negotiations; thus, subsequent EAs were more or less on a 'take it or leave it' basis. Because of the long process of ratification of the EAs, trade provisions came into force via interim agreements.

The EAs are preferential agreements of unlimited duration. They are intended to create free trade areas for industrial goods within a period of ten years and with a shorter timetable of liberalization on the EU side. Exception is, however, made for the so-called 'sensitive' sectors, such as coal, steel, and textiles for which EU liberalization is slower and/or more limited; and for agricultural products, for which Community preference continues to apply. These exceptions represent a substantial, albeit declining, part of CEEC exports. A difficult issue of contention in the early negotiations was the free movement of workers. Despite strong pressures from the associated countries, the EU has made no concessions in this area. The persistence of high rates of unemployment and growing social resistance to immigrants, combined with strong migratory pressures from many of the former communist countries, hardly allowed any room for flexibility.

The EAs also contain provisions for economic, cultural, and financial cooperation and the approximation of laws, although they fall short of the provisions made in the EEA agreement. Another feature of the Europe Agreements is the provision for political dialogue through regular bilateral meetings. Although the 'European vocation' of the CEECs was recognized, the Community/Union nevertheless drew a clear distinction between the status of an associate and a full member; and only more recently has it undertaken any specific commitment regarding the future accession of the associated countries.

The EAs fell short of the expectations of the associated countries which were pressing for better access to the Community market and a clear commitment to their early admission as full members (Saryusz-Wolski, 1994). The restrictions on sensitive products were strongly criticized by many economists who pointed to the welfare gains from trade liberalization and the very limited impact on EU producers which liberalization would have in the above sectors. According to Rollo and Smith (1993: 165), '[No] rational economic explanation for the EC's sensitivity with respect to trade with Eastern Europe emerges' (see also Faini and Portes, 1995). The frequent resort to anti-dumping action was also severely criticized.

The Community's policy *vis-à-vis* the CEECs gradually changed. Germany and the UK in particular acted as strong advocates of a more liberal policy, albeit not always in a consistent manner, and favoured an early new round of enlargement. There was, however, an important difference between the two: Germany insisted on the link between internal 'deepening' and enlargement, while the UK apparently saw no reason for this. As a result, a new version of the old and familiar debate about widening and deepening emerged (see Michalski and Wallace, 1992; Deubner, 1995). The Maastricht revision of the treaty failed to prepare the ground. After all, the Community was much preoccupied with internal issues at the time, most notably with EMU and the construction of the two new pillars, while the EFTA enlargement was already on the horizon. Thus, internal reforms as a precondition for the Community's enlargement to the East were left for the next IGC.

On the other hand, the transition to parliamentary democracy and the market economy soon proved to be a difficult and painful process. There was therefore little haste for opening the doors to problematic new members. Most people considered the policy based on EAs with some added embellishments to be sufficient. There were also attempts to offer substitutes for EU membership for those eagerly knocking at the door, in the same way as the EEA agreement had been presented as a substitute for membership to the EFTA countries. President Mitterrand's proposal for a 'European confederation' was of that nature.

Time was surely gained, but the policy had to change eventually. It was largely but not entirely the result of German pressure. Previous experience seems to suggest that it is extremely difficult to refuse an application for membership for very long, when the country concerned fulfils the basic political and economic criteria. The EU is, however, extremely good at procrastinating. Between the European Council of Copenhagen in June 1993 and that of Essen in December 1994, the main elements of a 'pre-accession' strategy were defined. They included improved conditions of market access for the exports of associated countries; the progressive integration of the CEECs in the internal market; a reorientation of the PHARE programme; a 'reinforced and extended multilateral dialogue' and a 'structured relationship' with EU institutions.

Trade liberalization moved at a rapid pace, and early enough the bulk of trade in industrial goods became free of any restrictions. The result was a spectacular growth of trade. In 1989, the Visegrad Four, plus Bulgaria and Romania, had accounted for 2.8 per cent of extra-EC exports and 2.7 per cent of extra-EC imports. By 1995, their share had risen to 6.5 and 5.8 per cent respectively (Commission data). The opening of the economies of the CEECs was accompanied by a major geographical shift in both exports and imports towards the EU and an increase in trade surpluses in favour of the latter. Germany emerged as by far the biggest trading partner of the CEECs, accounting in 1993 for 55 per cent of total EU exports to the area (Commission, 1994e). Among the CEECs, Poland, the Czech Republic, Hungary, and Slovenia are in descending order the most important trading partners of the EU. On the other hand, it should not be surprising, in view of the export subsidies associated with the functioning of the CAP and the adjustment problems in the CEECs, that the latter, with the exception of Hungary, have become net importers of agricultural products from the EU.

Another White Paper was presented by the Commission in May 1995 (Commission, 1995f), with a long and awe-inspiring list of the measures which the candidate countries will need to introduce progressively as the necessary preparation before the adoption of the *acquis*. Some provision was also made for technical assistance in order to facilitate this huge task. A cynical interpretation of this White Paper could be that the Commission was passing the buck on to the candidate countries.

The amounts committed to the PHARE programme were raised to 6.7 billion ECU for the period 1995–9, which will make a total of approximately 11 billion for 1989–99. One-quarter of the total amount committed can now be spent on infrastructural investment. Earlier on, a decision had also been taken to move away from an exclusive focus on the economics of transition, through the introduction of a democracy programme financed by PHARE. There are also other forms of EU assistance to the CEECs, such as balance of payments loans and loans through the EIB. The big bulk of financial assistance to Central and Eastern Europe (almost 70 per cent of total grants and credits from G-24) comes from countries of the European Union; but most of it is in the form of bilateral assistance which does not involve their common institutions. Member countries have jealously tried to retain the power to dispense with their assistance directly and thus also to gain from any leverage or influence that go with it. On the other hand, the PHARE programme has been subject to criticism, because most of the money is still in the form of technical assistance which goes mainly to highly paid Western consultants and also because of the many difficulties experienced by the Commission in matching the small staff available with the large sums of money involved.

The multilateral dialogue and the 'structured relationship' are meant to bring the candidate countries closer to EU institutions and the process of decision-making, while helping to familiarize them with multilateral fora and encouraging them to talk to each other. Regional cooperation in small or larger groupings has been strongly encouraged by the EU, although with relatively limited success. Bilateral relations in Central and Eastern Europe are not always the best, and are certainly in need of improvement. Furthermore, multilateral cooperation which does not extend beyond the region is viewed with great suspicion because of earlier experience with the CMEA and the Warsaw Pact and also because it is sometimes considered as an EU ploy to create another poor substitute for membership of the only European club worth joining. On the other hand, those multilateral meetings have not always been very well prepared, thus leading to a series of long monologues. The associated countries are perhaps learning the hard way that there is really no intermediate stage between association and membership; and they have always known which one they prefer (see also Sedelmeier and Wallace, 1996).

EU countries have also been active bilaterally and through multilateral organizations, such as the Council of Europe and the Organization for Security and Co-operation in Europe (OSCE). The latter will be responsible for the Stability Pact which was signed in Paris in March 1995, following an initiative of the former French Prime Minister, Mr Balladur. The Stability Pact is intended to create a broad political and security framework in Europe and to guarantee the protection of national minorities and the inviolability of frontiers. The very prospect of EU membership has very much influenced the attitude of CEEC governments on such highly sensitive issues by setting standards of politically correct behaviour. One example is the treaty signed between Hungary and Romania in September 1996, which guarantees the inviolability of frontiers and the rights of ethnic minorities; certainly not a minor achievement in view of the existence of a large Hungarian minority in Romania and the long history of tension between the two countries.

Admittedly, the prospect of EU membership has usually worked in tandem with that of NATO membership, both being the two still unattainable objects of desire of Central and Eastern European countries. Many EU countries have had mixed feelings about an early extension of NATO membership to the East, because of the strong reaction by Moscow and fears of destabilizing the region. On the other hand, the tragic war in Yugoslavia has shown the very serious limitations of the CFSP. The Europeans may sometimes play an active role in international diplomacy, when they decide to act in unison, which is not always the case. But faced with an armed conflict, they tend either to react separately or rally behind American leadership, thus leaving the CFSP pillar standing unceremoniously in a forgotten corner.

A clear commitment has finally been undertaken to admit the associated countries as members of the EU as soon as the countries concerned are able to satisfy the economic and political conditions for membership. These conditions include the stability of democratic institutions, respect for human rights and the protection of minorities, a functioning market economy, and last but not least, the ability to implement the *acquis communautaire*. No specific dates have been offered to the anxious candidates. Nevertheless, it has been specified that accession negotiations can only start after the conclusion of the new IGC which is expected to finish sometime in 1997, with the long ratification process following the signing of the treaties of accession.

This IGC is not about economic issues, at least not directly. Its agenda consists mainly of political and institutional reforms intended to deal with the Union's democratic deficit, its cumbersome decision-making procedures, and the ugliness and inefficiency of the pillar structure created at Maastricht. It is intended to prepare the ground for EMU and further enlargement. It may, however, prove unable to deliver the goods, taking place as it does only a few years after the traumatic experience of Maastricht, in an unfavourable economic and political climate, and while member governments are desperately trying to meet the convergence criteria for EMU. This would then mean that the big decisions will be postponed for yet another IGC, perhaps once EMU has already been in place and further enlargement is much closer: around the year 2000?

At the time of writing, there are fourteen applications for membership waiting on the table of the Council of Ministers; one short of the number of existing members. All ten associated CEECs applied between 1994 and 1996. They had been preceded by Turkey in 1987, Cyprus and Malta in 1990, and Switzerland in 1992. The application of Switzerland has been dormant since the 'no' vote in the referendum on the EEA agreement in December 1992.

Turkey's application has also been put in the deep freezer, following the

Commission's negative opinion in December 1989. A relatively low level of economic development, very high inflation and unemployment, a large and rapidly expanding population, a poor record in terms of human rights, bilateral problems with neighbouring Greece, and the continued occupation of the northern part of Cyprus have all combined to temper any enthusiasm that may have existed about Turkey's early accession (see also Redmond, 1993). Cultural and religious differences are the other important, albeit publicly unmentionable, factor behind European reticence. On the other hand, the strategic importance of the country, its membership of NATO, and its long institutional relations with the Community, not to mention fears of growing Islamic fundamentalism, make an outright rejection of Turkey's 'European vocation' well-nigh impossible, and also undesirable.

The Union has been subject to strong American pressures for the establishment of closer relations with Turkey (see also Stern *et al.*, 1996). Some difference of attitudes on this subject between the two sides of the Atlantic is perhaps understandable. What is for the United States an important although distant ally is for the Europeans a close neighbour and a potential member of the Union; hence the greater sensitivity shown by the Europeans on questions of democracy and human rights, not to mention the handling of bilateral relations with Turkey's neighbours. The decision to proceed with a customs union, which came into effect in January 1996, has provided an intermediate and perhaps temporary solution which has already come under strong criticism from the European Parliament. The combination of all the factors mentioned above will continue to complicate the Union's policy towards Turkey.

This leaves the EU with twelve active applications for membership. It has committed itself to begin negotiations with Cyprus and Malta six months after the end of the IGC. The Commission's opinions on the other ten applications from the CEECs are also expected soon after the conclusion of the IGC, 'so that the initial phase of negotiations can coincide with the beginning of negotiations with Cyprus and Malta six months after the end of the IGC, taking its results into account' (European Council in Florence, June 1996). Thus, we know that negotiations with the applicants will start more or less at the same time in 1998 at the earliest, assuming that there are no outright negative opinions which are subsequently endorsed by the Council. All applicants are therefore likely to start together, but nobody knows as yet if and when each one of them arrives at the finishing line.

Given the wide economic and political differences among them and also the different degrees of interest and support each one enjoys inside the Union (and the relative strength of their respective sponsors), the most likely scenario is that further enlargement to the East and the South will take place in successive rounds; and some applicants may have to wait for a long time. The length of accession negotiations is totally unpredictable and it is very much determined by political factors. For example, the negotiations of Austria, Finland, and Sweden were completed in only thirteen months, while the negotiations with Spain and Portugal had lasted almost seven years. Therefore, under normal circumstances and counting the minimum time needed for negotiations and the long process of ratifications which follows, the first new members might be able to join in the year 2001 or 2002. This is too far ahead to be able to make accurate predictions. In the meantime, EMU should also have happened; and this adds an important and unknown variable in the equation.

Among the candidates, Cyprus and Malta (will it remain a candidate after the election of a Labour government in October 1996?) present very few economic problems, because of their small size and also because of their more advanced level of development, particularly in the case of Cyprus. The prospect of entry of two more countries the size of Luxembourg raises some difficult questions about representation in the various EU institutions and the rotating six-month Presidency of the Council. The answer, if any, which the new IGC will give on this highly sensitive political issue is still unknown. The application of Cyprus is very much complicated by the continuing division of the island. Can membership be envisaged without a more permanent solution to the internal problem and is the Union ready to undertake an active role in this respect, having until recently opted for a back-seat position, with the United States and sometimes also the United Nations at the driving wheel?

Among the ten associated CEECs, there are considerable differences in terms of the progress made in their political and economic transition, their relative importance for the Union and its individual members, as well as their strategic importance or vulnerability. Poland, Hungary, Slovenia, the Czech Republic, and the Slovak Republic have been fast in liberalizing their economies (World Bank, 1996). Hungary accounts for a very large percentage of total FDI flows to the region, and all countries have experienced a major shift of their external trade towards the EU. They are expected to be on the fast lane in the membership race, with the possible exception of Slovakia where serious problems have appeared with respect to the functioning of democratic institutions.

Bulgaria and Romania have significantly lower levels of GDP compared with the above countries. They have also been slow in terms of economic liberalization, they have attracted little foreign investment (Romania has been more successful than Bulgaria), and their political system has shown signs of instability and/or some of the unsavoury features of the old regimes. To make matters worse, they seem to lack strong sponsors within the Council. On the other hand, their geographical contiguity to an unstable region increases the importance of their being part of the wider European system.

The Baltic countries present a different set of issues. Late starters in terms of economic liberalization, more recently they have been rapidly catching up. Small in size, they have low GDP levels which are close to those of Bulgaria and Romania. With large Russian minorities in their territories and located too close for comfort to big Russia, they are highly vulnerable to any pressures which Moscow may want to exert upon them. Russia has in fact drawn a distinction, as regards those countries, between EU membership to which it does not object and NATO membership to which it objects in rather strong terms.

The population of the ten CEECs is equivalent to 29 per cent of the population of the EU of Fifteen, while the CEECs' combined size is 33 per cent of the area of the EU. In contrast, their combined GDP is estimated to be less than 4 per cent of the GDP of Fifteen (approximately equivalent to the economic weight of the Netherlands). Therefore, the impact of their accession in terms of trade for instance should be very limited, even we if allow for high rates of economic growth and trade in the meantime; and this applies even to the so-called sensitive sectors. The burden of adjustment will, of course, fall mainly on the new members. For the EU, the main economic issues will be of a budgetary nature, especially as regards the financing of the CAP and the Structural Funds, and also with respect to the free movement of labour. On the other hand, the accession of new members is bound to accentuate already existing problems regarding the functioning of common institutions. Questions will also be asked regarding the ability of new members to implement and enforce the *acquis*. Further enlargement will unavoidably strengthen the calls for more flexibility and differentiation in terms of the common policies adopted by member countries.

Predictions of a very large budgetary cost associated with the accession of all CEECs, a cost which was considered to be politically unfeasible, led some people to look for alternatives to early membership (Baldwin, 1994). More recent estimates made by the Commission, coupled with the ingenuity of Brussels bureaucrats in looking for ways to bring the estimated costs down, have produced much reduced figures. Such estimates can only give a very rough idea of the orders of magnitude involved. There are still several years before the first round of further enlargement takes place, and accession has always been followed by a transitional period which is likely to last a minimum of five years. Thus, under normal circumstances, the full economic impact resulting from the accession of the first new members will not be felt before 2006 at the earliest. It takes a very bold person indeed to make economic predictions at such a distance.

In the ten CEECs which are already candidates for membership, approximately 25 per cent of the labour force is engaged in agriculture—more people in absolute terms than those engaged in agriculture in the EU of Fifteen. Prices are very much lower than EU support prices and production in most countries has registered a major decline because of adjustment problems after the switch away from the old collective system of farming. The prospect of enlargement will increase the international pressures that already exist for the Union to continue along the path set by the 1992 reform, leading to even lower support prices and a further decoupling of compensatory payments from production. This may combine with pressures for further renationalization of agricultural policies (see also Mahé *et al.*, 1995).

Should compensatory payments be made to farmers in the CEECs once they have joined, even though they do not suffer from any reduction in prices—precisely why compensation has been paid to their more fortunate fellow producers in existing member countries? This is perhaps an ingenious question and politically awkward, but it is bound to be asked. Should the money be used instead, for example, for programmes of rural development and environmental protection? In the meantime, the Union could make a concrete contribution to farmers in the associated countries by improving their access to EU markets and also by reducing the quantities of subsidized exports which are still being dumped in the markets of its associates. It might also envisage the financing of pre-accession modernization programmes for their agricultural sectors. This would, of course, involve an additional burden on the EU budget; but it might be considered a wise investment for the future of the enlarged Union.

All candidate countries will become major beneficiaries of EU structural policies upon their accession. They will all qualify for financial assistance from the Structural Funds under Objective 1 (being much below the present 75 per cent threshold of average EU GDP) and also from the Cohesion Fund (see also Besnainou, 1995). EU structural policies will come under review before the end of 1999, when the second Delors package runs out, and thus before any new enlargement takes place. This review will need to reconcile the interests of major contributors to the EU budget, most notably Germany; the present beneficiaries from EU structural policies, most particularly the four cohesion countries; and those waiting outside to join the feast. The difference between the amounts currently spent on the poorer countries and regions of the Union on the one hand and on the other, the associated countries which have been recognized as members-in-waiting and in much greater need than any insider, is very large indeed. It is a reflection of the importance of having a seat (and a vote) in the Council; it is also another illustration of the limited vision with which the Union has so far approached the political and economic transformation in Central and Eastern Europe.

It will not be easy to reconcile the interests of the North, the South, and the East with respect to the scale and nature of redistributive policies in an enlarged Union. Since the next review is scheduled to take place before further enlargement, the interests of existing members are bound to be given greater weight. '*Les absents ont toujours tort*': this is an old truth of social and political behaviour. Given the large gaps in terms of GDP per head which exist between the poorest members of the EU of Fifteen and most of the candidate countries, an extension of the existing rules would disqualify many of the present beneficiaries, which is politically unrealistic. And this would not be the only problem: the extension of current rates of assistance through the Structural Funds and the Cohesion Fund (which now represent approximately 3.5 per cent of GDP annually for Greece) to the candidate countries would produce transfers which would amount to 10–20 per cent of their GDP. Such numbers exceed the absorptive capacity of any country and its ability to provide matching funds.

Even with these qualifications, the distribution of funds among an increased number of beneficiaries will not be at all easy. It is interesting that the present Commissioner for regional policy, Mrs Wulf-Mathies, has thrown the idea of keeping the total amount for EU structural policy steady as a percentage of the combined GDP of the enlarged Union (expected to reach 0.46 in 1999), which should allow for some increase in real terms for total expenditure, although leaving (significantly?) less for the present beneficiaries. Given the long timetable envisaged for further enlargement, should the Union adopt a more generous pre-accession package than what is currently on offer through the PHARE programme? In times of budgetary consolidation, when all member countries are trying to meet the budget criterion set by Maastricht, this may sound extravagant and totally unrealistic. The broad budgetary lines have already been decided for the period until 1999. The new package which will be negotiated before the end of the decade will have to make provision for enlargement; how much is open to speculation.

The further enlargement of the EU is a long-term issue. It will be largely influenced by a whole range of variables which are still unknown: the outcome of the new IGC, entry into the final stage of EMU, the new budgetary deal, and the reform of structural policies, to mention only those which already figure in the equation. Rightly or wrongly, the Union has decided to deepen before it widens. The next few years should provide crucial answers as regards the nature and extent of this deepening.

Under the pressure of external events, the EU has been slowly giving shape to a European policy which is centred around the long-term goal of membership for all European countries which are able to meet the basic political and economic criteria, even though in some cases the long term may prove very long indeed. This European policy, which is the child of the post-cold war period, leaves much room for differentiation and for sub-groupings of countries with similar economic and political characteristics. There is the group of Eftans, which includes the few countries which have opted to stay outside the Union, at least for the time being; the two Mediterranean islands which are first in the queue to join; the ten associated countries of Central and Eastern Europe, which are further subdivided into smaller regional groupings and which have very different handicaps in the membership race; and Turkey which perhaps constitutes a category of its own, and a difficult one at that.

There are also the new republics which have emerged from the bloody war in greater Yugoslavia, and also Albania, the poorest country of Europe. As the situation in this turbulent part of the Balkans becomes more stable, the European policy of the EU will gradually be extended to those countries; and it will be directly linked to political and economic reform. If the EU can still do relatively little in terms of peace enforcement, even in its immediate neighbourhood, it has more powerful instruments at its disposal to influence transition in times of peace. Was that supposed to be the meaning of the term 'civilian power'?

There is still some ambiguity as regards the ultimate frontier of Europe to the East, since all the other frontiers are clearly demarcated by nature. The line drawn between the three Baltic states and the other newly independent republics of the former USSR implies an important political decision. It is the line that separates those countries which are eligible for membership of the EU and the rest. It reflects strategic and balance of power factors more than cultural or historical ones. Are Russia, Georgia, and the Ukraine more or less European than others? It is, however, very difficult to imagine any of them inside the Union fold, even in the more distant future.

The EU has also tried to influence the course of political and economic reforms in the countries which now belong to the Commonwealth of Independent States

(CIS), a loose regional grouping which has taken the place of the former USSR, minus Estonia, Latvia, and Lithuania. The EU has signed partnership and co-operation agreements with some of the CIS, including most notably the Russian Federation; it has dispensed economic aid and technical assistance, more generously than other Western donors, either bilaterally or through EU institutions (the TACIS—technical assistance to the CIS—programme being the counterpart of the PHARE programme for the CIS); and it has also tried to influence events through the use of more traditional tools of international diplomacy. The impact seems to be rather limited. The size of the problem is too big for the EU to handle effectively; member countries are usually tempted to act separately; the objectives jointly pursued are often vague and the message delivered abroad unclear and *sotto voce*; and last but not least, the American superpower leaves the EU little room for independent manoeuvre. As has happened in other parts of the world in recent years, the United States decides the policy and takes the action, while the European allies are invited to pay a large part of the bill. The Europeans seem so far to have reconciled themselves, albeit with little enthusiasm, to this kind of arrangement.

The EU is undoubtedly a major economic power at the global level, more so in trade than macroeconomic matters. It usually looks much stronger from outside than it does from inside. It commands more respect and it carries more influence in Africa than it does in Asia. But perhaps more importantly, it is a regional power with considerable political and economic influence on the rest of the old continent. EU external policies and the prospect of membership have helped to shape internal policies in many of the transition countries of Central and Eastern Europe. But it is certainly not a traditional power; and it will not be as long as it does not possess the instruments for a common security policy, which may not be the case for several years to come.

11

TEN THESES ON INTEGRATION

The analysis contained in earlier chapters leads to ten simple theses on integration, with the main emphasis on the interaction between economic and political factors. They are followed by a basic question in search of a political answer. The reader should, however, be warned: policy conclusions, explicit or otherwise, are not always value-free.

1. The old trade model of integration has continuously expanded to include not only goods but also services and factors of production. Regulatory, redistributive, and increasingly stabilization policies have entered the European agenda. As a result, an ever-growing number of economic agents and citizens have become directly affected, and integration has entered more and more into the heart of national sovereignty.

The foundations of European economic integration were laid in the aftermath of the Second World War. Since then, three main phases can be distinguished. The first one coincided with the long period of high growth, the golden years of the 1950s and the 1960s, when the creation of common institutions and the establishment of a new legal framework were coupled with the rapid liberalization of intra-European trade, a liberalization which affected mainly trade in goods. In economic terms, the emphasis was on the elimination of border controls, and more specifically the elimination of tariffs and quota restrictions. Active intervention by the common institutions was limited essentially to agriculture, because of the peculiar characteristics of this sector and its large size in the national economies of that period. Provisions for such active intervention also existed in the case of coal and steel, although little use was made of them in those early years.

The second phase was one of relative inaction. The long period of the economic boom came to an end in the early 1970s as the European economies were buffeted by oil shocks and the rapid disintegration of the international monetary order. It could also be argued that the period of rapid growth and high employment carried the seeds of its own destruction, to use a now unfashionable term of political discourse. At the same time, very little happened in terms of integration, and much of the effort of the architects was expended on preventing the collapse of the still very incomplete European edifice. Although those were the years when intra-European economic diversity became pronounced, stagnation is perhaps too strong a term to use since '*l' Europe des petits pas*' continued to move along; and some of those small steps, such as the setting up of the EMS, proved in the end to be very significant. Furthermore, the economic crisis did not prevent more countries from coming into the EC fold; and more rounds of enlargement followed in subsequent years.

The beginning of the third phase can be located around 1985, although some undercurrents of change had been noticeable earlier. The second half of the 1980s was marked by the relaunching of the process of regional integration and a remarkable change in the economic and political climate in Western Europe. Integration moved into new areas, such as economic regulation inside national borders, and also to services and factors of production. The European agenda kept on expanding, and this eventually included the creation of new redistributive instruments. At the same time, the return of high growth and the creation of many new jobs went hand in hand with a major restructuring of industry; and, unlike earlier periods, this restructuring was no longer confined within national boundaries. Although this economic boom proved rather short-lived (there was certainly no revival of the Golden Age which had lasted for more than two decades), the deterioration of the economic environment, accompanied by a resurgence of Euro-scepticism, did not prevent a further expansion of the European agenda. Preparations for a complete EMU are the dominant feature of the second half of the 1990s. The irrevocable fixing of exchange rates and the adoption of the Euro, assuming that they do materialize, will mark the beginning of yet another phase of European integration.

Steadily, the economic map of Western Europe has been transformed. Almost fifty years after the setting up of the first regional organizations, Western Europe is characterized by a high intensity of cross-border economic exchange. National economic frontiers have become less and less important, although they are still far from irrelevant. The transcending of economic frontiers applies not only to border controls but also increasingly to the various forms of indirect discrimination between producers and owners of factors of production on the basis of nationality, resulting from different regulatory frameworks in each country. Integration has slowly but steadily penetrated the area of mixed economy. Over the years, attention has shifted progressively from customs duties on goods to technical regulations and standards, to supervision rules of financial institutions and the opening of public procurement.

Trade liberalization, including the progressive elimination of a large number of NTBs, has helped to bring about a very high degree of trade interdependence among the countries of the EU; and this basically extends to all countries of Western Europe. Intra-European trade has generally grown faster than GDP and also faster than trade with the rest of the world. This interdependence is mainly true of goods, although it also increasingly applies to services which have been at the centre of the latest phase of integration.

The situation is, however, different with respect to capital and labour. Capital mobility has grown spectacularly over the years, but this is much more an international than a European phenomenon. The ability of national governments to influence the location of investment and capital flows in general has been severely curtailed, although it is still far from marginal in the case of FDI. Increased capital mobility has been accompanied by more cross-border mergers and acquisitions; however, with few exceptions, the emergence of the so-called Euro-champions is still a very doubtful proposition. There has been a progressive weakening of ties between firms and states, but here again, we have been witnessing an international and not a purely European phenomenon which sometimes tends to be exaggerated in the globalization literature.

On the contrary, labour mobility across national frontiers has remained low, and most migrants continue to come from outside Western Europe. Within the region, professionals are more mobile, and their mobility is expected to increase further as a result of recent liberalization measures. Largely because of low intra-EU labour mobility, national labour markets are still characterized by wide diversity in terms of legislation and power relations between employers and trade unions; in other words, the European labour market remains highly compartmentalized.

Meanwhile, the EU has also developed important redistributive instruments, mostly through the Structural Funds, which now result in sizeable transfers in favour of the less developed countries and regions. Furthermore, through the EMS and the provisions in the Treaty on European Union for the transition to a complete EMU, not only the exchange and monetary policies of the member countries but also their macroeconomic policies in general are directly affected by their participation in the European economic system.

Historical experience suggests that there is an element of spillover which operates between different areas of economic policy and also between economics and politics. To some extent, the integration process can be viewed as a series of dynamic disequilibria which create the conditions and the pressure for further extension and deepening. Looking for 'level playing fields' in different areas, as a means of protecting the interests of their national economic agents, governments have often created the need for common rules and the transfer of some powers to the centre. Yet, there is no automaticity about the process of spillover, nor is there any guarantee of its irreversibility in individual policy areas or sectors.

2. Integration has influenced the economic order by weakening the power of the state. This is true of the allocation, redistribution, and stabilization functions traditionally performed by state institutions. This also has wider implications in terms of trade-offs, such as the trade-off between efficiency and equality or efficiency and stability.

During the Golden Age, European integration was based on a symbiosis between external liberalization and the strengthening of the economic role of the state at the domestic level. This can be summarized in the phrase 'Keynes at home and Smith abroad'. However, another important consequence of this symbiotic relationship was that integration was essentially limited to trade in goods. This started to break down in the years of stagflation when industrial activism and other forms of national economic protectionism opened large holes in the European edifice. The internal market programme has ushered the EC, and later the EU, into a new phase of integration which is mainly about the mixed economy, while also leading to an extension of its powers in other areas such as social policy and the environment.

The progressive elimination of NTBs has been achieved so far through a combination of deregulatory measures, the wide application of the principle of mutual recognition, which has not, however, proved the magic recipe to cure all ills (and eliminate all barriers), and the adoption of common rules at the European level. Is it regulatory competition (sometimes implying a race to the bottom) or institutional harmonization? The emerging new 'regimes' vary considerably from one economic area to the other, as witnessed, for example, in the case of technical standards, financial services, telecommunications, and labour markets.

Broadly speaking, there has been a significant deregulatory element, although in most cases the jury is still out regarding the extent and the likely effects of this deregulation. The internal market programme has produced some transfer of powers from the nation-state to European institutions, although usually different in kind: the emphasis is on regulation and not on direct intervention. Thus, the EU has acquired a significant regulatory role, for example, in policy areas such as the environment where EU membership has led to a significant raising of standards in some of the less environmentally conscious countries. Thus, a two-tier regulatory structure has been created with a sometimes ambiguous division of powers between European and national authorities (Tsoukalis and Rhodes, 1997). Yet, there is little doubt that the internal market has produced an even more substantial transfer of power from the state to the market. This has been entirely consistent with international developments and the prevailing economic ideology. Nevertheless, the weakening of state power has been perhaps as much by design as by default. The shift in the balance between the state and the market can be at least partly attributed to the weakness of the European political system; sometimes the will is there but the instruments and the legitimacy are lacking.[1]

Europe's industrial policy consists mainly of competition policy which applies both to private enterprises and also increasingly to state aids and nationalized firms. Otherwise, public intervention at the European level is directed mostly at the promotion of R&D, especially in high technology sectors, and inter-firm collaboration across national borders. This is a very mild European version of the old policy of national champions which has become virtually obsolete as a result of growing international economic interdependence (or globalization, if the reader so prefers).

Agriculture is the exception to the rule. *Laissez-faire* in agriculture is not a serious political option. There are too many considerations, apart from narrow market efficiency, which exclude the complete dismantling of the CAP in the foreseeable future; and they have tended to change over time from food security to social and environmental considerations. Yet, for many years there was little correspondence between objectives and instruments, and this led to much wastage

---

[1] While acknowledging the effects which European integration and market liberalization among other factors have had on national economic autonomy, Cassese and Wright (1996) write about the 'restructuring' of the Western European state. See also Dehousse (1996) and Tsoukalis (1996).

of scarce resources, increased inequalities, and serious aggravation in relations with third countries. Since 1992, the CAP has taken the path of serious reform. The gradual shift from an almost exclusive reliance on the price instrument to a combination of lower prices and income subsidies is a move in the right direction; and it is likely to continue further under international pressure and the prospect of further enlargement. In the manufacturing sector, the only important example of a highly interventionist policy has been with respect to steel. It developed as a response to the deep crisis the sector experienced during the years of the long recession of the 1970s and it produced very mixed results at best. It is difficult to envisage such an elaborate system of European controls being put together again in the foreseeable future.

The weakening of state powers is also evident in the area of public finance and more particularly in the ability of national authorities to raise taxes, when there is a high degree of international mobility and hence the possibility of arbitrage across national frontiers. The problem arises because of the wide divergence in terms of national tax rates and the difficulties experienced with respect to harmonization at the European level. In the case of the VAT, this problem has largely, although not entirely, been dealt with through the adoption of the destination principle and the complicated arrangements introduced during the transitory phase which may last longer than originally expected. The problem is more acute with respect to taxes on capital, for which some governments are still insisting that harmonization is neither feasible nor indeed desirable. Taxation on capital incomes and capital gains has been substantially reduced almost everywhere. While all European governments are desperately trying to cut down their budget deficits, largely in order to meet the convergence criteria set at Maastricht, the increasing difficulty in raising taxes on capital presents an awkward political problem; and (why not?), it is also a question of equity.

Keynesianism seems to have been buried deep in the ground by the increasing internationalization of economic activity and also the accumulation of large public debts. The combination of those two factors, reinforced by a new economic orthodoxy which mostly stresses government and not market failure, leaves little room for an active use of monetary and fiscal instruments in order to influence aggregate demand. Integration has further tied the hands of national governments: the EMS and even more so the Maastricht treaty have imposed very narrow limits for government action in the macroeconomic sphere. Neither the political will nor the instruments exist at present to play such a role at the European level.

The strengthening of market forces at the expense of state power has been happening in the name of economic efficiency. Considerations about stability and equity have been gradually pushed into the background, although perhaps not for good. There are important issues which may eventually lead to a new re-ordering of political priorities. The stability of financial markets is one example; increasing income inequalities and the crisis of welfare systems are another.

3. European monetary integration has been driven by a search for stable exchange rates, while also serving as an economic means to a political end. The road to EMU goes through deflationary policies. The final stage also carries high risks, because of inadequate economic substitutes for the exchange rate as an instrument of adjustment and because of the underdeveloped nature of the European political system. If EMU does work, however, it will radically transform the process of integration.

Regional monetary integration has a long history. It has not been the result of a conscious transfer of economic power to European institutions. It can be much better understood instead as the attempt made by national governments to reconcile different and often incompatible economic objectives. In a world of increasingly global capital markets, a term which applies at least to foreign exchange and to a lesser extent to bonds, governments have to choose between fixed exchange rates and an autonomous monetary policy. European governments have generally opted for the former in an attempt to safeguard their external trade and also as a means of avoiding competitive devaluations.

This does not mean that they have always been successful in the achievement of their objectives. Time and time again, member governments have experienced major setbacks, when the particular combination of national policies was deemed by markets to be incompatible with fixed exchange rates. The victory of financial markets over governments has frequently little to do with the alleged 'rationality' or 'efficiency' of the former. It is more a question of relative weight. Be that as it may, it should be clear by now that solemn decisions reached in European Councils are not sufficient by themselves to secure the stability of exchange rates; and even less so, to guarantee a workable monetary union. Faced with the inherent instability of markets, public authorities may be tempted in the future to throw small quantities of sand in the wheels of international finance, although this idea is hardly compatible with the prevailing economic orthodoxy.

EMU has been inextricably linked with high politics, and money is generally considered as one of the foundation stones of the European construction. The political will now seems to be there and the EU is preparing for the big rendezvous of 1999, with national macroeconomic policies being adjusted to the requirements of the convergence criteria set out in the TEU. Unlike the internal market programme, which had a positive effect on market expectations, the road to EMU is littered with deflationary rocks. The conditions for sustainable growth are simply not there, and the efforts made to reach a European consensus on a broad framework of policies for higher growth have so far failed. Whether EMU happens or not (and when) will be determined by the continuous interplay of governments, societies, and markets.

The EU is not an optimum currency area; far from it. There are no adequate adjustment mechanisms, such as labour flexibility and large budgetary transfers, to act as effective substitutes for the exchange rate. There is, therefore, a major economic risk involved in a complete monetary union. A high degree of fiscal decentralization will be no match for the powers of the ECB in terms of monetary policy in the final stage. Furthermore, the viability of EMU is highly doubtful without a more developed European political system capable in turn of guaranteeing the legitimacy needed for the new institutions which will be called upon to manage EMU. Risks may, however, also be treated as a challenge. Thus, EMU could act as another powerful push on the accelerator in terms of both economic and political integration, precisely in order to deal with the problems mentioned above.

4. During the early stages of integration, European institutions concentrated on external liberalization, while national institutions retained responsibility for internal redistribution. Large transfers across national boundaries now form an integral part of the European package deal. The reduction of interpersonal inequalities remains, however, the exclusive responsibility of nation-states.

As mentioned above, the symbiosis between external liberalization and different versions of the mixed economy and the welfare state lasted for many years. It was a major characteristic, indeed a precondition, of the long economic boom of the postwar period in Europe. The progressive expansion and deepening of integration, coupled with increasing economic divergence resulting from successive enlargements, has led to the establishment of a close political link between liberalization and redistribution at the European level. The first important step was taken with the internal market programme and the next step with EMU. Redistribution through the EU budget is essentially on an inter-country and inter-regional basis and the transfers made through the Structural Funds have an important macroeconomic dimension for the poorer countries and regions of the Union. On the other hand, the EU has increasingly relied on differentiation in the application of common rules and policies, this differentiation usually taking the form of longer timetables and temporary derogations, in order to facilitate the adjustment of its weaker members.

In recent years, further liberalization has been accompanied by a very substantial increase in unemployment which seems to be the counterpart to the large increase in income inequalities experienced in the United States (and also the UK which has followed the American example in terms of labour market deregulation). Thus, the recent period of economic restructuring has produced an increasing number of losers and a large amount of uncertainty for many others who see themselves as potential losers in the future. As Europe (and the process of integration) becomes more and more identified with economic liberalization, those who perceive themselves as losers from this process tend to rally behind nationalist flags. Considerable evidence of this can be found in voting patterns and opinion polls of recent years.

Economic integration, and the process of internationalization more generally, coupled with technological change, puts a premium on skills and on the flexibility and mobility of factors of production. Capital should therefore be expected to gain more than labour, and professionals more than unskilled workers. There is already ample evidence pointing in this direction. In the words of Caporaso (1996: 44), 'the regionalization of the European economy, guided by the EU, is not a politically innocent process'. The internal political package deal of postwar European societies is therefore in the process of breaking down; and welfare systems are experiencing increasing difficulties in buying their way out of the problems created by massive economic restructuring.

Those who find it difficult to adjust to rapid technological changes and economic liberalization continue to turn to national institutions, because they simply have nowhere else to turn. Thus, the nation-state becomes a kind of 'Jesus rail' for the losers. Mortimer has a very vivid description: 'In this bewildering new world the nation-state is no longer the engine of modernisation. Instead, it has become the "Jesus rail"—the handle that a white-knuckled passenger clings onto shouting "Jesus", as the car he is travelling in hurtles round a blind corner' (*Financial Times*, 6 April 1994).

Under the pressure of high unemployment and/or growing income inequalities, resistance to further liberalization and the rapid economic change which it implies may grow stronger. This resistance is likely to be targeted against European institutions as the most immediately recognizable representatives and vehicles of change. There will always be a significant number of national politicians who will readily point the finger to Brussels as the main culprit for the social hardship suffered at home. A new European package deal may therefore have to combine liberalization with some of the objectives and instruments of national welfare systems. On the other hand, welfare policy has traditionally served as an important instrument of statecraft; and naturally enough, most national governments are bound to resist such a transfer of powers to the European level.

5. *The lack of a European labour market, coupled with the persistence of large differences in national regulatory systems and productivity levels, sets narrow limits for the development of a European social policy. Social dumping has been more of a political slogan than an economic reality. Yet, European integration needs to rely on a wide consensus as regards the economic and social model for Europe, even though broadly defined.*

Intra-EU labour mobility has remained low, largely because of cultural and linguistic barriers which cannot be legislated away. The labour market is one of the least integrated markets in Europe. National regulation is extensive but also very diverse, and the differences in productivity rates are very wide. Economic and institutional diversity in turn sets narrow limits on the production of European social legislation, generally in the form of minimum common standards and some rather symbolic gestures. It is interesting that much of European social policy has been essentially court-driven (Leibfried and Pearson, 1995), the ECJ being forced to adopt a more active stance than either the Commission or the Council.

The limits for the adoption of neo-corporatist arrangements at the European level are even narrower. They usually need able and willing social partners and strong political institutions to underwrite any agreements reached between them. All those conditions are still absent from the European scene. Political analysts usually tend to underestimate the constraints imposed by economic factors on the development of European social policies, while many economists tend to deal with the labour market as if it were like any other product market.

Social dumping has been the term coined in the more developed countries to give expression to fears about excessive deregulation of labour markets and unfair competition. To the extent that labour market deregulation has happened in recent years, it has been due much more to growing unemployment and/or international competition and less due to insufficient harmonization at the European level. The pressure towards further deregulation will persist as long as European economies cannot create enough jobs.

Many people refer to the existence of a distinct European economic and social model which was gradually created in the aftermath of the Second World War. In the words of Malinvaud (1991: 36), it is based on the philosophy 'that the economy is for the service of people, accepting the notion of a social welfare that values equality of conditions as well as protection against risks, and giving to the State the function of guaranteeing this social welfare'. Although this model needs to adjust to rapidly changing economic conditions, there seems to be a broad agreement in Europe, with some notable exceptions, however, that the fundamentals should remain the same. If the response of individual European countries were to develop very differently, this would most likely create serious tension inside the Union. After all, European integration has never been about the creation of a simple free trade area. A joint definition of a European model, with the development of the necessary policy instruments to back it up, requires a European political market which still does not exist.

6. European integration has contributed to international economic liberalization. 'Fortress Europe' has been one of the myths associated with the internal market programme; another is about economic globalization and the alleged absence of policy choices. While trade preferences are becoming increasingly irrelevant, new policy instruments have been developed. Most importantly, a European policy has gradually emerged, while the Union prepares for new rounds of enlargement.

High economic interpenetration among EU countries is combined with considerable openness *vis-à-vis* the rest of the world. Regional integration and international liberalization have been mutually reinforcing, and this was particularly evident in recent years with the internal market programme and the Uruguay Round. The former has led to lower levels of external protection in some areas, while also acting as a catalyst for multilateral trade negotiations. Thus, 'Fortress Europe' did not materialize, although the fears expressed by outsiders in the early phase of the internal market programme may have helped to attract more FDI inflows as a way of jumping over (imaginary) high fences.

Both the large restructuring of the manufacturing sector and the deregulation of financial services which have marked European economic developments in the more recent period are part of international phenomena; they have not, however, been unaffected by political decisions. And this is a very important point. European integration takes place within the context of growing international economic interdependence, which is more evident in the markets for capital rather than goods. Yet, economic internationalization (or globalization) can be easily exaggerated. The figures for extra-EU trade openness, for example, show a remarkable stability over a period of more than thirty years. There is still considerable room for public regulation and intervention, especially at the European level, and this has been repeatedly evident until now. The literature on economic globalization is often ideologically loaded: markets are always good and governments bad.

Having for years pursued a policy of trade preferences, sometimes for lack of better policy alternatives, the EU and its privileged trading partners have discovered that those preferences have rapidly been losing their economic effect. The Europeans have also realized that they had perhaps concentrated their policy efforts and their trade too much on countries with little economic dynamism, at least judging from the experience until now. Yet, privileged partners are often chosen by history or geography, and not necessarily on the basis of economic performance. The EU consists of countries with high levels of economic prosperity and considerable political stability. With very few exceptions, such as Norway or Switzerland, its immediate neighbours on the east and the south are very different. Low levels of income are coupled in many cases, mostly on its southern water frontier, with the reality or the threat of serious political instability. Demographic explosion, economic stagnation, and Islamic fundamentalism can produce a very explosive mixture in some Mediterranean countries; and this could lead among other things to large new waves of immigrants.

The EU is still very much constrained as an international actor. Internal divisions and the lack of common institutions and instruments in the more traditional areas of foreign policy and security set narrow limits. The tragic events in greater Yugoslavia have exposed the weakness of the CFSP. It is not enough to declare a common foreign and security policy for it to materialize. The economic giant has still not grown much in political terms. Nevertheless, its influence on European affairs is already considerable. Under the pressure of external events, it has progressively developed a European policy which is centred around the target of EU membership, even though the pre-accession period for some candidates may be prolonged.

7. Economic integration has always served wider political objectives. It helped West Germany to recover its sovereignty and exercise it within a European framework; and it later provided the anchor for a unified Germany. It also contributed to democratic consolidation and modernization in the countries of Southern Europe. Performing a similar role for the new democracies of Central and Eastern Europe still remains a challenge which so far has been only very partially met.

Economic integration has never been considered only as an end in itself, and this has been evident at every stage of the process. Wider political considerations have always occupied the most prominent position. Back in the 1950s, when the three Communities were set up, the emphasis on economic instruments was mainly for reasons of political expediency. European integration was seen primarily as a means of dealing with the German problem and the cold war and, only to a lesser extent, was it an instrument for tackling the collective weakness of European economies. Franco-German reconciliation and the successful incorporation of Germany into the European system owe a great deal to regional integration. Not surprisingly, the unification of Germany after the collapse of the postwar division in Europe has been directly linked to the further deepening of integration, mainly through EMU.

Although the process of integration originated in 'Carolingian Europe', which still remains the hub of political power and economic prowess, EU membership has in many respects meant much more for the peripheral and less developed countries, be they Ireland or Greece. It has offered those countries a stable multilateral framework and the opportunity to take an active part in the formulation of European policies instead of being reduced to the role of simple consumers of decisions taken elsewhere. The EC, and later the EU, has also acted as a force of stabilization and modernization for the young democracies of Southern Europe after the collapse of dictatorial regimes. Active participation in European institutions and the application of common rules have played a major role in this respect. Large transfers of funds have also facilitated the adjustment of previously heavily protected economies. The transformation of the Iberian countries has been really spectacular. Although there may still be a Southern problem, manifested in terms of lower income levels and a less satisfactory performance with respect to the convergence criteria—partly due to the relative weakness of their state institutions and the political system in general, a weakness which is often translated into higher rates of inflation and larger budget deficits—the gap with the rest of the EU has been gradually reduced. Broadly speaking, the integration of the new Southern European members should be declared a success.

The challenge presented by the countries of Central and Eastern Europe, which in recent years have been going through a difficult transition to parliamentary democracy and market economy, is undoubtedly much greater. There are many more countries involved—in fact, the final boundaries to the east may not as yet have been finally settled, and there are also candidates in the south of Europe; the difference in terms of levels of economic development is much greater; the experience with democratic institutions in some countries is virtually non-existent; and last but not least, it is all a question of establishing a new geopolitical order in a region of Europe which contains many sources of potential instability and which happens to lie next or close to the Russian border. Already the prospect of EU membership, distant though it may be, plays a major role not only in relation to economic policies (trying to come closer to the requirements of the *acquis communautaire*) but also in the treatment of minorities and the respect of human rights.

Preoccupied with internal problems, the EU has continued treating those countries as outsiders who may one day join; the day of accession being pushed slowly but surely into the more distant future. It has also shown relatively little generosity, and even less imagination, in parting with its money. The difference between intra-EU transfers and economic aid to prospective new members is absolutely striking. If the carrot is small, then the stick which may be sometimes employed as a form of sanction should also be of a similar size. The process of democratization and economic and social modernization of the countries of Central and Eastern Europe will unavoidably be linked to their progressive integration into the European system of which the EU constitutes the most important part. And for this to happen, without killing the hen that lays the eggs, major internal reforms of the EU will be required, coupled perhaps with a more flexible approach towards new members.

8. *Growing internal diversity, itself a product of successive enlargements, and the continuous expansion and deepening of integration have led to increasing differentiation in the application of EU rules. Any attempt to institutionalize a core group of countries could destabilize the Union. What is needed instead is an agreement on core interests and policies accompanied by the necessary institutional reforms. The accession of new members will, however, require special and more flexible arrangements.*

The EC/EU has relied extensively on differentiated rules and selective forms of membership with respect to individual policies in order to deal with growing internal diversity. Timetables of variable duration for the application of the *acquis*, numerous derogations as well as 'opt-ins' and 'opt-outs' have been used to cater for economic weakness, administrative difficulties, or simply different political preferences and tastes. Thus, the longer timetables accorded to cohesion countries for the liberalization of their telecommunications sectors are in recognition of concrete economic difficulties which may justify a longer period of adjustment; differentiated rules in much of European environmental legislation are a function of the economic costs involved, the administrative problems associated with its implementation, and different trade-offs in individual member countries; and the social protocol of the Maastricht treaty is mostly the result of different political preferences and ideologies.

Differentiation is not a recent development in the process of European integration. In fact, it goes back to the founding treaties and the numerous protocols attached to them. However, because of continuous expansion, both in terms of scope and numbers, EU institutions have been forced to rely more frequently on differentiated rules and selective membership of individual policies as a means of going forward. The SEA constituted an important step in this process. In the implementation of the internal market programme, European legislators have made ample use of the flexibility offered to them by the revised treaties. The provisions for EMU in the Maastricht revision have gone even further.

The new IGC which started in 1996 is meant to introduce the necessary institutional reforms in order to prepare the EU for monetary union, further enlargement, and also for a more active stabilization role in the new post-cold war Europe. Flexibility was a key word in early discussions, meant as an answer to growing political and economic diversity. Proposals have been put forward for the creation of a hard core of countries, consisting of those willing and able to lead the Union to the next stage of integration, with France and Germany forming the core of the core (Schäuble and Lamers, 1994; see also Deubner, 1995).

The literature is extremely rich in terms of the metaphors used to describe (and often prescribe) different models of integration, which all depart from the principle of uniform application and universal membership: flying geese and magnetic fields, hubs and spokes and concentric circles are some of the more recent additions in a collection which already included two-tier, multi-speed, and variable geometry models (see, for example, Wallace and Wallace, 1995, for a penetrating analysis and a useful taxonomy).

Some countries have been, of course, always more equal than others. A decision-making system which favours the smaller countries could not be sufficient by itself to compensate for real differences in political and economic power (and influence). Franco-German agreements have continued for many years to provide the basis for a large number of common decisions. The original members of the EC, and also increasingly Spain, have constituted an informal core group, while the UK has willingly excluded itself from it. On the other hand, monetary integration has highlighted the leading role of Germany, a role which has been further strengthened after the fall of the Iron Curtain and the Berlin Wall.

Geography, size, and economic strength place Germany in a very special position in the European system. Its ability to influence decisions has been reinforced by the reputation enjoyed by the Bundesbank, its continued (for how long?) willingness to act as the main funder of the EU budget, and also the greater familiarity of German politicians with a federal-type system. The *savoir-faire* and the remarkable ability of the French political establishment to come up with new ideas and initiatives may no longer be a match for such strong assets. Therefore, the crucial question remains how to integrate a big and powerful Germany inside a strong European Union, while removing the risk of domination over the other countries. This has become one of the main catalysts of the integration process; and EMU needs to be understood in this context.

An institutionalization of a core group of countries would undermine the foundations of the European construction. In fact, it would be a denial of so much that European integration has stood for until now. The crucial point is that participation in different policy areas should remain open to all those willing and able. Furthermore, flexible arrangements and solidarity mechanisms should be used as extensively as possible, without depriving common policies of any real sense, in order to maximize the number of those able to join in. This has been a crucial characteristic of European integration, which it would be a great pity to destroy. What the EU needs is not a hard core but the ability to take decisions on a (qualified) majority basis, with or without a change in the distribution of votes in the Council of Ministers. And this in turn means that the power of veto should be limited to very exceptional cases, while at the same time, the right of self-exclusion from common decisions or policies should be extended. The slowest or most reluctant members of the convoy should not be allowed to impose their speed on the others, unless there is a really vital interest at stake, which should be defined restrictively. Admittedly, such principles are not always easy to apply in concrete circumstances.

It has been suggested that, instead of core countries, we should think of core policies which would form the common base for all members, while participation in other policies would be open to all those willing and able (CEPR, 1995a). This idea may be appealing, at least on the surface, because flexibility is defined in functional and not in geographical terms. One problem would be, of course, to agree on the contents of the common base. Presumably, hardly anybody would dispute the need to include the internal market and all the associated regulatory activities, a reformed CAP, and external trade policy in the common base. It would now be difficult to imagine a European package deal without the Structural Funds; and there are strong economic reasons to include tax harmonization and perhaps more, although the accumulation of more functions and policies should not be an objective in itself. Assuming that an agreement could be reached on the above policies as forming part of the common base, some room for differentiation should also be allowed in order to cater for different needs and (why not?) tastes.

However, a very difficult problem would arise with respect to EMU. Should it also form part of the common base? The treaty sets strict criteria for admission to the final stage of EMU, which implies that several countries will remain in 'derogation' for some time. Moreover, two countries have already obtained 'opt-outs'. Thus, it has become politically accepted that EMU does not form part of this common base. The realism of this apparent compromise is extremely doubtful. If EMU does materialize and it lasts (there are, of course, two 'ifs' in this sentence), it will certainly not be like any other policy. It is bound to become the key element of the new stage of economic integration, while also acting as a powerful catalyst for political union. What would membership of the EU then mean, if the country concerned stayed out of EMU? It is difficult to imagine such a situation lasting for very long. Furthermore, complete independence in the conduct of exchange and monetary policies would be difficult to reconcile with participation in the internal market. The risks associated with competitive devaluations would be too high. Last but not least, the early participants would set the rules of the game which latecomers would subsequently have to accept. It has happened so many times before. On the other hand, the problem with social policy may be easier to tackle. As long as there is no major divergence of national policies, the discussions in Brussels will be more about symbolism than substance. If such a divergence were to develop, things would, of course, become much more complicated.

The long list of prospective new members presents a very real problem in trying to reconcile further deepening with enlargement. In most cases, early accession would necessitate only a partial adoption of the *acquis*, even with respect to the internal market legislation, and/or long transitional periods. The alternative would be to write the accession of several countries *ad calendas Graecas* (or in plain English, to postpone it indefinitely). It will be a difficult decision to take. A strong Union which has reached an internal agreement on the definition of core interests and policies (including a more real CFSP?) and which has also developed the institutions and the political system to back them up should be better able to show the necessary flexibility in order to pave the way for further enlargement.

9. The decision-making system of the EU puts the emphasis on the technical at the expense of the political. The growth of its regulatory function leads to a further trans-

fer of power to technical experts and independent specialized agencies. The creation of the ECB, in charge of monetary policy, will, however, constitute a step too far in this direction as long as it is not accompanied by the strengthening of European political institutions.

Decision-making in the EU tends to depoliticize issues through the use of an impenetrable legal jargon and the many layers of committees. Much of the European legislative process hardly ever catches the public eye: negotiations are usually done behind closed doors and in different committees of experts. It is very characteristic that the majority of decisions, although they are not presumably the most sensitive politically, are taken by the Committee of Permanent Represent-atives (COREPER), consisting of high-level officials and mostly diplomats, without any direct involvement of democratically elected representatives. The role of national parliaments remains extremely limited, while the European Parliament has only very partially succeeded in filling this democratic gap. In the words of W. Wallace (1996: 449): 'The structure of Community policy-making was designed from the outset to disaggregate issues wherever possible, to disguise broader political issues, to push decisions down from ministerial confrontation to official *engrenage*'.

The predominance of technocrats has become further strengthened by the considerable expansion of the EU regulatory role resulting mainly from the internal market programme. It is mostly about the elimination of NTBs in cross-border economic transactions and regulation at the European level. This usually requires specialized knowledge and the exercise of discretionary power. It is true of the world of technical standards and regulations, where the expert meets the interested party, and it is also largely true of environmental and competition policy. In fact, the pressure for the creation of independent agencies endowed with real decision-making powers, such as the European equivalent of the *Kartellamt*, has been steadily growing.

The gradual depoliticization of issues and the concomitant rise of the expert is a more general phenomenon which has also been witnessed at the national level. True enough, technical issues may hide different sets of values and preferences, but the question is how those values and preferences are translated into politics and policies. Wider questions about legitimacy and accountability in our demo-cratic systems are also raised. This problem is much more acute for the fledgling European political system, not only because the process of depoliticization has gone much further but also because the European system does not have the reservoir of legitimacy and the sense of belonging to a real (or imagined) community on which to draw. As the number of people directly affected by the process of integration grows, and so also does the importance of issues dealt with by European institutions, this problem will become more acute.

In the final stage of EMU, responsibility for monetary policy will be transferred from the national to the European level. Provisions have been made in the treaty for the creation of the European Central Bank which will run monetary policy in complete independence from political institutions, be they national or European.

Meanwhile, national central banks which will be part of a federal-type structure, will have also acquired the same degree of independence *vis-à-vis* national authorities. It is all about following the successful model of the Deutsche Bundesbank which enjoys a strong reputation in terms of its ability to deliver the public good of monetary stability.

There are, however, a few crucial differences. First, there will be no equivalent political counterpart to the ECB at the European level, and this absence will give the ECB a degree of real power and non-accountability not experienced by any other central bank in a national system. Secondly, the popular attachment to price stability may not be as strong in other European countries as it is in Germany, mainly for historical reasons. This means that popular attitudes towards trade-offs may also be different. The third follows directly from the second: when difficult (read unpopular) decisions need to be taken, decisions which imply a trade-off between price stability on the one hand and growth and employment on the other, even if many economists claim that such a trade-off can only exist in the short term, the ECB will not be able to draw on the reservoir of legitimacy which is usually available to its national counterparts. A newly independent Banque de France can still draw on the legitimacy of the French state, while there is no such equivalent as yet at the European level. The conclusion to draw is that a truly independent ECB will find it very difficult to function without a more developed European political system.

10. The gap between economic and political integration has been growing wider. The political game remains predominantly national and the permissive consensus on which European integration has relied for many years can no longer be taken for granted. EMU and further enlargement will require stronger and more efficient European institutions and a political system which rests on a more solid popular base.

The underlying theme in this concluding chapter has been the growing gap between economic and political integration which in turn raises questions about the next stage of integration. Economic issues have become increasingly European and international under the influence of autonomous market forces, technological change, and the lowering of economic barriers. National political forces have played an active part in this process. Yet, politics remains predominantly national and the political discourse generally implies that national units are much more independent economically than they actually are. Symbols and public money are still very much in the hands of national governments and this largely determines the direction of loyalties and expectations of their citizens. But there is also a clear time-lag in the perception of change by large sections of the national political élites and the public at large. National political discourse often has a striking sense of unreality.

Malinvaud (1989: 374) has argued that 'achieving European unification while maintaining national autonomy' is like a tragedy in the spirit of Corneille. National governments, together with their citizens, have been the main protagonists in a tragedy which is more and more about the expectations gap in terms of what national governments can actually deliver. The latter are increasingly unable to deliver the goods to which their citizens have become accustomed: steady growth, effective solidarity mechanisms for the reduction of inequalities, insurance against risks, and a wide collection of public goods. These are all functions which European states acquired during the long period of economic boom after the Second World War. And they were added to the more traditional functions of the state, such as the provision of security as well as acting as the embodiment of national identity.

This increasing inability to deliver the economic goods is, of course, directly related to the loss of effective control over the national economy coupled with rapid changes in the international economic environment which have resulted in an increasing number of losers. In the words of Streeck (1996: 312), 'As the gap between formal and effective sovereignty widens and the purchasing power of national citizenship deteriorates ... popular beliefs in the lasting efficacy of national democracy are bound to give rise to distorted expressions of collective preferences, perverse political alliances and self-defeating definitions of interest'. Populism and xenophobia would then be just around the corner.

European integration for long relied on some kind of permissive consensus which has become less solid than in the past. The pains caused during the ratification of the Maastricht treaty should have served as a clear warning sign. Integration now covers a very wide range of issues and policy areas, thus also having a direct impact on an increasing number of citizens. In times of low growth and high unemployment, European integration represents rapid change, associated with economic liberalization, together with restrictive macroeconomic policies and virtually non-existent solidarity mechanisms, except for those operating in favour of the less developed countries and regions. Thus, the European system is not perceived as being able to fill the gap left by the growing weakness of national governments.

Usually covered in their technocratic cloak, European issues remain out of bounds for the ordinary citizen. Political parties, still very much national in their outlook and internal organization, have largely failed until now to act as two-way transmission belts. And certainly, it is not the harmonization of standards which will send people waving banners down the streets of Newcastle and Cagliari; although there are many signs that EMU can achieve this in the streets of Paris, and certainly people do not go out to demonstrate in favour of European policies. Europe is being built from the top downwards and integration remains even now, despite the rapid expansion of the European agenda, largely an affair of élites; it is the privileged who tend to identify more with Europe. Business interests play a more active part than labour, and organized lobbies usually enjoy more favourable access than they do in national political systems.

There is no doubt that European institutions have acquired important functions. The EU is a unique example of a regional economic and political system which seems to defy classification. Schmitter (1995: 29) goes further: he calls it post-national, non-sovereign, polycentric, polymorphic, and neo-medieval. Perhaps, we should simply think in terms of a process of European governance which is being invented and which has not yet acquired a definite shape (see also Jachtenfuchs and Kohler-Koch, 1996). Yet, irrespective of how we describe it, this political system which has developed after almost fifty years of regional integration in Europe, does not seem to be able adequately to fulfil either the goals set by European politicians or the expectations of European societies at large.

Some of the main characteristics of this *sui generis* political system are the slow and inefficient method of decision-making, which is still close to an inter-governmental type of negotiation with multiple layers; poor transparency and accountability of its institutions; an administrative structure which has serious difficulty in coping with the wide range of functions and the financial resources entrusted to it; a large 'implementation deficit' which results from the highly decentralized nature of the system and the difficulties experienced in exercising effective control, accompanied by the threat of sanctions, over the proper im-plementation of decisions reached in Brussels; and perhaps more importantly, the lack of a solid popular base which goes hand in hand with the lack of democratic legitimation. There is no European political market, which means that there is also no proper public debate on European issues. Thus, choices continue to be made (even inertia implies choice) essentially on an intergovernmental basis. Transforming diplomacy into democracy has not proved to be at all easy (Laffan, 1996: 93); and democracy requires the existence of a *demos* and a shared identity which are certainly not there, at least as yet. Can they be created?

Bridging the ever-widening gap between economic and political integration is indeed a pre-condition for the establishment of a new European order based on democratic principles; a new order without hegemony which should eventually extend to the whole of the old continent, while also allowing the Europeans to play an active role in world affairs through their collective institutions. Furthermore, it is a pre-condition for the development of an effective system of governance between the nation-state and an increasingly global economy, which in turn implies that politics should not always genuflect to market forces. Economic and social change is too important to be left only to the market.

A weak European political system will not be able to deliver those goods. Thus, political integration is directly linked to the kind of society Europeans want to live in and the influence they wish to exert on their external environment. This link has not always been clearly spelt out in the public debate, largely because the debate has been confined within national boundaries. Will European politics adjust to economic change and to multiple outside pressures? This is not meant as a rhetorical question. There is no inevitability or automaticity in the process of integration. Only time will tell. The fundamental choices facing European citizens need to be made starker. This is where political action takes over from academic analysis; although, of course, there has never been anything like a clear line separating the two.

REFERENCES

Adams, Heinz, and Rekittke, Karl (1989), 'Ein weites Feld: Standort Europa'. In H. Adams (ed.), *Europa 1992: Strategien, Strukturen, Ressourcen*. Frankfurt: Frankfurter Allgemeine Zeitung.

Aglietta, Michel, Brender, Anton, and Coudert, Virginie (1990), *Globalisation financière: L'Aventure obligée*. Paris: Economica.

Albert, Michel (1991), *Capitalisme contre capitalisme*. Paris: Seuil.

—— and Ball, R. J. (1983). *Towards European Recovery in the 1980s*. Luxembourg: European Parliament, Working Documents 1983–4.

Allen, David (1996a), 'Competition Policy'. In H. Wallace and W. Wallace (eds), *Policy-Making in the European Union*. Oxford: Oxford University Press.

—— (1996b), 'Cohesion and Structural Adjustment'. In H. Wallace and W. Wallace (eds), *Policy-Making in the European Union*. Oxford: Oxford University Press.

Allsopp, C., Davies, G., and Vines, D. (1995), 'Regional Macroeconomic Policy, Fiscal Federalism, and European Integration', *Oxford Review of Economic Policy*, Summer.

Alogoskoufis, George (1995), 'The Two Faces of Janus: Institutions, Policy Regimes and Macroeconomic Performance in Greece', *Economic Policy*, April.

Anderson, Jeffrey (1995), 'Structural Funds and the Social Dimension of EU Policy: Springboard or Stumbling Block?'. In S. Leibfried and P. Pierson (eds.), *European Social Policy: Between Fragmentation and Integration*. Washington, DC: The Brookings Institution.

Atkinson, A. B. (1996), 'Income Distribution in Europe and the United States', *Oxford Review of Economic Policy*, Spring.

Aubry, M. (1989), *Relations sociales et emploi*. Paris: La Documentation Française.

Balassa, Bela (1961), *The Theory of Economic Integration*. London: Allen and Unwin.

Baldwin, Richard (1989), 'The Growth Effects of 1992', *Economic Policy*, 9, October.

—— (1994), *Towards an Integrated Europe*. London: CEPR.

Baltensberger, Ernst, and Dermine, Jean (1987), 'The Role of Public Policy in Ensuring Financial Stability: A Cross-Country, Comparative Perspective'. In R. Portes and A. K. Swoboda (eds.), *Threats to International Financial Stability*. Cambridge: CEPR/Cambridge University Press.

Bank for International Settlements (1995), *65th Annual Report*. Basle: BIS.

Bank of England (1989), 'The Single European Market: Survey of the UK Financial Services Industry', *Bank of England Quarterly Bulletin*, 3, May.

Banting, Keith (1995), 'The Welfare State as Statecraft: Territorial Politics and Canadian Social Policy'. In S. Leibfried and P. Pierson (eds.), *European Social Policy: Between Fragmentation and Integration*. Washington, DC: The Brookings Institution.

Begg, Iain, Gudgin, Graham, and Morris, Derek (1995), 'The Assessment: Regional Policy in the European Union', *Oxford Review of Economic Policy*, Summer.

Bensidoun, Isabelle, and Chevallier, Agnès (1996), *Europe-Méditerrannée: Le pari de l'ouverture*. Paris: Economica/CEPII.

Besnainou, Denis (1995), 'Les Fonds structurels: Quelle application aux PECO?' *Economie Internationale*, 62.

Bieber, Roland, Jacqué, Jean-Paul, and Weiler, Joseph, H. H. (eds.) (1985), *An Ever Closer Union*. Brussels: Commission of the EC/The European Perspectives Series.

Biehl, Dieter (1988), 'On Maximal Versus Optimal Tax Harmonization'. In R. Bieber, J. P. Jacqué, and J. Weiler (eds.), *1992: One European Market?* Baden-Baden: Nomos for the European Policy Unit, Florence.

Bisignano, Joseph (1992), 'Banking in the EEC: Structure, Competition and Public Policy'. In G. Kaufman (ed.), *Bank Structure in Major Countries*. New York: Kluwer.

Blanchard, O. J., and Muet, P. A. (1993), 'Competitiveness through Disinflation: An Assessment of the French Macroeconomic Strategy', *Economic Policy*, April.

Boltho, Andrea (ed.) (1982), *The European Economy*. Oxford: Oxford University Press.

—— (1994), 'A Comparison of Regional Differentials in the European Community and the United States'. In J. Mortensen (ed.), *Improving Economic and Social Cohesion in the European Community*. New York: St Martin's Press.

Borio, Claudio, and Filoca, Renato (1994), 'The Changing Borders of Banking: Trends and Implications', *BIS Working Paper*, No.23, October.

Boyer, Robert, and Drache, Daniel (eds.) (1996), *States Against Markets*. London and New York: Routledge.

Bressand, Albert (1990), 'Beyond Interdependence: 1992 as a Global Challenge', *International Affairs*, January.

—— and Nicolaïdis, Kalypso (1990), 'Regional Integration in a Networked World Economy'. In W. Wallace (ed.), *The Dynamics of European Integration*. London: Pinter for The Royal Institute of International Affairs.

Buigues, Pierre, and Goybet, Philippe (1989), 'The Community's Industrial Competitiveness and International Trade in Manufactured Goods'. In A. Jacquemin and A. Sapir (eds.), *The European Internal Market*. Oxford: Oxford University Press.

Camps, Miriam (1964), *Britain and the European Community 1955–1963*. Oxford: Oxford University Press.

—— (1967), *European Unification in the Sixties*. London: Oxford University Press for the Royal Institute of International Affairs/Council on Foreign Relations.

Caporaso, James (1996), 'The European Union and Forms of State: Westphalian, Regulatory or Post-Modern?', *Journal of Common Market Studies*, March.

Cassese, Sabino, and Wright, Vincent (1996), 'La restructuration des États en Europe occidentale'. In V. Wright and S. Cassese (eds.), *La recomposition de l'État en Europe*. Paris: La Découverte.

Cecchini, Paolo (1988), *The European Challenge: 1992*. Aldershot: Wildwood House.

CEPR (Centre for Economic Policy Research) (1993), *Making Sense of Subsidiarity: How Much Centralization for Europe?* London: CEPR.

—— (1995a), *Flexible Integration*. London: CEPR.

—— (1995b), *Unemployment: Choices for Europe*. London: CEPR.

Cline, William (ed.) (1983), *Trade Policy in the 1980s*. Washington, DC: Institute for International Economics.

—— (1995), 'Evaluating the Uruguay Round', *The World Economy*, 18.

Cnossen, Sijbren, and Shoup, Carl (1987), 'Co-ordination of Value-Added Taxes'. In S. Cnossen (ed.), *Tax Co-ordination in the EC*. Deventer: Kluwer.

Cohen, Benjamin (1994), 'Beyond EMU: The Problem of Sustainability'. In B. Eichengreen and J. Frieden (eds.), *The Political Economy of European Monetary Unification*. Boulder, Colo., San Francisco, and Oxford: Westview.

—— (1995), 'The Triad and the Unholy Trinity: Problems of International Monetary Co-operation'. In J. Frieden and D. Lake (eds.), *International Political Economy: Perspectives on Global Power and Wealth*, 3rd edn. New York: St Martin's Press.

Colchester, Nicholas, and Buchan, David (1990), *Europe Relaunched: Truths and Illusions on the Way to 1992*. London: *The Economist* Books/Hutchinson.

Coleman, William, and Underhill, Geoffrey (1995), 'Globalization, Regionalism and the Regulation of Securities Markets', *Journal of European Public Policy*, September.

Collins, Doreen (1983), *The Operation of the European Social Fund*. London: Croom Helm.

—— (1985), 'Social policy'. In A. El-Agraa (ed.), *The Economics of the European Community*. Oxford: Philip Allan.

Collombet, Michel (1995), 'L'Europe bancaire reste à construire', *Banque*, July–August.

Commissariat du Plan (1980), *L'Europe: Les Vingt Prochaines Années*, Paris: La Documentation Française.

Commission (1985a), *Completing the Internal Market. White Paper from the Commission to the European Council*. Luxembourg: Office for Official Publications of the European Communities, June.

—— (1988a), 'The Economics of 1992', *European Economy*, 35, March.

—— (1988b), 'Creation of a European Financial Area', *European Economy*, 36, May.

—— (1989), 'Facing the Challenges of the Early 1990s', *European Economy*, 42, November.

—— (1990a), *Second Survey on State Aids in the European Community in the Manufacturing and Certain Other Sectors*, Luxembourg: Office for Official Publications of the European Communities.

—— (1990b), 'The Impact of the Internal Market by Industrial Sector: The Challenge for the Member States', *European Economy*, Special Edition.

—— (1990c), 'One Market, One Money', *European Economy*, 44, October.

—— (1993a), 'Stable Money—Sound Finances: Community Public Finance in the Perspective of EMU', *European Economy*, 53.

—— (1993b), 'The Economics of Community Public Finance', *European Economy*, Reports and Studies, 5.

—— (1993c), 'The European Community as a World Trade Partner', *European Economy*, 52.

—— (1993d), 'International Economic Interdependence' (Discussion Paper). In European Parliament, *Economic Interdependence—New Policy Challenges* (Proceedings of the public hearing held by the Committee on External Economic Relations, 28 September). Brussels: European Parliament.

—— (1994a), 'Annual Economic Report for 1994', *European Economy*, 56.

—— (1994b), *Growth, Competitiveness, Employment: The Challenges and Ways Forward Into the 21st Century* (White Paper). Luxembourg: Office for Official Publications of the European Communities.

—— (1994c), 'Competition and Integration: Community Merger Control Policy', *European Economy*, 57.

—— (1994d), *Competitiveness and Cohesion: Trends in the Regions*. Luxembourg: Office for Official Publications of the European Communities.

—— (1994e), 'The Economic Interpenetration between the EU and Eastern Europe', *European Economy*, Reports and Studies, 6.

—— (1995a), *Employment in Europe*. Luxembourg: Official Publications of the European Communities.

—— (1995b), 'Annual Economic Report for 1995', *European Economy*, 59.

—— (1995c), *The Single Market in 1994*. Brussels: COM (95) 238.

Commission (1995*d*), 'Mergers and Acquisitions', *European Economy*, Supplement A, March.

—— (1995*e*), *Social Protection in Europe 1995*. Luxembourg: Office for Official Publications of the European Communities.

—— (1995*f*), *Preparation of the Associated Countries of Central and Eastern Europe for Integration into the Internal Market of the Union* (White Paper). Brussels: COM (95) 163, May.

—— (1996*a*), *XXVth Report on Competition Policy—1995*. Luxembourg: Office for Official Publications of the European Communities.

—— (1996*b*), *First Cohesion Report, Preliminary edition*. Brussels: European Commission, November.

—— (1996*c*), *The Structural Funds in 1994*. Luxembourg: Official Publications of the European Communities.

—— (1996*d*), *The Community Budget: The Facts in Figures*. Luxembourg: Office for Official Publications of the European Communities.

—— and UNCTAD (1996), *Investing in Asia's Dynamism: European Union Direct Investment in Asia*. Brussels.

Cooper, Richard (1994), *Foreign Trade, Wages, and Unemployment*. Harvard Institute of Economic Research Discussion Paper, 1701.

Cosgrove, Carol (1994), 'Has the Lomé Convention failed ACP Trade?' *Journal of International Affairs*, Summer.

Cox, Andrew, and Watson, Glyn (1995), 'The European Community and the Restructuring of Europe's National Champions'. In J. Hayward (ed.), *Industrial Enterprise and European Integration*. Oxford: Oxford University Press.

Crafts, Nicholas, and Toniolo, Gianni (1996), 'Postwar Growth: An Overview'. In N. Crafts and G. Toniolo (eds.), *Economic Growth in Europe Since 1945*. Cambridge: Cambridge University Press.

Dahrendorf, Ralf (1988), *The Modern Social Conflict*. London: Weidenfeld and Nicolson.

Dashwood, Alan (1983), 'Hastening Slowly: The Community's Path Towards Harmonisation'. In H. Wallace, W. Wallace, and C. Webb (eds.), *Policy Making in the European Community*, 2nd edn. Chichester: Wiley.

Davenport, Michael (1982), 'The Economic Impact of the EEC'. In A. Boltho (ed.), *The European Economy*. Oxford: Oxford University Press.

—— Hewitt, Adrian, and Koning, Antonique (1995), *Europe's Preferred Partners? The Lomé Countries in World Trade*. London: ODI Special Report.

Davis, E. *et al.* (1989), *1992: Myths and Realities*. London: London Business School.

de Cecco, Marcello (1989), 'The European Monetary System and National Interests'. In P. Guerrieri and P. C. Padoan (eds.), *The Political Economy of European Integration*. Hemel Hempstead: Harvester Wheatsheaf.

de Grauwe, Paul (1992), *The Economics of Monetary Integration*. Oxford: Oxford University Press.

—— (1994), 'Towards European Monetary Union without the EMS', *Economic Policy*, April.

Dehousse, Renaud (1996), 'Les États et l'Union européenne: les effets de l'intégration'. In V. Wright and S. Cassese (eds.), *La recomposition de l'État en Europe*. Paris: La Découverte.

de la Fuente, Angel, and Vives, Xavier (1995), 'Infrastructure and Education as Instruments of Regional Policy—Evidence from Spain', *Economic Policy*, April.

de la Serre, Françoise, Lesquesne, Christian, and Rupnick, Jacques (eds.) (1994), *Union Européenne: Ouverture à l'Est?* Paris: Presses Universitaires de France.

Delors, Jacques (1994), *L'Unité d'un Homme. Entretiens avec Dominique Wolton*. Paris: Odile Jacob.

Delors Report (Committee for the Study of Economic and Monetary Union) (1989), *Report on Economic and Monetary Union in the European Community*. Luxembourg: Office for Official Publications of the European Communities.

Dermine, Jean (ed.) (1990), *European Banking in the 1990s*. Oxford: Blackwell.

Deubner, Christian (1995), *Vertiefung der Europäischen Union: Wie Dringend, Wie Weit, und Mit Wem?* Baden Baden: Nomos.

Deutsches Institut für Wirtschaftsforschung (1995), *Economic Bulletin*, November.

Dolado, Juan *et al.* (1996), 'The Economic Impact of Minimum Wages in Europe', *Economic Policy*, October.

Drees, Burkhard, and Pazarbasioglu, Çeyla (1995), 'The Nordic Banking Crises: Pitfalls in Financial Liberalization?' *IMF Working Paper*, June.

Duchêne, François (1973), 'The European Community and Uncertainties of Interdependence'. In M. Kohnstamm and W. Hager (eds.), *Nation Writ Large*. London: Macmillan.

Duff, Andrew (1994), 'Ratification'. In A. Duff, J. Pinder, and R. Pryce (eds.), *Maastricht and Beyond*. London and New York: Routledge for The Federal Trust.

Eichengreen, Barry (1990), 'One Money for Europe: Lessons from the US Currency Union', *Economic Policy*, 10, April.

—— (1996), 'Institutions and Economic Growth: Europe after World War II'. In N. Crafts and G. Toniolo (eds.), *Economic Growth in Europe Since 1945*. Cambridge: Cambridge University Press.

—— and Wyplosz, Charles (1993), 'The Unstable EMS', *Brookings Papers on Economic Activity*, 1.

Emerson, Michael (ed.) (1984), *Europe's Stagflation*. Oxford: Oxford University Press.

—— (1988), *What Model for Europe?* Cambridge, Mass.: MIT Press.

Faini, Riccardo, and Portes, Richard (eds.) (1995), *European Union Trade with Eastern Europe: Adjustment and Opportunities*. London: CEPR.

Forster, Anthony, and Wallace, William (1996), 'Common Foreign and Security Policy'. In H. Wallace and W. Wallace (eds), *Policy-Making in the European Union*. Oxford: Oxford University Press.

Franklin, Mark, Marsh, Michael, and McLaren, Lauren (1994), 'Uncorking the Bottle: Popular Opposition to European Unification in the Wake of Maastricht', *Journal of Common Market Studies*, December.

Franks, Julian, and Mayer, Colin (1990), 'Capital Markets and Corporate Control: A Study of France, Germany and the UK,' *Economic Policy*, April.

Fratianni, Michele, and Peeters, Theo (eds.) (1978), *One Money for Europe*, London: Macmillan.

Funabashi, Yoichi (1988), *Managing the Dollar: From the Plaza to the Louvre*. Washington, DC: Institute for International Economics.

Fursdon, Edward (1980), *The European Defence Community: A History*. London: Macmillan.

García, Soledad (1993), 'Europe's Fragmented Identities and the Frontiers of Citizenship'. In S. García (ed.), *European Identity and the Search for Legitimacy*. London: Pinter for The Eleni Nakou Foundation and The Royal Institute of International Affairs.

Garrett, Geoffrey (1994), 'The Politics of Maastricht'. In B. Eichengreen and J. Frieden (eds.), *The Political Economy of European Monetary Unification*. Boulder, Colo., San Francisco, and Oxford: Westview.

Garton Ash, Timothy (1993), *In Europe's Name*. London: Jonathan Cape.

George, Ken, and Jacquemin, Alexis (1992), 'Dominant Firms and Mergers', *The Economic Journal*, January.

Giavazzi, Francesco, and Giovannini, Alberto (1989), *Limiting Exchange Rate Flexibility: The European Monetary System*. Cambridge, Mass.: MIT Press.

—— and Pagano, M. (1988), 'The Advantage of Tying One's Hand: EMS Discipline and Central Bank Credibility', *European Economic Review*, 32.

—— and Spaventa, Luigi (1990), *The 'New' EMS*. CEPR Discussion Paper, 369.

Giersch, Herbert (ed.) (1983), *Reassessing the Role of Government in the Mixed Economy: Symposium 1982*. Tübingen: Mohr.

—— (1985), *Eurosclerosis*. Kiel: Kiel Discussion Paper, 112, October.

Gilpin, Robert (1987), *The Political Economy of International Relations*. Princeton, NJ: Princeton University Press.

Giovannini, Alberto (1989), 'National Tax Systems versus the European Capital Market', *Economic Policy*, 9, October.

Glyn, Andrew (1995), 'The Assessment: Unemployment and Inequality', *Oxford Review of Economic Policy*, Spring.

Goodhart, Charles (1993), 'The External Dimension of EMU'. In L. Bekemans and L. Tsoukalis (eds.), *Europe and Global Economic Interdependence*. Brussels: Presses Interuniversitaires Européennes for the College of Europe and the Hellenic Centre for European Studies.

—— and Smith, Stephen (1993), 'Stabilization', *European Economy*, Reports and Studies, 5.

Goodman, John (1992), *Monetary Sovereignty: The Politics of Central Banking in Western Europe*. Ithaca, NY and London: Cornell University.

Goybet, Philippe, and Bertoldi, Moreno (1994), 'The Efficiency of Structural Funds'. In J. Mortensen (ed.), *Improving Economic and Social Cohesion in the European Community*. New York: St Martin's Press.

Grabitz, Eberhard (ed.) (1984), *Abgestufte Integration: Eine Alternative zum herkömmlichen Integrationskonzept?* Kehl am Rhein: Engel.

Greenaway, D. (1993), 'Trade and Foreign Direct Investment', *European Economy*, 52.

Gros, Daniel, and Thygesen, Niels (1992), *European Monetary Integration: From the European Monetary System Towards Monetary Union*. London: Longmans.

Haaland, Jan, and Norman, Victor (1992), 'Global Production Effects of European Integration'. In A. Winters (ed.), *Trade Flows and Trade Policy After 1992*. Cambridge: Cambridge University Press.

Haas, Ernst (1958), *The Uniting of Europe*. London: Stevens.

Hayward, Jack (1995), 'Introduction: Europe's Endangered Industrial Champions'. In J. Hayward (ed.), *Industrial Enterprise and European Integration*. Oxford: Oxford University Press.

Helm, Dieter (1993), 'The Assessment: The European Internal Market: The Next Steps', *Oxford Review of Economic Policy*, Spring.

Helpman, E., and Krugman, P. (1985), *Market Structure and Foreign Trade: Increasing Returns, Imperfect Competition and the International Economy*. Cambridge, Mass.: MIT Press.

Héritier, Adrienne *et al.* (1994), *Die Veränderung von Staatlichkeit in Europa. Ein regulativer Wettbewerb: Deutschland, Grossbritannien und Frankreich in der Europäischen Union*. Opladen: Leske und Budrich.

Hill, Christopher (1993), 'The Capability-Expectations Gap, or Conceptualizing Europe's International Role', *Journal of Common Market Studies*, September.

Hine, R. C. (1985), *The Political Economy of International Trade*, Brighton: Harvester.

—— and Padoan, Pier-Carlo (1997), 'External Trade Policies'. In A. Smith and L. Tsoukalis (eds.) (1997), *The Impact of Community Policies on Economic and Social Cohesion*. Bruges: College of Europe/Sussex European Institute/Synthesis.

Hirst, Paul, and Thompson, Grahame (1996), *Globalization in Question*. Oxford: Blackwell.

Hoekman, Bernard, and Kostecki, Michel (1995), *The Political Economy of the World Trading System: From GATT to WTO*. Oxford: Oxford University Press.

Hoeller, Peter and Loupe, Marie-Odille (1994), 'The EC's Internal Market: Implementation and Economic Effects', *OECD Economic Studies*, Winter.

Hooghe, L. and Keating, M. (1994), 'The Politics of European Union Regional Policy', *Journal of European Public Policy*, 1/3.

IMF (1993), *International Capital Markets: Exchange Rate Management and International Capital Flows*. Washington, DC: IMF.

Issing, Otmar (1996), *Europe: Political Union Through Common Money?* London: Institute of Economic Affairs.

Jachtenfuchs, Marcus, and Kohler-Koch, Beate (1996), 'Einleitung: Regieren im dynamischen Mehrebenensystem'. In M. Jachtenfuchs and B. Kohler-Koch (eds.), *Europäische Integration*. Opladen: Leske & Budrich.

Jacquemin, Alexis, Buigues, Pierre, and Ilzkovitz, Fabienne (1989) 'Horizontal Mergers and Competition Policy in the European Community', *European Economy*, 40, May.

—— and Sapir, André (1988), 'European Integration or World Integration?' *Weltwirtschaftliches Archiv*, 124/1.

—— —— (eds.) (1989), *The European Internal Market: Trade and Competition*. Oxford: Oxford University Press.

—— —— (1990), 'La Perspective 1992 et l'après Uruguay round', *Economie prospective internationale*, 44.

—— and Wright, David (eds.) (1993), *The European Challenges Post-1992*. Aldershot: Edward Elgar.

Johnson, Christopher, and Collignon, Stefan (eds.) (1994), *The Monetary Economics of Europe*. London: Pinter for the European Parliament.

Julius, DeAnne (1990), *Global Companies and Public Policy: The Growing Challenge of Foreign Direct Investment*. London: Pinter/The Royal Institute of International Affairs.

Kapstein, Ethan (1994), *Governing the Global Economy*. London and Cambridge, Mass.: Harvard University Press.

Kay, J. A. (1989), 'Myths and Realities'. In E. Davis *et al.*, *1992: Myths and Realities*. London: London Business School.

Keen, Michael, and Smith, Stephen (1996), 'The Future of Value-Added Tax in the European Union', *Economic Policy*, October.

Keohane, Robert, and Hoffmann, Stanley (1991), 'Institutional Change in Europe in the 1980s'. In R. Keohane and S. Hoffmann (eds.), *The New European Community: Decisionmaking and Institutional Change*. Boulder, Colo., San Francisco, and Oxford: Westview.

Kjeldahl, Rasmus, and Tracy, Michael (eds.) (1994), *Renationalisation of the Common Agricultural Policy?* Copenhagen: Institute of Agricultural Economics/Agricultural Policy Studies, Belgium.

Krasner, Stephen D. (1982), 'Structural Causes and Regime Consequences: Regimes as Intervening Variables', *International Organization*, 36/2.

Krugman, Paul (1986), 'Introduction: New Thinking about Trade Policy'. In P. Krugman (ed.), *Strategic Trade Policy and the New International Economics*. Cambridge, Mass.: MIT Press.

—— (1987), 'Economic Integration in Europe: Some Conceptual Issues'. In T. Padoa-Schioppa Report, *Efficiency, Stability and Equity*. Oxford: Oxford University Press.

—— (1990), 'Policy Problems of a Monetary Union'. In P. de Grauwe and L. Papademos (eds.), *The European Monetary System in the 1990s*. London: Longman for CEPS and the Bank of Greece.

—— (1994*a*), 'Competitiveness: A Dangerous Obsession', *Foreign Affairs*, March/April.

—— (1994*b*), *Peddling Prosperity: Economic Sense and Nonsense in the Age of Diminished Expectations*. New York and London: W. W. Norton & Co.

Kruse, D. C. (1980), *Monetary Integration in Western Europe: EMU, EMS and Beyond*. London: Butterworths.

Lafay, Gerard *et al.* (1989), *Commerce international: La fin des avantages acquis*. Paris: Economica.

Laffan, Brigid (1996), 'The Politics of Identity and Political Order in Europe', *Journal of Common Market Studies*, March.

—— and Shackleton, Michael (1996), 'The Budget'. In H. Wallace and W. Wallace (eds.), *Policy-Making in the European Union*. Oxford: Oxford University Press.

Lagrange, Maurice (1971), 'L'Europe institutionelle: Réflexions d'un témoin', *Revue du Marché Commun*, June.

Lamfalussy, Alexander (1989), 'Macro-Coordination of Fiscal Policies in an Economic and Monetary Union in Europe'. Delors Report, *Report on Economic and Monetary Union in the European Community*. Luxembourg: Office for Official Publications of the European Communities.

Lawrence, Robert Z. (1996), *Regionalism, Multilateralism, and Deeper Integration*. Washington, DC: The Brookings Institution.

—— and Schultze, Charles L.(eds.) (1987), *Barriers to European Growth*. Washington, DC: Brookings.

Leibfried, Stephan, and Pierson, Paul (1995), 'Semisovereign Welfare States: Social Policy in a Multitiered Europe'. In S. Liebfried and P. Pierson (eds.), *European Social Policy: Between Fragmentation and Integration*. Washington, DC: The Brookings Institution.

Leonardi, Robert (ed.) (1993), *The Regions and the European Community*. London: Frank Cass.

Lindberg, Leon N. (1963), *The Political Dynamics of European Economic Integration*. Stanford, Calif.: Stanford University Press.

Ludlow, Peter (1982), *The Making of the European Monetary System*. London: Butterworths.

McArthur, J. H., and Scott, B. R. (1969), *Industrial Planning in France*. Cambridge, Mass.: Harvard University Press.

MacBean, A. I., and Snowden, P. N. (1981), *International Institutions in Trade and Finance*. London: Allen & Unwin.

MacDougall Report (1977), *The Role of Public Finance in European Economic Integration*, i and ii. Brussels: Commission.

McGowan, Francis, and Seabright, Paul (1989), 'Deregulating European Airlines', *Economic Policy*, 9, October.

McKinnon, Ronald (1963), 'Optimum Currency Areas', *American Economic Review*, 53.

Maddison, Angus (1982), *Phases of Capitalist Development*. Oxford: Oxford University Press.

Mahé, Louis-Pascal *et al.* (1995), 'L'Agriculture et l'élargissement', *Economie Internationale*, 62.

Majone, Giandomenico (1993), 'The European Community between Social Policy and Social Regulation', *Journal of Common Market Studies*, June.

—— (1994), 'The Rise of the Regulatory State in Europe', *West European Politics*, 17/3.

Malinvaud, Edmond (1989), Comment on A. Giovannini, 'National Tax Systems versus the European Capital Market', *Economic Policy*, October.

—— (1991), *Macroeconomic Research and European Policy Formation*, Jean Monnet Chair Papers. San Domenico: The European Policy Unit at the European University Institute.

Maravall, José Maria (1993), 'Politics and Policy: Economic Reforms in Southern Europe'. In L. C. Bresser Pereira, J. M. Maravall, and A. Przeworski, *Economic Reforms in New Democracies: A Social-Democratic Approach*. Cambridge: Cambridge University Press.

Markovits, Andrei (ed.) (1982), *The Political Economy of West Germany*. New York: Praeger.

Marsh, David (1994), *Germany and Europe: The Crisis of Unity*. London: Heinemann.

Marshall, T. H. (1975), *Social Policy*. London: Hutchinson.

Mattera, Adolfo (1988), *Marché unique européen: Ses règles, son fonctionnement*. Paris: Jupiter.

Mayes, David (1989), 'The Effects of Economic Integration on Trade'. In A. Jacquemin and A. Sapir (eds.), *The European Internal Market*. Oxford: Oxford University Press.

Mény, Yves (1995), 'Conclusion'. In Y. Mény, P. Muller, and J. L. Quermonne (eds.), *Politiques publiques en Europe: Une nouvelle division de travail*. Paris: L'Harmattan.

Messerlin, Patrick (1987), 'The European Iron and Steel Industry and the World Crisis'. In Y. Mény and V. Wright (eds.), *The Politics of Steel: Western Europe and the Steel Industry in the Crisis Years (1979–1984)*. Berlin: Walter de Gruyter.

—— (1989), 'The EC Anti-Dumping Regulations: A First Economic Appraisal, 1980–1985', *Weltwirtschaftliches Archiv*, 125/3.

—— (1995), *La Nouvelle Organisation mondiale du commerce*. Paris: Institut Français des Relations Internationales.

Michalski, Anna, and Wallace, Helen (1992), *The European Community: The Challenge of Enlargement*. London: Chatham House Discussion Paper.

Micossi, Stefano, and Padoan, Pier-Carlo (1994), 'Italy in the EMS: After Crisis, Salvation?' In C. Johnson and S. Collignon (eds.), *The Monetary Economics of Europe*. London: Pinter for the European Parliament.

Millon, Chantal (1993), *La Subsidiarité*. Paris: Que sais-je?

Milward, Alan S. (1984), *The Reconstruction of Western Europe 1945–51*. London: Methuen.

Minford, Patrick (1985), *Unemployment: Cause and Cure*, 2nd edn. Oxford: Blackwell.

Monnet, Jean (1976), *Mémoires*. Paris: Arthème Fayard.

Montagnier, Gabriel (1995), 'Harmonisation fiscale communautaire', *Revue Trimestrielle de Droit Européen*, April–June.

Moravcsik, Andrew (1991), 'Negotiating the Single European Act'. In R. Keohane and S. Hoffmann (eds.), *The New European Community: Decisionmaking and Institutional Change*. Boulder, Colo., San Francisco, and Oxford: Westview.

Mortensen, Jørgen (1990), *Federalism vs. Co-ordination: Macroeconomic Policy in the European Community*. Brussels: Centre for European Policy Studies, CEPS Paper, 47.

Müller, Jurgen, and Owen, Nicholas (1989), 'The Effect of Trade on Plant Size'. In A. Jacquemin and A. Sapir (eds.), *The European Internal Market*. Oxford: Oxford University Press.

Mundell, Robert (1961), 'A Theory of Optimum Currency Areas', *American Economic Review*, 51.

Myrdal, Gunnar (1956), *An International Economy*. London: Routledge and Kegan Paul.

—— (1957), *Economic Theory and Underdeveloped Regions*. London: Duckworth.

Nell, Phillippe (1990), 'EFTA in the 1990s: The Search for a New Identity', *Journal of Common Market Studies*, June.

Neven, Damien (1990), 'EEC Integration towards 1992: Some Distributional Aspects', *Economic Policy*, 10, April.

—— (1994), 'The Political Economy of State Aids in the European Community: Some Econometric Evidence', CEPR Discussion Paper, 945.

—— Nutall, Robin, and Seabright, Paul (1993), *Merger in Daylight: The Economics and Politics of European Merger Control*. London: CEPR.

Nicol, William, and Yuill, Douglas (1982), 'Regional Problems and Policy'. In A. Boltho (ed.), *The European Economy*. Oxford: Oxford University Press.

Noelke, M., and Taylor, R. (1981), *EEC Protectionism: Present Practice and Future Trends*, i. Brussels: European Research Associates.

O'Brien, Richard (1992), *Global Financial Integration: The End of Geography*. London: Pinter for The Royal Institute of International Affairs.

Odell, Peter (1986), *Oil and World Power*, 8th edn. Harmondsworth: Penguin.

OECD (1995*a*), 'Financial Markets and Corporate Governance', *Financial Market Trends*, November.

—— (1995*b*), *OECD Economic Outlook—June 1995*. Paris: OECD.

Ohmae, K. (1990), *The Borderless World*. London and New York: Collins.

Olson, Mancur (1982), *Rise and Decline of Nations*. New Haven, Conn.: Yale University Press.

Owen, Nicholas (1983), *Economies of Scale, Competitiveness and Trade Patterns in the European Community*. Oxford: Clarendon Press.

Padoa-Schioppa, Tommaso (1994), *The Road to Monetary Union in Europe: The Emperor, the King, and the Genies*. Oxford: Clarendon Press.

—— (1987 Report), *Efficiency, Stability, and Equity*. Oxford: Oxford University Press.

Page, Sheila (1981), 'The Revival of Protectionism and its Consequences for Europe', *Journal of Common Market Studies*, September.

Pearce, Joan, and Sutton, John (1986), *Protection and Industrial Policy in Europe*. London: Routledge and Kegan Paul for the Royal Institute of International Affairs.

Pelkmans, Jacques (1980), 'Economic Theories of Integration Revisited', *Journal of Common Market Studies*, June.

—— (1984), *Market Integration in the European Community*. The Hague: Martinus Nijhoff.

—— (1987), 'The New Approach to Technical Harmonization and Standardization', *Journal of Common Market Studies*, March.

—— (1990), 'Regulation and the Single Market: An Economic Perspective'. In *Governing Europe*, i. Brussels: Centre for European Policy Studies.

—— and Winters, Alan (1988), *Europe's Domestic Market*. London: Routledge and Kegan Paul for The Royal Institute of International Affairs, Chatham House Papers, 43.

Perroux, François (1959), 'Les Formes de concurrence dans le marché commun', *Revue d'économie politique*, 1.

Pipkorn, J. (1986), 'Die Mitbestimmung der Arbeitnehmer als Gegenstand gemeinschaftlicher Rechtsentwicklung'. In H. Von Lichtenberg (ed.), *Sozialpolitik in der EG*. Baden-Baden: Nomos.

Pisani-Ferry, Jean, Italianer, Alexander, and Lescure, Roland (1993), 'Stabilization Properties of Budgetary Systems: A Simulation Analysis', *European Economy*, Reports and Studies, 5.

Prest, Alan (1983), 'Fiscal Policy'. In P. Coffey (ed.), *Main Economic Policy Areas of the EEC*. The Hague: Martinus Nijhoff.

Prud'homme, Rémy (1993), 'The Potential Role of the EC Budget in the Reduction of Regional Disparities in a European Economic and Monetary Union', *European Economy*, Reports and Studies, 5.

Pryce, Roy (1994), 'The Treaty Negotiations'. In A. Duff, J. Pinder, and R. Pryce (eds.), *Maastricht and Beyond*. London and New York: Routledge for The Federal Trust.

Puchala, Donald (1972), 'Of Blind Men, Elephants and International Integration', *Journal of Common Market Studies*, March.

Putnam, Robert *et al.* (1993), *Making Democracy Work: Civic Traditions in Modern Italy*. Princeton, NJ: Princeton University Press.

Redmond, John (1993), *The Next Mediterranean Enlargement of the European Community: Turkey, Cyprus and Malta?* Aldershot: Dartmouth.

Rhein, Eberhard (1996), 'Europe and the Mediterranean: A Newly Emerging Geographical Area?' *European Foreign Affairs Review*, July.

Rhodes, Martin (1992), 'The Future of the "Social Dimension": Labour Market Regulation in Post-1992 Europe', *Journal of Common Market Studies*, March.

—— (1995), 'A Regulatory Conundrum: Industrial Relations and the Social Dimension'. In S. Leibfried and P. Pierson (eds.), *European Social Policy: Between Fragmentation and Integration*. Washington, DC: The Brookings Institution.

Robson, Peter (1987), *The Economics of International Integration*, 3rd edn. London: Allen and Unwin.

Rollo, Jim, and Smith, Alasdair (1993), 'The Political Economy of Eastern European Trade with the European Community: Why So Sensitive?' *Economic Policy*, April.

Romero, Federico (1990), 'Cross-Border Population Movements'. In W. Wallace (ed.), *The Dynamics of European Integration*. London: Pinter for The Royal Institute of International Affairs.

Rosenblatt, Julius *et al.* (1988), *The Common Agricultural Policy of the European Community*, International Monetary Fund, Occasional Paper, 62, November.

Rosenthal, Douglas (1990), 'Competition Policy'. In G. C. Hufbauer (ed.), *Europe 1992: An American Perspective*. Washington, DC: Brookings.

Sachs, J., and Wyplosz, C. (1986), 'The Economic Consequences of President Mitterrand', *Economic Policy*, 2.

Saint-Paul, Gilles (1996), 'Exploring the Political Economy of Labour Market Institutions', *Economic Policy*, October.

Sala-i-Martin, Xavier, and Sachs, Jeffrey (1992), 'Fiscal Federalism and Optimum Currency Areas: Evidence for Europe from the United States'. In M. Canzoneri, V. Grilli, and P. Masson (eds.), *Establishing a Central Bank: Issues in Europe and Lessons from the US*. Cambridge: Cambridge University Press/CEPR/IMF.

Sandholz, Wayne, and Zysman, John (1989), '1992: Recasting the European Bargain', *World Politics*, October.

Saryusz-Wolski, Jacek (1994), 'The Reintegration of the "Old Continent": Avoiding the Costs of "Half-Europe"'. In S. Bulmer and A. Scott (eds), *Economic and Political Integration in Europe: International Dynamics and Global Context*. Oxford: Blackwell.

Scharpf, Fritz (1995), *Negative and Positive Integration in the Political Economy of European*

Welfare States, Jean Monnet Chair Papers. San Domenico: Robert Schuman Centre, European University Institute.

Schäuble, Wolfgang, and Lamers, Carl (1994), *Reflections on European Policy*. Bonn: CDU/CSU Fraktion.

Schmitt von Sydow, Helmut (1988), 'The Basic Strategies of the Commission's White Paper'. In R. Bieber, J. P. Jacqué, and J. Weiler (eds.), *1992: One European Market?* Baden-Baden: Nomos for the European Policy Unit, Florence.

Schmitter, Philippe (1995) 'Quelques alternatives pour le futur système politique européen et leurs implications pour les politiques publiques européennes'. In Y. Mény, P. Muller, and J. L. Quermonne (eds.), *Politiques publiques en Europe: Une nouvelle division de travail*. Paris: L'Harmattan.

Schuknecht, Ludger (1992), *Trade Protection in the European Community*. Chur: Harwood.

Sedelmeier, Ulrich, and Wallace, Helen (1996), 'Policies towards Central and Eastern Europe'. In H. Wallace and W. Wallace (eds.), *Policy-Making in the European Union*. Oxford: Oxford University Press.

Servan-Schreiber, Jean-Jacques (1967), *Le défi américain*. Paris: Denoël.

Shackleton, Michael (1990), *Financing the European Community*. London: Pinter for The Royal Institute of International Affairs.

Sharp, Margaret (1990), 'Technology and the Dynamics of Integration'. In W. Wallace (ed.), *The Dynamics of European Integration*. London: Pinter for The Royal Institute of International Affairs.

—— (1997), 'RTD and Cohesion'. In A. Smith and L. Tsoukalis (eds.) (1997), *The Impact of Community Policies on Economic and Social Cohesion*. Bruges: College of Europe/Sussex European Institute/Synthesis.

—— and Shearman, Claire (1987), *European Technological Collaboration*. London: Routledge and Kegan Paul for The Royal Institute of International Affairs, Chatham House Papers, 36.

Shonfield, Andrew (1976) International Economic Relations of the Western World: An Overall View'. In A. Shonfield (ed.), *International Economic Relations of the Western World 1959–1971*. London: Oxford University Press for The Royal Institute of International Affairs.

Siebert, Horst (1991), 'German Unification: The Economics of Transition', *Economic Policy*, October.

—— and Koop, Michael (1993), 'Institutional Competition versus Centralization: Quo Vadis Europe?' *Oxford Review of Economic Policy*, Spring.

Smith, Alasdair, and Tsoukalis, Loukas (eds.) (1997), *The Impact of Community Policies on Economic and Social Cohesion*. Bruges: College of Europe/Sussex European Institute/Synthesis.

—— and Venables, Anthony (1990), 'Automobiles'. In G. C. Hufbauer (ed.), *Europe 1992: An American Perspective*. Washington, DC: The Brookings Institution.

Smith, Stephen (1993), 'Subsidiarity and the Co-ordination of Indirect Taxes in the European Community', *Oxford Review of Economic Policy*, Spring.

Sørenson, Peter (1993), 'Coordination of Capital Income Taxes in the Economic and Monetary Union: What Needs to be Done?' In F. Torres and F. Giavazzi (eds.), *Adjustment and Growth in the European Monetary Union*. Cambridge: Cambridge University Press/CEPR.

Spahn, Bernd (1993), 'The Consequences of Economic and Monetary Union for Fiscal Federal Relations in the Community and the Financing of the Community Budget', *European Economy*, Reports and Studies, 5.

Stern, Richard, Asmus, Ronald, and Larrabee, Stephen (1996), *The European Union and the Mediterranean: New Challenges and Implications for U.S. Policy.* Santa Monica, Calif.: RAND.

Strange, Susan (1976), 'International Monetary Relations'. In A. Shonfield (ed.), *International Economic Relations of the Western World 1959–1971.* London: Oxford University Press for The Royal Institute of International Affairs.

—— (1985), 'Interpretations of a Decade'. In L. Tsoukalis (ed.), *The Political Economy of International Money.* London: Sage for The Royal Institute of International Affairs.

—— (1988), 'A "Dissident" View'. In R. Bieber, J. P. Jacqué, and J. Weiler (eds.), *1992: One European Market?* Baden-Baden: Nomos for the European Policy Institute, Florence.

Strasser, Daniel (1992), *The Finances of Europe.* Luxembourg: Official Publications of the European Communities.

Straubhaar, Thomas (1988), 'International Labour Migration within a Common Market: Some Aspects of EC Experience', *Journal of Common Market Studies*, September.

Streeck, Wolfgang (1995), 'From Market Making to State Building? Reflections on the Political Economy of European Social Policy'. In S. Leibfried and P. Pierson (eds.), *European Social Policy: Between Fragmentation and Integration.* Washington, DC: The Brookings Institution.

—— (1996), 'Public Power beyond the Nation-State: The Case of the European Community'. In R. Boyer and D. Drache (eds.), *States Against Markets: The Limits of Globalization.* London and New York: Routledge.

Sun, Jeanne-May and Pelkmans, Jacques (1995), 'Regulatory Competition in the Single Market', *Journal of Common Market Studies*, March.

Synthesis (1996), *Evaluation of the Impact of Structural Policies on Economic and Social Cohesion of the Union— Greece* (study commissioned by the European Commission). Athens: Synthesis.

Tarditi, Secondo, and Zanias, George (1997), 'Agriculture'. In A. Smith and L. Tsoukalis (eds.), *The Impact of Community Policies on Economic and Social Cohesion.* Bruges: College of Europe/Sussex European Institute/Synthesis.

Taylor, Christopher (1995), *EMU 2000?: Prospects for European Monetary Union.* London: The Royal Institute of International Affairs.

Taylor, Paul (1983), *The Limits of European Integration.* London: Croom Helm.

—— (1989), 'The New Dynamics of EC Integration in the 1980s'. In J. Lodge (ed.), *The European Community and the Challenge of the Future*, London: Pinter.

Thurow, Lester (1992), *Head to Head: The Coming Economic Battle among Japan, Europe, and America.* New York: Morrow.

Thygesen, Niels (1979), 'The Emerging European Monetary System: Precursors, First Steps and Policy Options', *Bulletin of the National Bank of Belgium*, April.

Tinbergen, Jan (1954), *International Economic Integration.* Amsterdam: Elsevier.

Tindemans, Leo (1975), 'Report on European Union', Supplement to *Bulletin of the EC, 1.*

Tracy, Michael (1989), *Government and Agriculture in Western Europe 1880–1988*, 3rd edn. London: Harvester Wheatsheaf.

Tsoukalis, Loukas (1977*a*), *The Politics and Economics of European Monetary Integration*, London: Allen and Unwin.

—— (1977*b*), 'The EEC and the Mediterranean: Is "Global" Policy a Misnomer?' *International Affairs*, July.

—— (1981), *The European Community and its Mediterranean Enlargement.* London: Allen and Unwin.

Tsoukalis, Loukas (1991), *The New European Economy: The Politics and Economics of Integration*. Oxford and New York: Oxford University Press.

—— (1993*a*), *The New European Economy: The Politics and Economics of Integration*, 2nd rev. edn. Oxford and New York: Oxford University Press.

—— (ed.) (1993*b*), *I Ellada kai i Europaiki Koinotita: I Proklisi tis Prosarmogis* [Greece and the European Community: The Challenge of Adjustment]. Athens: Papazissis for the Hellenic Centre for European Studies.

—— (1996), 'Intégration européenne et autonomie économique nationale'. In V. Wright and S. Cassese (eds.), *La recomposition de l'État en Europe*. Paris: La Découverte.

—— and Rhodes, Martin (1997), 'Economic Integration and the Nation State'. In M. Rhodes, P. Heywood, and V. Wright (eds.), *Developments in West European Politics*. Basingstoke: Macmillan.

—— and Strauss, Robert (1985), 'Crisis and Adjustment in European Steel: Beyond Laisser-Faire'. *Journal of Common Market Studies*, March.

Tyson, Laura d'Andrea (1992), *Who's Bashing Whom: Trade Conflict in High-Technology Industries*. Washington, DC: Institute for International Economics.

VerLoren van Themaat, Pieter (1988), 'The Contributions to the Establishment of the Internal Market by the Case-Law of the Court of Justice of the European Communities'. In R. Bieber, J. P. Jacqué, and J. Weiler (eds.), *1992: One European Market?* Baden-Baden: Nomos for the European Policy Unit, Florence.

Vernon, Raymond (1971), *Sovereignty at Bay*. New York: Basic Books.

Vogel-Polsky, Eliane (1989), 'L'acte unique ouvre-t-il l'espace social européen?, *Droit social*, February.

Wallace, Helen (1983), 'Distributional Politics: Dividing up the Community Cake'. In H. Wallace, W. Wallace, and C. Webb (eds.), *Policy Making in the European Community*, 2nd edn. Chichester: John Wiley.

—— (1996), 'Politics and Policy in the EU: The Challenge of Governance'. In H. Wallace and W. Wallace (eds.), *Policy-Making in the European Union*. Oxford: Oxford University Press.

—— and W. Wallace (1995), *Flying Together in a Larger and More Diverse European Union*, Working Documents. The Hague: Netherlands Scientific Council for Government Policy.

Wallace, William (1990), *The Transformation of Western Europe*, London: Pinter for The Royal Institute of International Affairs.

—— (1996), 'Government without Statehood'. In H.Wallace and W.Wallace (eds.), *Policy-Making in the European Union*. Oxford: Oxford University Press.

Wegner, Manfred (1985), 'External Adjustment in a World of Floating: Different National Experiences in Europe'. In L. Tsoukalis (ed.), *The Political Economy of International Money*. London: Sage for The Royal Institute of International Affairs.

Weiler, Joseph (1983), 'Community Member States and European Integration: Is the Law Relevant?' In L. Tsoukalis (ed.), *The European Community: Past, Present and Future*. Oxford: Blackwell.

Werner Report (1970), 'Report to the Council and the Commission on the Realization by Stages of Economic and Monetary Union in the Community', Supplement to *Bulletin of the EC, 3*.

Winham, Gilbert R. (1986), *International Trade and the Tokyo Round Negotiation*. Princeton, NJ: Princeton University Press.

Winkler, Bernhard (1995), *Towards a Strategic View on EMU: A Critical Survey*, EUI Working Papers, Robert Schuman Centre. San Domenico: European University Institute.

Wood, Adrian (1994), *North–South Trade, Employment and Inequality: Changing Fortunes in a Skill-Driven World*. Oxford: Clarendon Press.

Woolcock, Stephen (1994), *The Single European Market: Centralization or Competition among National Rules*. London: The Royal Institute of International Affairs.

—— and Hodges, Michael (1996), 'EU Policy in the Uruguay Round'. In H. Wallace and W. Wallace (eds.), *Policy-Making in the European Union*. Oxford: Oxford University Press.

Woolley, John (1994), 'Linking Political and Monetary Union: The Maastricht Agenda and German Domestic Politics'. In B. Eichengreen and J. Frieden (eds.), *The Political Economy of European Monetary Unification*. Boulder, Colo., San Francisco, and Oxford: Westview.

World Bank (1996), *World Development Report*. Washington, DC: World Bank.

Wyatt-Walter, Andrew (1995), 'Globalization, Corporate Identity and European Technology Policy', *Journal of European Public Policy*, September.

Wyplosz, Charles (1990), 'Macro-economic Implications of 1992'. In J. Dermine (ed.), *European Banking in the 1990s*. Oxford: Blackwell.

Yannopoulos, George (1989), 'The Management of Trade-Induced Structural Adjustment: An Evaluation of the EC's Integrated Mediterranean Programmes', *Journal of Common Market Studies*, June.

Zavvos, George (1988), 'The EEC Banking Policy for 1992', *Revue de la banque*, March/April.

INDEX

accountability of EU institutions 4, 41, 238, 273, 276
  ECB 184
  EC budget and 209, 219, 222
ACP (African, Caribbean, and Pacific countries) 228, 245–7
additionality and EC regional policy 122, 199, 203, 206
agriculture, *see* CAP
airlines:
  effects of the internal market 77
  liberalization 86
  state aids 91
Albania 257
anti-dumping 231, 233, 236–7, 238, 239–40, 249
approximation 44
  of indirect taxation rates 43, 67
ASEAN (Association of South-East Asian Nations) 241
Asian NICs 28, 228, 234, 237
asymmetry:
  in the EMS 38, 158–61
  in the international monetary system 142
Australia 115
Austria 27, 142, 227
  convergence criteria and 179
  EFTA and 15
  ERM entry 160
  EU accession 59–60, 243, 253
  intra-EU trade and 181
  unemployment 34
automobiles 28, 35, 236

balance of payments 9, 15, 93
  effects of the internal market 70–1
  EMU and 139–40
  Treaty of Rome 138

Balladur, Edouard 251
Baltic States 249, 254, 257
Banca d'Italia 159
Bank for International Settlements 101
Bank of England 73, 153
banks and banking:
  capital-asset ratios 98, 99
  corporate control 89
  effects of the internal market 77
  first and second banking directives 97–9, 101
  mergers and acquisitions and 100
  own funds directive 97
  prudential control 97–9, 167
  regulation of 94–5
  single banking licence 97, 98
  solvency ratios 97, 98
  universal bank model 95, 97, 98
  see also financial services
Barcelona conference (1995) 245
Barre plan 139
barriers to trade and the internal market 43
  physical, technical, and fiscal 62–8
  see also NTBs; White Paper (1985)
Basle Committee on banking regulations and supervisory practice 98
Basle–Nyborg agreement 158
Belgium 82, 84, 208
  banking system 95
  capital controls and 96
  EC budget and 217
  EMU and 139, 171, 176, 179
  foreign residents 119
  social charter and 126
  tax harmonization and 107
  see also Benelux countries
Benelux countries 27, 75, 84, 105, 106, 142, 155, 181
Brandt, Willy 28n.

Bretton Woods 9, 15, 138–9, 159
    collapse of 28, 141
BRITE (Basic Research in Industrial
    Technologies for Europe) 36, 85
Brussels summit (1985) 43
Brussels summit (1988) 48, 59, 200, 211
Brussels summit (1993) 130
budget, of the EC 209–22, 265, 271
    ability to pay principle 211, 216–17
    'British problem' 31, 40, 210
    CAP and 198, 210–14
    Delors package 48, 200–1
    Edinburgh reforms 59, 201–2
    EMU and 183, 185, 186, 210, 220–2
    Fontainebleau reforms 42, 210
    foreign aid and 232
    further enlargement and 232
    juste retour principle 210, 219
    redistribution and 209–22
    stabilization and 211, 221–2
budget deficits 38, 57, 263, 269
    convergence criterion 169, 175–6, 219
    Delors Report and 165
    effects of the internal market 70–1
    excessive deficit procedure 52–3, 167–8
    German unification and 156
Bulgaria 249, 250, 254
Bundesbank 156, 158, 161, 173, 271, 274
    1992–3 ERM crisis and 159
    role model for ECB 165, 167, 184

cabotage 63
CAP (Common Agricultural Policy) 17,
    22–3, 24, 30, 198, 229, 272
    CEECs and 250, 255–6
    exchange rates and 62–3, 139
    expenditure 40–1, 210–14
    export restitutions 235
    GATT and 28, 29, 235, 239
    impact on cohesion 197, 212–14
    Mediterranean countries and 199, 244
    reform of 42, 48, 58, 213, 214, 216, 235,
        239, 262–3
    Treaty of Rome 13
    variable import levies 235
capital controls 94, 96, 142
    in the EMS 152, 155, 158
capital movements 260–1
    data on 81

EMU and 50, 164, 168
    liberalization of 14, 23, 45, 49, 50, 58, 75,
        96, 230
    taxation and 107–8
    Treaty of Rome 93–4
Cassis de Dijon 43, 109, 111
CCP (common commercial policy) 13,
    28–9, 62, 231–2
    see also CET; trade
Cecchini Report (1988) 68–72
    economies of scale and 86
    financial services and 93
    J-curve unemployment effect 123
    standards and technical regulations and
        108–9
CEECs (Central and Eastern European
    Countries) 3, 29, 240, 268, 269
    1995 White Paper 250–1
    applications for EU membership 60, 252,
        253
    CAP and 250, 255–6
    collapse of communist regimes 40, 51,
        164, 248
    conditions for EU membership 252
    economic assistance to 202, 245, 258
    EU agreements with 59, 248–9
    integration with EU 228, 245
    labour costs 135
    labour migration 119
    NATO membership 252, 254
    pre-accession strategy 250
    Structural Funds and 255, 256–7
    technical assistance to 248, 250–1, 258
    trade with EU 230, 235, 237, 247, 249,
        250, 255
CEN (Centre Européen de Normalisation)
    64, 111, 238
CENELEC (Centre Européen de
    Normalisation Électrotechnique) 64,
    111, 238
CET (common external tariff) 16, 23, 216,
    223, 231, 233
CFSP (Common Foreign and Security
    Policy) 222, 224, 272
    Maastricht Treaty 1n., 52, 54
    Yugoslavia and 56, 252, 268
China 228, 237, 240
CIS (Commonwealth of Independent States)
    257–8

citizenship of the Union 52
CMEA (Council for Mutual Economic
    Assistance) 244, 251
Cockfield, Arthur 44
co-decision procedure 52
cohesion, economic and social 46, 54, 122–3,
    187–222
Cohesion Fund 59, 201, 202, 203, 207, 256
    Maastricht Treaty 54, 168
cohesion report 192, 201
cold war 3, 40, 54, 243, 248, 268
Committee of the Governors of Central
    Banks 166
Committee of the Regions 201
Community Initiatives 207
Community preference:
    principle of the CAP 22, 235, 249
Community trade mark 65
company law 74, 89
comparative advantage 72, 76, 189, 192,
    233
    in agriculture 235
    new trade theory and 234
competition policy 13, 23, 86–92, 262, 273
    international dimension of 238
    see also state aids
competitiveness 26, 27, 31, 57, 214, 230
    1993 White Paper 130–1
    effects of internal market 70
    cooperation among firms and 91, 92
    monetary policy and 156, 161, 174, 183
    real effective exchange rates 153–5
    social policy and 124, 125, 126, 127
concentration, industrial 76, 86
    in banking 95
convergence:
    of inflation and interest rates in the EMS
        143–52
    Maastricht criteria 53, 166, 168, 169–70,
        174–9, 201, 219, 263, 264, 269
    real economic convergence 57, 176–7
cooperation procedure 46
Copenhagen summit (1993) 250
COREPER (Committee of Permanent
    Representatives) 273
Council of Europe 10, 15, 43, 126, 251
Council of Ministers 24, 41, 43, 52, 128, 209,
    211, 220
    CCP 231

EC budget and 209, 211
    further enlargement and 252, 253, 254,
        256
    Structural Funds and 199, 207
    voting procedures 44, 45–6, 47, 48, 67,
        105, 108, 110, 111, 125, 134, 210, 271
    see also ECOFIN
countervailing duties 231, 233
Court of Auditors 209, 217, 220
CSFs (Community Support Frameworks)
    203–7
customs union 17, 62, 117
    creation of in EC 14
    GATT and 23, 29
    theory of 18–20, 68–9
Cyprus 208, 243–4, 252, 253, 254
Czech Republic 208, 249, 250, 254

Davignon, Etienne 30, 36
Delors, Jacques 42, 51, 130, 219, 244
    EMU and 170
    social policy and 115, 125, 126, 129, 133
Delors package 48, 200, 201
Delors Report (1989) 50, 165–6, 172, 185,
    220
democratic deficit 41, 46
Denmark 74, 76, 84
    CAP and 213
    EC accession 25
    EC budget and 219
    EFTA and 15
    EMU and 169, 171, 178–9, 181
    Maastricht Treaty and 53, 55, 153
    part-time employment in 133
    SEA and 44, 45
    snake and 142
    tax harmonization and 105
deregulation 37, 237, 240, 243, 262
    of financial services 32, 92–102, 232, 267
    internal market and 43, 73, 79
    labour markets 135–6, 265, 266–7
    see also liberalization
differentiation 75, 265, 270–2
    see also multi-speed and -tier Europe; opt-
        out clauses; variable geometry and
        speed
Dooge Committee 44
Dublin summit (1990) 51
dynamic effects of integration 20, 69, 71

EAGGF (European Agricultural Guidance and Guarantee Fund) 198, 200, 212
EBRD (European Bank for Reconstruction and Development) 248
ECB (European Central Bank) 52, 102, 166, 167, 168
  credibility of 176–7, 180, 184
  independence of 165
  legitimacy of 184–5, 273–4
  monetary policy and 186, 264
ECJ (European Court of Justice) 24, 43, 87, 109, 117, 121, 266
ECOFIN 167–8, 178, 185
Economic and Social Committee 129–30
economic growth 9, 16, 33, 34, 49, 77, 173, 274, 275
  1993 White Paper 131
  internal market and 50, 70–1
  labour markets and 116, 119
  liberalization of financial services and 93
  popular support for integration and 56
  Structural Funds and 202, 204–5
  trade and 18–20
economies of scale:
  banking 100
  customs union theory and 20
  internal market and 71, 77, 86
  and learning effects 35, 69, 188–9
  trade theory and 72, 234, 237
ECSC (European Coal and Steel Community) 1n., 11–12, 14–15, 86, 117
  High Authority 11, 24, 209, 211
ECU (European Currency Unit):
  creation 38
  in the ERM 144–5, 146, 158
  Euro and 171
  SEA 46
EDC (European Defence Community) 12
EDF (European Development Fund) 211, 246
Edinburgh summit (1992) 59, 201, 211
EEA (European Economic Area) 60, 242–3, 249
EEC, *see* Treaty of Rome
effective rates of protection 233
efficiency wages 188
EFTA (European Free Trade Association) 3, 25, 26, 37, 40
  after 1995 enlargement 60

creation of 14–15
FDI 84
technical standards and 111
trade agreements with EC 242–3
trade with EU 227
EIB (European Investment Bank) 13, 145, 168, 197, 198, 200, 212
  CEECs and 251
  Mediterranean countries and 245
electronics 28, 35–6, 233, 234, 236
EMCF (European Monetary Cooperation Fund) 145, 158, 168
EMI (European Monetary Institute) 53
  tasks 168–9
  technical preparations for EMU 173
empty chair crisis 24
EMS (European Monetary System) 6–7, 143–62, 259, 261, 263
  1992–3 crisis 58, 152–62
  asymmetry 38, 156–61
  CAP and 62, 139
  creation 38
  deflationary bias 159–60
  divergence indicator 145, 158
  monetary stability 146–52
  role of central bankers 172
  SEA 46
EMU (Economic and Monetary Union) 7, 24–5, 163–86, 223, 227, 260, 264, 273, 274, 275, 276
  1996 IGC and 60, 175, 252
  banking structure and 101
  costs and benefits 180–6
  Delors Report 50, 165–6
  differentiation and 270, 272
  Germany and 268, 271
  labour markets and 120, 136
  Maastricht Treaty 52–3, 54–5, 166–70, 261
  political union and 51, 139, 164, 185
  redistribution and 31, 170, 189–92, 201, 202, 208, 210, 219, 220–2, 265
  Werner plan 139–41
energy, EC policy 27–8, 198
  energy tax proposal 131, 221
  liberalization 74
  TENs 53, 131
enlargement 2, 48, 260, 270, 272, 276
  first (1973) 25, 31, 198, 210

fourth (1995) 59–60, 202, 211, 243
further enlargement 208, 220, 222, 225, 248–58, 263, 269
second and third (1981, 1986) 32, 40, 42, 49, 199–200
environment, EC policy 262, 270, 273, 274
1993 White Paper 131
Cohesion Fund and 201
Maastricht Treaty 54
SEA 46, 111
EOTC (European Organization of Testing and Certification) 112–13
EPC (European Political Cooperation) 24, 32, 41, 44, 46, 54
EPU (European Payments Union) 9–10, 12
ERDF (European Regional Development Fund) 31–2, 198–9
redistributive impact 200, 204, 208
ERM (Exchange Rate Mechanism) 38, 144–62
1992–3 crisis 58, 152–62
convergence criterion 169, 176, 179
EMU and 168, 173, 174
ERP (European Recovery Programme) 10
ESCB (European System of Central Banks) 52, 167
ESF (European Social Fund) 13, 31, 117, 122, 198, 200, 206
ESPRIT (European Strategic Programme for Research and Development in Information Technology) 36, 85
Essen summit (1994) 136, 250
essential requirements 43
banking 97, 98
standardization 110, 111, 113
ETSI (European Telecommunications Standards Institute) 111, 112, 238
ETUC (European Trade Union Confederation) 134
Delors address to 126, 129
Euratom (European Atomic Energy Community) 1n., 12
EUREKA (European Research Co-ordinating Agency) 37
Euro 171, 173, 174, 180, 260
Euro-champions 80, 85, 91–2, 237, 261
Euro-euphoria and -optimism 56, 164, 172, 204
Europe Agreements 248–9

European Commission 24, 42, 52, 232
1993 White Paper 59, 130–1
Barre plan 139
CEECs and 248, 250
competition policy and 36, 65, 69, 85–92
conduct of CCP 231, 232, 233
EC budget and 209, 210, 211, 219, 220
EMU and 166, 168, 169, 170, 172, 176, 180, 220–1
implementation of EC legislation and 74
internal market and 33, 43–4, 50, 61, 68–73
Kennedy Round and 16–17
opinions on membership applications 253
poor internal coordination 206, 224
social policy and 117, 125, 126, 127, 128–9, 132, 133, 136, 266
standardization and 110, 111
steel crisis and 30
Structural Funds and 46, 199, 200, 201, 203, 207–8
tax harmonization and 67, 103–8
European company statute 65, 126, 128–9, 133
European Council 32, 43, 46, 52, 67, 169
European Parliament 199, 253, 273
direct elections 32
EC budget and 211, 219
powers 24, 25, 41, 44, 46, 52, 209
social policy 125, 128, 266
Euro-pessimism and -scepticism 5, 33, 50, 51, 56, 58, 153, 237, 260
Euro-sclerosis 33, 115
excessive deficit procedure 167–8, 171
exchange rates 263–4
CAP and 62–3, 139
effectiveness as a policy instrument 181–3
real effective exchange rates 153–5
speculative attacks 15, 58, 152–62
Treaty of Rome 138
see also EMS; EMU; ERM; snake
excise taxes 66–7, 103, 104, 106
extraterritoriality 238

FDI (foreign direct investment) 49, 81, 84–5, 205, 230, 244, 254, 260, 267
effects of internal market on 73, 76

federalism 10, 24, 33, 210
  fiscal federalism 104
  Maastricht Treaty and 55
  social policy 116, 124
FIFG (Financial Instrument for Fisheries
    Guidance) 200
financial services and markets 6, 262, 263,
    264
  capital adequacy directive (1993) 99
  deregulation of 37, 92–102, 232, 267
  globalization and 230
  insurance 66, 97
  internal market and 58, 70, 77
  investment services 97
  investment services directive (1993) 99
  see also banks and banking
Finland 227
  convergence criteria and 176, 179
  ERM entry 176
  EU accession 59–60, 243, 253
  intra-EU trade and 181
  regional disparities 192–3, 196
  unemployment 34
fiscal policy:
  demand management 14, 21, 27, 263
  EMS and 160
  EMU and 140, 165, 166, 167–8, 183, 184,
    185–6, 221
  international coordination 232–3
  SEA 46
  tax harmonization and 105
Fontainebleau summit (1984) 42, 210, 216
foreign aid, EU 232
Fortress Europe 7, 76, 85, 237, 267
France 42, 51, 76, 89, 230, 270, 271
  banking system 95, 99
  CAP and 24, 213
  capital controls and 94, 96
  EC budget and 217
  EMS and 38, 58, 152, 155, 156, 158
  EMU and 53, 139, 170–1, 174, 175,
    177–8
  EU external policy and 245
  Euratom and 12
  FDI 84
  Hague summit and 24–5
  industrial policy and 21n., 36n., 83, 85,
    237
  merger control 87, 88, 89

referendum on Maastricht Treaty 55–6
  regional disparities 193, 199, 203
  Schengen agreement and 75
  snake and 142
  social policy and 117, 124, 126
  taxation and 106, 107
Franco-German initiatives 11, 24–5, 38, 51,
    124, 143, 171, 271
fraud 206, 219–20
functionalism 12, 50, 92
  functional spillover 108, 165

G-7 (Group of Seven) 232
G-24 (Group of Twenty-Four) 248, 251
GATS (General Agreement on Trade in
    Services) 240
GATT (General Agreement on Tariffs and
    Trade) 28–9, 216, 233, 240
  agriculture and 235, 239
  Article XXIV 29, 241, 247
de Gaulle, Charles 17, 23–4, 209
Genscher-Colombo proposal 41
Georgia 257
Germany 20, 25, 28, 48, 49, 75, 76, 83–4, 189,
    220, 230, 270, 271
  capital controls and 94
  banking system 89–90, 95
  CAP and 213
  CEECs and 249, 250
  EC budget and 42, 48, 210, 217–18, 256
  EC regional policy and 192–3, 200–1, 203,
    207, 208
  EMS and 38, 58, 143, 145, 148, 150,
    156–7, 159, 160
  EMU and 53, 140, 164, 170–1, 174, 177–8,
    180, 181
  EU external policy and 245
  internal market and 74, 79
  inflation and 27, 274
  merger control 87, 88, 89
  ratification of Maastricht Treaty 56
  snake and 142
  social policy and 119, 120, 124–5, 126,
    128, 129, 132, 134
  taxation and 106, 107
  unification 51, 58, 148, 150, 156, 164,
    192–3, 219, 268
  West–East monetary union 183–4
Giscard d'Estaing, Valéry 38, 148, 171

globalization 2, 37, 85, 93, 223, 230–1, 240, 261, 262, 267
'Golden Age' 16, 20, 26–7, 49, 198, 260, 261
Greece 32, 37, 38, 44, 72, 74, 75, 76, 106, 109, 243, 269
  banking system 95
  CAP and 213
  capital controls and 96
  EC accession 40, 244
  EC budget and 217
  EC regional policy and 42, 189, 192–3, 196, 199, 201, 203, 204–5, 207
  EMU and 176, 179, 181
  ERM and 150, 160
  labour migration 118
  social charter and 126
  state aids and 65
  Turkey and 253
GSP (Generalized System of Preferences) 247

Hague summit (1969) 24–5
Hallstein, Walter 11, 24
Hanover summit (1988) 50, 165
harmonization 262, 275
  in banking 97–102
  of economic policies 139, 140
  internal market and 49, 64
  new approach 43–4, 110–11
  of professional qualifications 66
  of social security 66, 117
  of social standards 132, 135, 267
  of taxation 66–7, 74, 80, 102–8, 263, 272
de Havilland affair 88
HDTV (high definition television) 85
health:
  public, Maastricht Treaty 53
  regulations as NTBs 63
  and safety 46, 111, 112, 122, 132
Heckscher–Ohlin trade theory 233–4
high technology 230
  barriers to trade 63
  EC policy 35–7, 70, 262
  effects of the internal market 72
  national champions and 21–2, 35, 36
home country control, of banks 97, 98
Hungary 248, 249, 250, 252, 254

Iceland 60, 75

IGC (intergovernmental conference) 276
  1996 IGC 55, 60, 136, 175, 222, 225, 250, 252, 270
  Maastricht 46, 50–1, 116, 130, 166, 172
  SEA 44–5
IMF (International Monetary Fund) 14, 155, 232
IMPs (Integrated Mediterranean Programmes) 42, 199–200
income inequalities 135, 231, 263, 265, 266
India 240
industrial policy 13, 21, 30, 70
  competition policy and 81–92, 262
  high technology and 36–7
  Maastricht Treaty 53–4, 92
  trade policy and 234
inflation 16, 26, 27, 38, 140, 153, 155, 156, 269
  convergence criterion 169, 175
  convergence in the EMS 143–52
  effects of the internal market 70–1
information technology 34, 36
integration, negative and positive 68
interest rates, long-term:
  convergence criterion 169, 176
inter-industry trade 19–20, 72
internal market programme 1, 5, 48–50, 57–8, 61–78, 85, 219, 230, 264, 273
  anticipation effect of 73, 100
  barriers to completion 61–8
  cooperation among firms and 86, 92
  creation 33–4
  credibility of 96, 180
  as a deregulatory exercise 79
  EFTA and 242
  ex ante studies 68–73
  ex post studies 75–8
  extension of EC powers and 92, 261–2
  external dimension of 237–9
  flexible integration and 270, 271, 272
  implementation 73–5
  redistribution and 34, 71, 189–92, 200, 202, 223, 265
  SEA 45, 47
  see also Cecchini Report; White Paper (1985)
intra-EC trade 9, 17–18, 29, 30–1, 34, 49, 57, 181, 192, 216, 227, 259, 260
  in agricultural products 22

intra-EC trade (*cont.*):
  internal market and 43, 68–9, 72, 76
intra-industry trade 19–20, 76, 228
investment 20–1, 26, 33, 34, 47, 49, 57, 204
  effect of integration 20
  effects of internal market 44, 50, 70
  liberalization of financial services and 93
Ireland 31, 269
  CAP and 213
  EC accession 25
  EC budget and 217
  EC regional policy and 193–6, 201, 203,
    204, 205, 209
  EMU and 172, 178, 181
  ERM and 145–6, 152, 155
  FDI 84, 205
  Maastricht Treaty and 55
  merger control 87
  SEA and 44, 45
  state aids and 65
  tax harmonization and 105
Israel 243, 244
Italy 27, 42, 45, 89, 96, 203, 205, 219, 245
  banking system 95, 100
  CAP and 213
  EC budget and 217
  EC regional policy and 189, 196, 197,
    198, 199
  EMS and 38, 58, 150, 152, 153, 157, 158
  EMU and 176, 179, 181
  labour movements 23, 117, 118, 119,
    120
  mergers and acquisitions 83, 84
  merger control 87, 88
  Mezzogiorno 13, 117, 189, 197, 203
  state aids and 65

Japan 15, 34, 225
  alliances with EC firms 84, 85
  banking system 98, 101
  car transplants in UK 236
  EC R&D programmes and 86, 234
  EC VERs with 236
  EU anti-dumping and 237
  expenditure on social protection 115
  import quotas 62
  protectionism against 28, 29
Jenkins, Roy 143
justice and home affairs 1n., 52, 54, 63

Kennedy Round 16–17, 23
Keynesian economics 10, 14, 37–8, 263
  1993 White Paper and 59, 131
Kohl, Helmut 51, 170

labour markets 22, 26, 114–37, 261, 262
  deregulation and flexibility of 38, 59,
    266–7
  regional problems and 188
  see also social policy
labour mobility 23, 117–21, 261, 266
  regional disparities and 188, 189–92, 197
Lamfalussy, Alexander 168
legitimacy of EU institutions 4, 262, 264,
    273, 274, 275
  EMU and 184–6
  industrial policy and 234
  social policy and 134
liberalization 85–6, 92, 204, 240, 261, 265,
    266, 267, 275
  of capital movements 14, 23, 45, 49, 50, 58,
    75, 96, 230
  of financial services 58, 92–102
  internal market and 73, 74, 76
  regulation and 22, 79–80, 93
  of telecommunications 58, 74, 75, 270
  of trade 5, 10, 20, 29, 33, 67, 189, 198, 223,
    247, 259, 260
  see also deregulation
Libya 245
Liechtenstein 60, 107, 243
Lomé conventions 29, 246–7
Luxembourg 192
  banking system 95
  EMU and 131, 171, 178
  financial sector 99
  foreign residents 119
  tax harmonization and 105–7
  see also Benelux countries
Luxembourg agreement (1966) 24, 47

Maastricht Treaty 1n., 5, 51–5, 58, 173–4, 224
  capital mobility and 96
  cohesion and 201
  the ECU and 144
  EMU and 166–70
  industrial policy and 92
  ratification 55–6, 153, 275
  taxation and 108

MacDougall Report 220
macroeconomic policy coordination 14, 23, 27
  in the EMS 155–6, 159–60
  in EMU 139–42, 183, 185–6, 221
  international 232–3
  Treaty of Rome 138
Madrid summit (1989) 50, 166
Madrid summit (1995) 173–4
Major, John 53
Malta 243–4, 252, 253, 254
market for corporate control:
  Anglo-US versus German model 89–90
Marshall Plan 9–10
MCAs (monetary compensatory amounts) 62–3
Mediterranean countries 228, 268
  EC agreements with 29, 59, 243–5, 246, 247
  labour migration 23, 119
MERCOSUR 241
merger control regulation (1989) 87–9
mergers and acquisitions 37, 49, 73, 81–92, 261
  in banking 95, 100
  European Company Statute and 128
METS (minimum efficient technical scale) 69
Mexico 101
Mezzogiorno 13, 117, 189, 197, 203
MFAs (multifibre arrangements) 29, 62, 235
MFN (Most Favoured Nation) treatment 241, 248
Middle East 244
Milan summit (1985) 43, 44
minimum wage 127–8
Mitterrand, François 51, 171, 250
mixed economy 5, 20, 22, 62, 116, 260, 261–2, 264
  European model and 124
  internal market and 79
  redistribution and 187
  standards and 109
  trade liberalization and 67
Monetary Committee 138, 166
monetary policy 37, 73, 142, 263, 273
  banking regulation and 97
  demand management 14, 21, 27

  in the EMS 38, 145–52, 155–6
  in EMU 52, 53, 140, 164–5, 166–7, 168, 174, 180–3, 184, 272
  international coordination 232–3
  liberalization of capital movements and 93
  regional disparities and 189–92
  Treaty of Rome 138
Monnet, Jean 17
moral hazard:
  in banking 94
  Structural Funds and 205, 208–9
multilateralism:
  EU trade and 225
  in GATT 23, 29, 241
  in US policy 10
multi-speed and -tier Europe 28, 41, 46, 53, 75, 130, 161, 169, 179, 270–1
  see also differentiation; opt-out clauses; variable geometry and speed
mutual information directive (1983) 110, 112
mutual recognition 43, 64, 81, 262
  in banking 97–102
  difficulties with 74
  international agreements 238
  of qualifications 23, 49, 66, 120
  of standards and technical regulations 110–13

NAFTA (North American Free Trade Agreement) 241
national champions 21–2, 81, 82, 83, 85, 86–7, 262
  in high technology 28, 35, 36
  in steel 30
nationalized firms 91, 262
NATO (North Atlantic Treaty Organization) 54, 252, 253, 254
neoclassical economics 4, 19, 188
Netherlands 20, 84, 196
  absence of capital controls 94, 142
  EC budget and 217
  EMU and 140, 171
  merger control 87
  monetary policy 157
  part-time employment 133
  workers' participation 128, 129
  see also Benelux countries

new approach to harmonization 43–4,
    110–11
NICs (newly industrializing countries) 16,
    28, 228, 234, 237
NIEO (New International Economic Order)
    246
NIS (New Independent States) 240
North Africa 118, 135, 244, 245
Norway 3, 142, 268
    EEA and 243
    EFTA and 15
    referenda on EC accession 15, 60, 243
    Schengen and 75
NTBs (non-tariff barriers) 22, 260, 262, 273
    GATT and 233, 239
    internal market and 43–4, 67–8, 69, 72, 92
    to labour mobility 117, 120
    the new protectionism and 28–30
    preferential agreements and 245
    standards and technical regulations 36,
        109, 110
NUTS (nomenclature of territorial units for
    statistics) 192

OECD (Organization for Economic
    Cooperation and Development) 9, 75
OEEC (Organization for European
    Economic Cooperation) 9–10, 12, 15
oil shocks 27–8, 30–1, 34, 259
OPEC (Organization of Petroleum
    Exporting Countries) 31, 228
openness of EC economies 181–2, 227
    of EU as a whole 225, 267
optimum currency area 180–1, 264
opt-out clauses 53, 130, 170, 270, 272
orderly marketing arrangements 28
OSCE (Organization for Security and
    Cooperation in Europe) 251
own resources 40–1, 214–16
    creation of 24, 25, 32, 209–10
    Edinburgh reforms 59, 201
    Fontainebleau reforms 42, 210–11

Paris summit (1972) 141
PHARE (Pologne, Hongrie, assistance pour
    la restructuration économique) 248,
    250, 251, 256–7, 258
Plaza agreement 146
Pleven Plan 12

Poland 248, 249, 250, 254
political union 7, 51, 91
    EMU and 139, 164, 185–6
    Maastricht IGC 166
Pompidou, Georges 24
Portugal 32, 75, 109, 132, 134, 181, 199, 243
    banking system 95
    CAP and 213
    capital controls and 96
    EC accession 244, 253
    EC budget and 217
    EC regional policy and 189, 192–3, 196,
        201, 203, 204
    EFTA and 15
    EMS and 150
    FDI 84
    inter-industry trade and 72, 76
    labour migration 118
    state aids and 65
PPSs (purchasing power standards) 192
preferential trade agreements, EU 241–8, 268
    see also Europe Agreements
productivity 26, 41, 266
    labour costs and 134
    regional disparities and 188–9, 193–6
protectionism 10, 37, 237
    in agriculture 235
    in the EU 238–9
    the new protectionism 28–30, 233
    in textiles and clothing 235
public debt 57, 263
    convergence criterion 169, 175, 219
public expenditure 20, 38, 115, 136, 212
public procurement 232, 238
    concentration and 76
    GATT and 233, 240
    as a NTB 22, 64–5
    implementation of EC legislation 74, 75
pyramid of privilege 247

qualified majority voting:
    harmonization and 64
    Maastricht Treaty 52
    SEA 45, 48, 111, 271
    social policy and 53, 130, 132
quantitative restrictions 233, 235, 239

RACE (Research in Advanced
    Communications for Europe) 36, 85

Reagan, Ronald 37, 40, 123, 146
reciprocity:
  banking regulation and 97, 99, 237
  preferential trade agreements and 242–7
  takeovers and 90
  Uruguay Round and 237
redistributive policies 2, 7, 122, 187–222,
    260, 261
  cohesion impact of the CAP 212–14
  EMU and 31, 170, 189–92, 201, 202, 208,
    210, 219, 220–2, 265
  enlargement and 256
  internal market and 34, 71, 189–92, 200,
    202, 223, 265
  Treaty of Rome 14, 187
  see also EC budget; regional policy;
    Structural Funds
referenda:
  Denmark 45, 55, 153, 169
  France 55–6
  Ireland 45, 55
  Norway 25, 60, 243
  Switzerland 60, 243
regime theory 101
regional disparities in the EC 27, 188–200
  economic growth and 205
  first enlargement and 31
  MacDougall Report and 220
  SEA and 46
regionalism in world trade 248
  regional integration arrangements 228,
    240–1
regional policy 21, 198
  EC regional policy 13, 187–8, 196–209
  see also IMPs; Structural Funds
regulation 2, 5, 73, 262, 268, 273
  of banking 94–5, 97–102
  of labour markets 6, 22, 114–37
  liberalization and 22, 79–80, 93
  of stock exchanges 89
  technical regulations 63–4, 81, 108–13,
    260, 273
regulatory competition 64, 262
  in banking 98, 102
  fiscal competition 106–7, 108
  in standards 113
  see also social dumping
research and development 262
  1993 White Paper and 59, 131

expenditure 212, 214
Maastricht Treaty 54
multi-annual framework programmes 85
SEA 46
see also BRITE; ESPRIT; EUREKA; RACE
Romania 249, 250, 252, 254
Rotterdam–Antwerp effect 217
Round Table of European Industrialists 37,
  73
rules of origin 15, 29, 62, 236
  preferential trade agreements and 244,
    245, 246
Russia 252, 254, 257, 258, 269

safeguards, in GATT 29
Santer, Jacques 59, 136
Schengen agreement 75, 120
Schiller, Karl 139, 141n.
Schmidt, Helmut 38, 143, 148, 170–1
Schuman, Robert 51
Schuman Plan 11–12
SDI (Strategic Defence Initiative) 37
SEA (Single European Act) 45–8, 54, 55, 64,
    111, 122–3, 200, 270
seigniorage gains 180
services 260
  freedom of movement and establishment
    65–6
  GATS and 240
  GATT and 239
  internal market and 92, 232
  trade in 230, 260
Slovakia 249, 254
Slovenia 208
Smithsonian agreement (1971) 141
snake 28, 141–2, 145
social action programmes 121, 127, 129, 130
social dumping 124, 134–5, 137, 266
social policy 6, 114–37, 262, 266, 272
  equal opportunities 117, 121, 126, 127,
    132
  internal market and 34, 50
  Maastricht Treaty 53, 130
  SEA 46
  social charter 126–8
  social dialogue 122, 124, 126, 129–30,
    133–4
  social protocol 130, 133, 270
  UK opt-out 53, 130

social policy (*cont.*):
  workers' participation 128–9
sovereignty 25, 60, 150, 259, 268, 275
  EMU and 163, 179, 209
  free movement of labour and persons and
    63, 120
  internal market and 44, 67
  liberalization of financial services and 93
  social policy and 126
  Structural Funds and 206
  taxation and 80, 104, 107, 108
Soviet Union 40, 164, 248
Spain 32, 37, 75, 77, 84, 109, 181, 199, 230,
    243, 245, 271
  banking system 100
  CAP and 213–14
  EC accession 244, 253
  EC budget and 217
  EC regional policy and 193–6, 201, 203,
    204, 208
  EMS and 150, 153
  FDI 84
  labour migration 118
  merger control 87
  social charter and 126
Stabex 246
Stability Pact, OSCE (1995) 251
stagflation 26, 262
standardization 36, 81, 108–13, 260, 262,
    273
  conformity assessment 109, 112–13
  internal market and 63–4, 75, 232, 238
state aids 13, 23, 29, 65, 90–2, 197, 262
steel 11, 28, 30, 62, 91, 236, 237, 249, 263
stock exchanges 89–90, 95
Strasbourg summit (1989) 51, 126, 166
Stresa conference (1958) 23
Structural Funds 122, 200, 202–9, 211, 214,
    261, 264, 272
  CEECs and 255, 256–7
  Delors package 48, 200
  Edinburgh reforms 59, 201–2
  internal market and 50
  Maastricht Treaty 54
  SEA 46, 200
  see also EAGGF; ERDF; ESF; FIFG;
    Cohesion Fund
Stuttgart Declaration (1983) 47
subsidiarity 55

1993 White Paper and 131
corporate tax harmonization and 106
EMU and 165
Maastricht Treaty 54
mutual recognition and 64
social policy and 127, 132–7
Structural Funds and 206
supply-side economics 26–7, 37, 38, 107
  1993 White Paper and 131
  internal market programme and 43, 44,
    50
Sweden 142, 227
  EFTA and 15
  ERM and 160, 179, 181
  EU accession 59–60, 243, 253
  unemployment 34
Switzerland 3, 27, 107, 268
  EU application 252
  EFTA and 15
  rejection of EEA 60, 243
Sysmin 246
systemic risk, in banking 94, 101

TACIS (technical assistance to the CIS) 258
takeovers 89–90, 128
taxation 263
  1985 White Paper 66–7, 103–4
  clearing house system 104, 105
  common market principle 104
  corporate 103, 106–7, 129
  destination principle 63, 66–7, 102–3,
    104, 105, 263
  energy tax proposal 131, 221
  fraud 105
  harmonization 66–7, 74, 80, 102–8, 263,
    272
  on investment income 103, 107–8, 263
  Maastricht Treaty 108
  origin principle 106, 221
  tax revenue 136
  worldwide principle 107
  see also VAT
telecommunications 35, 37, 65, 66, 234, 262
  effects of the internal market 72, 77
  liberalization 58, 74, 75, 270
  TENs 53, 131
TENs (trans-European networks) 221
  1993 White Paper and 59, 131
  Cohesion Fund and 54, 201

Maastricht Treaty 53
TEU (Treaty on European Union), *see* Maastricht Treaty
textiles and clothing 28, 62, 72, 229, 233, 244
  Uruguay Round and 235, 239
Thatcher, Margaret 37, 45, 47, 51, 126, 210
Tindemans, Leo 28n.
Tokyo Round 29, 233
trade 29, 230
  contribution to welfare and growth 18–20
  creation and diversion 18, 22, 23, 68, 76, 238
  deflection 15, 104
  EC agreements with third parties 23, 29
  EC integration and 18
  EU trade patterns 225–30
  EU trade policy 231–41, 272
  EU trade preferences 241–8, 268
  inter-industry 19–20, 72
  intra-industry 19–20, 76, 228
  liberalization 5, 10, 20, 29, 33, 67, 189, 198, 233, 247, 259, 260
  new theories of 71–2, 189
  social anti-dumping clauses 135
  strategic trade policy 234
  see also intra-EC trade
trade unions 22, 26, 115, 125, 127–8, 261
  1992 process and 50
  power of 38, 115
  social dialogue and 129–30, 134
transatlantic free trade area 248
transport policy 23, 45, 197
  barriers to the internal market 63, 66
  TENs 53, 54, 131
  see also airlines
Treaty of Paris, *see* ECSC
Treaty of Rome 1n.
  competition policy 86
  creation of 12–17
  liberalization of capital movements 93–4
  macroeconomic policy 138
  regional policy 196–7
  social policy 117–18
  standardization 109
  taxation 102–3
  trade and association agreements 241
TRIMs (Trade-Related Investment Measures) 240

TRIPs (Trade-Related Intellectual Property Rights) 240
Turkey 118, 119, 135, 237, 243–4
  customs union 257
  membership application 252–3

UK 17, 27, 56, 79, 85, 230, 271
  capital controls and 94, 142
  banking system 95
  CAP and 30, 213
  CEECs and 249
  deregulation of labour market 135
  EC accession 24–5, 198–9
  EC budget and 31, 40–1, 42, 48, 210–11, 217, 219
  EC regional policy and 203, 207
  ECSC and 11
  EC social policy and 53, 125–6, 128, 129, 130, 132, 133
  EFTA and 14–15
  EMS and 38, 58, 143, 150, 152, 160
  EMU and 166, 169, 172, 174, 179
  FDI and 75, 84
  financial sector 99
  IGCs and 43, 50, 51, 166
  inequalities in 135, 265
  Japanese car transplants 236
  market for corporate control 89–90
  merger control 87, 88
  mergers and acquisitions 83, 84
  SEA and 45
  tax harmonization and 104, 106, 107
Ukraine 257
unemployment 2, 16, 26, 27, 33, 34, 38, 49, 56, 135–6, 221, 231, 243, 265, 266, 275
  1993 White Paper and 59, 130–1
  CEECs and 249
  effects of internal market 70–1, 75, 123
  ESF and 122
  'insiders' and 'outsiders' 127–8, 135–6
  labour mobility and 119
  minimum wage and 127–8
  regional disparities and 193–6
  solidarity and 115
  Structural Funds and 202
UNICE (Union des Confédérations de l'Industrie et des Employeurs d'Europe) 126, 129, 134

unilateralism 236, 238
United Nations 254
United States 15, 16, 17, 23, 34, 37, 40, 146,
    186, 225, 253, 254
  alliances with EU firms 84, 85
  American model 135–6
  anti-dumping 236, 240
  banking system 95, 98, 101
  'benign neglect' 141, 144
  Bretton Woods and 138–9
  EC research programmes and 86, 234
  EMU and 164
  expenditure on social protection 115
  federal budget 220
  inequalities in 135, 265
  investment in Europe 20, 84
  leadership 240, 252, 258
  Marshall Plan 9–10
  oil shocks and 28
  regional disparities 192
  role in postwar reconstruction 9–11
  stock exchange 90
  Uruguay Round and 235, 237
Uruguay Round 58–9, 216, 232, 233, 237,
    239–40, 267
  EU–US agreement on agriculture 58, 235,
    239
  internal market programme and 239
  textiles and clothing 235, 239

variable geometry and speed 42, 46, 75, 130,
    137, 161, 169, 271
  see also differentiation; opt-out clauses;
    multi-speed and -tier Europe
VAT (value added tax):
  approximation 67

  as EC budget resource 25, 32, 42, 210, 211,
    216–17, 221
  harmonization 66–7, 102–6, 221, 263
  second and sixth VAT directives 103
VERs (voluntary export restraints) 28, 236
Visegrad Four 249, 250
Vredeling directive (1980) 129, 133

Warsaw Pact 251
welfare state 5, 20, 22, 26, 59, 116, 265
  1993 White Paper 131
  financial pressures 2, 115
  regulation of labour markets and 114
Werner, Pierre 139
Werner Report (1970) 139–41, 165, 185
WEU (Western European Union) 40, 54
White Paper, *Completing the Internal
    Market* (1985) 42–5, 61–8
  barriers 61–9
  financial services 93, 95–6
  mutual recognition 64
  new approach 43–4, 110
  taxation 66–7, 103–4
White Paper, *Growth, Competitiveness and
    Employment* (1993) 59, 130–1, 134
White Paper on the integration of the CEECs
    into the internal market (1995) 250–1
withholding taxes 107
WTO (World Trade Organization) 59, 225,
    232, 238, 240, 241
Wulf-Mathies, Monika 256

X-inefficiency 69

Yaoundé convention 246
Yugoslavia 56, 118, 249, 252, 257, 268